Data Warehousing

Data Warehousing

Strategies, Technologies, and Techniques

Rob Mattison

Technical Editor: Rick Alaska
Illustrator: Brigitte Mattison

McGraw-Hill

New York San Francisco Washington, D.C. Auckland Bogotá
Caracas Lisbon London Madrid Mexico City Milan
Montreal New Delhi San Juan Singapore
Sydney Tokyo Toronto

McGraw-Hill

A Division of The McGraw-Hill Companies

Library of Congress Cataloging-in-Publication Data

Mattison, Rob.
  Data warehousing : strategies, technologies, and techniques / by
Rob Mattison.
    p. cm.
  Includes index.
  ISBN 0-07-041034-8 (h)
    1. Database management. 2. Databases. I. Title.
QA76.9.D3M3872 1996
658.4'038'028574—dc20   96-4040
                                                             CIP

1 2 3 4 5 6 7 8 9 0   DOC/DOC   9 0 0 9 8 7 6

ISBN 0-07-041034-8

The sponsoring editor of this book was Jennifer Holt-DiGiovanna, the book editor was John C. Baker, and the executive editor was Robert E. Ostrander. The indexer was Jodi L. Tyler. The director of production was Katherine G. Brown. This book was set in ITC Century Light. It was composed in Blue Ridge Summit, Pa.

Printed and bound by R. R. Donnelley & Sons, Crawfordsville, Indiana.

McGraw-Hill books are available at special quantity discounts to use as premiums and sales promotions, or for use in corporate training programs. For more information, please write to the Director of Special Sales, McGraw-Hill, 11 West 19th Street, New York, NY 10011. Or contact your local bookstore.

Product or brand names used in this book may be trade names or trademarks. Where we believe that there may be proprietary claims to such trade names or trademarks, the name has been used with an initial capital or it has been capitalized in the style used by the name claimant. Regardless of the capitalization used, all such names have been used in an editorial manner without any intent to convey endorsement of or other affiliation with the name claimant. Neither the author nor the publisher intends to express any judgment as to the validity or legal status of any such proprietary claims.

MH96
0410348

To my darling wife, Brigitte, whose integrity, intelligence, faithfulness, and courage have proven to me just how special she really is and caused me to love her more each day, and whose vigilant contribution to the preparation of this book has made it as good as it is.

Contents

Acknowledgments

I would like to express my deepest appreciation to those individuals who contributed to make this book possible.

First, the contributors who provided material for the section on data mining:

Chapter 14, "Multidimensional analysis of warehoused data": Richard Tanler, Chairman, and Karen Drost, Marketing Manager

Information Advantage, Inc.
7401 Metro Boulevard
Minneapolis, MN 55439
Phone: 612-820-0702
Fax: 612-820-0712

Chapter 15, "Statistical analysis": Elan Long, Director of Corporate Marketing, and Douglas Dow, Director of Strategic Partnerships

SPSS, Inc.
444 N. Michigan Avenue
Chicago, IL 60611-3962
Phone: 312-329-3500
Fax: 312-329-3668

Chapter 16, "Neural networks and business data systems": Steve Russell, Senior Principal Consultant

dbINTELLECT Technologies
1536 Cole Boulevard
Golden, CO 80401
Phone: 303-275-6900
Fax: 303-275-2135

Chapter 17, "Neural networks: Net-modeling market": Kathy Pippert, Documentation and Training Manager, and Donna Bartko, Marketing Manager

Advanced Software Applications
333 Baldwin Road
Pittsburgh, PA 15205
Phone: 412-429-1003
Fax: 412-429-0709

Chapter 18, "Putting the data warehouse on the enterprise Intranet": Richard Tanler, Chairman

Information Advantage, Inc.
7401 Metro Boulevard
Minneapolis, MN 55439
Phone: 612-820-0702
Fax: 612-820-0712

Chapter 19, "Visualization in data mining": Jim Aucoin, Product Manager

Advanced Visual Systems, Inc.
300 Fifth Avenue
Waltham, MA 02154
Phone: 617-890-4300
Fax: 617-890-8287

Chapter 20, "Prediction from large data warehouses": Dr. Kamran Parsaye, CEO

Information Discovery, Inc.
2461 W. 205th Street
Suite B202
Torrence, CA 90501
Phone: 310-782-3340
Fax: 310-782-7565

Next, I want to thank the support people who helped assemble this "work of art."

To Brigitte Mattison, who has so painstakingly participated in the development of this book from beginning to end. It was Brigitte's organizational skills, word smithing, and administrative assistance that has made it possible for this book to be delivered with the quality, quantity, and aesthetics it currently shows. It is no exaggeration to say that this book is as much hers as mine. She probably spent more time on it than I did, and her influence shows throughout.

To Rick Alaska, the technical writer and editor, who went through the meticulous process of editing and rewriting all of the logically contradictory ramblings that my writing style evokes. It is Rick who helped make this book as coherent and well-organized as it is.

Third, I would like to thank those other individuals who contributed through their support and highly valued feedback. The list includes Paul Hoyt, Steve Russell, Steve Molsberry, Bob Smith, Bob Fetter, Pete Estler, and the entire dbINTELLECT/EDS organization whose support helped make it possible to deliver this book.

Last but not least, thanks to my family, Dustin and Peter Mattison, Chris and Johnny Yesulis, Stephanie, Tony, Raquel and Lil' Tony Cirrincione, and to all the others who put up with the fanaticism that always accompanies the development of this kind of project.

Introduction

For someone who has spent the last twenty years working in the data-processing industry, it is amazing to witness, first hand, the incredible impact the computer has had on business and on the lives of individuals. Twenty years ago, the computer was an extremely large, extremely complex, cumbersome piece of machinery, running with tubes, wires, and punch cards. The principal means of programming was to rearrange the tubes or to rewire the guts of the machine. The effect of the computer on the individual's and business's lives was minimal. Only the largest, most sophisticated organizations could afford what the computer had to offer.

Since those early days, we have seen the computer and the microchip change, not only how we compute things, but the actual way we live and even the way we perceive reality. Wow! Think about it. The computer has changed how we look at things, what we think of as important, and what we consider to be "reality." The computer has changed our experience of life itself. Computers make it possible for us to do more kinds of work and enjoy more kinds of recreation than ever before imaginable. They have made it possible for us to land on the moon, create more fuel-efficient cars, and design and create buildings, bridges, and basilicas that defy what used to be known as the world of physical reality. At the same time, computers have made it possible to cure diseases, perform surgery with laser beams and microscopic scalpels, and even to begin to manipulate the very genes that generate life so that we can now grow corn that is genetically resistant to insects and tomatoes that grow to the size of watermelons.

Of course, all of this incredible exponential increase in our capacity to do things has come with a cost. At this point, and for some time to come, the price that we pay for this power is confusion, disorientation, and chaos. The reason for this is clear. As the computer continues to become more and more powerful and as our sense of reality becomes challenged again and again, we find ourselves in a constant state of readjustment. As new things become possible, we must figure out how to make them fit into our already overly complicated lives.

One very critical component of this process of re-evaluating and re-creating our reality is information. Information is what we use to make decisions. Information is what we use to evaluate reality. The gathering of information, analyzing it, and making decisions because of it is, in one sense, what life itself is all about. We are thinking animals and, thus, we process information.

In a very real sense, what the computer revolution has done is provide us with the ability to collect, analyze, and effect changes in the real world on a phenomenal scale. The computer is *not* a thinking machine but is an information storage and processing engine. We use computers to enhance our own capacity in that regard. Conceptually, the computer is an artificial extension of our own thinking process.

Of course, this explosion of information collection, storage, and processing capacity has not occurred in a logical, well-thought-out manner. It is happening continuously and in a myriad of directions all at the same time. Our problem is to try to figure out how to control this process of data collection, storage, and analysis in a way that makes it manageable and versatile.

This is exactly the set of problems that the data-warehousing approach attempts to address. Unfortunately, the process of figuring out how to harness all of this information and make it easy to examine and utilize is tied to a whole lot of rules of physical, economical, social, and organizational realities. It is these pre-existing conditions that make the job so incredibly difficult. We have physical laws of science that still limit us in what we can do. While computers are powerful, they are not omnipotent. They increase our capacities by leaps and bounds, but these leaps too have their limits.

Not only must we deal with the physical realities of what the computer can do, but we also must constantly check with the economical realities of the process. While in the ideal world we would want to warehouse all of the data in the universe, the economic reality is that we cannot afford to.

No matter how hard we might try to make data stores a neutral and coldly logical kind of collection of information, the fact is that these stores are the product of a social and organizational system. These systems have rules of their own, and they also dictate what can and cannot be done with them.

Add to all of these conflicting conditions and frameworks the fact that the computer technology continues to grow in its capacity. Each time the capacity and capabilities are increased, we are forced once again to re-evaluate all of the assumptions that we made about all of our previous decisions.

This then is the real world of data warehousing. The objective is to capture and make available oceans of information. The constraints involve chaos in the form of ever-changing laws of physics, economics, society and organization.

It is the objective of this book to develop for the reader a set of tools, concepts, and approaches that make the process of conceiving, designing, and constructing the data warehouse a significantly less chaotic and frustrating experience than it has proven to be in the past.

What we *cannot* do is provide you with a simple recipe book or to-do list where you simply can "follow the instructions" to successfully deliver the perfect data warehousing solution. That would be impossible.

We *can* provide you with a framework for understanding what a data warehouse is, what it takes to put one together, and how to understand and negotiate all of what it takes to make it a successful implementation.

Data warehousing is complicated, but we can help make it less so. Data warehousing is challenging, but we can help you at least understand more clearly what the challenges are and how to address them.

My primary objective in writing this book has been to provide the would-be developer of a warehouse with a tool that fights the chaos so endemic to the undertaking of projects of this nature. We have tried to provide you with a framework for understanding what you are doing and why, and we have tried to give you a vocabulary and a problem-solving paradigm set that should make it possible for you to attack the process of data warehousing with a clearer vision of what you are trying to do.

We have organized this book into three major sections. The first section (chapters 1 through 3) deals with the concepts of data warehousing and the situational and environmental constraints and objectives that any project of this type entails. The second section (chapters 4 through 12) gets into the detail of how to structure a data warehousing project, how to identify the different components of any data warehouse, and the detail about how to design and develop each of these components. The third section (chapters 13 through 20) is dedicated exclusively to the topic of data mining. This section is radically different from the rest of the book in that it is made up, almost exclusively, of contributions from other writers who spend at least part of their time talking about individual products. Because the subject area of data mining is so diverse and complicated, we felt that you would benefit from getting as many different perspectives as possible.

The Big Database in the Sky
What Is a Data Warehouse Anyway?

Los Angeles, 1994: After we had waited around for a good 20 minutes, the maitre d', dressed in a Hawaiian print shirt and sandals, showed us to our table. It was an incredible view—plate glass window walls on three sides. To the left was a building with a huge whale painted on it; to the left and straight ahead, the Pacific Ocean in all its tumultuous glory. We settled in, ordered drinks, and talked about the weather for a little while. Finally, our host (I will call him Preston) was ready to get down to business.

Preston is the CFO (Chief Financial Officer) for a major consumer goods manufacturer. He is well known in his industry, has many years of experience, and has a reputation for being sharp, innovative, and aggressive. Preston is no pushover. He is one bright businessman. Yet Preston felt that he needed to have this little "informal" meeting to share some of the concerns and visions that he has. By many standards, Preston could be considered to be among the brightest minds in business today. Despite his success and apparent competence, however, he has come to the point of being completely overwhelmed with the problems that he is currently experiencing in struggling with his information systems.

Oh, taken as individual systems, his information systems probably would be considered some of the best in the business. They are efficient, well-run, and dependable. These systems, without a doubt, keep the business running and are no small part of the reason why Preston's company enjoys the strong market and financial positions that it currently enjoys. With all of these positive factors going for him, it would seem that the last place that Preston would be concerned would be in the area of computer systems operations. After all, Preston is a financial specialist, not a systems specialist. Why is he even getting involved in these kinds of issues?

You see, Preston is stuck in a serious dilemma. On the one hand, he certainly would like to contain costs and keep the existing organization running as well as possible. On the other hand, however, he sees all kinds of opportunities to make things two, five, or even ten times better than they are today, if only he could get those ugly, old Legacy computer systems to cooperate!

So, as the Pacific Ocean roared and crashed on the rocks outside our window, Preston roared on about his frustration over his current computer challenges. "Ultimately, it all comes down to my databases!" he raved. "No matter what we do, we always end up shackled by what these databases can or cannot do."

Preston then took a little time to educate us as to his understanding of what a database was. Of course, as an accounting type, the database to him was little more than a very large spreadsheet, but he failed to understand why he could not "have it his way" considering all of the time, money, and energy that gets spent on these systems. "I have this vision in my head," he said, "of this huge database in the sky. A place where all of the information that I need is stored for future reference. I mean, I understand about all the complexities and problems involved in working with my operational information in place, but why can't I just make a copy of it all and play with that?"

Preston, a person with no information-systems background and no previous exposure to data warehousing conferences and seminars, has intuitively figured out that somehow, his imaginary database in the sky (a data warehouse) is the solution to many of his problems.

So, for whatever reason, we find that corporations are turning, en masse, to this intuitively obvious solution to the problem of trying to get more and better information for the development of better, more flexible information systems.

The Data Warehouse Phenomenon

If you're involved in information systems development in the corporate world today, then you most probably have been exposed to this, the most recent phenomenon to take the business by storm. Data warehouses are the hottest new topics in the industry today.

Around the world, conferences geared to educating the masses on the how, what, where, when, and why of data warehousing are springing up. These conferences espouse the many different benefits that a data warehouse can bring to your organization and feature speakers who are "expert" in the construction of such systems.

A typical brochure for such a conference includes headlines such as:

- Applying Client/Server, Object Technology, Open Systems and Relational/ Multidimensional DBMS to Provide Next-Generation Decision Support Systems—Proven Strategies and Fresh Insights from Industry Experts and Early Adopters
- The OLAP (On Line Analytical Processing) Forum—How OLAP can benefit you and your organization

and includes seminar topics like:

- Data Warehousing—The Competitive Advantage
- How to Build a Better Data Warehouse
- Critical Factors for Implementing Data Warehousing
- . . . and dozens more

Well, if you didn't think that data warehousing was a big deal with a solid discipline and thousands of backers with clearly established track records and construction disciplines in place, then a quick browse through any of these brochures would certainly convince you. Of course, these dozens of seminars are backed by an equally impressive onslaught of data warehousing exposure in the industry media.

The media

Magazines are deluged with article after article of helpful hints and tips about how to build these data warehouses and how to manage them once they're built. Special issues, supplements, and even data-warehousing publications and newsletters are stuffing the mailboxes of corporate offices. A recent special supplement to a major industry weekly was entitled "Data Warehousing—A Mandatory Initiative for IT Survival."

Data-warehousing products

The manufacturers of computer hardware and software are equally committed to the advocacy of the data-warehousing solution as the means to helping your organization meet its data processing needs. Almost without fail, hardware vendors are touting vast, expansive data warehousing support products and approaches, from the highly specialized data warehouse multi-CPU (SMP or MPP) platforms of the UNIX-based hardware vendors to the vaunted halls of IBM with its mainframe-based data warehouse solutions.

Many of the software vendors are getting into the act as well, from the "Data Warehouse Compatible" or "Data Warehouse Ready" stickers that show up on database products, to the grandiose data-warehouse management systems that claim to provide a complete data warehouse kit (just buy this product and add data). One software vendor recently announced plans to invest $45 million in the creation of a whole new line of data-warehouse interface products, and new software companies are springing into existence daily, each claiming to meet some aspect of your data warehousing needs.

Business planning and the warehouse

As if all this clamor were not enough, recent surveys of several major corporations reveal that businesses are planning on spending big on the data warehouse as well. The sample survey consisted of organizations from the manufacturing, financial, health, retail, utility, government, banking, and telecommunications fields. The percentage of revenue spent on information systems averaged out to approximately 5% per year. Of those firms surveyed, a whopping 90% were involved in some stage of data warehousing system development.

If 90% of all businesses are building data warehouses in some shape or form, then it must be *big*. Some more information about these data warehouses might be helpful:

- Of the organizations working on data warehouse projects, over 60% are planning on storing data involving more that 20 gigabytes of data, and over 10% are looking to build systems that involve more than 300 gigabytes. Some actually are planning their systems in the terabyte range.

- Budgets for these systems range from a modest $250,000 at the low end to several million dollars at the high end.

- The number of users to be supported is measured in the tens, hundreds, and sometimes even the thousands.

Well, these statistics certainly would seem to indicate that there is a data warehouse in just about everybody's future.

However, with so much hype and so much activity, what is by far the most perplexing thing is that, although everyone knows that data warehouses are good—not essential to survival—and although there are literally millions of pages and thousands of hours being spent on talking about how to build one, there is a definite lack of information about exactly what a data warehouse is.

What is a data warehouse anyway?

So clearly, if a book is going to claim to tell you something about how to build a data warehouse, then it makes sense that we start with some kind of definition of what a data warehouse is. Coming up with a good definition for a data warehouse actually is going to be pretty difficult. Certainly not because of a lack of information about what people think it is, but more so because of an abundance of it. There is no force at work, no single authority, no regulating agency, that will establish a definition to which everyone can agree. As opposed to relational technology, which had its "inventor" Dr. Codd to act as the ultimate source of authority on the topic, and as opposed to object technology, whose definition is monitored and controlled by several standards groups and agencies, data warehousing *kind of just is*.

The closest that we can come to an original source of information about data warehouses is a series of books written by Bill Inmon and Richard Hackathorn. These books represent the first time that the data warehouse was identified as such and given the name "data warehouse." Unfortunately, as you will see after closer inspection, the underlying concepts and principles of the data warehouse really can be traced back to a much broader base and to much earlier roots.

Therefore, the clearest "official" definition of a warehouse that we can derive is the best approximation of what the term means as it is used in the industry today. It is a combination of the foundational work done by Inmon/Hackathorn as modified by its practical use in business today.

A data warehouse is a database that:

- Is organized to serve as a neutral data storage area
- Is used by data-mining and other applications
- Meets a specific set of business requirements
- Uses data that meets a predefined set of business criteria

Obviously, we will need to be a little more specific before we can claim to have provided a useful definition of a data warehouse. So we will begin by coming to grips with exactly what we mean by the term *database*. Put into even simpler terms, a data warehouse really is nothing more than a big database that holds copies of data from other systems and that then is made available for use for other applications.

What Is a Database?

A data warehouse can be many things to many people and can involve a lot of different parts, but everybody seems to agree that one of the critical components of any data warehouse is that it is some kind of a database. However, before we can make such a bold statement, we first will need to examine just exactly how difficult it is to even come up with a definition of what a database is.

The term *database*, as well as the term *data warehouse*, is a name for a thing. However, because of the extremely complex nature of the world of data processing these days, they are names that can communicate very different things for different people. Let us provide you with some examples.

The technician's view

My own personal background is extremely technical in nature. As an experienced COBOL programmer, we had several years of experience working with programs and files before the term *database* ever came into existence.

Some time in the late 1960s and early 1970s, hardware and software vendors had found that they could create specialized data-management software, called *database products*, that would handle a lot of the cumbersome data-management tasks for the programmer. These original databases—with exciting names like IMS (Information Management System), IDMS, ADABAS, and Model 204—were the first generation of software that made it possible for organizations to manage large amounts of data with ease.

So these were the first generation of database software products, known generically as "databases." As the technology advanced, new generations of these products came out: relational databases, object-oriented databases, and others. These databases still were databases in the classical sense. All they did was manage data for programs. The programs did the work and interfaced with the user, and the database simply managed the data.

In more recent years, a new type of database software product came on the scene. These "databases," mostly working on personal computers, managed the data for the programmer but came included with programming languages and features all their own. The programming part of the database and the data management part became enmeshed. So, when talking with someone about a database software product, you might get some very different answers about what they can or cannot do depending upon the experience of the person with whom you talk.

Now this little progression of the term *database* is one that makes sense from a technical perspective. However, there is another use of the term, a business use, that has a very different meaning.

The business person's view

A business person is completely unconcerned with the technical details about programming languages and database software. To the business person, that is all just "technical stuff." From a system user's perspective, a database is the collection of all of the information about a population of interest to them, regardless of where or how it is stored. For example, as far as a marketing person is concerned, all of the information about his or her customers that can be found within any of the computer systems run by the company are considered to be part of the corporate "database."

There is a customer database that consists of all of the information about who buys their products, a sales database with information about purchases, and a product-inventory database. This "database," from the business person's perspective, is not part of any physical file or database software structure, and it is not even seen as being tied to any specific applications, screens, or systems. It is simply all of the information that exists somewhere "in the system."

This more generalized application of the term *database* actually can be the cause of some pretty humorous exchanges. I'll never forget the hours-long discussion that I had with a woman named Debbie, who worked for a marketing database company. We both were considered to be "database experts" and yet it took us over 30 minutes just to figure out that what she called a database was only remotely related to what I called a database. She didn't know what ORACLE was, and I couldn't figure out why a person who "built databases" would be concerned with the standard postal codes for zip codes.

So, while at first, it might seem that telling you that a data warehouse is a type of database might be a useful bit of information, it turns out that this observation is useful only when made more specific. A data warehouse is a database in two senses—technical and business. One of the things that makes a data warehouse unique is that, at the heart of a data warehouse, there is a clearly defined physical database (technical understanding), which holds within it all information of interest to specific groups of business users (business understanding).

What Is the Specific Set of Business Requirements?

So you know that a data warehouse is a type of database. The next thing that you need to know is what people want to do with them once they are built. Again, we are left with no solid set of criteria from which to work. However, what we can do is point to a set of certain key assumptions that most people make when it comes to data warehouse construction.

In general, when people talk about making use of the information within a data warehouse, there are two uses to which it is to be put. First, they usually begin talking about "user friendly" query tools: Executive Information Systems (EIS), On Line Analytical Processing (OLAP), and Decision Support Systems (DSS). This impressive list of acronyms has become known generically in the industry as *data-mining applications*. Second, they often demand that the data stored in the data warehouse be formatted and exported for use by other systems. Sometimes these systems are new; sometimes the information is shipped back to its sources in a validated form.

So, to be more specific, a data warehouse is a database, designed to be utilized by data-mining products and applications and to serve as a staging area for the extraction of that data by other applications.

Data-mining applications

There are several reasons why data-mining applications have become as important as they have over recent years, and their application is so specialized and complex that we will be dedicating a fair portion of this book to their understanding and utilization.

By including data-mining applications in our list of prerequisite components for a data warehouse, we find that it becomes much easier to explain why people are interested in building a data warehouse in the first place. Data-mining applications have some very specific requirements for the data that they utilize. The data must be clearly defined, easily accessible, and stored in a specific format. The data-warehousing approach makes that much easier to do.

For many organizations, it might be said that a data warehouse simply is a database built to support the use of data-mining technologies.

Data mining: The controversy

There is a raging debate currently underway in the IT community. Like so many "buzz words" and "buzz technologies" before it, the term *data mining* is the subject of considerable discussion. While some "truists" maintain that the term should be used to define only a very limited subset of data-analysis tools and techniques (only the "hard" disciplines of artificial intelligence, neural networks, and data discovery), another, even larger group of people maintain that the term should be utilized to define any of the vast assortment of products and approaches that involve any kind of query, reporting, or data exploration, no matter what form it takes. We have purposely deferred our discussion of this matter until the later chapters of this book, specifically chapters 13 (which provides you with our definition of the term) through 20.

Staging data for use by other applications

There also are many reasons why organizations would find it useful to create a system to serve as a kind of data "clearing house" for other systems. With many different systems at work and so many different versions of the same data floating around, it becomes impossible to coordinate them all without some kind of special staging area to get things organized.

While data-mining applications and the desire to create a neutral storage area for data can result in a wide variety of approaches and applications, the format for the storage of the data that is needed must meet several specific characteristics. For operational and efficiency reasons, the data needed by these applications must be stored in an area separate from the operational systems that created them.

In the case of data-mining applications, this separate area is crucial because these applications tend to be very resource-intensive when it comes to data, and attempts to share data between these applications and the legacy systems that create the data have ended in performance disasters.

Characteristics of data within the data warehouse

My consideration of the primary purpose of a data warehouse to serve as a staging area for other applications leads us to the first of our observations about the nature of the data within the data warehouse itself. If the data warehouse is to function as this form of "neutral" data storage area, then we can conclude: "A data warehouse produces no new raw information. It serves only as a storage area for the information produced by other systems." This certainly is consistent with its name, data "warehouse." A data warehouse is not a data factory.

Historical data

Not only do data-mining and other types of applications require their own set of data to function, they usually require much more data than the amount that legacy systems are used to carrying. Operational systems cannot afford to keep track of all of the changes that occur to the data as time goes on. The systems would "choke" from the sheer volume of data needing to be managed. So, in general, operational (legacy) systems are designed to run "efficiently."

Data-mining operations, on the other hand, are meaningful only when they have access to a lot of the historical information that legacy systems traditionally have discarded. Therefore, the second characteristic of the data within the warehouse is that it will contain not only current copies of information, but also historical copies as well.

For the most part, people do not build data warehouses for the sole purpose of supporting only one data-mining application. Although certainly possible, it has been determined that it can be much more efficient to design the warehouse to hold data that several different applications can use simultaneously. To make this possible, the data warehouse must be designed in such a way that this "sharing" of data is simplified. The third characteristic of the data in the warehouse is that it is organized in a way that makes it easy for people to find and manipulate.

While the definition proposed so far might seem a bit general, it needs to be, because the scope of data-warehousing applications is so broad that it is difficult to define it in any more specific terms.

Diagram of a Data Warehouse

Therefore, you can see that a data warehouse project really is made up of three major components (see Figure 1.1).

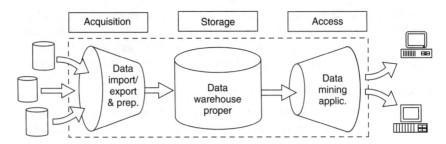

Figure 1.1 The three components of the data-warehouse system.

The first component and the center of any data-warehousing system is the data warehouse itself: a large, physical database that holds a vast amount of information from a wide variety of sources. The data within it has been organized in a way that makes it easy to find and use and is updated frequently from its sources.

The second component of the data-warehouse system is the data importing and exporting component. This portion of the system includes all of the programs, applications, data-staging areas, and legacy systems interfaces that are responsible for pulling the data out of the legacy system, preparing it, loading it into the warehouse itself, and exporting it out again, when required.

The third and most important component of the system includes all of the different data-mining applications that make use of the information stored in the warehouse.

This simple schema provides you with a basic overview of the makeup of *any* data-warehousing application.

Examples of data warehousing applications

Businesses today are making use of the data-warehousing approach to systems construction to solve a wide variety of problems and to meet a broad range of business needs. Some examples can help illustrate how this is being done.

Case 1: Quality control (petrochemicals). This company is in the business of purchasing several different grades of "raw materials," then subjecting those materials to a lengthy, complex series of refining steps, resulting in the ultimate production of several "grades" of end product.

Because of the intricate and specialized nature of these processing steps and the constant changes in the technology, the firm found itself in the position of needing to maintain dozens of independent quality-control software packages, each measuring different things, and each working at a different phase of the manufacturing process.

Because these systems had each been developed at a different time, making use of different technologies and testing for different things, it was exceedingly difficult for production control to ever figure out exactly how well products were moving through the system or to anticipate what kinds of shortages they might find at a future date.

It was determined that the best solution would be a data warehouse. The design of the data warehouse was straightforward. Pertinent information about the progress of different "batches" through the factory was identified within each of the disparate quality-control systems. The critical information from each system was copied daily to a centrally defined quality-control tracking data warehouse. A selected set of data-analysis tools then was used by production control to analyze the status of each batch and to help anticipate raw materials requirements for the next week's production runs.

Case 2: Integrated marketing (telecommunications firm). This firm, a large telecommunications provider, was having a lot of trouble keeping track of its relationships with customers. It seems that the company had several different systems, each managing different aspects of the customer-management process. The billing system had one set of records. The direct mail department had their own customer list. The telemarketing group maintained yet another set of customer contact records, and the service department maintained yet another.

The problem was that these systems did not communicate very well with each other. If a customer tried to tell someone about a change of address, depending upon who they talked to, different copies of the customer information would be changed at different times.

In some situations, a customer might put in a call to customer service complaining about the service and demanding that the phones be removed. Two weeks later, they would receive a letter stating "Thank you for being such a good customer." In other situations, bad credit risks were given unlimited credit because of anomalies in the system.

The solution that this organization opted for was a data warehouse that established a primary source of information for all customer information.

First, a customer master list was compiled. This was developed by extracting and comparing all of the customer lists provided by each of the legacy systems. These lists were consolidated into one master list. Then the critical information about these customers was identified. This information was extracted, "sanitized," and formatted for storage within the warehouse. Finally, applications were developed that could take advantage of this new consolidated customer view.

Case 3: Financial systems control (banking). This organization found itself deluged with synchronization problems between dozens of different accounting systems. While each different division of this bank had accurate accounting, it was becoming increasingly difficult to create consolidated financial statements that made sense.

As part of an overall re-engineering of the bank's information systems, a financial-systems data warehouse was constructed that would make it easy to balance one system against the others.

A recognizable pattern

The previously cited examples are only a few of the many different ways that organizations are trying to apply the data-warehousing approach to their systems challenges. It can be informative at this point to note the similarities in the situations that are being faced.

In all of the situations cited, and in the vast majority of cases, businesses are turning to data warehouses to integrate data across disparate legacy systems. The subsequent goal is to use the consolidated data to better understand, coordinate, and estimate their organizations.

The "classical" problem being addressed by data warehouses today is known as "vertical silos" of information. See Figure 1.2.

In this scenario, the operational systems that run the company are pictured as vertical stacks, each of which is dedicated to the efficient execution of some aspect of the business' operations. The data warehouse then is utilized as a way to "bridge" these vertical silos and to integrate the information that each holds into new, more synergistic, and more meaningful ways. For example, in the case of the petrochemical company, each of the different testing and quality-control applications represented a different vertical stack of information. See Figure 1.3.

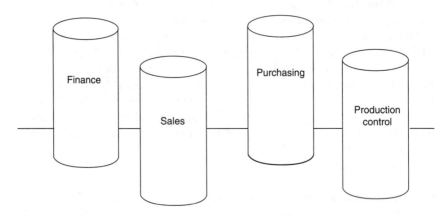

Figure 1.2 Silos of information.

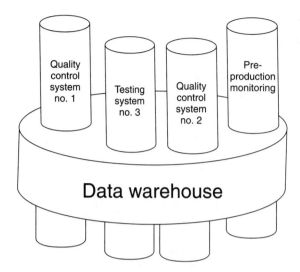

Figure 1.3 Silos of quality-control data.

The data warehouse was created to integrate the information being collected and make it available to those people responsible for the overall process.

A sense of déja vu . . . perhaps

By now, anyone who has been involved in the development of large-scale information systems for any length of time probably is reeling. These veterans of systems integration are probably thinking "Now wait a minute! Is that all there is to this data warehouse thing? Why we've been building systems like this for years!" For the most part, these grizzled veterans would be correct.

The data-warehouse concept is not new. It is almost as old as corporate data processing itself. We are aware of dozens of projects that attempted to do the same thing, years before the term *data warehouse* was even coined. We can even recall several articles in *Computerworld* and other industry publications as far back as 1985 that played with the data warehouse theme.

Therefore, the question that comes to mind is: Why all the fuss about data warehousing at this particular point in time? Why is this approach, which seems logical and which has been successfully utilized hundreds of times in the past, suddenly being treated like the greatest new approach to systems development?

While it might be impossible for anyone to believe how a phenomenon like this builds this kind of momentum, several factors probably have contributed significantly. To discover the roots of data-warehousing mania, we can turn back to the days of the mainframe computer system.

A Storm on the Horizon: 1975

Back before the wholesale incursion of UNIX servers and personal computers onto the data-processing scene, the mainframe computer ruled as the unchallenged king of corporate computing. At that time, data processing was quickly becoming a well established, stable, and dependable science. Business was in love with large, centralized computer systems, and corporate success could be gauged by how many mainframes you had and how many CICS terminals you had attached to them. As businesses continued to exploit this environment, it became clear that some limits were being reached in what could be accomplished.

It was obvious that the largest limiting factors on the continued expansion of these corporate systems was the data that they managed and the database software that managed it. The IMS, IDMS, and other navigational databases could hold only so much data at one time. More importantly, to manage that data well, the data had to be predetermined, preformatted, and stored within a solid, hard-coded database environment.

Visionaries try to prevent impending data doom

Several people saw how large, unmanageable, and inflexible these systems had become, and they began to try to figure out ways to break the bottleneck. They proposed approaches to the solution of the problem, and these proposals fell under two major categories.

The first category concentrated on coming up with a different kind of database software product. The strongest case was made by Dr. E. F. Codd with his relational-database approach. Dr. Codd proposed that the main reason for this data intransigence was the software that managed it, and with his new, freer-formed database, the bottleneck could be broken.

The other group of proposals to solve these problems came under the category of information-engineering solutions. Advocates of these solutions said that the problems of data glut and over-utilization could be resolved by coming up with a way to identify and catalog all of the data, thereby making it easy to manage through the use of data dictionaries or data repositories.

So corporations dutifully went off attempting to get around their data problems by creating new relational databases and/or by initiating different kinds of enterprise-modeling excursions. The enterprise modeling advocates were quickly followed by a large group of CASE (computer-aided software engineering) advocates, who claimed that, once the data was successfully cataloged, you would be able to automate even the software creation process through the use of their products.

Ultimately, despite many years of effort and millions of dollars, the information engineering approach has yet to yield any significant fruits. Most organizations have all but abandoned the enterprise modeling and CASE approaches to managing their data.

However, relational databases fared much better, but there is no way for us to know whether they would have ever reached their current level of acceptance without some help, because just as the relational databases began to reach acceptance, we found the halls of corporate computing being assaulted from several new sources.

Those were the days of the UNIX and personal computer revolutions. While corporate computing continued along its merry way, a new class of computer systems came onto the scene. Suddenly, there were hundreds and thousands of computers within the walls of the corporation that the computer departments knew nothing about. These systems landed on every desktop and in every department, supported by completely different groups of computer specialists, with a completely different perspective on data processing. Riding on the crest of this wave was the relational database.

Relational databases were the only databases that anyone knew about in these environments. As the acceptance of the personal computer and UNIX server grew, so did the acceptance of relational databases. Today, almost every major new system, on any platform, is built using relational technology.

Unfortunately, with the rise of the nontraditional (nonmainframe) computer platforms, and the more free-form relational databases came the breakdown of something else. The biggest fatality of the relational and personal computer revolutions was a process known as the *systems development life cycle*. This process, which was perfected over many years of experience, was the road map, the template, the instruction manual for the way that people were supposed to build computer systems.

For all its weaknesses, the SDLC gave people a set of guidelines, which when followed, allowed them to develop large, complex computer systems with some predictability. However, with the explosion of non-SDLC-based hardware products and databases came the ultimate breakdown of the methodology. We lost the instruction book for how to put systems like this together. The net result was that people continued to build newer, bigger, and more expansive systems, but these systems were less integrated with the previous systems than ever before. More and more data got duplicated across more and more systems, with less control.

The impending doom has arrived

So the problems that were cited as major concerns back in the 1970s have become problems that are hundreds of times worse than any of those people could have imagined. Organizations literally are buried in data that they cannot use, because it is stored in so many different places. Not only is the data scattered all over the place, but no one is sure what it all means. Because of the failure of the information engineering disciplines to take hold, no one has created any kind of catalog of where data is or how it is being used.

So, corporations are desperate. Desperate to get control of their data. Desperate to make better use of it. Desperate to figure out where it is, what it is, and what they can do with it. Coupled with this lack of control is a tremendous amount of pressure to do more things with the data. New approaches to marketing, just-in-time manufacturing techniques, and sophisticated statistical analysis and projection software give business people the potential to make their businesses more efficient and profitable then ever before. However, they need data to do it. They need more data then ever before, from more sources then ever before. They need it, and they need it now. They cannot wait three years or even three months.

Coupled with the power and potential of these new tools has come the latest of the revolutions: client/server. Now all of these disparate personal computers, UNIX servers, and mainframe computers can be tied together into a huge network of computers. The physical barriers that used to isolate all of these systems have broken down. Every computer now is physically tied to every other computer. However, it still is unclear as to why this should be done, because no one can figure out where all the data is and how it should be used.

Data Warehouses: The Only Viable Solution

Only the bravest, boldest, and most trusting of corporations will even attempt to get control of their data through the necessary investment in far-reaching, long-term enterprise-planning and -modeling programs. The track record of these initiatives is abysmal, and no short-term benefits are likely.

Some of the bravest have begun to embrace object-oriented approaches. While these at least have a chance of long-term payback, the start-up cost is very high. For the most part, businesses cannot afford to continue to re-engineer their existing systems anymore. Those systems, some of them currently housing 20 years worth of "fiddling," simply cannot be modified cost-effectively, and yet businesses cannot afford to replace them. They are too critical to their operations and too delicate to mess with.

So, ultimately, most corporations are stuck. Data warehousing, at this point in time, seems to be the only viable option if they are to continue to expand their systems capabilities without taking a major setback in their budgets and time tables.

The Future of Data Warehousing

Given the alternatives, data warehousing, no matter how ineloquent a solution, provides a viable alternative to the continued, less-than-cost-effective alternatives. If you carry this trend to its logical conclusion, you can see that what we are doing, through the wholesale creation of data warehouses, is creating a new, artificial baseline of data, against which whole new genera-tions of software can be written. Ultimately, these new data warehouses probably will become the foundations for the next generation of business applications. See Figure 1.4.

This more relaxed vision of the data warehouse—as the solution to many of the problems of data management faced by organizations today—has a lot of merit to it. Under this more liberal interpretation of the term, we ac-tually can envision the warehouse as supporting not only simply decision-support and query-intensive kinds of applications in a direct access manner. We also can see how the data warehouse could be used as the provider of input into a whole new generation of operational systems. It is this broader perspective of the warehouse that holds more excitement and potential for the future than the "warehouse as decision support delivery vehicle" view.

In the pages to come, we will be exploring the possibilities provided by this not-so-new approach to data and systems management and will provide you with some insights into the issues and approaches that can make data warehousing a viable alternative to systems development problems.

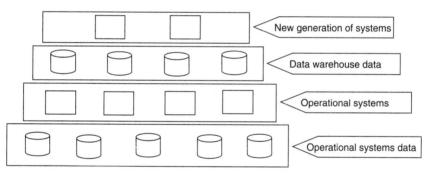

Figure 1.4 The data warehouse pyramid.

2

The Immutable Laws of Systems Development

Detroit, 1993: The client was not pleased, to say the least. We were sitting around a conference table behind the movable walls of a makeshift conference room that had been plopped into the middle of a renovated factory building. The client, an executive with several years of experience, had called this meeting to check on the status of our "audit" of her company's latest data warehousing initiative.

"Would you repeat that, please," she said slowly in an exaggeratedly calm voice.

I cleared my throat, looked around nervously and said, "Yes. Our initial findings are that you would be better off scrapping this project and starting over again."

She grimaced, "Do you mean to say that the hundreds of thousands of dollars that we have sunk into this project so far have been wasted?"

I managed a strained smile before I replied, "Well, certainly there are some things that can be salvaged and re-used, but for the most part the answer is, *yes*."

The scene that I have just described is not a pretty one. Sadly, it actually is representative of the fate of most major computer systems initiatives in business today. The records show that, if a corporation undertakes a major systems development initiative, chances are good that it will fail completely or, at the very least, end up costing considerably more, taking much longer, and doing a lot less than initially envisioned. Statistics indicate failure rates as high as 60% for even small- to medium-sized initiatives. As the projects get larger, so does the likelihood of failure. Some sources suggest that the failure rate for multimillion dollar, multiyear projects might be in the 90% range.

It is critical, for several reasons, that we address these issues at the onset of this investigation into the construction of data warehouse projects. The main objective simply is to establish validity. Anyone who claims to tell you how to build something as large and complex as a data warehouse also should be able to tell you why the approach being submitted would not result in the kind of scene that we described earlier. In our opinion, a discussion about how to avoid these failure traps is a prerequisite to any proposed project.

Unfortunately, it is in the very nature of systems-development theory and practice today to try to ignore these sobering statistics at almost any cost. The industry and the press are deluged with experts, opinions, products, and approaches to systems development that either fail to address the issue at all or allude to grandiose schemes that claim to provide a safe, predictable path for systems development; however, in the final analysis, they fall just as short as any of their predecessors.

Clearly, what is needed before we begin to talk about how you should approach the building of a data warehouse is a much better understanding of some of the fundamental forces that drive people to participate in failed project after failed project.

There are two questions that we would want answered before going any further:

- We would want to know why corporations continue to participate in systems-development initiatives that are clearly (based on experience) very high-risk ventures. Why does a company choose to risk so much in the pursuit of a data warehouse, or any other kind of system for that matter?

- We would want to know how the proposed approach to data warehouse construction is going to give us some sense of assurance that the results will be successful.

To create a framework for this investigation, we will consider the problem through the identification and explanation of several of the "immutable laws" that seem to govern and drive the corporate systems-development process today. These laws, some well-known and some simply implied, should provide you with some valuable insight into the how and why of building a data warehouse in today's high risk environment.

Murphy's Law

The first law that seems to apply in the world of computer systems development would clearly seem to be Murphy's Law: "If anything can go wrong, it will." Unfortunately, although we certainly have seen Murphy's Law at work on almost every project that we have participated in or audited, the law in and of itself provides us with very little insight into what we can do about it.

Some obvious conclusions that we can draw from our continued exposure to the consequences of Murphy's Law as we continue to build computer systems are that we are participating in a high-risk endeavor and that we should exercise as much caution and reduce as much risk as possible. While we will attempt to apply this rule of conservatism to our approach whenever possible, we will see that, in many cases, it is simply not possible to do so.

Why Do People Take the Risks?

The first objective then is to try to determine why people continue to participate in a seemingly endless parade of disastrous systems development projects.

To understand this superficially obvious need of major corporations to invest willy-nilly in a wide range of high-risk, low-success projects, you need to take a step back and try to understand this process from a larger perspective. You need to understand something about the relationship between businesses and their computers.

The Introduction of the Computer to Business

Back in the early days of business, before the introduction of the first Burrough's or IBM mainframes, businesses were run by people and by paper. The bigger the organization got, the more paper needed to be created, and the more people were required to take care of it. Take a simple function like accounting. Corporations needed dozens of payroll clerks, who spent their time adding, subtracting, journaling, and ledgering all of the different financial transactions that drove the business along its merry way.

Then came the first computers. They were large, sensitive, and very expensive, but these computers, with their simple punch cards as input and output, provided the business with the opportunity to process a lot more paper a lot more quickly and with a lot more accuracy than they could with human computing. So the first mainframes made their appearance.

The result was staggering. Corporations got an incredibly lucrative return on the investment that they made in these systems.

Because it worked so well the first time, they did it again and again and again. Soon, as computers became bigger and better, smart corporate executives were able to capitalize on those capabilities, too. Each new generation of computer capability enabled large corporations to gain efficiency, reduce costs, and grow larger.

This pattern has continued to this day. As computers become faster, more powerful, and more efficient, opportunistic business people take advantage of those capabilities.

Moore's Law

Therefore, the next law that we will consider is Moore's Law. Moore examined the relationship between computer power and cost and found them to be inversely related. In fact, he identified a pattern. The details of the pattern vary depending upon the variables that you include, but it generally states that, every few years, the power of computers increases exponentially with a corresponding drop in the cost to provide that power. (See Figure 2.1.)

Moore's Law tells us that, until some kind of wall is reached in the current progression of computer capabilities, there will continue to be drastic growth in the computer capabilities area.

Darwin's Law

While Moore's Law provides us with the ability to understand what has been happening with computer technology itself, it does not explain the relationship of business to that capability. To understand that, we will make an application of Darwin's Law of evolution.

Charles Darwin was the first to propose the theory of evolution. We will be able to draw many parallels between Darwin's observations about how living systems change and grow over time and help you understand how business systems do the same thing. The first application of this law is Darwin's basic observation that the species that survive are the ones best

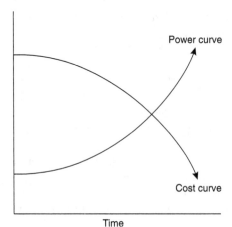

Power curve

Cost curve

Figure 2.1 Moore's curve. As the power of computers increases, the cost of that power decreases.

Time

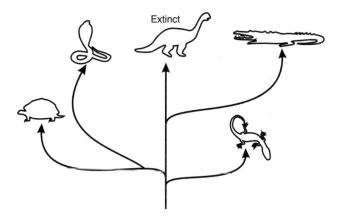

Figure 2.2 Reptile evolution.

able to take advantage of the opportunities presented to them. This is Darwin's "survival of the fittest" theory. In the same way that different kinds of animals were able to survive by capitalizing on their environment better than others, so too does this rule apply to business.

Since the wholesale acceptance of the computer as an integral part of business, it has become clear that the businesses that thrive and survive are those that are best able to take advantage of computer capabilities. No major business organization could survive today without its computer systems. Also, the companies with the better systems do better. Just look at any industry: transportation, finance, manufacturing, etc. All are driven by the computer technologies that hold them together.

So, the answer to the question about why businesses keep taking on these high-risk computer systems projects is clear. They do so because they must to survive in a highly competitive marketplace. Just as evolution has shown that species evolve through a process of trial and error, so too do computer systems. (See Figure 2.2.)

Just as the paleontological history of each species is peppered with dozens of "dead end" evolutionary adjustments that failed (causing the extinction of the species), businesses must experiment with untested and risky systems-development projects if they hope to beat their competition to the next plane of existence. (See Figure 2.3.)

Going back to the computer power/cost curve proposed by Moore's Law, we can draw a parallel curve to indicate the progression of corporate computer systems. The corporations that survive will be the organizations that exploit their systems' capabilities along the ever-changing computer power/cost curve. (See Figure 2.4.)

This analysis provides us with some valuable ground work for developing a better understanding of why organizations are spending the kind of

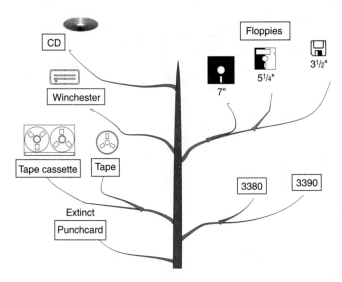

Figure 2.3 Evolution of computer systems.

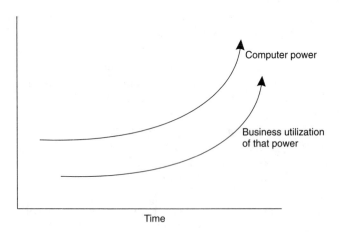

Figure 2.4 To survive, a business must strive to keep up with the available computer power.

money that they are and taking the risks that they take. The trick is to figure out how to keep your company on the curve. To spend too much money or to invest in dead-end approaches can mean the end of the business, but so can being too conservative and allowing the competition to gain an irretrievable advantage by moving along the curve faster or better.

Moore's Complement

Armed with the insights provided by Moore's and Darwin's Laws, you can begin to develop an appreciation for why things are done the way they are. Business people know that they need to continue to improve their computer systems to survive. They also know that the process will be risky and that they will have to take some leaps of faith to move along the evolutionary scale. Yet, in and of itself, this need to change does not fully explain the chaotic and tumultuous environment that surrounds most projects of this nature. To understand that, you need to gain access to a couple more of the laws that seem to drive this industry and a more detailed understanding of the process of systems development.

The building of any large computer system for business these days is an incredibly large and complex exercise. The deployment of a large system can involve the concentrated efforts of dozens, and sometimes hundreds, of people, all working to make the vision of the new proposed system a reality.

Given this foundation, you can begin to develop an appreciation for what some of the underlying pressures are to drive organizations to undertake these projects. To get an even better picture, we will turn once again to some of the fundamental laws that drive the process.

While Moore's Curve allows us to anticipate the progression of computer systems capabilities, there is a hidden aspect of this curve. Moore's Law tells us about the raw processing power that improved capabilities provide, but it says nothing about the complexity of the processing that is being done. As businesses learn to exploit each new generation of technology, they do so with ever more complicated sets of processing tasks.

In the early days of computer processing, computer capability was measured in simple terms. A computer could execute only so many instructions per second. Because of the limitations that those capabilities imposed, processing was very simple, focused, and linear. A certain number of cards were read and written per hour.

As more computer power became available and as the ability to share data through disk packs and databases developed, the complexity of the systems increased tremendously.

In other words, in the early days, the computer could do little more than compute percentages and store the totals for a payroll. With improved capabilities, systems could perform comparisons of different salaries, operating efficiencies, and so forth.

Today, these simple tasks are taken for granted, and the computer is expected to extrapolate, interpolate, and perform sophisticated statistical analysis, linear algebra, and other extremely complex processing.

The increase in computer power that is attained is not simply applied to the tasks that were previously being done. The new power available with the second generation of computers was not utilized to get those computers to read tapes faster and enhance the overall batch processing approach. Instead, the newly available power was used to create a new more complicated type of processing: real time, direct disk access.

At the same time, the amount of information that needs to be processed is continuously increasing. While the original computer systems were expected to keep track of all of the most recent transactions, many of today's systems are expected to "remember" everything that ever happened.

Not only is each new generation more complex and makes use of more data than previous generations, but to provide new, improved value over previous systems, they must be bigger and work with more of the processes and data collected by earlier systems than ever before. By definition, a new system that provides a new kind of value must make use of the things done by the earlier generations of systems.

We again can identify parallels in the natural world. If you were to take a look at the different components of the human brain, you would find that it is organized in many layers. At the core is a small area of the brain that takes care of only the most basic and rudimentary of processes. This core area makes sure that we breathe, that our heart pumps, etc. The next layer, which surrounds this core and interfaces with it, takes care of a second more complex set of functions. The process continues until we reach the outermost layer, which is the largest and the most complex and which handles all of the higher functions: thinking, creating, organizing, and communicating.

What evolutionary biologists have found is a correlation between each of these layers of the brain and the evolutionary progress of different forms of lower animals. We find that we can attribute the construction and functionality of each layer to the full thinking capability of our lower-level cousins on the evolutionary ladder. (See Figure 2.5.)

In the same way, each new generation of computer systems is built upon the foundations of the systems that came before it. Those systems are never eliminated but simply are re-integrated in new ways to feed and support the higher functions.

So, what is not obvious from the Moore Curve is the assumption that, as computer capabilities increase and costs go down and as businesses fight to stay as close to the curve as possible, there is a corresponding increase in the complexity of what the systems are expected to do, in the volume of information that they must process to do it, and in the interdependencies with older systems that must be integrated. (See Figure 2.6.)

Brooks' Law

These lessons of the biological world provide us with some valuable insight into the reasonableness of what we can or cannot try to accomplish. It is clear that Mother Nature wastes little and that systems that get the job

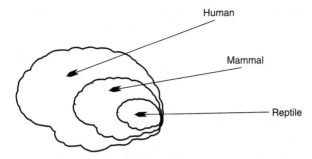

Figure 2.5 Layers of the brain.

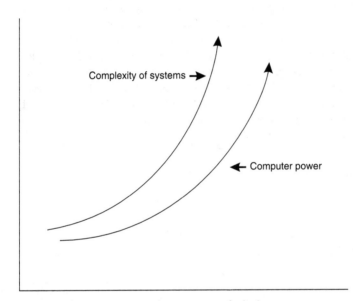

Figure 2.6 As computer power increases, complexity increases.

done are kept. By contrast, our experience to date has shown that organizations are finding it impossible to eliminate old antiquated systems. While this observation appears obvious, it forces us to turn to yet another of our basic truths and that is the one proposed by Frederick P. Brooks, Jr.

Back in 1975, Brooks was the author of a book called *The Mythical Man-Month*. In this book, Brooks, a project manager for a very large computer operating-systems development project, cited many of the inconsistencies and counter-intuitive forces that seemed to be at work in the development of computer software. These observations were incredibly insightful and are more valid in the systems development world today than they were in the 1970s. In his book, Brooks observed that the bigger a project got and the more complicated it became, the more time would be required just to keep all of the system developers in synch with each other as the system grew. (See Figure 2.7.)

Again, it only makes sense that, as more people become involved in the process, it will take more of the energy of each resource to stay coordinated with the others.

However, what does this mean when we combine this insight with the conclusions drawn from Moore's Complement? It means that, by definition, each new generation of system will be harder to build, will take longer, and will dedicate more and more of its resources to figuring out what has been done by previous systems. It means that systems will get more expensive, more coordination-dependent, and more subject to failure, based not upon technical problems, but upon the inability to coordinate and synchronize the activities of hundreds of people and dozens of other computer systems. (See Figure 2.8.)

Nobody needs to develop a new system to process purchase orders twice as quickly as the previous system. You can fix that with a simple upgrade to your computer's memory. Nobody needs a system that does what an earlier generation of system did, using the latest and greatest Windows-based, mouse-driven screen. It provides no new value to the company and, therefore, does not make economic sense.

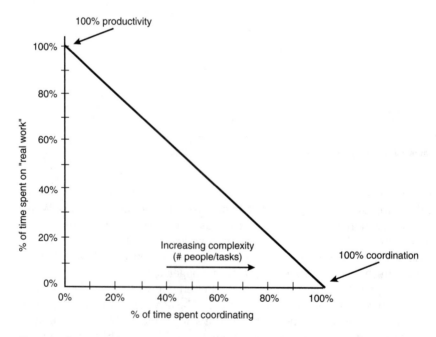

Figure 2.7 Percent of time spent on "real work" as complexity increases.

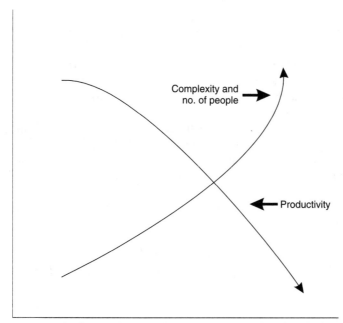

Figure 2.8 As the complexity of the systems goes up, the productivity of participants goes down.

What people need, to continue the climb up the evolutionary scale of computer systems, are systems that coordinate and mediate better.

The Consequences

Up until this point, our exploration of the laws that drive computer systems development has proceeded along a basically logical line of reasoning that no one could argue with. The observations and applications are clear, logical, and easily supported by a huge body of evidence. However, it is at this point that we can begin to uncover some of the insidious counter-assumptions and counter-claims that make the world of computer systems development as risky as it is.

The Human Need for Simplicity and Categorization

While no one could argue with the assumptions that we have made so far, you will find an incredible amount of discord when asking people what we are supposed to do about it. It is here that the rubber meets the road, and we will provide you with some viable approaches to undertaking data-warehouse construction.

In the past several pages, we have provided you with a basic understanding of the underlying forces that motivate people to do the things that they do when it comes to systems development. What we have not yet done is provide you with the detail about the complexities that underlie each of these observations. It is this complexity and the very human desire to simplify complexity that sets us up for most of the problems that we encounter when trying to build a system.

Let's face it, computer systems and businesses today are extremely complex animals. A typical corporate computer system today involves the use of thousands of computers (from mainframes to minis to personal computers), billions of lines of computer code, and billions upon billions of bytes of stored data.

It is not even humanly possible for anyone to understand it all. You would have to be an accounting genius, marketing guru, manufacturing maven, have years of experience in dozens of disciplines, and be technically competent in dozens of languages, operating systems, applications, and network technologies. No one can take it all in, and this is where the real problems begin.

The Participants in the Systems Development Process

To help you understand the process a little better, we will attempt to oversimplify the case and say that there are basically three groups of participants in any systems development initiative: management, operations, and systems.

Management defines all the people involved in the control and direction setting functions of the business. They usually are executives and are commissioned with responsibility for setting the direction of the business, monitoring its progress, and approving its major initiatives and expenditures. Management is always involved whenever large sums of money or major operational modifications are concerned.

We will use the term *operations* to identify those people within the business who are commissioned with the day-to-day execution of the duties that make the business run. We usually identify different operational units as divisions or departments. Each is commissioned to perform some set of tasks that help the corporation get its job done.

The final group involved in systems development includes the people that work on computer systems themselves. These are the people that run the *systems*, write the programs, and make the computer systems vision a reality. (See Figure 2.9.)

To effectively deploy a new, major computer system, these three groups each have a vital role to play. In general, it is the job of management to be aware of the marketplace, to know what the competition is doing and is likely to do, and to set the agenda for operational enhancement that will

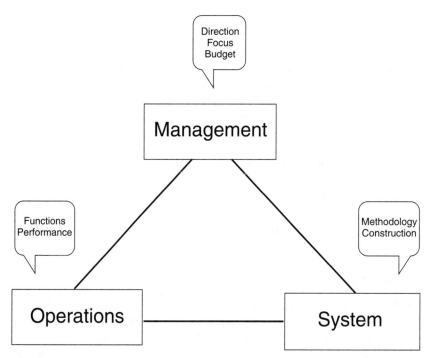

Figure 2.9 Balanced roles.

help the organization grow or at least survive. It is the job of the operational group to provide systems developers with the knowledge and experience necessary to deploy a new system that will be effective. It is the job of the systems group to take the direction provided by management and the input provided by the operational group to build a system that meets the requirements of both groups.

This model provides us with the starting point for the development of a better understanding of what goes wrong when large systems are built.

The Systems-Development Life Cycle

Given that, by definition, new technology systems are going to be extremely large and complex, will involve individuals from management, operations, and systems, and will provide new levels of functionality and interdependency than ever before attempted, we are faced with our next problem, which is figuring out who should have input to the decision-making process.

Historically, we find that most large systems initiatives have been proposed and are sponsored by individuals from any of the three groups, or jointly between them all. In other words, sometimes it is management's idea; sometimes operations; and sometimes the driving force to build a system comes from the systems group itself. As the systems-development cycle continues, however, it is clear that participation from all three groups will be mandatory. Because it is not possible for anyone to really understand all of the consequences of what will be involved in the systems development, people assume that they can trust that those things that do not make sense to them have reasons that members of the other groups do understand.

It is this tendency to have faith that leads us to the last law that we will consider. Ultimately, the process is driven by the systems people. They are the people charged with responsibility for the delivery of the software and hardware, so they ultimately must orchestrate the development. So, in the final analysis, it is systems developers and their systems development methodologies that are relied upon to coordinate the systems-development cycle.

Unfortunately, it is here that we find the application of the last and most insidious law.

Barnum's Law

P. T. Barnum was considered by many to be the greatest showman of all time. He was responsible for creating the "Greatest Show on Earth" and really revolutionized the entertainment industry in the days before movies, radio, television, and video games. Probably the most famous statement that Barnum ever made about people and their seeming willingness to believe any kind of atrocious nonsense that he created was that "There's a sucker born every minute."

We place Barnum's Law at the top of the list of laws to take into account when considering this topic. For wherever you have chaos, high risk, and a large group of people who do not know what needs to happen but that trust that somebody else does, you create the opportunity for all manner of circus acts to dominate your planning horizon.

Let me begin by saying that I truly believe that the vast majority of the people involved in computer systems development are hardworking, honest people with a high degree of intelligence and integrity. However, these characteristics notwithstanding, what seems to be happening again and again is that people, on an industry-wide basis, are making decisions that involve the dedication of billions of dollars and millions of man-hours of effort with almost no assurance that what they are doing will yield anything remotely resembling tangible, usable results.

Our industry has been plagued by generation after generation of dead ends along the evolutionary scale. While some organizations have been able to avoid doing themselves any serious damage, many have found the experience to be painful and frustrating.

It is precisely because the environment that we are in is so complex, confusing, and chaotic that organizations try so desperately to place their bets on approach after approach. This tendency for people to "set themselves up" in this way was best identified by the ancient Greek philosopher Demosthenes when he observed that "A man is his own easiest dupe, for what he wishes to be true he generally believes to be true." In more modern times, Samuel Johnson stated that "We are inclined to believe those whom we do not know because they have never deceived us before."

While these approaches vary in their assumptions and solutions, they all have the same basic set of claims associated with them, and, as shall be evident, these claims themselves mark the approaches as doomed to failure.

Claims

It is intrinsic in the way that the computer systems industry works, or at least how it has worked up until this point, that people are looking for ways to make the process easier to live with. Because of this, we are bombarded with generation after generation of magic solutions that are guaranteed to:

- Simplify the development process
- Reduce the cost of systems development
- Make it possible to maintain and modify code for less
- Develop systems very rapidly

In other words, no matter what the claim happens to be, whether it be:

- CASE
- Relational databases
- Client/server
- Object oriented
- Repository
- Enterprise modeling
- Data warehousing

all claim that, if you simply do it their way, all of the problems that you are experiencing with your new systems development process will magically go away.

Now the fact of the matter is that each of these approaches has merit. Each can, and has, contributed to the progression of organizations up the evolutionary scale of computer utilization.

However, the following facts are equally true:

- None of them has simplified anything. Each has added another layer of complexity on top of what already was there.

- None of them has resulted in the ability to build large, complex systems more quickly or for less money or effort.

- None of them has managed to reduce the risk involved in undertaking new systems projects (most of them actually add significantly to the risk, time, and expense).

The reasons should be obvious. As we have already discovered, it is within the very nature of what we are trying to accomplish to continuously add to the cost, complexity, and time. There is simply no way to get around that.

We refer to these approaches under the section "Barnum's Law," not because they have no value, but because people in the management, operational, and systems side are all too likely to embrace these new approaches based upon their promises, without considering the consequences.

At least when P. T. Barnum introduced you to the three-headed dog boy from Mars, you were amazed and entertained for your trouble. In our case, the results are anything but amusing.

When you take all of the different factors that are simultaneously working against the builder of a new system, it actually is quite amazing that anything gets done at all. By combining the ever-increasing capabilities as indicated by Moore's Law and the concomitant complexity demanded by the entrepreneurial "survival of the fittest" approach that business takes to computers, if you add a few dashes of Brooks' Law and Barnum's, you have all the makings of a first class fiasco.

Any proposal that claims to provide you with a road map that can help you successfully build a data warehouse had better include, in its very core, the ways and means to address the many weaknesses that we have so far expounded.

There are certain assumptions about any systems-development approach that we dismiss immediately as being infeasible, and there are certain characteristics of the process that, by definition, must be included in the planning if the system is going to be successful.

Survival of the Fittest for Computer Systems

At first glance, it will seem that the effect of all of these laws on our attempt to develop a new computer system would result in nothing but chaos and failed systems. Yet, computer systems do get built, and businesses do function by making use of them. Somehow, yet another law would seem to be in effect.

To understand how this law works, we will need to take a few steps back and take a brief look at the history of computer systems and the business.

The Early Days of Computing

If we go back to the early days of computers in the business, we can begin to gain some insight into how this law originally was established and see how it still is at work today. In the days of business before computers, the corporation was driven and managed by paper. Accounting, sales records, production control, everything was managed by people and paper. Obviously, this resulted in a lot of paper and in the need to have very large staffs of people who simply managed that paper. Not only were these businesses driven by paper, but they also were driven by computation. Big companies had scores of accounting personnel, whose jobs it was to add, subtract, and tally all of the different transactions that had to take place.

A good mental image of any large, precomputer business would have to include the existence of incredibly large buildings, whose only purpose was to house filing cabinets full of records and large rooms full of accountants with adding machines on their desks. People's jobs involved scurrying about gathering up papers, adding things up, creating new papers, and passing them on to the next group.

Into this paper and manually intensive environment were introduced the first business computer systems. When the first computers were brought into the business world, the people involved had no idea just how big and complicated this whole process would get. The business people of those days were looking at very specific, tactical business problems and expenses, and the early computers provided good, simple tactical solutions.

We began to see large, bulky, punch card-driven computers being introduced to the business. These early applications were very simple (by today's standards) and very limited in scope. For many businesses, the payroll system was the first one to be introduced. Payroll was a perfect application for the computer. It was simple, straightforward, repetitive, and time-consuming. So the payroll systems moved in, and the payroll clerks moved out. The same kind of pattern occurred in other operational areas at other times. (See Figure 2.10.)

Although these early computer systems were very expensive, the businesses that brought them in did not seem to mind. The reason? Simple; the deployment of these systems resulted in a very good return on the initial investment. The money saved was far greater than the money spent, and usually within a very short time frame.

So business' love affair with the computer was started. Of course, as the technology became more mature and it became obvious that even more savings and efficiencies could be gained, businesses brought in more systems. These applications were brought in one at a time and always on a good return on investment basis. (See Figure 2.11.)

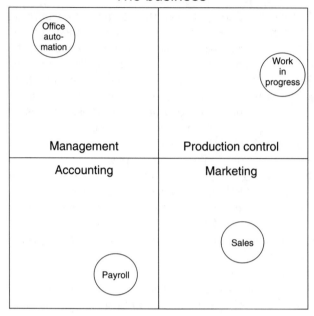

Figure 2.10 Initial deployment of computer systems. Specific, tactical, high return on investment.

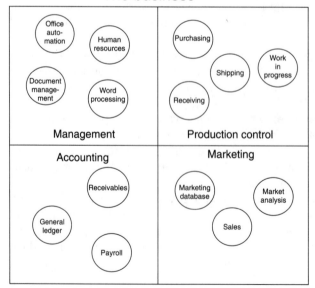

Figure 2.11 Proliferation and creation of functional clusters.

At some point in this process, it became obvious to someone that a new kind of efficiency could be accomplished. People found that, if you took the data from one system and fed it into another one, these new kinds of "dependent" systems also yielded great returns, so the next phase, the data-integration phase, began. (See Figure 2.12.)

The integration of data also created value. New kinds of systems that did nothing but integrate data from other sources began to be popular.

The important thing to realize is that, since the earliest days of computer systems, the one thing that has always been true is that the driving force behind business' decisions to deploy computer technology has been to use it to address short-term, tactical kinds of problems.

By this statement, we do not mean that long-term computer systems strategies are undesirable. On the contrary, the history of most successful corporations today includes the presence of a sound, long-term strategic computer systems vision. We also do not mean that businesses are unwilling to spend large amounts of money on large scale applications.

What we do mean is that history has shown repeatedly that the only computer systems strategies that have stood the test of time have been based upon the business' need to address specific, tactical problems. (See Figure 2.13.)

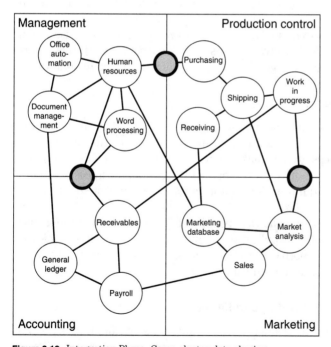

Figure 2.12 Integration Phase. Cross-cluster data sharing.

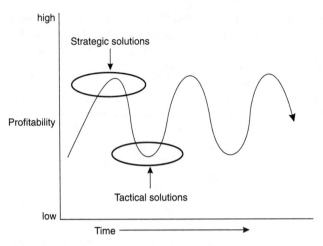

Figure 2.13 Economic cycles and systems.

The Drive to Achieve Tactical/Operational Efficiency

The entire history of data processing has been based upon the application of systems to the solving of specific problems. You could say that it is the fundamental principle upon which the entire business/computer relationship is based.

What this means is that, no matter how hard we try to do otherwise, we ultimately are going to end up favoring those solutions that get us the best short-term benefit, no matter how good the longer-term benefits might sound.

Opposition Forces at Work

What we have seen with this historical perspective is that there are two forces at work within the data-processing environment: the drive on the part of each business area to make their own internal processes more and more efficient and the drive on the part of the overall business to attempt to integrate more and more of this information to accomplish greater overall efficiencies.

In the long run, this means that people will continue to build more isolated, highly specialized applications while at the same time achieving greater integration. In both cases, only those solutions that provide the most value to the overall organization will survive.

The Death March of Strategic Initiatives

The history of data processing is full of strategic visions and initiatives that claimed to provide the solution to a lot of business' computer system problems: CASE, structured programming, enterprise modeling, and a host of others. Each of these disciplines claimed that, if the business could only take a "strategic" view of their corporate resources and develop a long-term vision that treated the data as a precious corporate resource, they eventually could get to a higher level of efficiency within their systems overall.

Unfortunately, regardless of the theoretical merit of these approaches, the end result has been failure after failure. At first glance, this might not seem to make a lot of sense. It would seem that, if you approached the problems of data processing from a scientific perspective (as opposed to the rather short-term-driven, almost random perspective that the systems have been based upon up until this point), efficiencies could result. Alas, that never seems to happen.

Economic Cycles

Unfortunately, when people begin to operate their business off of visions that are far removed from the day-to-day tactical realities of the business, they tend to take on initiatives that cannot stand the test of time. One way to look at this is to consider the fact that every business undergoes business cycles. For certain periods of time, the business will be forced to be "lean and mean" under the pressure of intense competition, shifting markets and the need to change their means of production. At other times, the business will be very prosperous—high revenue, high growth, and a bright future.

When the business is at one of the high points of the cycle, it has the time, available resources, and keen interest in the development of long-term strategic kinds of solutions. It is during this time that the business is most subject to the workings of Barnum's Law.

On the other hand, no matter how well the strategic vision has been set up, the economic profile of the business eventually shifts, and suddenly everyone is forced back into "lean and mean" mode. When this happens, the strategic implementations are the first to go. (See Figure 2.14.)

The long-term effect of this cycle is that the only systems that end up standing the test of time are those that meet specific tactical objectives. These applications form the basis of the corporate information systems infrastructure, not the more strategic, "big picture" kinds of approaches.

Ultimately, therefore, our law states that:

> The only strategic system initiatives that will stand the test of time are those tied to the solution of specific tactical problems.

In other words, only those systems with tactical relevance will make any sense. This law certainly will make sense to any manager of computer systems in the business environment. Everyone is hearing the same story these days: Don't offer me solutions that do not solve today's problems.

Like this

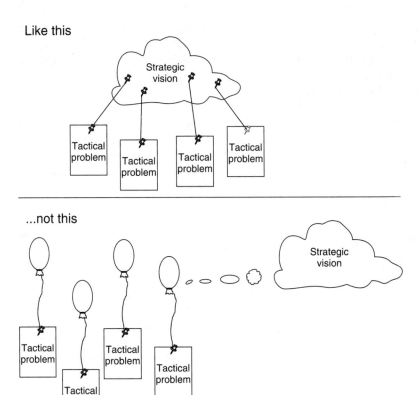

...not this

Figure 2.14 Tactical problems. Successful strategies—tactical relevance.

Applicability of the Law of Tactical Relevance to Data Warehousing

The implications of this law for the developer of a data warehouse should be clear, and the role of the warehouse defined in terms of this model. A data warehouse is the ideal approach to take when trying to integrate information between disparate systems. The warehouse can easily meet many of the data integration demands of the business on a strategic and tactical level. On the other hand, warehouse developers should stay away from any attempts to subrogate the role of already efficiently running tactical, operational systems. These systems need to be left alone as much as possible. The greatest implication for the developer of the warehouse, however, is that he needs to stay sensitive to the tactical implications of what is being built and base its construction upon that foundational strategy.

Conclusions

This discussion about the immutable laws of systems development has provided us with the ability to make certain assumptions about what we will and will not be able to accomplish with the process of data warehouse development.

To start with, we will assume that the data-warehouse project will be:

- Large
- Financially risky
- Difficult to manage
- Complex
- Resource intensive
- Time intensive

In response to these known and accepted characteristics, we will build the following safeguards into our approach:

- We will manage the problems and risks associated with its large size by developing an approach that allows us to partition the job of building one into a collection of smaller, more manageable tasks. These tasks will be autonomous of each other and will involve the production of tangible, functional deliverables.

- We will manage the financial risk by tying the finances of the project to each of the individual pieces of the process.

- We will manage the problems and risks associated with its unmanageability by organizing a structure that holds management, operational, and systems personnel responsible for different aspects of its construction, and we will tie that accountability to each of the deliverables and tasks identified.

- We will manage the problems created by overwhelming complexity by designing a structure that allows people to maintain their focus and direction. We must create a blueprint for a way to build a data warehouse that makes it possible for people to concentrate on discrete pieces of the whole while being assured that the system will work when completed.

- We will manage the risks associated with underestimating the complexity, financial cost, or time required to get the job done by being thorough in our understanding of what it actually will take to get the job done.

To say the least, these objectives are not easily met. However, it is our hope that, in the next few chapters, we will be able to deliver on the promises.

3

So You Want to Build a Data Warehouse?

The Data Warehouse Development Life Cycle

Boston, 1995: The scene is the cafeteria of a major financial services firm. The people sitting around the table are enjoying a break from their work day. They all are involved in different aspects of the construction of a financial data warehouse for their firm.

"So, how's the programming progressing on that new data-warehouse system?" an innocent bystander asks.

"Don't ask," replies the disgruntled programmer, sipping a cappuccino and snorting in disgust. "I've never seen such a screwed up project in all my life. Here we are, four weeks into the development of the screens, and it turns out that the database people don't have requirements for any of the data that we need. I don't know what they expect my programs to work with. To top it off, we just found out that it doesn't really matter because the users have just changed their minds about what we're supposed to be doing anyway. We just got word that half of the screens we've been working on are going to be changed so much that we have to just start over."

The resident database person then chimes in "Yeah, well, we would've had what you wanted if the people writing the programs that take the stuff out of the legacy system had gone after the right data in the first place! What they got for us is all wrong. Bad dates, missing fields, it's just about all garbage. . . . Why, did you know that, by the time we got through with those name and address files, we found out that only about 100,000 of the 1 million records had usable state codes? There's no way to fix it. Someone is going to have to go in and change all those records manually."

"So when do you think this project is going to be finished?" asks our clueless bystander.

"How about in, say, five more years" replies the programmer.

"But the project is scheduled to be done by November," he persists.

"It will never happen," responds everyone at the table, in unison.

This little snippet of a discussion is typical of the conversations that occur daily within the ranks of people building data-warehousing projects (and most systems-development projects). This conversation does little more than echo the sobering findings that we cited earlier: Most large data-warehousing projects turn into organizational and financial disasters. If we try to develop a strategy for how to build a successful data warehouse, we must first map out a plan to prevent this scenario.

At this point, the more traditional writer might jump into yet another tirade about "how to build a data warehouse the right way." Indeed, it is tempting. We could quite easily slip into a rhetoric here whereby we describe the different phases of a data-warehousing project (don't worry, we will get to that, but not quite yet). We then could proceed to give you all sorts of technical detail about how to build this feature and what not to do with this or that situation.

All of the information would be useful, and I am sure that a lot of it would help you in the process of building your own system. However, by diving into that level of detail right away, we will be missing the forest for the trees. I will end up making the mistake that so many authors, in trying to tell people how to build systems, have made in the past. I basically would be describing how to use a screwdriver without telling you anything about when, where, how, or why to use one. The results will most likely be the same. You will end up trying to use a screwdriver when you should be using a hammer and vice versa.

So, before I begin expounding on the way a data warehouse should look after it has been built, we will invest some time in understanding how they get built and how we approach building them in a better way.

What's Wrong with the Way We Build Systems?

The first step in this process will be for you to get a basic understanding of how people go about the process of building large-scale business computer systems in general and data warehouses specifically. We will approach this exploration, not from within the confines of any predefined methodology or belief system or by regurgitating thousands of pages of diatribe that dictate how things should be done, but by considering how things really happen in the business world today.

However, we will use the traditional systems-development life cycle as a starting point. This process describes the process of systems development as:

- Development of concept
- Feasibility study
- Analysis
- Design
- Construction

Starting with this framework will be useful for many reasons. First, it makes logical sense to do things this way; second, it is a framework with which everyone can identify and, therefore, can serve as a common point of reference; third, it allows you to better understand how the process can go awry so often.

In our examination of the way things really get done, we will be especially sensitive to those situations that support the observations and rules that we have discussed in previous chapters. We will try to identify the ways that the approach actually seems to be designed to create failed system after failed system.

We will try to identify the major factors that contribute to the demise of so many warehouse projects. Mainly, these include:

- Failure to control the scope of the project (focus)
- Failure to assign responsibility for the varied aspects of the construction process (accountability)
- Failure to accurately estimate the many different costs of system development including the:
  ~Financial cost
  ~Time investment of systems, management, and operational personnel
  ~Time required to complete each phase

Specifically, we will look for the different ways that people fail to:

- Plan for the time necessary to coordinate and integrate business information.
- Plan for the time necessary to develop complex technical solutions.
- Coordinate the phases of the actual construction process.

I then will propose an approach that will allow you to avoid many of these pitfalls. What you will find is that, in general, these failures occur because of the way we approach the building of warehouse systems themselves. Therefore, if you want to build a successful data warehouse, then you had better figure out how to get around those problems.

An Approach Specific to Data-Warehouse Construction

At this point, you might be wondering if this topic might be more appropriate for a book that is not focused specifically on data warehouse building. Isn't this topic better suited for a book on how to build computer systems in general?

My response to that is simple. Although many of the reasons for the failure of data-warehouse projects are the same reasons for the failure of so many other systems development projects, the solutions for them will be unique to the data-warehouse construction process. The approach that we will propose here will provide a good solid framework from which people can undertake the construction of a good system, but the solutions that we consider will not work to help in the construction of other types of systems. It is possible to develop this kind of solution only because data-warehousing applications have a large number of characteristics that are similar, no matter where they are being built or for what reason. Therefore, we can leverage what we know about this process and assist the developer in the process of building similar systems. The insights and approaches that we propose certainly can be useful in trying to develop approaches for the construction of other types of systems, but that is beyond the scope of what we are trying to accomplish.

How are systems built today? The process of building a system is started long before the first analyst sits down and begins mapping out specifications.

Phase one: The concept is born

The first phase in the life of any system occurs when someone, somewhere has an idea about how a computerized, automated process can help the business make more money or run more efficiently. This idea then is bantered about, and if enough people think that it is a good idea and enough momentum builds up, someone eventually proposes that the system should be built. In our case, that idea will be an idea for a data warehouse.

One of the first things to take note of is who has proposed the system in the first place. Depending upon the corporate culture and the specific situation, it might be a person from the management, operational, or systems group.

Phase two: System justification—feeble or feasible?

In many cases, if enough people think that the idea for a data warehouse is sound, the next thing that will happen is that some kind of feasibility study will be commissioned. Unfortunately, the quality of most such studies leaves much to be desired, and it is here that the seeds of failure are sown for the majority of the future warehouse-development projects.

Feasibility studies can be done by the internal systems people or by the operational people. Often an outside consulting firm will be commissioned to do it. The objective of this study is to determine whether or not building the warehouse makes sense.

More often than not, what actually happens is that the half-developed concepts and unsubstantiated beliefs of the project sponsors simply are regurgitated and formalized through the process. The net result is a decision to move ahead on the construction process based upon very weak business justification, if any.

A well executed feasibility study will tell people:

- What the system is supposed to do

- How much it will cost

- What the benefit will be when it is done

Probably the biggest shortcoming of most feasibility studies is that they are much too general in their scope and not nearly specific enough in their claims.

If an idea sounds "good enough" or if the momentum is simply high enough, organizations will not even bother with the feasibility phase at all.

Phase three: Consensus building

Phase three is a new phase and one that is not part of the SDLC. The reason this phase has been added is because the way businesses run has changed since the SDLC was first developed. In the "olden days," organizations were extremely hierarchical in nature. There was a chain of command. Different people had responsibility for different things, and you knew who could approve what.

Today's business world does not work that way. Businesses are much more democratic and decentralized. The lines of demarcation have blurred considerably, and everyone has a say in decisions that affect their area. Therefore, if you want to get a system built these days, you need the buy-in of all the different people that will be affected.

A good example of this autonomy and democracy in action can be found in the process of computer systems development itself. Within most organizations, any department can buy its own UNIX server, if it has the money, and basically create its own mini data center. Individual departments and individuals all have their own personal computers, and it is common business practice for these departments to commission their own systems, independent of the larger corporate information systems staff. So, if you want to build a large data warehouse, then you are going to need everyone's approval and participation.

It is here that the process becomes particularly interesting because a data warehouse is a pretty flexible kind of thing. The whole objective of building the warehouse is to store a lot of data so that a lot of people can "do their own thing" with it.

Therefore, the temptation with a project like this is to begin promising everybody that everything they want can be "piggy-backed" onto the system, either now or later. As a consequence, the original "vision" of the warehouse becomes more and more blurred as more and more "future promises" are traded for buy-in and funding approval today.

At this point, it becomes very difficult to control the direction in which the data warehouse ultimately will go. There is very little written documentation, and the "vision" usually is in a constant state of flux as more and more things are added and the vision grows larger and larger.

Of course, feasibility studies generally are not done on any of these alternative realities. If a study was done, everyone assumes that their little extra piece is not going to change the baseline numbers. The reality is that the warehouse concept usually has become so large by the time that it gets out of the consensus-building phase that it is unrecognizable.

Another damaging aspect of this informal consensus-building process is that, because it is informal, no real, formal consensus gets reached. At best, everyone involved has agreed that you can proceed with the next phase, but the process does little to appraise the level of commitment that each party makes to the process. The danger here is that the implicit buy-in of many individuals can easily be misinterpreted and considered to be an explicit buy-in. Sometimes, this comes back to sabotage the system-development process when a party chooses to pull out its support at a later date. It also can cause the advocates of the system to assume that their informal extrapolations about the benefits the new system will provide are valid, when they actually are speculative.

At this point in time, no one has seriously looked at any of the real operational parameters upon which the system is going to be based. If you are lucky, there might be some diagrams of some screens and maybe some lists of anticipated benefits. In general, however, no rigor has yet been applied.

Phase four: Getting some estimates—the pandemonium stage

It is at this stage that most organizations make their biggest tactical blunder. It is at this stage that the seeds for the destruction of the vast majority (probably over 90%) of projects are planted.

Your organization has decided that it makes sense to find out about what it will cost to build a system of this kind. At this stage, you have very little information about the details of how the system will work, and a significant investment of time and energy will be necessary to work out these details.

Unfortunately, corporate computer systems development culture has a pat solution to that problem. It is time to put the system out for bid.

The process of developing cost estimates for large-scale systems projects has got to be the sorriest excuse for a "discipline" that anyone has ever invented. There is simply *no way* for someone to tell you how much it is going to cost to build a huge system—one that involves hundreds of users and thousands of system components with dozens of operational business details to re-engineer—based upon the haphazard collection of screen layouts and benefits statements that most people start out with. Yet, that pretty much describes what most people expect. I have participated in the process of responding to hundreds of corporate RFPs (Request For Proposals) for all manner of different systems-development initiatives, and I have yet to see one that contained enough information to develop a conscientious bid.

At this point, organizations will invite different people to participate in the bidding process. Sometimes they invite the "Big Six" consulting firms or the big-name system integrators. Sometimes they involve the specialty consulting firms or independents. Often, the RFP is used as the "honey" to attract hardware and software vendors to participate in the process. In some cases, the systems people simply are asked to "put some numbers together." In all cases, people are being asked to estimate when they have no real way of knowing what it will take to build the system.

The reasons for this have nothing to do with the ability, integrity, or veracity of the people developing the estimates. They have everything to do with the false assumptions that people make about the integrity of the systems-development life cycle.

It is here that the immutable laws of data processing come to full bloom. The system being developed, by definition, must be more complex and involve more components than any system developed before it; however, for some reason, everyone seems to feel that "this one will be different" or that "this will be an easy one."

The data-warehousing project is a typical example of a system that ends up becoming oversimplified in people's minds. "How hard can it be?" the thinking goes. "Just copy the data and go to town!" This kind of thinking dooms the systems' sponsors to typically disastrous conclusions.

Complexities and Dependencies

We know, based on our application of Darwin's Law and Moore's Complement, that the new system will most likely involve the coordination of people's activities in ways never before accomplished. If it didn't, then people either didn't need it or didn't think of it before. You cannot count on people being able to draw on past experience. This means that you will have to spend a lot of time figuring it out and that you are going to have to take up a lot of those people's time to help you do it. It also means that you really cannot be sure of what the system is going to do until after that has been done.

In addition to the unworked-out details about what the system needs to do, you also will get into problems based upon unanticipated technical complexities. Building the new system is going to involve making use of the latest technologies. This means that, by definition, there is no track record upon which to base a history of how long it takes to do things. It also means that there is no depth of expertise available to build the system. It even means that no one can predict what kind of hardware or software you will need to buy, and you also need to know, in specific detail, what the system is going to do. In the old days of data processing, it was much easier. You had fewer variables than today, and the business itself was much more stable.

So how can you estimate what it will cost when you are not sure what it is going to do? Ultimately, you end up with the classic chicken-and-egg scenario. You cannot develop a reasonable estimate of the cost without knowing what the system needs to do and how you are going to build it. However, you cannot decide whether you actually want to build it or not until you know what it will cost.

Many times the people who have agreed to provide estimates for the project agree to take on this dilemma. The big question is: How do they do it? The easiest way to solve this dilemma is to use several of the scientifically sound estimation techniques and the old standby technical solutions that have been developed over the years in the data-processing industry. These are known as the *WAG technique* for estimating and the *PFM technique* for answering the question of how will it work.

The acronym WAG stands for "Wild Absolute Guess." In other words, when you don't have anything to base an estimate on, make something up. It works like a charm. You get an answer every time. Unfortunately, you also live with the consequences further down the road. The second acronym, PFM, means that "Pure Freaking Magic" is the answer to any technical question that you can't answer any other way. How will you do it? PFM will take care of that problem!

For the most part, there is nothing wrong with a little application of PFM or WAG to an estimating situation. Obviously, you are going to have to do some guessing and make some assumptions about how the system is going to fit together. The problem is that, over time, as systems have become more and more complex and as technical information has become more and more diverse and obscure, the level of PFM and WAG has reached astronomical proportions. The numbers that they usually come up with are pretty close to meaningless.

How much will it cost? How much have you got?

By far, the most common estimation technique is for the bidder (internal Information Systems, or I/S, department or outside consultant) to base the bid amount on their best guess estimate of how much the organization will be willing to spend. The rationale goes something like this: "First we will get the project awarded, then we will figure out what it will do." Even more blatantly, "How much you pay us determines how much we will get done. We will simply keep building until the money runs out. Then you can either ask us to stop, or you can give us some more to finish."

Estimates of this nature can lead to all kinds of abusive situations. There are firms that will get a contract awarded and then continue to push out the scope of the project further and further, just to avoid actually having to do anything. Such projects become perpetual analysis and design projects that are halted only when the sponsors cannot stand it anymore.

Blatantly abusive situations notwithstanding, even in the best of cases, you establish a situation where a serious disconnect is set to occur between the systems, operational, and management people. Imagine the situation. A group of managers has agreed to a "vision" for the new system based upon early investigations and payback scenarios. Over the course of time, as the consensus-building process continues, this "vision" has turned into several mini-visions held by the different people who have been involved in the discussions. Finally, when systems or a vendor is asked to come up with an estimate, it is based upon a WAG that is based upon a little bit of each.

A touch of reality?

If you were to accept that the preceding scenario is accurate, how would you try to inject some reality into the situation? It is extremely difficult because of the way the stage has been set.

First of all, if the bidders want to get the work, then the last thing they are going to admit is that they cannot come up with an estimate because their understanding is unclear or that not enough information is available. What about all the other bidders? Internal systems people, consulting firms, vendors—there are plenty of people willing to stand up and say "I'll do it for this much." This is a kind of high-stakes version of "Name That Tune." If you can't bid on this, it is a reflection of your ability, not a reflection of the vision.

If the sponsors of the project were actually to listen and believe that there is not enough information to develop a good estimate, they then must go back to management and say, basically, "To get an estimate for this project, we have to figure out what it is going to do in better detail first." In other words, you have to invest a sizable amount of money in the execution of the analysis and design phases before it can be estimated. Pay for half of it up front, then we will tell you how much it is going to cost!

This is not an easy proposition to sell to anyone, no matter how trusting or farsighted they are. The irony of this situation is that the "how do we build the data warehouse" game actually is rigged to favor the building of systems with low returns on investment or even none, simply because they are much easier to estimate and control.

However, I digress. We now will continue with our examination of how system building is approached today. After the sponsors of the project have examined all of the proposals, there are several things that they can recommend:

- Walk away from the project because it will cost too much
- Award the building of the system to a bidder
- Sponsor a study to figure out more of the detail

We will ignore the first and third options as these are rare occurrences. In the case of option three, the study might or might not end up being enough to prevent the problems cited. If the job that is done is not thorough, and the project is commissioned anyway, you still will find yourself in the same position.

Phase five: Catch up—the application of a "customized" SDLC

Assuming that someone (internal systems or a contractor) has been awarded the data-warehouse contract, the pandemonium begins to really take hold. Because the bidder is aware that a whole lot of up-front analysis and design needs to be done before he or she really can figure out how to build the system, they propose the execution of some kind of modified SDLC. In theory at least, this customized approach will attempt to involve all of the parties required from management, operational, and systems areas to determine the details of the vision.

At this point, management and the operational group assume that their participation is over. They have approved the project; the systems people that are building it must be aware of what they wanted, so now they can go on to other business.

Now the operational and management people begin being drawn into an endless death march of JAD (Joint Application Development), RAD (Rapid Application Development), and in general very SAD analysis and design sessions. Despite whatever window dressing of hype that has been associated with these methodologies, the reality is that these sessions are conducted for one reason: to try to figure out what the system really is supposed to do.

It is at this time that all of those "pesky little details" about how the system is going to work, how the operational people will do their job differently, how the system is going to impact existing systems, and where the data is to support the vision that people had of the system begin to unravel. For the most part, as people participate in more and more of these sessions, the original vision gets foggier and foggier. It is at this time that people begin to discover the real cost of the system in terms of their investment of time and energy in the coordination of activities and the changing of their work environment. It also is at this time that the systems people begin to realize just how complicated and thorny the design, loading, and delivery of the data warehouse really are going to be.

Of course, by now it is too late. Commitments have been made. No one wants to take the bull by the horns and go back to the project sponsors and management and say "Boy, were we off! It is clearly going to take four times longer and cost five times more than we agreed to!"

No, no one wants to do that, and usually no one does. Usually, they try to defer the inevitable as long as possible and simply hope that something will happen to salvage the situation. It hardly ever does.

There are several symptoms of a project that indicate that this kind of stall-out has occurred. First, the users who are supporting the design process find less and less reason to participate in the process. They would much rather go without the system than continue with the painstaking, back-breaking work of constantly revising their visions over and over again while the necessary interchange between systems, operational groups, and management takes place. In general, people would rather do anything than participate in the grueling process of trying to figure out how to rectify literally hundreds of discrepancies between what people thought they were going to get and what they are going to have to live with.

Eventually, the project gets to the point where everyone involved in the process of building it knows that the objectives that were set will never be met. Severe frustration and a loss of motivation set in, and the whole process gets even harder to move along.

Phase six: Compromise and surrender

After things have gotten bad enough, enough has gone wrong, enough excuses have been made for enough mistakes, and enough people have been blamed, management steps in and declares a compromise. If anything at all is going to be delivered, then clearly the scope of the vision is going to have to be severely trimmed and the delivery schedule will be greatly lengthened. This is the first sign of compromise: the extending of deadlines and the cutting of what the system is to deliver.

In the more adroit corporate culture, this will be disguised via the creation of new "phases." ("Oh yes, of course, the system will do that; it was just moved over into phase two.") If the company is committed enough to the project, then the addition of phases will become the camouflage that hides the infusion of fresh budget into the project. With persistence and very deep pockets, a company actually might get the system that it went after, but never on time nor on budget.

Alternative Approaches to the Process

First of all, let me assure you that the systems-building life cycle that we have just described is accurate. It is a cycle that has been repeated hundreds of times at corporations around the world. The question we must ask ourselves is whether or not we care.

If you simply accept this as the way things are done, then you can certainly skip the next section of this book. If, on the other hand, you would like to consider some approaches that will allow you to build a data warehouse while avoiding a lot of the waste, frustration, and false expectation setting that accompanies projects of this kind, then read on. You will not be able to prevent all of these problems, but you certainly can come up with a game plan that minimizes them.

My initial premise then will be that, if you want to build a data warehouse effectively, you must develop an approach that avoids a lot of these problems. While an explanation about how all of the different pieces should work with the system certainly is useful, it actually is quite meaningless if there is no way for you to reasonably expect that you actually can get there.

Therefore, the approach that we will consider will be much broader in its scope than most discussions. I actually will take responsibility for helping you figure out not only how the data warehouse will work, but also how you will build it.

This approach therefore will include the following:

- It will be based on a set of assumptions about how systems really get built. It will not be based upon any kind of false reliance on typical systems-development life cycle approaches.

- It will include the definition of specific areas of accountability and responsibility for management, operational, and systems participants and will attempt to fill in many of the gaps that most approaches leave between these groups.

- All phases will be tied off to specific deliverables. I have little tolerance for endless analysis and design adventures that yield no tangible benefit.

- It certainly will include techniques for guaranteeing that all of the different parties (management, operations, and systems) and all of the different components of the computer system itself will be coordinated and integrated. Computer-component integration includes all of the issues relating to the hardware, software, network, and application development within all three areas of the warehouse: the legacy systems interface, the data warehouse proper, and the data-mining front end.

- Most importantly, it will be an approach specifically laid out to assist in the construction of data warehouses. I will leverage my extensive experience and the relatively consistent nature of such projects to tie down a lot of the variables that make large-scale systems development difficult.

Organizing the Data Warehouse Construction Teams

As we have stated previously, the data warehouse is made up of three major components:

- The Acquisitions Component—A "back end," which consists of the legacy system interfaces.

- The Storage Component—The warehouse itself, which usually consists of a specially identified hardware platform that runs a specific database software product. Into this environment, you will load and store all of the information of interest.

- The Access Component—The "front end," which will consist of any number of different custom-built data-warehouse applications and any data-mining tools.

What is especially useful about this breakdown of the system is that the skills and experience required to support construction in these three areas correspond to three different personnel.

The people designated to work in the legacy systems interface area will need to have a good business understanding of the way those legacy systems work. Additionally, for most organizations, they will have to be familiar with all of the different facets of working in a basically older, mainframe-type environment.

To be effective in the construction of the new data warehouse, team participants will need to be experts in the database software product and the hardware that is being utilized. The skills of a relational database DBA and data analyst are far removed from the skills required in the legacy systems interface area.

Developers and designers assisting with the construction of the data-mining and data-warehouse applications need to be specialists in the actual business environments within which these tools will be used. The level of business and technological sophistication necessary to effectively build these supercharged front-end applications is pretty high, and the technical and design issues faced are very different from those in the other areas.

Experience has shown that, when putting together the data-warehouse construction team, it is a very bad idea to try to get the same person to work on more than one of these three areas (except in the case of three special roles that we call the *cross-component specialists*: data mapping, infrastructure, and architecture). The amount of work and the amount of detail in each area is quite different. It has been tried to "cross-pollinate" people to reduce costs or to increase coordination between the groups and have paid the consequences. Ultimately, the person ends up concentrating on one area of the three, and the other two areas suffer for it.

If you are going to build a data warehouse, then you might as well accept from the outset that you are going to need three different, autonomous types of people, each commissioned to execute a different part of the construction process. (See Figure 3.1.)

The Traditional Data Warehouse Construction Approach

Having accepted the need for three autonomous, specialized development teams, we will consider how you should set this project up. We will begin by returning to the model of how the "typical" data-warehouse project gets set up so that we can draw some comparisons.

Your data-warehousing project has been awarded to a consulting company, software vendor, or the internal systems department. The next thing that they are going to do is map out a development plan. While there can be many variations on the theme, the plan will look something like this:

1. Analysis (four weeks)—Recruit users into JAD sessions to develop data requirements and screen layouts.

2. Design (two weeks)—Normalize the data, generate DDL, and build tables.

3. Identify sources (one week)—Identify where the data should come from.

4. Data extraction (three months)—Find some programmers to read the data out of the old system for loading into the new.

5. Load (one week)—load the extracted into the tables.

6. Install the data-mining product (one month)—Install the data-mining product and point it towards the right tables.

7. User training (one week)—Send the users to a one-week training class in how to use the tool.

8. Project done.

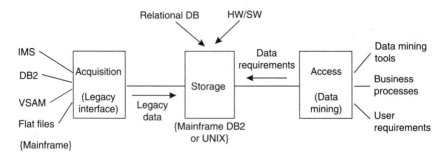

Figure 3.1 Data-warehouse teams.

What a great plan! It makes sense, it puts everything in the right order (according to the systems-development life cycle anyway), and it creates a nice, short, easy-to-understand 13-week project timeline.

Unfortunately, this project plan will never work! We already have considered, at a higher level, why this kind of plan is doomed to failure, but now we will dig right down to the detail level and see how those principles work in reality.

We will consider this project plan one phase at a time and try to figure out what the false assumptions are that lead to making these mistakes.

The first place where you will get into problems is that this project plan assumes that each phase will go to completion before the next phase begins—a basically serial plan. First you will do analysis and then, if you do a really good job, you will be able to stop the analysis process and begin the design. After design, you can begin construction, etc.

Well, unfortunately it doesn't work that way. To help develop a better understanding of why this linear approach to building data warehouses in this kind of environment cannot work, we will take a moment to track one of the many processes involved in construction to see just how complicated and interdependent things can get.

Following the Life of a Single Data Element

For our first example, we will try to follow the life of a single data element from the time that it is first conceived until that element actually shows up on an actual personal computer screen.

Operational users usually have a pretty good idea about the kinds of data that they want or need. It is not very difficult to get them to tell what these things are and what they are used for. Many times, they'll even have some ideas about where the data can be found in the legacy systems. However, there are problems that will arise after you have gathered this information.

Data-mining analysis: Multiple meanings for the same thing

The first problem will be that the users' ideas about the information that they want usually are not in sync with the information that other users want. Take a relatively simple element, like "sales." A user will say that he or she wants to see the daily, weekly, monthly, and annual sales numbers for a given product line. Seems simple enough. However, when you go and talk to a different user who also wants to see product sales information, there is a chance that he or she might not mean the same thing.

For one person, the periodic sales number that he or she wants to see is gross sales before expenses. Another might want to see a net sales number where the amount has been adjusted for variable sales expenses (take out commissions and sales overhead), while yet another might want to see the sales number with an additional adjustment, removing a percentage of the fixed costs. Sometimes people want the sales amount adjusted to reflect returns; sometimes they don't. Therefore, the first challenge is to get everyone to agree on exactly what it is they want to see, and that is not easy. It takes a lot of time and discussion to sort through all of the disagreements.

Data warehouse analysis: Mapping all the data into the warehouse

After you get all the users to agree on what needs to be in the warehouse, you are ready to create a data model that maps each of these data elements into a proposed collection of data tables. During this phase, a number of inconsistencies will be found between the individual pieces and the big picture. The way to resolve these things is to go back to the users and, once again, develop a consensus.

Legacy system analysis: Mapping the legacy system to the warehouse

So you have mapped the users' wishes into the warehouse. Now you must develop a map that tells us where all the data is going to come from.

Multiple Potential Sources for the Same Piece of Information

Let's assume that the users have all gotten together and agreed upon the one, true meaning for each of the data elements that they want to see. Now you get into the next set of problems: figuring out where to get the data from.

It is in the nature of most legacy systems that information is duplicated many times. The number for sales might be carried in dozens of systems, and each system might or might not apply some minor adjustments to it based on what they are trying to accomplish. The challenge that you must face is deciding which one of those numbers to use for the warehouse.

To do this, you often will end up backtracking through a number of systems, trying to figure out which number you want. This is an arduous and time-consuming task not only for the people investigating the legacy system, but for the data modelers working on the warehouse itself and for the users who originally developed the requirements.

Every time you run into these inconsistencies, you must go back to the ultimate users of the data. "You said you wanted the data from here, but that was no good because of this reason. We can get what we think you want from here instead. Is that okay?" At this point you either get approval, or you get sent back to keep looking.

Problems with History

Another problem is getting historical information. Unless you are very lucky, it is unlikely that the system has kept track of all the history. In many cases, no history is available at all. In others, you find that your primary, preferred source of the most accurate data holds no history but that other, less accurate systems do. You end up either having no history or needing to blend data from several sources.

Again, every deviation from the plan requires the involvement of data warehouse modelers and the original operational users.

Problems with Post-Extraction Legacy System Coordination

While the previously cited cases define the worst of what it is going to take to get your data loaded into the warehouse, you still have several additional things to consider. After pulling the data into the system for the first time, how are you going to keep it updated and in sync with the original systems? When you begin blending different sources of data, how do you get them to "unblend" for auditing and validation purposes?

So you've located the data, mapped it back to the warehouse, and even found it where you were told it would be. Now comes the next problem: How "clean" is the data?

We use the term *data cleanliness* to identify how accurate and consistent the data stored in the legacy system actually is. It might come as a surprise to many, but just because a file or database has a field called "Sales," for example, and just because the users and the programs say that this is the correct value for their purposes, this does not mean that you can be sure that all of the sales information that you want is in there or that all of the sales information that you don't want can be excluded.

Legacy systems tend to do interesting things with data over time. Fields are bridged, recycled, dummied-up, and in general fudged by any number of legacy-system programs. The fact is that nobody really knows what is in the underlying files that make up these systems until you actually dump them out and start trying to use them. If you are smart, you will check these things out early and head off some problems. If not, you will find out at the last minute and panic. When the data files are dumped and dirty data is found, you have no choice but to once again go back to the users and find out what they want to do about it.

The Case of the Missing Data

It is not uncommon to find users requesting information that doesn't exist anywhere. Remember, to operational users, the "database" is this big, amorphous thing that holds all of the information that they think they need. It is not uncommon to have to scrap 50% of a data-warehouse model because no valid, clean, accurate source for the desired data could be found. These are only a few of the dozens of data issues that crop up when building a warehouse.

As you can see, the process of identifying and pulling data into the data warehouse is not a linear process. It requires the continuous interaction of operational users, data-mining people, data-warehouse people, and legacy-systems people to validate, map, and sanitize the thousands of elements that make up a typical warehouse.

The Dump-and-Run Model of Data-Warehouse Building

Now, if all this checking, validating, cleaning, and fussing about individual data elements seems like a terribly tedious and painful process, you are absolutely correct. However, what is even more interesting is the way that a great many advocates of data-warehouse construction believe that you can avoid these problems by using what we will call the dump-and-run model. (See Figure 3.2.)

According to this model, the best way to build a data warehouse is to simply dump everything that you possibly can into it, then let the users sort it all out at their leisure. Under this plan, a team of highly trained data analysts "attacks" the legacy system's files, identifying the elements and deriving the nature of the tables being built within the warehouse based on what they discover. The thinking goes that, because you have dumped everything into the warehouse, you don't need to be so selective. Let the users figure it out.

Anyone attempting to build a warehouse in this manner is naive to say the least. There is no way that anyone can look at a bunch of data file layouts and systems documentation and "derive" what the data contained there really means. It is simply impossible. Systems documentation is never

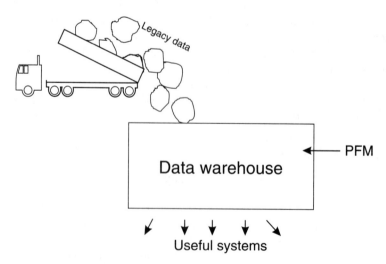

Figure 3.2 The "dump and run" model.

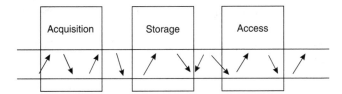

Figure 3.3 Minimizing and controlling the thrashing.

accurate (if it exists at all), and the programs will be no better off. The only way that an approach like this could work is if the users were asked to participate in every decision about every field being pulled, which is not likely.

Multiple Levels of Complexity and Multiple Dependencies

The whole problem here is that, to make the warehouse work, you have got to go through the painful, detailed process of mapping each and every element against a plethora of dependencies, then you have to map those against a barrage of technical and operational issues before you ultimately deliver a system.

There are certain realities here, and one of them is that people can keep track of only so much detail and so much interdependency at one time. When the load gets too great, they go on overload and begin assuming, guessing, and filling in the blanks with inaccuracies. It is this information overload that really brings large systems to their knees. It simply is not humanly possible to manage that much complexity.

Going back to the Brooke's Law curve, you can see that, when projects get to a certain size, everyone has to spend all their time coordinating and no work can get done. In the computer hardware world, we call this condition *thrashing*. (See Figure 3.3.)

The Autonomous Value-Based Segmentation Approach (AVBS): Building the Warehouse One Piece at a Time

My proposal will be to approach the construction of the data warehouse in such a way that you can avoid the problems caused by this kind of thrashing. Our principal assumptions will be that the data warehouse must provide real value to the corporation during each stage of its development and that there is no way that this can be done all at once. Our second assumption, therefore, will be that the data-warehouse project will be made up of several smaller subprojects and that each of these subprojects must be:

- Autonomous—It can be built without the benefit of any other subprojects except for those that already have been completed.

- Value based—With the exception of the first two subprojects (the Project Planning and Infrastructure/Prototype subprojects), each subproject will provide a real value to the corporation in and of itself. In other words, each subproject can be cost-justified based on what it will deliver to the business in added value.

While the traditional and popularly held approach to warehouse construction views the project in terms of the systems-development life cycle, the autonomous value-based segmentation (AVBS) approach views the project as a series of smaller, more manageable, self-contained mini-projects, each of which can build on the work done in mini-projects before it.

Under the AVBS approach, there is no investment in large, drawn-out, unfocused development efforts. The project is divided up into several mini-projects. Each project then must be justified to management as having its own inherent pay back. Each subproject, therefore, requires very little "sell job" at all because it is clearly understood by everyone how much benefit will be derived when it is completed.

This kind of approach puts an entirely different perspective on data-warehouse construction for everyone. You are no longer going to ask management to try to figure out how to "justify" a multimillion dollar budget to get the delivery of an unknown or immeasurable system at the other end. Instead, you are going to present management with a menu list of subproject options, each of which should deliver a different, tangible, and economic benefit to the corporation in its own right.

The question is no longer one of needing to take one tremendous leap of faith and hoping that things will work out as you planned. Instead, it becomes a process of allowing management to approve the construction of each piece of the warehouse and withholding commitment on future pieces until the pieces that have been completed are delivering as promised.

Several Types of Projects

Of course, the payback from different kinds of subprojects is going to be different. In fact, there will be four kinds of projects that need to be developed:

- Planning and Evaluation Projects—Projects whose objective is to define what needs to be done, estimate the effort to develop it, and assess the benefit it will yield.

- Validation Projects—Projects whose sole purpose is to validate the assumptions made by a planning project. These projects exist to help minimize the risk of subsequent development steps and help clarify everyone's understanding of what is to be done.

- Infrastructure Development Projects—Projects designed to create an environment within which the warehouse functions can be executed.
- Warehouse Applications—The "real" applications that make the warehouse useful.

The Overall Warehouse Development Project

The first project that we propose is one that we will use to actually develop the specifications for the overall data warehouse itself. It is the one that takes all of the "pre-bid" aspects of traditional data-warehouse construction into account. As you will see, this project actually is the most important one for many reasons.

The output of the first project should be several items. The first set of output from the warehouse-development process will be the identification of a collection of value propositions. Each of these value propositions represents a different business application that will be developed through the use of the warehouse. The second output of the process will be a plan for the development of these applications and the warehouse itself. The third output will be the specifications for the infrastructure upon which the warehouse will run. (See Figure 3.4.)

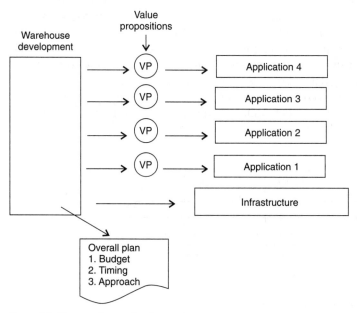

Figure 3.4 The warehouse-development process.

The most important single deliverable out of the first project is a plan that clearly identifies a series of subsequent projects, each of which will result in the construction of one, and only one, piece of the data warehouse. No project should take longer than six months to deliver, and each project should do something and provide some real value. Each should be cost justifiable as a standalone project and should make sense from a business perspective outside the context of the bigger data warehouse. In other words, it should be a real, viable project in and of itself.

Not only do you want to have your project divided into a series of smaller, autonomous projects, you actually are going to demand that they be done serially for the most part. Get the first project done before starting the second. If the projects in question are not related to each other, they obviously could be done in parallel; however, if they must be tied together, then they must be done separately and one before the other. (See Figure 3.5.)

There are many reasons for recommending this kind of approach. One of the biggest is that, by forcing the developers of the system to focus on a much narrower deliverable, you allow them to concentrate on the delivery of that piece. More importantly, this kind of "scope boxing" allows you to manage the amount of thrashing that can occur. (See Figure 3.6.)

The art and science of figuring out how to "box" the scope of these projects is something that we will consider later. Suffice it to say that determining the right scope is not easy.

To help illustrate the difference between these two approaches a little more clearly, we will develop a case study for a fictitious company that we will continue to use throughout this book. We'll call this company XYZ Motors and assume that they make automobiles. We will draw upon our experience building data warehouses for financial institutions, insurance companies, and other types of organizations as well as the many automotive warehouses that have been built, but the examples will help us make the topic easier to relate to.

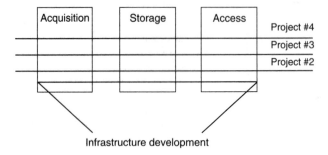

Figure 3.5 Subsequent projects.

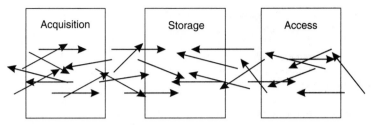

Figure 3.6 Systems-development thrashing.

The project plan originally proposed for XYZ fit perfectly into the model of what we have described as a "dump-and-run" or "traditional" construction approach. When the warehouse was put out for bid, the "vision statement" associated with it read as follows:

> The XYZ Motors data warehouse is being built to serve as a common location to house information about customers, sales, and vehicles and will make use of information from over 25 legacy systems, in addition to rented customer lists from a half dozen name providers. The information contained within the system will be used to help coordinate sales and marketing efforts and to provide the Marketing and Customer Service departments with more accurate, timely, and robust sets of information to enable them to do their jobs better.

What a wonderful vision of a warehouse! However, what does it really tell you? Not much. What it tells you is that a lot of data is going to somehow be dumped together in a common location and that a lot of people are going to somehow make good things happen when they access it. You can see the earmarks of a disaster in the works just by reading through this statement. There is simply nothing truly tangible, accountable, or measurable about the way it is being defined.

Let's take a look at the vision and subsequent plan as detailed under the autonomous value-based segmentation approach. First, the vision statement will be a lot more specific. It will include a brief summary of what each of the subprojects intend to deliver. Second, the vision statement will include a series of value propositions, one for each subproject. (A *value proposition* is a statement that specifies what the new subproject is supposed to do and what economic or operational value it will bring to the company when it is complete.)

By preparing the pre-bid project plan in this way, you guarantee that everyone understands what each subproject is supposed to accomplish, and you assure that everyone knows how to tell whether the subproject is worth doing or not. The vision statement for XYZ Motors, using this approach, might read as follows:

> The data warehouse project for XYZ Motors is being designed to serve the needs of the Marketing and Customer Service departments in the execution of

their responsibilities. The warehouse itself will consist of the information necessary to support the following business functionalities:

1. A customer-tracking system that will provide the customer-service agent with up-to-date information about customer transactions over the past five years. Included in this history will be information from the Warrantee, Sales, and Customer Service databases. The system will allow the Customer Service department to provide better and more timely responses to problems that customers might have. Research has indicated that this increased level of support should result in an improvement in the retention rate of our current customer base, resulting in the firm's ability to hold on to 10% of those customers who might otherwise defect to other manufacturers. This would result in a projected 10-year increase in sales of over $7.5 million, while at the same time allowing us to reduce up front, traditional marketing expenses by $100,000 per year.

2. A marketing database engine that will house the firm's current population of over 20 million "prospect names" in the support of direct-mail campaigns. It is estimated that the development of this capability will allow the firm to eliminate $2 million a year in fees to outside service bureaus who provide that service at this time.

As you can clearly see, these vision statements provide the reader with a much better idea of exactly what it is the system is supposed to provide. It also breaks the whole data warehouse down into its subsequent parts and provides a basic cost justification for each piece.

The Second Project: The Infrastructure Development Phase

I stated earlier that the data-warehouse project would be made up of a collection of autonomous, cost-justified, and value-based subprojects, except for the first two. The first one, the subproject that ultimately delivers a plan, makes perfect sense and in many ways fits right in with the traditional SDLC. The second subproject, however, is a little more difficult to justify and is immeasurably more difficult to do.

After you have determined the different subprojects that eventually will contribute to your data warehouse, you still have one barricade to really figuring out what all is going to be involved in the construction and execution. In the vast majority of cases, you will need to sponsor a small project, to be done before the others, that allows you to establish the infrastructure and architecture for all of the projects to come.

You will recall that we earlier established that you will need three teams of people to build the warehouse, one associated with each component: a legacy systems interface team, a data-warehouse team, and a front-end data-mining and application development team. If you are going to expect people to build small, short-lived, high-impact data-warehouse subprojects, then you are going to have to provide them with a framework within which to do it.

Working out the details before you begin

The data warehouse that we are talking about building here is not a one-shot-deal kind of system. It is large, complex, and expensive. It is not as if you can simply tell a bunch of strangers to go off and build it and expect that anything but chaos can result. What you need to do is create an environment within which each of these teams can get themselves organized and figure out how they are going to work together.

Roles and responsibilities issues

I said that the biggest drain on the resources of any project team is the number of variables that they must deal with and the number of details that they must try to reconcile at the same time. One of the major investments made by a new project team is the time that it takes to figure out who will be responsible for doing what and how they will "hand off" things to each other. The time spent figuring this out is "wasted time" as far as the individual subprojects and their value propositions are concerned. The subproject cost estimates will be based on the assumption that everybody working on this project already has figured out these organizational fundamentals before the real work begins.

If you create a "straw man" project—one that is very simple in scope but that forces all participants to work together and iron out these details—you can shave months off the duration of future projects.

Among the most important roles and responsibilities to work out are those of the three types of cross-component specialist. These individuals will concentrate their efforts on guaranteeing that what happens across the boundaries between components happens smoothly and accurately. These specialties include:

- Data Disciplines Expert—The person responsible for tracking the identity of data from the user workstation all the way back to the source legacy system, making sure that the values that the users see actually are the values that they think they are seeing.

- The Infrastructure Expert—The person who makes sure that you have built into the data warehouse everything to make it a smoothly running production environment, as opposed to the slip-shod, thrown-together collection of isolated functions that plague most large warehouses.

- The Architecture Expert—The person who makes sure that all of the hardware, network, and software components are working together as a cohesive whole.

Data discipline issues

We already have considered, in some detail, exactly how complicated and tedious the process of mapping data back to its origins can be. If you do not make one person or group of people responsible for this, then you are going to end up with a lot of disconnects from one end of the system to the other.

Infrastructure issues

In addition to all of the organizational issues that must be worked out between the data-warehouse builders and users, there are a plethora of system and project reporting, software management, environmental support, and other types of infrastructure issues that must be solved. One of the biggest pieces of this component of the system is the development of the software that eventually will manage the warehouse itself and provide information to the users about the data within it. These aspects of the system also are "overhead" type characteristics, and it would not be reasonable to burden any one subproject with the cost.

Architecture issues

Finally, there are an unbelievable number of architectural issues that involve the computer hardware, network, and software environment that also must be established. The best and most efficient way to do this is to create some kind of small project that allows the members of each team to run their pieces of the system through its paces. Most warehouse projects involve the integration of personal computers (over several sizes and types), one or more LANs, a warehouse platform, and however many legacy system platforms you might have to deal with. Setting things up for the huge volumes of data that you want to transport from one platform to the next can be quite challenging.

Pay Now or Pay Later and Later and Later

Undoubtedly, people are going to have their biggest problem with this aspect of our proposed approach. All of the other pieces will fit very nicely into the preconceived fantasies that are supported by the traditional SDLC. However, the irony is that the traditional SDLC was developed at a time when people did not need to spend all that extra time figuring out their organizational and operational relationships, building a project infrastructure from the ground up, and creating a computer systems architecture. During the days when the SDLC was invented, all these things were a "given" for most organizations. There was a stability and track record in place back then that does not exist today. There is simply no way of getting around the fact that it must be done.

If you were to diagnose dozens of the failed data-warehousing projects over the past few years (and I have), you would find that, more often than not, it is the failure of people to take these issues into account at the front end that led to the project's ultimate demise. Unfortunately, the other major cause—the failure to realistically account for what it really will take to execute an individual subproject—also is present, making for a truly disastrous undertaking.

Rationale

There are several ways that you can rationalize the demand that the first subproject to be one that has no "hard value" except to get the organization, infrastructure, and architecture in place for the subsequent subprojects.

The first is that this work should be done only once for everyone. It is incredibly wasteful to start five project teams, each working in parallel, then force each of the five to invent their own brand of infrastructure, procedures, and architecture. This should be done once, first and for all.

The second is that it really is not fair to place the burden for figuring these things out on any single, tactical subproject. This cost should rightfully be spread across the lifetime of the warehouse and all business units that eventually will use it.

Objections

For data-warehouse construction, our first and most important recommendation then is that you break the overall data-warehouse project into a series of smaller mini-projects, each of which will provide, on its own, some deliverable value to the organization (in other words, the mini-project should have a return on investment profile that cost-justifies its existence) and that can be delivered without the benefit of all of the other pieces.

This actually is a pretty revolutionary proposal, and it flies in the face of a lot of the "seasoned logic" that drives computer systems development today. This approach defies the vast majority of the "understood rules" that drive the industry and challenges many of the "sacred cows" (like the SDLC, CASE, Enterprise modeling, and many data-warehousing approaches) as well. The first thing that you are going to hear when you propose an approach like this is all of the reasons why it can't or shouldn't be done that way. The more polite individuals will say "Wow, this all makes perfect sense in theory, but it will never work!" The more intransigent will simply dismiss what you are saying as heretical and ignore it completely.

There certainly is cause for skepticism when anyone proposes that you change the accepted logic of how things are done, especially in this industry at this time. It is clear that the ways we have approached data-warehouse building in the past have not worked too well, and a radical departure like this will raise everyone's eyebrows.

Let's consider some of the more obvious objections that are going to come up as the result of this proposal and consider them for their merit.

Objection 1: It can't be done. To those that say this approach cannot be done and will not work, all I can say in response is that variations of this approach have been successfully utilized many times in the past.

Objection 2: It's inefficient. For those who cringe at the supposed waste that an approach like this fosters (with the thinking that it is more efficient to do all of the analysis first, then do all of the design, etc.), I simply would point to the abysmal track record that approach has left in its wake.

Objection 3: It's too complicated or has too many interdependencies. For those who feel that such an approach makes the building of the data warehouse overly complicated, my only reply is that my model reflects the "true" complexities involved much better than any other that I have seen (except maybe for RAD). The fact of the matter is that a data warehouse is very complicated and trying to pretend and structure it into something simpler and more easy to understand is *not* going to make it so.

My approach does one thing to make the process a lot less complex: We concentrate on stabilizing one piece at a time before moving on to the next. First, we stabilize the team itself, the infrastructure, and then the hardware, then we build one narrowly defined component, get all of its legacy systems coordination issues and user utilization issues stable, then move on to the next level of complexity.

My response to the first three objections was to basically refute the claims that they made, showing that the approach actually produces the opposite of the effect that they fear. On the other hand, my response to the next three objections is different.

Objection 4: It will cost more than the "big bang" approach. My response to this is simple. Although the proposed plan for a project run in this way is indeed much more expensive, the reality of what this will cost versus what the others eventually will cost is not even an issue, because the odds are very good that the "traditionally" run project has a very good chance of failing and never being delivered. At least, with my approach, you can stop at any time after the first real subproject is complete and have something to show for it. You can stop at any time with a minimal investment at risk.

Objection 5: It will take longer than the other way. The argument here is pretty much as it was for the cost issue. It might show up on the drawing board as taking longer, but how confident are you that the other way will work at all?

Objection 6: It's not the way we do it! What can one say to this kind of argument?

Ultimately, our response to objection numbers four, five, and six is one word: Tough.

Yes, it will take a long time; yes, it will be expensive; and, yes, it is a different way of doing things. However, it is my belief that this approach much more accurately and equitably appraises the situation as it really stands. Up until this point, we have been able to establish several of the fundamental concepts that I feel are key to understanding and effectively building data warehouses. We have spent some time in considering the basic principles that underlie the warehouses' construction. We also have presented several arguments regarding what the best approach to building that warehouse should be.

We also have begun to propose a very specific data-warehouse system-development life cycle. Now we actually are ready to define and formalize this cycle and to begin describing the different phases.

Iterative Autonomous Project Development: The Application Development Phase

Only after you have developed a clear vision of the role that the warehouse is going to play within the business and an equally clear vision of how it is going to work should you actually begin to make use of the warehouse by populating it with real data and providing that data to end users.

The last phase of the process is the continuous construction and deployment of discrete applications within the warehouse framework.

The data-warehouse development life cycle

We have established a basic set of premises regarding system construction.

Premise 1. In the vast majority of cases, the construction of a data warehouse in the corporate environment today will involve the development of extremely large, complex systems.

Premise 2. The abysmal record of failures that haunt most large systems-development projects requires that you develop some kind of understanding of why those failures occur and that you develop an approach that greatly reduces the risk that your warehousing project will suffer the same fate.

Premise 3. The root cause of most large systems failures could be traced back to three fundamental areas of concern: complexity, coordination, and cost justification.

Complexity. Systems are becoming more and more complex. In most cases, the sponsors and directors of these projects fail to take that complexity into account. When a system reaches a certain level of complexity, all of the people involved in the project end up spending all of their time trying to coordinate and resolve issues and have no time left for actual system construction. We also proposed that, in most cases, the systems will be so complex that, even under the best of conditions, they could not be done given the specified time frames and resource availability (Brooke's Law).

Coordination. Even when the complexity of the system is simplified, you are going to have an equally difficult time keeping the people from different areas of the business in synch about what the system can and should do. The systems-development life-cycle methodologies have broken down and no clear "game plan" exists for developers to follow. Somehow, you must come up with an approach that allows management, operational, and systems people to all understand what their roles are in the process and how they are to inter-relate.

Cost justification. The computer systems industry in general, and data-warehouse construction in particular, is a discipline void of any meaningful cost-justification criteria. Generally, people build systems based on whether they think it is a good idea or not, not on hard numbers that indicate the relationship between cost and benefit.

Premise 4. The best way to try to ameliorate these circumstances, decrease your risk, and increase your chances of success is to develop an approach to warehouse construction that forces everyone to limit their scope to a reasonable level, while at the same time providing all participants with the means to coordinate their activities.

We have identified three levels of complexity that must be dealt with:

- You must deal with the complexity that comes when a large group of people struggle with trying to develop a common vision of what the warehouse is supposed to do.

- You must deal with the technical and procedural complexities that a data warehouse itself must deal with.

- You must address the specific complexity of each of the individual applications that are added to the warehouse.

In all cases, you should attempt to manage this complexity by:

- Breaking big problems down into smaller parts
- Providing everyone involved in the process (management, operational groups and systems development) with a clear understanding of their roles and responsibilities within the process

- Providing a clear focus, tangible objective, and measurable deliverables for each step

- Requiring that managerial and fiscal responsibility be assigned for each stage

We have defined the data-warehouse development life cycle as being made up of the following phases:

- Overall warehouse development
- Infrastructure development
- The development of applications

The overall warehouse development phase

One of the first and biggest challenges that the builders of a warehouse face is the incredible amount of miscommunication and misunderstanding that develops as people go through the creative idea development process. Without doubt, the failure to get everyone to agree, at the outset, to a common vision of what the warehouse should be will cause innumerable problems as the system develops. During the overall warehouse-development phase, you can arrive at a consensus between all participants regarding the size, scope, complexity, approach to construction, and value of the warehouse project.

The infrastructure development phase

After you have determined how big the warehouse will be and what will be included within it, your next challenge is to figure out how it will be delivered technically. In the past, it was relatively easy to determine the appropriate infrastructure for a system (because that infrastructure relied heavily upon an already stable and functioning mainframe environment). In today's world of object-oriented, client/server, relational databases and personal computer-based data-mining tools, this technical environment can easily turn into a nightmare of tremendous proportion.

During the infrastructure development phase, all of the technical, managerial, and system-support issues are resolved. The physical infrastructure is built and tested, and it is staffed with the appropriate support personnel. Only after the infrastructure has been stabilized will you actually begin to try to use the warehouse.

The application development phase(s)

The last phase of warehouse development actually is an iterative phase that never ends. During this phase, you begin to add usable applications to the warehouse, one application at a time. This is the part of the warehouse development process that most people associate with systems development. During this phase, tables are designed, programs are written, and specific business needs for information are met.

In future chapters, I will provide much of the detail that goes into each of these phases, as well as a lot of the rationale for using this particular approach.

While this approach might not seem to be the most efficient or logical, when considered against the backdrop of how things really work in the systems development world today, it should quickly become apparent that it is the only approach that has a good chance of success.

Chapter

4

The Components
and Construction

April 1994 (excerpt from an RFP for a data warehouse):

> The data warehouse will consist of an Oracle database, running on an HP9000 platform. The existing customer, sales, warrantee, and tracking data will be loaded into the database, and the users will make use of Excel to process the warehouse data.

While this description might give all the appearances of being a complete physical specification (it does describe the input, processing, and output mechanisms), it clearly falls short of providing the builders of the system with any idea of the complexity and challenges that this project eventually will entail.

Before we can continue with our discussion of how to set up and manage the individual subprojects within a data-warehouse project, you will have to develop a better understanding, in much greater depth, of exactly what issues and challenges you really will be facing when you undertake to build one.

In this chapter, I will attempt to provide this requisite background information. First, I will set the stage for further discussion by dissecting a little more of the detail surrounding the workings and techniques for building each of the three major data-warehouse components (the import/export [acquisition], data warehouse proper [storage], and applications front-end [access] components). Then I will take an introductory look at the construction of the data warehouse itself and at the structural layers upon which it is based (the infrastructure and data disciplines layers) and see how those will make it possible for your warehouse to function smoothly.

You need this information before you begin discussing the details of how to set up the warehouse project, because once you start this setup work, you immediately will create expectations in the minds of management, the users, and the builders of the system. It is critical that, as you establish those expectations, people have a clear understanding of what they are going to get, how it is going to work, and how much it is going to cost in time and effort. Errant expectations at the early stages will lead to nothing but disappointment, miscoordination, and other kinds of problems at the later stages.

The Storage Component

We'll now consider for a moment just exactly what we mean by the data warehouse itself. What is it? What are its component parts and what are the tricks to building it correctly?

Tables

For the vast majority of data warehouses built today, the structure that underlies the label "data warehouse storage area" is a collection of relational database tables. Each of these tables will hold a different subset of the information that people want to have access to.

Of course, just because data is in a relational database does not make it a data warehouse by default. There are certain characteristics that data-warehouse tables share that are not common to other types of systems.

The characteristics of data warehouse data

In general, if you are building a data warehouse, your data will meet the following criteria:

- The tables will be extremely large.
- The data in those tables will have a high degree of interdependency with the data in other tables.
- The principal means of accessing these tables will be *ad hoc* (as opposed to predefined) access.
- Not only will the tables within the warehouse be large, but there will be a large number of tables available to access.
- The data is accessed in a read-only mode from the user's perspective.
- The data will need to be refreshed periodically from multiple sources.
- Much of the data collected will be historical (therefore time-dependent).

You can group these characteristics into three categories of concern, each of which will require you to consider some specific organizational assumptions as you proceed with the construction process:

- High-volume/*ad hoc* access
- Complexity of the environment
- Time sensitivity (one aspect of the complexity)

High volume/*ad hoc* access

Anyone with any experience at all dealing with relational database systems knows that the combination of high volumes and a lot of *ad hoc* access can be toxic to the performance of any kind of database. The paradox is that, while relational databases can make it easy for a user to ask for any kind of combination of data that he or she wants, it also is true that the user therefore can put in any number of requests that can tax the capabilities of the largest machine and bring the system's performance to a screeching halt. Simply stated, there is a trade-off between flexibility and system performance. The more power you give the users to do things, the more opportunities you create for users to bring the system to its knees.

Addressing the performance/flexibility trade-off

From the very outset of data-warehouse construction, therefore, you must be sensitive to this trade-off and come prepared with some approaches to managing the consequences.

One of the ways that you can try to head off these kinds of problems is to anticipate the worst possible case and engineer the system to take that into account (i.e., get a computer with 10 times as much power as you think it will need). This obviously is the weakest kind of solution, as experience has shown that users will always find ways to max out any hardware configuration that you can imagine.

Therefore, it is incumbent upon the data-warehouse builder to develop some restriction or structuring strategies that will allow the users some considerable freedom in their activities without letting them become too *ad hoc*.

Some organizations have tried to create this kind of structure simply by training the users in the proper use of SQL and making them responsible for monitoring the performance of what they do. In some rare cases, this can work, but the users usually are not interested in becoming relational database experts.

Some of the more useful structuring approaches have included:

- The use of query regulators that monitor the work load that an individual user is putting on the system and that can cancel the activity if it gets out of control.

- The creation of query templates that are predefined SQL commands. They accomplish the major navigational aspects of a query but allow the user to change certain parameters within it. These queries also are *ad hoc* but within the confines of the templates that are provided to the user.

- Staged tables, another solution to the problem, are for the manufacturers of the data warehouse to pre-execute and store parts of queries, thereby identifying and isolating a subset of data that the user then can access in a true *ad hoc* fashion.

The deployment of any of these techniques requires that you construct the warehouse differently and that you allocate a certain amount of time, energy, computer power, and disk space to each. Each has consequences for the ultimate user of the warehouse as well.

For example, a query-regulator solution implies that the major burden for SQL query generation will fall upon the user. This can be good or bad depending on how those users feel about SQL. The query-template solution takes a lot of the burden off the users but requires that you allocate time and resources for someone to actually go through the process of identifying, building, storing, and making the templates available to the user. The staged-tables solution has the same consequences as the query-template solution, with the additional need to allocate a lot of extra disk space and management time to include the extra tables in the warehouse itself.

Managing the complexity of the environment

One of the biggest traps that data-warehouse builders fall into is that they fail to appreciate how complicated the management of the ongoing environment really will turn out to be. This false confidence in the ease of complexity management is supported by the prototype development approach.

The most common way for people to kick off a warehousing project is to take a few critical data tables, put them into the warehouse, and let a select group of expert users have access to it. These projects usually are considered to be great successes by everyone involved.

Unfortunately, because you started with a small number of tables and a small number of users, you managed to avoid much of the impending complexity issues that you will have to face at a later time.

It is easy for 3 users to keep track of 12 tables. It is a much different matter to expect hundreds of users to keep track of hundreds or even thousands of tables.

Many layers of complexity

We now will consider some of the different kinds of complexity that you will need to manage within this full-blown warehouse solution.

The sheer number of tables. A full-scale data warehouse will involve hundreds of data tables. As the number of tables grows, it becomes more and more difficult for people to know what each one contains. Therefore, a catalog of tables must be developed that is not simply a list of contents. It must be organized in a way that makes it extremely easy for people to zero in on what they need to find.

Table interdependencies. Besides the problems of simple table inventory management, you also will need to find a way to allow users to understand what the relationships between those tables are. This can raise the level of sophistication required from your catalog many times over.

In general, a large number of the data-warehousing products that flood the market today concentrate on, or at least provide, the purchaser with a lot of the capabilities for catalog management that we have been talking about. The key word associated with these capabilities is "meta data" management. (Meta data is information about your information.)

Timing. An additional set of complexities arise around the issues of timing. The data warehouse is not time stagnant by any means. You will have to keep track of hundreds of tables being refreshed at different times. The time frame that applies to a given population of data is critical to the users' analysis, and the time at which each table is refreshed also is key. Therefore, you must develop the means to track and report on these time and synchronization complexities, for the sake of the users and for the administrators of the warehouse.

The solution to these problems, again, will vary upon the system. However, some kind of software will need to be developed or purchased to help keep track of it all. Some data-warehousing products include data synchronization and timing monitoring as part of their offering as well as the meta data-management capabilities. However, a lot of organizations end up building their own customized solutions.

No matter how it is identified and delivered, the software that manages these things is critical to the ongoing efficient operation of the warehouse. When you tie these kinds of data-warehouse support capabilities with their complementary functions in the data-mining and legacy systems interface area, you begin to have an idea of exactly what the data-warehouse infrastructure is all about.

Legacy Systems Interface: The Acquisitions Component

The second component of the warehouse that we will consider will be the "back end" or the data import and extract facilities that we formally dub the *acquisition component.*

While some of the issues that were apparent in the dissection of the data warehouse itself will create complementary issues on this side, there are additional problems that you will need to track.

We will begin by developing an understanding of the steps required for you to make the data available.

The phases of the data extraction and preparation process

When looking at this process from a high-level perspective, the premise seems very simple: Identify the data that you want to load into the data warehouse, unload it, then load it into the warehouse table. Unfortunately, it is never that simple.

Whether you are pulling data into your warehouse from a mainframe DB2 system, a VSAM file, a UNIX database, or someone's Excel spreadsheet on a personal computer, experience has shown that several things are going to have to happen before that data is ready to be loaded.

Data extraction. Data extraction involves the actual removal of data from its source (purchased or rented tape, mainframe file structure, personal computer etc.) and the placement of that data within the processing area.

There actually are two types of data extraction that you need to be concerned about. First, there is the process of initially extracting the data and making it suitable for the initial load. Then there is the establishment of a regularized data-extraction procedure that will be executed again and again throughout the lifetime of the warehouse, as you constantly refresh it.

Data cleansing. Most people have no appreciation for exactly how "dirty" most data is. Dirty data occurs when the values stored in individual fields are inconsistent, missing, unreadable, or wrong. There are many ways that stored data values can be wrong. They can be plain inaccurate (wrong address, wrong color, etc.), they can be wrong in the way that they relate to other fields (a customer key that does not match up with customer file), or they might not fall within an acceptable value range (i.e., a person who is 200 years old).

The data-cleansing process also comes in two forms. The first and most grueling process occurs after you have made your initial data extraction. At this time, you will want to spend a considerable amount of time figuring out what is not clean about the data and then getting it cleaned up.

The second form occurs when you take the basically manual cleansing process that you performed the first time and turn it into a regularly scheduled integrity-checking and data-cleansing routine, which recleans the data each time that you make a fresh extraction.

Data formatting. Just because you have extracted and cleaned the data does not mean that it is ready to load. The next challenge that you face is how to format the data so that it is laid out in a way that the warehouse will accept. Included in the list of formatting issues are:

- The sizes of fields
- The data types for those fields
- The order in which fields are positioned in the record

Merge processing. Sometimes, if you are very lucky, all of the data that you want to load into a data-warehouse table will come from the same source file or database. Often, however, the data for one warehouse table actually comes from many different sources. In these cases, you must preprocess each of the disparate partial sources of the data, then merge the files together to get the population that you need.

Key processing. A primary reason for building a data warehouse is to provide the organization with a more coordinated, consolidated view of its information. One major obstacle to this ability to have a "common view" is that disparate systems and subsystems tend to use different sets of keys to uniquely identify the core data groups upon which the rest of the system is based.

Some examples of core data groups would include customer records and the subsequent customer numbers for a marketing system or parts and their part numbers in a manufacturing system. It is not uncommon to find corporations with dozens of different customer numbering key systems or half a dozen part-numbering schemes.

In organizations fraught with these kinds of situations, the ability to cross-reference all of the different keying schemes into one consolidated keying structure can have immense value. Therefore, it is not uncommon to find incredibly large and complex key-synchronization and merge-processing steps as a critical piece of the data extraction and loading process.

Purge processing. Not only do you end up needing to merge different files together to get the right collection of fields for a table, but many times you also will need to do some form of processing that compares the values in two files and eliminates certain records from the ultimate warehouse population.

For example, you might want to load up your customer table but decide that you do not want to include the customers that have failed to pay their bills for the past three months in the mix. In this case, you will run a purge process that compares a late-payment customer list to a list of all customers. The customers that match up with the first list then are purged from your data warehouse load.

Stage. The last step is the staging process, which is the moving of all the data (in the form that the data warehouse wants to load it) to the place from where the warehouse ultimately will read it.

Some observations about the extract process

It is important to note that, while we have identified several distinct steps in the data-extraction and -preparation processes, there is no reason that they must be done in any set order or that they must even be done as separate steps. Many people have successfully incorporated many of the steps into the execution of a single, extract/cleanse/format/merge/purge/stage program. Others have done merge/purge first, then cleanse, then format, and finally stage.

The actual order and nature of these steps depends on the nature of the data being extracted and processed.

Back-flush capabilities

In many situations, the fact that you actually have cleaned up the data and standardized the keys across all of the organization's different subsystems makes the output of the data-extraction process much too valuable to simply pass on to the warehouse and leave. In those situations, organizations will want to build in a "back-flush" capability where the end products of the sanitation and preparation process actually are fed back into the legacy systems that originally provided them, to help cleanse and consolidate the legacy systems themselves. (For example, if you clean up all of the names and addresses for customers, you will want to return those accurate addresses to the source systems so that they can benefit from the best available information also.)

Therefore, it is important that you plan for and develop fully functional data back-flush capabilities with the same degree of thoroughness and manageability as you build the forward-directed process.

Complexity and tracking in the import/export component

This brief exploration into the workings of the data-extraction process (we will spend significantly more time later) presents you with a set of complexity-management issues similar to those explored in the area of management in the data warehouse itself. While it would be a simple matter for you to build a data-warehousing system that involves the extract and load of a dozen or so files without too much of a problem, it will be an entirely different matter to try to manage such an environment when you are trying to keep track of the simultaneous processing of hundreds of these job streams, all at the same time.

What will be sorely needed in this environment is the means to track and manage the progress of each and every extract file as it moves through these steps. For the most part, you will need to *build* this management and tracking capability for yourself, but it will become a critical facet of your successful, full-blown data-warehousing system.

Data Mining and Delivery: The Access Component

The last component of the data warehouse to be considered is the "front end." Included in this component are all of the data-mining access techniques utilized by the end user to make the data warehouse usable. As with the other components, you will see that even this area is not as simple as it first seems.

Different means of access

When most people think about data warehousing, one of the first images that come into their minds is a specific set of data-mining or warehouse access tools. These tools, in many cases, are very high-powered data-analysis and executive information-system products that provide the user with all sorts of new ways to view, analyze, and explore the information that runs their business.

These flashy front-end products are not the only data-mining tools to be considered, and they usually represent only a small percentage of the tool sets that will be utilized to view and explore the information that the data warehouse provides. In the vast majority of cases, the real payoff that can be gained from the warehouse will come from the more mundane, day-to-day, simple query operations that allow people to do their jobs better.

Therefore, we will define the class of data-mining and warehouse access products and tools into the following major categories:

- Simple *ad hoc* query interfaces
  ~Traditional query managers (QMF, QBE, MS-Query)
  ~Query-management facilities embedded in other products (Excel, Access, etc.)
  ~Traditional report generators
- Custom warehouse access applications
- Sophisticated data-mining applications
  ~Visualization facilities
  ~Advanced traditional statistical-analysis packages
  ~Data-surfing facilities
  ~Quasi-artificial intelligence
  ~Simulations
- Autonomous business packages

With such a wide variety of products and data-access approaches to choose from, it is difficult to develop any kind of generalized view of how the front end of the data warehouse is going to have to be built. However, because in most cases we are going to have to assume that some of the approaches from each of the categories are going to end up being included, we can say something about how you will have to structure and manage this "hybridized" environment.

Feedback mechanisms. Just as the acquisition components need to feed information back to the legacy systems that feed it, there will be situations where the access component will need to provide the same kind of capability. These feedback mechanisms must be planned for and built into the infrastructure of the system itself.

Data and architectural characteristics of each category. While it does not make sense, at this point, to get into the details about how each of the possible products that might work with your warehouse will need to interface with it, we can draw some conclusions about each of these categories to set the stage for that discussion at a later time.

Simple *ad hoc* interfaces. At first glance, it might appear that you finally have found a portion of the warehouse construction process that is going to be relatively easy to implement. You simply will install the query manager type product, hook it up to the warehouse, tell the users which data to go after, then move on to the next part of the project. Of course, it is never that simple. There are several reasons that the implementation of even the simplest of query or report manager packages is going to present you with challenges.

The first set of challenges revolves around those issues that we identified under the section about the data warehouse itself. You will remember that we said that the data that needed to be accessed was going to be of a high volume in nature and that the *ad hoc* access, by definition, was going to present some problems. We offered several solutions to those problems (query regulators, "parametrized" queries [templates], and prestaged tables). At no time did we talk about how those would be managed and implemented. That is because the management of these solutions must be tied to the many different access techniques that users are going to be employing.

No matter how you decide to protect the integrity of the system's performance, you are going to have to implement it in such a way that access to the users is easy. The users should not care about how you are going to improve the performance of their systems; they should care only about finding the information that they need.

Therefore, what you will need to do is provide the user with a way to gain access to the catalog and data-management environment that we talked about building as a part of the data warehouse itself and incorporate its use into the functionality of whatever query-management tool they might employ.

In addition to the need to make the process of finding their data easy for the users, in most cases, you also are going to have to make the process of accessing all of the different data-access tools as easy as possible. A typical user might end up needing to use Excel, Access, Q&E, Lotus, Forest and Trees, and any number of other data-accessing tools depending upon the work that they are trying to accomplish. It does not make sense to simply leave them on their own to figure out how to get all of these products to work together.

A third area of complexity will come about when users begin to want to save the results of those queries in their own private data-storage areas. No user wants to execute a simple query. What they really want is to extract several different pieces, then combine those results to create yet another set. It is not practical to expect the warehouse itself to provide all of that capability. Therefore, you must incorporate a personal data storage and retrieval area into the user's desktop and provide them with the means to manage that as well.

Sophisticated statistical analysis and visual packages

The users of the more sophisticated data-mining tools—like SAS, DSS Agent, S-Base, or a long list of others—are going to run into all of the same problems as the simple query-tool users, and then some. Most of these products are built to force people to pull in different subsets of data, then perform multiple recursions of processing against that self-contained subset of data, before yielding the results that they want.

If the providers of the data warehouse services expect to be in business for very long, then they are going to have to help the users figure out how to use these as well.

Custom warehouse access applications

Ultimately, most organizations end up building their own customized applications to work with different specific parts of the warehouse. For example, most marketing or customer-information warehouses include a customer look-up facility, which allows a customer service or sales person to page through all of the different kinds of historical information about the customer that is available.

The data-access and -management challenges that are created when you begin to tie these kinds of applications into the warehouse are entirely different than those in the previous two cases.

Autonomous applications

In some situations, people actually will purchase fully functional applications systems (i.e., human resources, financial accounting, etc.) and expect these systems to make use of warehouse information input. Again, there is another set of criteria to consider.

User view of the "back room" warehouse processes

In addition to all of the explicitly defined warehouse access methods that users will incorporate into their work stations, it eventually will become incumbent upon the warehouse managers to provide those end users with access to the "back room" warehouse information. The information that users are looking at usually is very time-sensitive. Before they can do a good job of using that information, they will need to know exactly how up-to-date each of the tables that they are using really are.

For example, a user trying to make a report that tells them about the current balances in each of a customer's various checking, savings, and investment accounts will need to know how recently each of those was refreshed. If the savings account table is refreshed only once a month and the checking account table is refreshed once a week, then that user will need to know when the last refresh occurred and maybe even when the next one is scheduled.

The user's need for information about how timely their information is goes even deeper than that. No matter how much we would like to fool ourselves into believing that computer systems are these large, dependable-as-clockwork machines, the reality is that computer systems, especially very large, very complex ones, have failures all the time. What if the user is desperate to finish some end-of-month reports? The user checks and finds out that two of the files have not been refreshed as they should be. The next set of questions that the user is going to have are:

- What went wrong?
- Is it being fixed?
- The big question: When do I get my data?

The people responsible for managing the warehouse will have to make a choice. You can either put yourself in the business of constantly needing to respond to questions and researching the answer for the users, or you can provide them with the means to find out for themselves. With a system of any size and complexity, the latter option makes infinitely more sense.

The user workbench environment

The long-range solution that many people develop to address all of these issues is to create an integrated user workstation application that ties together all of these disparate pieces. A user workbench of this kind usually will start out with some kind of a menu- or icon-driven interface that allows the user to easily and seamlessly navigate through the catalog, select tables to work on, and tie their identity over to the reporting or query tool of choice, then allows them to schedule, execute, store, and continue to process the results. At the same time, this workbench can create an environment where this same user can check on the status of the updating of each of the tables that they have targeted and to inquire as to the next scheduled refresh time.

Tying the components together

In the previous four sections, we attempted to summarize some of the issues and complexities that the builder of the data warehouse is going to face, within each of the components of the system. With this information in hand, we now are ready to consider the many layers of issues that are going to crop up when you actually try to build the warehouse and coordinate the construction of each of the components.

It should come as no surprise that the three components of the warehouse that we have described are roughly analogous to the three major functions that any real-world warehouse would perform.

Every warehouse has a receiving function where goods are accepted, checked for damage, broken down into storable chunks, and placed within the warehouse itself. Every warehouse also has an inventory-management function, whereby the locations of goods are tracked and their storage organization kept optimized. Finally, every warehouse has an inventory checkout, packaging, and shipping function. We will continue to develop this analogy to help you understand how the data warehouse needs to be built.

Building a Warehouse

A commonly asked question is, "If you're going to build a data warehouse, where should you begin?" Most people think that you should start with the data itself. These "data-driven" advocates believe that you first must develop a logical model of all of the data that the warehouse will hold before you begin figuring anything else out. Well, in some ways, this is correct; however, for the most part, it is not.

When a company decides that it needs to build a new warehouse for their inventory, they do not start out by developing a list of everything that they want to keep in it. That would be silly. A warehouse is a transient thing. Materials move into and out of the warehouse at a rapid pace, and what you store in the warehouse is going to change over time.

Step 1: Figuring out whether you need a warehouse or not

Before any business person would begin to build a real warehouse, he or she would have first determined whether the company actually needed one or not. It would be senseless to go out and buy a new building if you didn't need one. How does a company decide that a warehouse is needed? It's simple. Companies build warehouses when they are having trouble managing their inventory. There actually are several ways that this "inventory-management pain" can manifest itself.

Inventory overload. Some companies find that they simply no longer have enough room to keep products and files. Their manufacturing facilities take up more and more space of storage, while their retail outlets cram the back rooms full of items that they don't need. Both sides of the supply chain eventually find that they are spending more and more of their time managing inventory and less and less time doing their jobs. Manufacturers want to make products, and retailers want to sell them. Neither of them wants to manage the inventory of the other.

Breakdown and consolidation services. In other situations, the company might find that it needs to set up a facility that can "preprocess" inventory before forwarding it to its destination. For example, a clothing-store chain found that it could save money on women's jeans by purchasing them by the train carload from a manufacturer. Unfortunately, after it purchased the jeans, it had to send the jeans somewhere to get the load broken down into the different smaller-sized packages for each of their stores. Other organizations put warehouses in place so that multiple, smaller orders for disparate goods can be consolidated into larger, more efficient shipments.

Prudent reserve. Another reason to build a warehouse is to create a storage area where you can store production overruns or simply allow the factory to run at a higher volume and higher level of efficiency. The warehouse serves as an inventory buffer, allowing the company to have a prudent reserve of their goods in between production runs.

The bottomless inventory pit. Despite the presence of so many good rationalizations for building a warehouse, the manager will always approach the decision to build a new one with care. The reason is simple. There are many organizations that have built warehouses that turned into bottomless inventory pits. These inventory pits become places where worthless inventory accumulates for extended periods of time, taking up more and more space and becoming a large liability to the company, instead of being an asset. Data warehouses can easily turn into the same thing.

Searching for alternatives. The decision to build a data warehouse is a big one. It should not be approached with any less analysis or caution than the building of a real warehouse. There always are alternatives to warehousing, and the sponsor of a warehousing project must be convinced that the alternatives are worse than the cure before advocating this kind of solution.

Step 2: Developing criteria for determining the value of the data warehouse

Ultimately, the value of the data warehouse needs to be measured with the same criteria as a real warehouse. How do companies decide whether a warehouse has value or not? There are several criteria, but the most prevalent is a measurement called *turns*.

In a real warehouse, the term *turns* refers to the measurement of how many times a specific cargo moves into and out of the warehouse over a given period of time, or how many turns per time period. A high number of turns means that items of the category being measured have moved into and out of the warehouse several times for the given time period. A low number of turns means that it moved in and out very few times.

For example, when you are warehousing fresh vegetables, you need to have a high turn rate. Vegetables should "turn" every few days, or they will rot. On the other hand, expensive jewelry moves at a much lower turn rate. If you move one a week, you are doing well.

The data warehouse also needs to be measured in turns. Data with a very low turn rate probably should not be warehoused at all. (For example, it has happened in the past that people have dumped millions of records into a data warehouse and never looked at it at all.) Data with a very high turn rate might be handled more appropriately via some other mechanism. (For example, if millions of rows of data are completely refreshed daily, it would be prudent to question the process.) Of course, figuring out what kinds of turn rates are acceptable, and developing the infrastructure to measure that, is a different story.

Step 3: Determine where the inventory will come from (legacy systems inventory)

Along with needing to know how much the warehouse will hold, you will need to know what the different sources of goods for the warehouse will be.

Step 4: Determine where the inventory will go (accessibility requirements)

Of course, you also need to know where goods are going to be shipped.

Step 5: Sizing

When a manager decides to put a warehouse together, it is because he or she knows that there are some items that need to be stored, processed (unbundle, rebundle, etc.), and forwarded to another location. This manager will begin by deciding exactly how big the warehouse will need to be. To make this decision, he or she will need to know what kinds of products will be stored and what kinds of volumes of this item to expect. In other words, the first thing that you do is size the warehouse.

Just as the manager will size the warehouse by getting some rough estimates from the different departments that will be the intended users of the building once it is completed, so too must the data-warehouse manager get some rough estimates as to the size, shape, quantity, and throughput of data to be managed.

Step 6: Determining the type of warehouse

The manager does not need to know what brand of microwave ovens or which designer's clothing will be kept in the warehouse. He or she needs to know only if the warehouse is for appliances, clothing, electronic parts, or maybe a combination of all three.

Obvious conclusions about the kinds of turns that you expect will come as a part of this decision. In general, the more valuable or complicated the product, the fewer turns to expect. Conversely, the less valuable the product, the more frequent the turns. Early on in the process, these criteria must be explored.

Step 7: Determine the location

After figuring out approximately how big the warehouse needs to be and what types of things will be kept in it, the next step will be to determine where the warehouse should be located. Obviously, placing a warehouse in Hong Kong when all of your distributors are in Kokomo, Indiana, is not a real good idea. (See Figure 4.1.)

The physical location of the data warehouse is going to be important for several reasons. The first and most obvious location issue will have to do with the warehouse's proximity to either the users or the sources of data or both. Despite the perceived notion that, with modern computer equipment, location is not an issue, the reality is that it still can have a big impact on the effectiveness of the warehouse.

A second, more nefarious, but equally important issue revolving around location has to do with determining where the warehouse will physically reside from a political and organizational perspective.

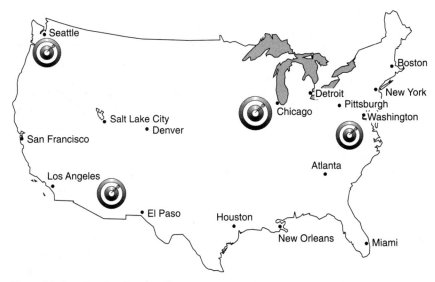

Figure 4.1 Location, location, location.

For example, should the warehouse be located in the computer room on the mainframe with the other legacy systems? Should it be located in the user area? This decision will determine a lot about how people will perceive it and also will influence the decisions about who is going to be responsible for supporting it.

Step 8: Build, modify, or buy?

Now that you know where the warehouse should be and know some of the requirements for its construction, it is time to make a decision about where to get it. Maybe you can take an existing building or a part of one of your other facilities and turn it into a warehouse. Maybe you can buy something that already meets your needs. Perhaps you just have to build your own.

The build/modify/buy decision is a tough one, and it is especially tough for the data warehouse procurer. Just as the business person must weigh a vast number of variables to make this determination, so too must the data warehouse advocate.

Step 9: Build the warehouse itself

Assume that, for whatever political, physical, capacity, or requirements reasons, you have decided to build a new warehouse and that you are ready to begin the specifications process. This is the point where our analogy to the physical warehouse construction process begins to diverge. In the real world, your manager simply can call architects who specialize in warehouse construction, give them the requirements, and wait for some blueprints to review. (See Figure 4.2.)

In the computer systems world, this process is complicated by several factors. First, there is no such thing as a set of blueprints for a computer system. People have tried, but they have consistently failed to spec out the process anywhere near as well as the construction planner. Second, the entire design and construction industry is based upon a series of well-established principles and guidelines for how to make use of those plans. The odds of a group of programmers following the specifications given to them actually is pretty rare for a large number of reasons.

In the pages to come, however, I will propose a set of blueprint documents that can be used to accomplish the same thing as the architect's drawings.

Specify hardware and network architecture. During the previous steps, the manager in charge of the warehouse project has collected a significant number of starting points for you. Because this homework has been done in advance, you can begin immediately to specify the critical components of the system.

Because you know where the warehouse will be, approximately how big it will be, the number of turns to expect, the people that will use it, and the places that the output will go, you will be in a position to specify all of the hardware and networking components necessary to support what has been proposed.

It is critical that this be specified as soon as possible because every subsequent decision is dependent upon these decisions. In other words, if you change one of these decisions later on, it is going to force you to redo a lot

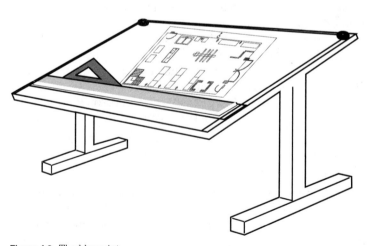

Figure 4.2 The blueprint.

of your planning and construction work, with the subsequent complete loss of anything that has been accomplished.

Determine the data architecture. After you have laid your foundation, built the walls, and created all of the access roads, you will be in a position to actually begin to lay out the warehouse. You need to figure out where the different kinds of goods are going to be stored, you need to figure out where people will walk, where they will drive forklifts, and where and how they will inventory little things, big things, fragile things, and expensive things.

Laying out the data warehouse is no different. Before you begin to actually try to manage data, you had better have thought through all of the same kinds of issues. Where will I place big tables? How will I manage little ones?

Determine staffing requirements. When you know how the warehouse is going to be laid out, you then can determine how many people it will take to support it. How many office people? How many people in receiving? How many in shipping?

Who will manage the warehouse? You cannot expect it to run itself. It actually is amazing how many people think that they simply can skip this step when it comes to building a data warehouse. It is a fatal mistake to ignore this issue.

Develop and install warehouse management policies and procedures. In tandem with the development of personnel requirements comes the need to determine the rules for how the warehouse will be used. In the real warehouse, people are given roles, and they fulfill them. In the data warehousing world, you create software (the infrastructure management software) that fulfills this same need.

Install bins, paint, and lines and bring in the forklifts. Finally, you are ready to bring in the equipment and tools and begin making the warehouse functional. (See Figure 4.3.)

Step 10: Begin the inventory management process

Only now should you actually consider bringing product into the warehouse. Have you ever heard of people trying to use a warehouse before it was finished? Have many people been pleased with the results when they sent valuable merchandise to an incomplete warehouse and lost the goods because they were stolen or got wet because the warehouse had no roof yet? Unlikely.

So too, must you fight the urge to use the warehouse before it is ready.

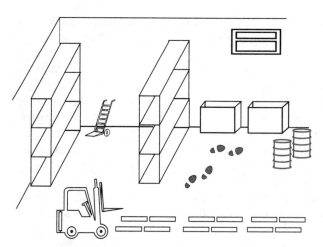

Figure 4.3 The real warehouse.

A Model for the Data Warehouse

Webster's Dictionary, 1995

> model (mod'l) –n 1. a standard or example for imitation or comparison 2. a representation, generally in miniature, to show the construction or appearance of something.

Up until this point in our consideration of the data warehouse, we have remained very general in nature. Now, we are ready to get more specific about how your warehouse actually will be put together and to start to develop a model.

To begin with, we already have established that the warehouse can be viewed as consisting of three major "vertical" components (Figure 5.1):

- Acquisitions Component—Responsible for the extraction of data from a variety of sources as well as for the cleansing, validation, formatting, and staging of that data for loading into the warehouse.

- Storage Component—Consists of a collection of relational database tables.

- Access Component—Made up of an assortment of analysis, query, visualization, and manipulation tools that make the warehouse useful to the business.

We also have established that you could further dissect the warehouse in terms of its horizontal layers. The lowest level, the one that forms the foundation for the entire warehouse structure, represents the physical infrastructure, or systems architecture.

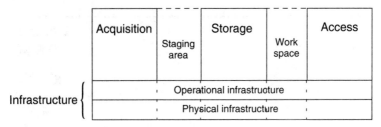

Figure 5.1 The core data warehouse.

Specifically, we will identify the following as being part of the physical infrastructure (Figure 5.2):

- Computer hardware that hosts the acquisitions, storage, and access components
- Network configuration that ties the pieces together and ties the system itself to the outside world (legacy systems at the acquisitions end and end users on the access side)
- Operating system (OS) or network operating system (NOS)
- Systems-level utilities and procedures that work in this environment (i.e., copy programs, sort programs, file-management systems, database software, etc.)
- Support staff that keep this environment running
- Roles, responsibilities, and procedures that make the environment manageable
- Management structure that defines who will be responsible for keeping all of the parts working and communicating with each other

The operational infrastructure overlays the physical infrastructure layer of the system. While the physical infrastructure is concerned with the mechanical, fundamental functionality of the computer system's aspect of the system, the operational infrastructure defines how the warehouse itself is going to run.

We can use the real warehouse analogy to help explain the difference. The first layer of the real warehouse is the physical building itself: the concrete floors, the walls, the ceiling (the computer hardware), and the roads, railway accesses, and loading docks (the network aspects). Within the real world warehouse, you must build this infrastructure before you can do anything.

However, after you have gotten the "physical plant" in order, you must figure out how the warehouse is going to be run. You need to know what the flow of material through the warehouse will be. Which docks are for loading? Which are for unloading? Where will you park the trucks that are waiting to pull up to the door? You need to draw lines on the floors so that forklift truck drivers know where to drive. You need to install bins and shelving units and stock up on an inventory of pallets. You also need to figure out how many dock workers you will have, how you will check in and check out merchandise and, in general, figure out how the warehouse will work. You need to have completed all of this before you begin receiving merchandise.

In the same way, you need to have all the "how this warehouse will work" issues settled before you can begin using the data warehouse. We call this collection of assorted warehouse management requirements the *operational infrastructure* (Figure 5.3). It consists of:

- The staff who will support the operation of the warehouse itself (DBAs, data analysts, job schedulers, etc.)

- The rules and procedures that will govern warehouse operation

- A customized set of software that will be responsible for keeping track of your data warehouse "inventory" and the progress of data through the different components

- Feedback mechanisms that send warehouse data back to the legacy systems

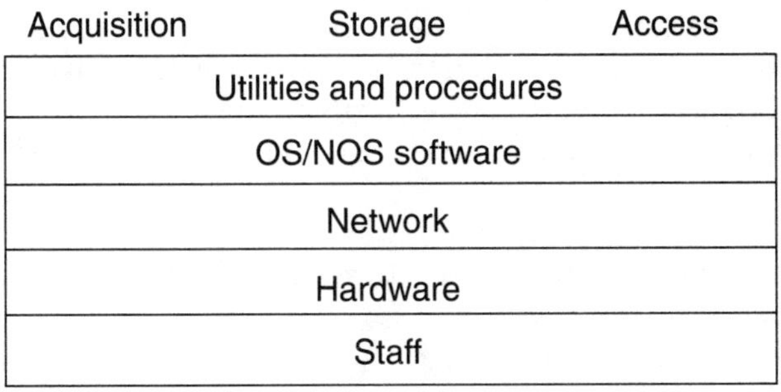

Acquisition	Storage	Access
Utilities and procedures		
OS/NOS software		
Network		
Hardware		
Staff		

Figure 5.2 Components of the physical infrastructure.

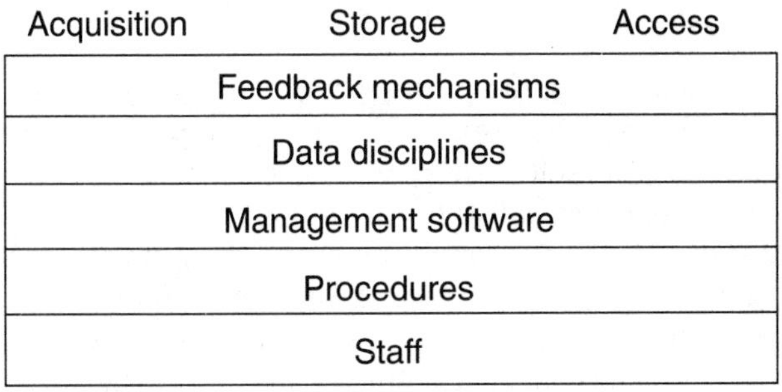

Acquisition	Storage	Access
Feedback mechanisms		
Data disciplines		
Management software		
Procedures		
Staff		

Figure 5.3 The operational infrastructure.

Feedback Mechanisms

In addition to the data disciplines, you have one other set of responsibilities that is considered to be part of the operational infrastructure, and those are related to the problems presented by feedback mechanisms.

Inadvertently, no matter how hard you try to avoid it, it will become necessary for the builder of the warehouse to feed information back into the system that sent the information in the first place. Although it will be necessary, it is important that you have a clear set of rules for how and where this kind of feedback will occur; otherwise, you jeopardize the very foundations upon which our warehouse has been built.

The dangers involved in allowing feedback mechanisms into the warehouse are diverse. First of all, the warehouse has been built in a certain way to optimize certain characteristics. In general, you want the warehouse to be a read-only operation so that you can optimize the storage of data for access, query, and analysis. By burdening the system with backward-moving data (data that moves from the user to the warehouse to the legacy systems), you make it impossible to tune the system for optimum query performance.

Second of all, you have designed the warehouse to serve as a neutral data storage area that insulates end users and analysts from the idiosyncrasies and requirements of operational legacy system's performance. If you allow your warehouse to work directly with those systems, you tie them to those systems in violation of the fundamental principles upon which you based the reason for the warehouse in the first place. In effect, you would turn the warehouse into an extension of whatever legacy system for which you are providing feedback.

In general, if you allow any but the most severely restricted type of feedback mechanism into the warehouse, you risk turning the warehouse into an operational system.

One might think of the data moving through the warehouse as creating a current, or a flow (Figure 5.4).

The entire purpose of the warehouse is to optimize the process of moving data from the one end to the other as efficiently as possible. Any attempts to push data "against" the flow are going to slow it down and muddle its efficiency and operational focus.

Despite your best intentions, people are going to insist that some kinds of feedback mechanisms to the warehouse exist. There are just too many situations where it makes sense. Therefore, from the outset, you must define what kinds of feedback mechanisms will and will not be allowed and build from there. However, what you can do is limit the ways that you will allow these kinds of feedback mechanisms to be worked into the warehouse.

We will propose three feedback mechanisms to build into the warehouse infrastructure: the back-flush mechanism, feedback loop, and the workspace area. Experience has shown that these approaches can protect the

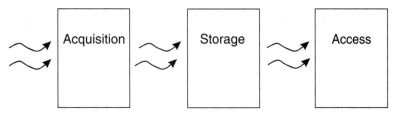

Figure 5.4. "Flow" through the data warehouse.

warehouse from too much "dilution" of function, while allowing people to do the things that they need to do.

Back-Flush Mechanisms

The first type of feedback mechanism that we will consider is the one that I call a *back-flush mechanism*. A back flush occurs when it becomes apparent that the data that the acquisitions component of the warehouse has prepared for loading has been cleaned, prepared, and validated in a way that will be of value to the legacy systems that sent the data in the first place.

An example from the development of a typical customer database should help explain this situation. In the building of customer data warehouses, it often is necessary to do quite a bit of cleaning up of the names and addresses. This is known as name and address hygiene. When legacy systems store name and address information, it is not uncommon to find that the information has become inaccurate or was never quite complete. To make this information useful to your warehouse, you will need to go through the process of getting all of that information corrected.

At this point, the people using the legacy system will end up having worse information than the warehouse. So what they usually require is that the now-sanitized name and address information be fed back into the legacy system so that the users of the operational systems have the benefit of the latest and most accurate information.

Back-flush mechanisms usually consist of nothing more than the creation of a special additional file that is written at the same time that the data being loaded is sent to the staging area. This file then can be picked up and applied to the legacy systems by the managers of the legacy systems themselves. (See Figure 5.5.)

Feedback from the Access Component:
Loops and Workspace Areas

The other types of situations where feedback is required are a lot trickier. When your warehoused information is accessed by users, there is always

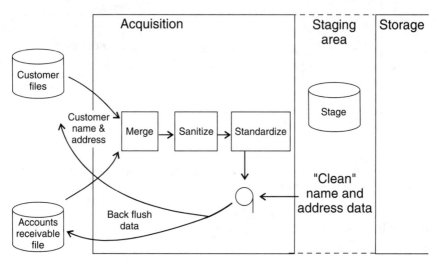

Figure 5.5 Back-flush mechanism.

the chance, and often the requirement, that the users will need to update that information. In some situations, people will want to make changes to the information and then send those changes back to the legacy systems at the same time. For example, suppose a customer calls, advising the customer service person of a change in address. The natural assumption is that the user simply should make the appropriate changes to the warehouse itself. Unfortunately, this could create a disaster. You then would have some information in the warehouse that you do not have in the legacy systems. Somehow, you need to figure out how to get the new address information back to all of the legacy systems that need it too.

The second situation is even more complex. In some cases, people will want to make changes to the warehouse data and then immediately allow other users to be aware of those changes. For instance, in the execution of mailing-list scoring algorithms, it is critical that people assign relative "weights" to each potential mail recipient and then make a selection of only those customers with a high enough score.

There are no easy solutions to these kinds of problems. Any attempt to read the warehouse backwards, back into the legacy systems, is going to result in an operational and performance nightmare. At the same time, you do not want to ignore the convenience of simply allowing the user to make the change in place and move on to the next problem.

We will provide two solutions to these feedback challenges. In the first case, our solution will be to create mechanisms that capture the changes to the warehouse data and send them back to the acquisitions component for processing. (I call this solution a *feedback loop*.) Specifically, you must capture all of the changes made to the warehouse storage area at the point that they are created and send copies of those changes to a "holding file" that will be utilized by the acquisitions component for the next full warehouse load/refresh cycle. This is akin to making a rule for a real warehouse that says that, if you want to check things back into the warehouse, you must send it to the receiving dock, not the shipping dock.

While the logistics of building this kind of feedback loop can be inconvenient and complicated, establishing this discipline is going to save you from dozens of complexities and inconveniences later on in the life of the warehouse. (See Figure 5.6.)

In situations where you must allow people to drastically change the nature of the warehouse data, it does not make sense to allow all of these in-place changes to the warehouse to occur. You should make use of workspace areas instead. (See Figure 5.7.)

In these cases, the subset of data that the users want to manipulate is copied into a temporary workspace (either database tables or flat files). The users then can manipulate, change, share, and alter the contents of the workspace as much as they want without endangering the integrity of the warehouse storage area itself.

At key points in the process, the workspace area can be cleaned up and the changes sent back to the acquisitions component for loading into a hold file and for eventual inclusion in the acquisition and warehouse loading process.

Infrastructure Conclusions

Taken as a whole, this collection of procedures and approaches defines your operational infrastructure. When you combine this operational infra-

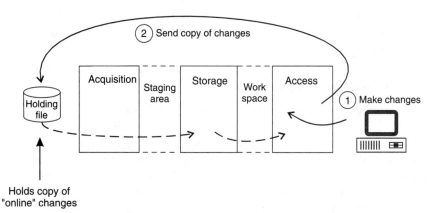

Figure 5.6 A feedback loop.

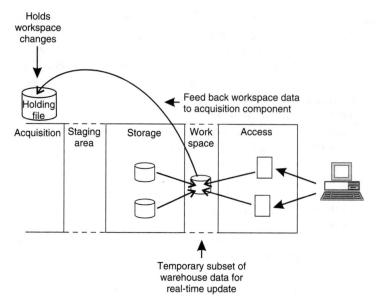

Figure 5.7 The workspace solution.

structure with the physical infrastructure, you will have defined the overall warehouse infrastructure that will be prerequisite to your being able to actually use the warehouse to do any real work.

It is critical at this point to note that no one would try to utilize a real warehouse until all of the grounds, building, personnel, and storage areas were defined. No one would dream of using a warehouse where the storage locations weren't cataloged and the part numbers of the goods being managed weren't clearly displayed and understood by the warehouse support staff.

In the same way, it will be critical in your construction of a data warehouse that you build this infrastructure before you start trying to do any warehousing work.

Data-Warehousing Applications

Assuming that you have developed your infrastructure, you now will be in the position to begin entertaining the thought of taking on some real warehousing work. The next issue that you face when deciding how to construct the data warehouse is how to manage the process of putting real, usable data into the warehouse. I have a very specific set of recommendations, and they do not correspond to the approaches that many people try to take. Before we go into details about our recommended approach, we will consider some of the alternatives.

Building up the warehouse inventory

Returning to the real-world warehouse example, when someone starts up a new warehouse, he or she does not simply open the doors on day one, fill it up with materials on day two, then start using it. That approach is too simplistic and doesn't take the realities of logistics and utilization into account. The view that you want to take of your data warehouse is not so much of a big storage locker where things are placed and then forgotten, but more of a merchandise conduit through which things pass. A viable, well-run warehouse is measured, not by how much it holds, but by how much passes through it. Looking at it from this perspective, it doesn't make any sense to think of your warehouse as being loaded up all at once.

Therefore, the advocates of data warehousing all have their own recommended approaches for how to structure the warehouse construction process. While we could identify an endless array of variations on the basic themes, in general, these approaches are either model driven or application driven.

The model-driven approach to warehouse construction

The basic operational assumption of the model-driven approach to warehouse construction states that you first need to develop a data model that defines what the warehouse should hold, fill it up with data, then allow people to use it. This approach bases most of its assumptions on the validity of data modeling, enterprise modeling, and the data-engineering disciplines in general.

Proponents of this approach believe that it should be possible to develop a logical model of all of the data that the warehouse should need, and only after this model has been perfected should you consider loading and making use of it. Of course, if you were to carry this logic out to its natural conclusion, you would find that you needed to model all of the data within the organization before you could start construction. (Any organization participating in the development of enterprise models knows how long that can take.)

In recognition of this inconvenience, most model-driven practitioners begin by saying that you do not have to model everything at once but that you can break down the task of global modeling into smaller pieces and build the warehouse one section at a time, by logical subject area. (For example, you might build a warehousing component in support of accounting first, then take on production control data and after that personnel information.)

While this approach certainly makes some sense, it unfortunately ignores several key practical considerations.

First, no enterprise-level mapping scheme to date has ever been successfully completed. There are a number of reasons for this; the main one is that no organization stays stagnant long enough for the modeling effort to near completion. While people are busily trying to figure out the information in existing systems, new systems are being built simultaneously. You can never catch up.

Second, the practical value of databases and data models, developed in a vacuum without the benefit of the knowledge of what people want to do with it and why, is to be seriously questioned. Experience in the development of hundreds of systems has shown that you cannot model useful databases without knowing what they will be used for.

Third, and most importantly, an approach like this makes it incredibly difficult for the builders of the system to focus on what they are to deliver, and scope management becomes the biggest concern. Those projects that have taken the model-driven approach to warehouse construction have met with failure more times than not. If you look upon your data warehouse as you would look upon a real-world warehouse, instead of as an exercise in data-processing theory, you would see very quickly why these approaches do not make sense.

The people who build real-world warehouses do not begin by figuring out how many screws, nails, nuts, bolts, and other items the warehouse will hold. They know that the actual contents of the warehouse are going to vary constantly and often quite dramatically. No company plans on needing vast amounts of inventory. If you could predict what you were going to need to store, you would head off the problems and eliminate the need for the warehouse in the first place.

We propose taking the same attitude toward the data warehouse. It is not something to be planned out and forgotten. It is a necessary evil, a stop-gap measure. When you condescend to build a data warehouse, what you really are saying is that you cannot predict where the ups and downs in inventory are going to be but that, with a warehouse, you can smooth out the spikes and valleys and provide your customers with a more dependable flow of information.

Another good analogy for the data warehouse is to think of it as a library. You want to store all of the information that people might need and simply provide them with an inventory of books, a Dewey Decimal system, a card catalog to help them find information, and some librarians to keep order. When you view the data warehouse as a service, instead of as an application, you begin to create an entirely new paradigm for figuring out how to approach it.

The application-based approach

I advocate an entirely different approach to warehouse construction—one that is logical and intuitively obvious but that flies in the face of what is considered the "right way to do things" in the data-processing world.

Instead of looking at your data-warehousing project as a stagnant one that is built, turned over to production, and ignored, I view the process of providing a warehouse to the organization as the development of a new support service that will be continually upgraded, changed, and tuned to meet the needs of the organization. In other words, we will view the data warehouse as a critical component of the organization's overall information systems infrastructure. I see it not as a tactical application to meet a specific set of short-term needs but as a facility through which you can build dozens, or even hundreds, of low-cost, rapidly deployed tactical applications. The managers of your warehouse eventually will become the managers of an extensive inventory of small, high-impact, highly sophisticated applications, each designed to meet a specific set of tactical business objectives.

This view of a data warehouse, not as an application, but as a vehicle for the mass production of applications, provides a totally different framework from which to consider the whole construction process. If you are going to accept this second, much-broader vision of the warehouse as being valid, then you are going to have to rethink some of the traditional assumptions about system construction and support.

You cannot afford to approach the data-warehouse project as a one-time deal. You cannot plan on one analysis phase, one design phase, one data model, etc. You must assume that the warehouse itself and the warehouse support team will be in a continual state of mapping data, cleaning, loading, and delivering it to end users.

Once you accept the premise that this will not be a one-shot project, then you must rethink your assumptions about how the system is going to be staffed and built from the very start. Taken from this perspective, you can see that the warehouse is not a monolithic block of data attached to another monolithic block of end-user access mechanisms, but instead it is a collection of discrete applications, each of which provides a different set of functionalities to end users. You can view each of these discrete applications as adding another layer to the warehouse. As you add more and more of these layers, the warehouse becomes more and more robust. (See Figure 5.8.)

By changing your perspective to this more incremental kind of approach, you create an environment that will allow you to increase the probability of success for each of the subsequent applications, while still building up a synergy that allows you to eventually benefit from having a critical mass of data within the warehouse itself.

The Need for a Data Discipline

Just because we claim that an application-driven approach to warehouse construction makes more sense than a model-driven approach does not mean that we intend to build the warehouse without the benefits of data modeling and the other data-management and data-architecture disciplines. Far from it. Indeed, the process of building each application must be driven entirely by a collection of disciplines that I refer to as the *data disciplines*.

Acquisition	Storage	Access
	"Application 3"	
	"Application 2"	
	"Application 1"	
	Infrastructure	
	Architecture	

Figure 5.8 Data-warehouse "applications."

Just as you would never dream of trying to run a real warehouse without some kind of method for identifying individual parts as well as all of the different storage locations within the warehouse so that you could keep track of what comes in and where it gets stored, so too must you have a similar inventory management approach to run your data warehouse.

In the real warehouse environment, everything that needs to be managed already has some kind of identifier. The process of building the data warehouse is a little more complicated. Part of the job of running this warehouse actually is finding the data that people need, tagging it appropriately, then bringing it into the warehouse for their use.

There are several data disciplines that must be in place. The list of these disciplines includes:

- Data-analysis processes
  - ~Data sourcing—Identifying where the data that people want currently exists and validating that what they think they will find really is there
  - ~Data-integrity validation—Verifying that the data extracted is accurate, valid, and usable
  - ~Data synchronization—Making sure that the multiple sources of data synch up with each other (including the development of back-flush mechanisms)
  - ~Data-transformation mapping—Verifying the identity and applicability of the data as it travels from one end of the data warehouse to the other
  - ~Data modeling—Cataloging an inventory of all of the data within the warehouse
  - ~Data design—Figuring out how the data will be arranged in the new warehouse relational tables (including the development of a data architecture)
  - ~Data-metrics gathering—Determining how much data will be managed and at what access rate

- Data-transformation processes
  ~Data extraction—Pulling the data out of its source and into a ware-house-usable form
  ~Data cleansing—Correcting errors in the accuracy, validity, and usability of extracted data, including merge, purge, and formatting programs
  ~Data loading and storage—Loading data into tables and data chains

It is critical that the people running the warehouse have a clear set of procedures for how and by whom these disciplines are to be performed before you actually can begin doing any real warehousing activities. (See Figure 5.9.)

Reconciliation of the Application-Driven Approach with Enterprise Modeling and Data Administration

At this point, you can anticipate a loud hue and cry from those corporate organizations that advocate a data-driven approach to systems development. Your adherence to an application-driven method might appear to be in direct opposition to corporate initiatives aimed at the management of data as a corporate resource.

On the contrary, it is my claim that this approach can fit quite nicely with these corporate initiatives. The only difference is that the integration with these systems must occur after the business-determined demands of the warehouse itself have been met.

With this approach, it is our intention to minimize data redundancy and to increase the manageability of data just as much as, if not more than, the "purist" data administration advocates espouse. The only difference is that you will create this environment of shared data resources by adding applications in a serial fashion, making sure that, as each application is added,

Acquisition	Storage	Access
		Solution development
		Data identification
Data sourcing		Data sourcing
Data integrity validation		Data integrity validation
Data synchronization	Data synchronization	
Back flush development		
	Storage topology mapping	Storage topology mapping
Data transformation mapping	Data transformation mapping	Data transformation mapping
Data metrics gathering	Data metrics gathering	Data metrics gathering
	Data modeling	
	Database design	

Figure 5.9 Data disciplines.

any data that has been pulled under the warehouse umbrella is utilized by as many different applications as possible. The details of how we propose to accomplish this data administration vision of data utilization are illustrated in the following sections.

We begin this process by considering, from this perspective (in a little more detail), what we mean by a *warehouse application*.

An overview of an application

Before looking at a few more rules for deciding what should or should not be included as an application for your warehouse, let's see what this application looks like.

Remember that, up until this point, your warehouse has held no data. All you have done is assemble the hardware and software necessary to run it; figure out how it would work; determine the rules for the treatment of management, monitoring, and data discipline; predefine your feedback mechanisms; and educate your staff in how to run the warehouse. Now it is time to see what it really looks like (Figure 5.10). (In the following paragraphs, the numbers in parentheses correspond to the numbers in the figure.)

Notice that you finally have begun to include real legacy systems, real programs, real data stores, real access programs and tools, and real users in your conceptualization. You begin with the identification of all of those legacy systems and the underlying legacy system data files that hold information critical to the warehouse (1).

Data from these systems is extracted and passed through a series of acquisitions programs (2). (These programs perform your keying, hygiene, validation, cross referencing, formatting, and storage functions.)

At this time, any back-flush programs that will be required to feed clean data back to the legacy systems also are developed (3). This includes those programs that will apply the clean data to those legacy files (4).

Eventually, you are left with a collection of staged data, ready to load into the warehouse (5). This staged data then is loaded into the actual storage area—usually relational database tables (6). Any summary, cross-reference storage tables are generated as well (7).

In some cases, workspace tables also will be automatically created and loaded (8), although this also can be postponed until the user specifically requests it.

A critical aspect of the workspace area of the warehouse is the inclusion of the workspace feedback mechanism, which periodically updates the acquisitions portion of the warehouse with the real-time information changes that the workspace contains (9). Basically, the contents of the workspace need to be sent to an acquisitions component staging file (10), where those changes can be included in the next reload/refresh of the main warehouse itself.

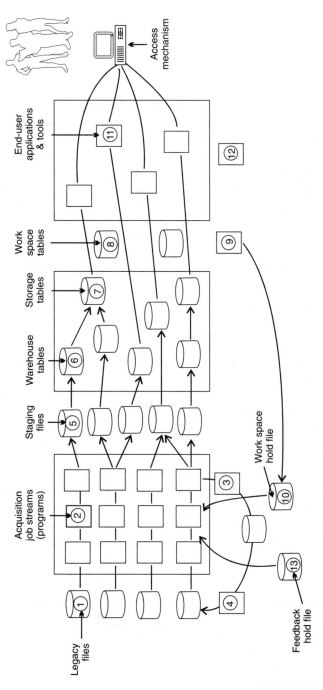

Figure 5.10 The components of an "application."

Finally, different end-user applications and tools (11) can access those subsets of data that they require. These facilities also might include a feed-back mechanism (12) similar to the one supporting the workspace area. In this case, each specific change made to the base warehouse tables also is recorded in a file (13), which eventually is fed back into the warehouse load process.

Data-warehouse applications and scope control

Given this more complete picture of how the application will be put to-gether, we now will turn to a more formal definition of what makes up each of the applications that eventually will make use of the warehouse.

Remember, the reason that we are taking this approach is because experience has shown that complexity and the lack of focus is what has led to the demise of most warehousing systems. Therefore, it is critical that you establish a set of rules for the definition of each of the applications so that these problems can be avoided. Remember also that we said the warehouse would be designed as an environment within which a great many applications could be added and that it was not to be considered as one application.

Rule 1: Contiguity

A warehouse application is a contiguous assembly of acquisition, storage, and access components that, when taken in their entirety, provide an end user with a functional set of data, delivered in a form that is usable. (See Figure 5.11.)

At this point, it is important to notice what we have and have not included in the definition of a warehouse application. First of all, we said that an application is a contiguous assembly of components, meaning that each warehouse application must include a data-acquisition, data-storage, and data-access component, each of which is dependent on the others. In other words, you cannot create a warehouse application that consists only of acquisition and storage components. (See Figure 5.12.)

Unfortunately, many people believe that this is exactly what a data-warehousing project is about. The thinking goes something like this: "We'll identify the data, extract it, and load it into the warehouse. The users can figure out later what they are going to do with it."

> A data warehouse "application" is a contiguous assembly of Acquisition, Storage and Access components which, when taken in their entirety, provide the user with a functional set of usable data.

Figure 5.11 What is an "application?"

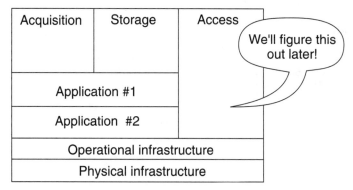

Figure 5.12 Don't do this:

This approach is destined for challenges, cost overruns, and eventual failure for two reasons:

- It ignores the complexity of data-access tools and their specific requirements.
- It ignores the problems of data acquisition, validation, and storage.

In general, it greatly oversimplifies everyone's understanding of the process. The fact of the matter is that you cannot acquire and store warehouse data that is usable unless you know what people are going to do with it. Therefore, we will never advocate the building of an application that does not include an access component.

There is another way that some will try to attack warehouse construction in a piecemeal fashion. (See Figure 5.13.) In these cases, users and the advocates of specific data-mining and data-analysis solutions develop a set of requirements and a whole lot of expectations about how a data-access component is going to work. These individuals say, "We will figure out exactly what we want to do with the information first, then build the warehouse to back it up."

This approach will fail just as quickly as the first approach. The designers will spend an inordinate amount of time figuring out how the data-access portion is supposed to work only to find that the information that they need is either not available or too expensive.

For example, I worked on one customer information system where, after nine months of design work, the builders of the system found that the only way to get the data that they required loaded into the system was for a team of business people to input the five million rows of data by hand. This was not a feasible solution, and the system had to be abandoned.

So the first criterion for selection of applications is that they be contiguous across all components. This guarantees that all of the parts of the warehouse are going to be synchronized when it is time to use the system.

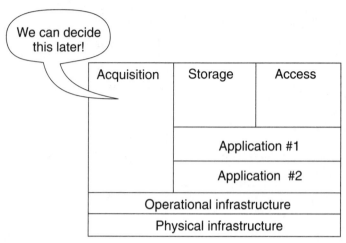

Figure 5.13 And don't do this:

Rule 2: Business Focus and the Decomposition of Business Cases

Our second rule is applied to help make our definition of the application even more specific in scope. While saying that each application must be contiguous provides a guideline for what not to do when determining the scope of a project, it does little to provide the means to limit the scope. The application of the second rule will provide this limitation. Rule 2 states that every application must be based upon a single, business-sponsored value proposition. To understand this rule, you obviously will need to develop an understanding of what a value proposition is.

Complexity in systems today

Every business computer system is designed to meet some kind of business need or collection of needs. In the early days, the name of the system often provided a good understanding of what it was designed to do. For instance, the Payroll system is designed to manage the process of recording people's time and issuing them paychecks. The Accounts Payable system was built to keep track of the corporation's debts and the payment of its bills. In each case, there is an implied business function that the system has been built to support.

As systems became more complex, it became more difficult to name them and have those names correspond to specific functions. Before too long, we began naming systems with acronyms. The GENESIS system might be the General Engineering and Sales Integration System, PRMS identifies the Purchasing and Receiving Management System, etc.

Clearly, as systems have become more complex and multidimensional in nature, their purpose and focus have become less and less discernible. You might recall that, in chapter 2, we spent a considerable amount of time discussing this aspect of business computer systems today. Systems have and will continue to become more and more complex, solving problems that involve the coordination of efforts of hundreds of different people and systems.

In today's development environment, it is not uncommon to find large numbers of people working on systems with no clear idea as to what the real reason for building the system is. To understand what the system is supposed to do requires that you read through pages and pages of descriptions. Many times, the core reason for the system is so obfuscated that you cannot figure it out unless you ask someone.

If you are going to build your warehouse in the incremental manner that we have described, you are going to have to figure out some way to break down these extremely complex business problems and solutions into small, well-focused parts. The only way to accomplish this is to decompose the business problems themselves into smaller, more manageable pieces.

Understanding business problems

Based on the following assumptions:

- Most of those applications that will be considered as candidates for the warehouse will be extremely large and complex in nature
- It is neither an obvious nor trivial process to break these extremely complex candidates into a collection of smaller parts

You are going to need to develop an approach that allows you to perform this decomposition process as quickly as possible.

The business environment and systems projects

To help develop just such an approach, we will begin by examining the typical business environment today as it relates to business systems and especially to data-warehouse development. To start with, you must recognize that business people could care less about data warehouses. A data warehouse is a systems-development concept, not a business concept. Business people live and focus in a world of business problems. While we have referred repeatedly to the confusing and contradictory nature of the systems-development environment, we have yet to discuss just exactly how confusing and contradictory the business environment itself has become.

In the early days of the large corporate environment, businesses were organized around clear, hierarchical lines. The business could be viewed as collections of departments, each performing specific tasks, and each of those tasks contributing to some greater business good. These days, however, with the advent of matrix management, unstructured team approaches, steering committee mania and the flat, managerless organizational structure, we find that business people are in just as constant a state of flux as the computer systems people are. In an environment of this type, it is very difficult to define clear, well-organized plans. Therefore, it also is difficult to develop requirements for a warehouse that are clear and well-organized.

In most business environments, people are wearing a variety of different hats. The lines between sales, marketing, accounting, production control, etc. are becoming ever more blurred. As a consequence, the ideas about how to make use of a data warehouse will tend to be equally fuzzy and undefined.

In a typical environment, there will be a large number of users and managers from a diverse set of business areas, each of whom sees a completely different, but equally believable, way in which the warehouse can solve their problems. Each of them will advocate a different assortment of propositions of how the warehouse should be used to meet their needs.

However, if you were to take this collection of propositions at face value, you immediately would become embroiled in all sorts of business and technical problems. Unless you apply some kind of discipline and rigor to the prioritization and treatment of these propositions, you will end up trying to please everyone and ultimately will please no one.

The decomposition of business propositions

Therefore, our assumption will be that, as soon as business people begin to understand what a data warehouse is and how it can help them, they immediately will come up with dozens of propositions describing ways that the warehouse can be of use.

Your job will be to help them to diagnose what those propositions really entail and to come up with some kind of a scheme for placing a value on each proposition and a priority list for which should be done in what order.

Value-proposition prioritization

I refer to each of the proposals made by a business person to make use of the warehouse to solve a business problem as a *value proposition*. Therefore, the first step in determining which applications to place into your warehouse will be to gather up these propositions, determine the merit of each, determine the relative cost of each, assign relative values to them, then rank them according to their priority of importance. Figure 5.14 shows a diagram of how this process works.

In some cases, the process of identifying, analyzing, and ranking value propositions will be managed as a formal project or as part of a feasibility study. In other cases, the systems-development people will simply, on an informal basis, gather up the candidate proposals and select those with the

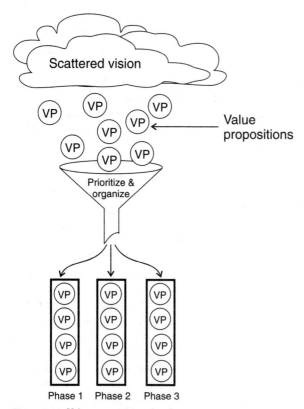

Figure 5.14 Value-proposition development.

most value. Ultimately, the process of soliciting, analyzing, and ranking value propositions needs to become part of the ongoing service that the administrators of the data warehouse provide. Remember, we said that the data warehouse is to be considered an ongoing service to the corporation. The identification and development of value propositions is the first and most important part of that process.

We also said that, if you were going to attempt to assess the value of the warehouse, then it should be based, not on how much information it holds, but on how often or how appropriately the information moves through the warehouse. The identification and implementation of more and more value propositions is the purpose of the warehouse.

Of course, simply identifying a collection of value propositions does not, in and of itself, guarantee you any kind of good scope management. You must apply some rigor to those definitions. The rules about value propositions that we will apply are discussed in the following sections.

Rule 1. Each value proposition must be a specific business problem. A value proposition cannot be a collection or "laundry list" of unrelated problems strung into the same sentence. For example, the proposition that the warehouse application will make it possible to keep track of customer inquiries, develop geo-economic segmentations of the market, and provide for the consolidation of customer data from 25 different source systems is not one value proposition; it is three. One regards customer inquiries, another market segmentation, and the third the integration of disparate information.

Rule 2. Each value proposition must have a single, responsible sponsoring business organization. Consider, for instance, the following: "The data-warehousing application will make it possible for customer service personnel to respond more quickly when customers call in with questions, while at the same time making it possible for the marketing department to keep track of which customers have received what promotional item." This is not one value proposition; it is two: one for customer service and one for marketing.

Rule 3. Each value proposition must define a specific, tangible benefit that the application will provide. It is preferred that they be financial in nature, but benefits can be less tangible as well (i.e., market share, efficiency, etc.).

For example, the following value proposition is incomplete: "The data-warehousing application will make it possible for customer service personnel to provide customers with immediate information about the status of their account." To complete it, you would need to add the following: "We estimate that this additional level of service will make it possible for us to prevent the loss due to customer dissatisfaction by approximately 2% of our market per year." Now this proposition would be complete.

Rule 3: The Sequencing of Application Development

The first two rules for the definition of an application tell you what an application should and should not be. However, they say nothing about the order in which these applications are to be added.

In the worst case, people might define a collection of value propositions, turn them into application plans, then attempt to build them all at once (Figure 5.15).

This one-shot approach to warehouse development defeats the purpose of identifying distinct value propositions in the first place. By forcing the sponsors of each warehouse application to specify exactly what it is that they want an application to accomplish, you have greatly reduced the complexity. If you were to try to develop them all at once, the majority of that complexity then would return.

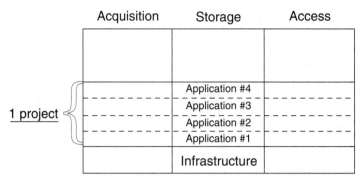

Figure 5.15   The build-all-at-once approach.

Therefore, rule number three states:

Applications that are dependent upon each other must be added to the warehouse serially.

In other words, if you have defined two applications and they share any common acquisition, storage, or data-access components, then they must be added to the warehouse one at a time. The first must be finished before the second is begun, etc.

Why demand serial development? This is one of the places where a lot of systems developers are going to have trouble with our approach. There basically are two reasons why people do not want to make this development serial. First, it forces the warehouse project to take longer. Instead of jumping on everything at once, you are telling people that they must get one part working before they begin the second. Second, many people believe that there are wonderful "economies of scale" to be gained by piggybacking one of these projects on another, especially if there is a lot of overlap between the corresponding acquisition, storage, and access components.

While the arguments behind these cases might be vehement, it is my staunchest belief that, except in the most trivial of cases, to allow developers to attack interdependent applications using any approach other than a serial one greatly increases the chances for failure.

We have discussed these reasons several times, but it basically boils down to the problems of increased complexity and intersystem interdependency. By attacking these applications one at a time, you make it possible for developers to stabilize the first set before taking on the second.

This is not to say that, when you build the second application, you cannot make use of the components developed for the earlier applications. Absolutely not. In fact, if you were not going to try to leverage the code that was generated, data that was stored, and access mechanisms that were developed, then it would be foolish to build a warehouse in the first place. No, all we are saying is that the first one needs to be working and stable before you begin messing with the second. That way, all of what you learned during the first project will make you that much smarter when it comes to doing the second.

It is in this area where we can get into many arguments about the "economies of scale" in systems design and the waste of people's time and efforts in apparently doing the "same job" twice, while forcing the delay of the ultimate system. (See Figure 5.16.)

There are many ways that subsequent applications can leverage work done in earlier efforts. Most obviously, data formatted and stored for the use of one application can be included for use by others, many times with little or no effect on the first system. Also, it is possible to make use of previously developed data formatting, cleansing, and validating programs from the acquisition component, as well as programs, interfaces, and tools that were utilized in the data-access component. In other words, the efficiency and ability to leverage warehouse resources are not curtailed by our serial development rule. However, they *are* delayed and forced within our structure for the sake of risk minimization and complexity containment.

Rule 4: Developing More Than One Application at the Same Time

In some situations, because of time constraints or other imperatives, people will insist that more than one application be developed at a time. You can allow this to take place, but only under a certain set of conditions.

This leads to our next rule about warehouse layer construction. Rule number four states:

> You can develop applications simultaneously, as long as they are completely autonomous.

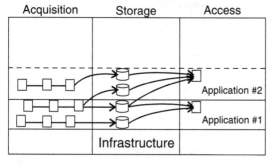

Figure 5.16 Serial development. Second application making use of components developed by the first.

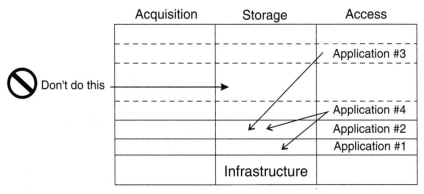

Figure 5.17 Simultaneous, autonomous development.

In other words, if you are going to build two or more systems simultaneously, then do so without leveraging the work of the others still in process. Obviously, there is nothing wrong with developing those applications to leverage work that has been done on applications that already are completed; just stay away from the other development teams.

The reason for this rule should be obvious. Two teams trying to meet their own system requirements while constantly shifting their solutions to respond to another team's similar fluctuations is a guaranteed formula for failure. (See Figure 5.17.)

"But what about the wasted effort?", skeptics will say. "If these applications are using the same data source, then aren't we doing double work?" The answer is a sympathetic but firm: "Yes." Unfortunately, there is no way around this dilemma. As soon as you allow for the crossing of these boundary lines, you court disaster.

However, what do you do if it is imperative that these two applications share the same data? What if part of the value is in their use of a common storage area? The only solution to this is to plan for a data integration project that eliminates the redundancy after the two systems are developed.

Wasted Effort and Extra Expense

At this point, there is a good chance that a lot of readers already have slammed this book shut and said, "Ridiculous! This approach is too slow, too wasteful, and too conservative. Surely, there must be a better way!"

My only response is that, despite 25 years of research and investigation into every methodology, every CASE tool, every systems-development life cycle, and every "new, latest, and greatest" technology under the sun, no one has been able to come up with a way to make anything that's incredibly complex and interdependent simple and easy to build. I am anxious to hear about any approaches to these problems that really have worked in a production environment that did not involve a lot of extra integration expense and without a lot of time delays due to the failure to estimate the true nature of this complexity.

The real advantage of this approach is that the risk, the cost, and the delays are predictable and manageable. The biggest shortcoming of all of the other approaches is that they do nothing to protect you against that risk.

Certainly, you can get lucky, or you might be blessed with an extremely competent staff, an extremely simple and straightforward problem set, or an incredibly motivated and competent user community. Any combination of these might allow you to ignore our application-layering rules. However, for the typical corporation, facing the typical set of business challenges, this is the only way that offers any chance of success. If nothing else, with this approach, you can minimize your risk.

Flipping the problem domain

Another way to look at these issues is to turn the tables on the advocates of big scope systems.

To the developers, I say: "Why should I believe that you can handle the construction of an extremely large and complex data-warehousing application if you are unable to develop a small, tightly defined one?" If the advocates of the "big scope" solutions are so sure of their approach, then let them do two things:

- Explain how you will avoid the impending complexity gridlock that is going to occur.

- Develop a small one and prove that you can manage that first, then come back to talk about bigger ones.

In a similar vein, to the business sponsors of these big solutions, I say: "Why should I believe that this big, multidimensional business solution is going to accomplish all of what you have stated? If the solution is sound, then surely there must be a way to implement a part of it to prove that the assumptions are sound. Prove the small concepts, and the big concepts will fall into place."

In other words, in both cases, the maxim that I would apply is this: If the concept is sound, then it should be provable on a small scale.

Disclaimers

At this point, let's be clear about some assumptions behind this current train of thought. Remember that we are talking specifically about data warehouses, not about computer systems in general. Clearly, there are hundreds of types of applications where you must deal with a high degree of complexity and establish a critical mass to show any value. For example, would any airline reservation system be useful if it only recorded flights but didn't record seating, flight schedules, etc.? Of course not. However, that system is an operational system, not a data warehouse.

We can afford to be more stringent with our warehouse-construction rules for several reasons. First, it is a passive information-access system, and therefore the synergy that it provides is of a different nature than operational systems. Second, it has a limited set of specific business problems that it can address. A data warehouse is not the answer to all of your data-processing needs; it is simply an option. Therefore, only in the rarest of situations will it make sense to violate the rules that we have laid out.

Summary of approaches to application layering

Given this understanding of what a value proposition is and of how our rules about how to define each of the applications that can be placed within the warehouse, you are ready to figure out how the warehouse is going to be built. I will call this process of laying one application on top of the other *warehouse-application layering.*

We already have considered two of our approaches:

- Autonomous layering—Where each application layer is added independent of the others

- Serial layering—Where you add each application layer in a predefined sequential order.

Of course, there are other ways that you can add applications as well.

Access-only applications. Another type of application that can be added to the warehouse is one that provides the user with an entirely new access mechanism but that makes use of data already collected and stored by a previously completed application. (See Figure 5.18.)

At first glance, the reader might suspect that the access-only application is a violation of our first rule about applications, where we said that each had to be contiguous. In fact, the access-only application does not violate this rule, because it consists of an access, storage, and acquisition component just like any other application. Just because it is making use of previously developed components does not make it incongruous.

Data-only applications. In the same way that you can develop a new application by leveraging previously developed storage components, so too can you leverage previously developed access components. There is no reason that you could not add the functionality of a new value proposition to an existing system simply by creating some new sets of stored data and allowing previously developed access mechanisms to use it. (See Figure 5.19.)

As in the previous example, our contiguity rule is satisfied because the application is complete.

Hybrid approaches. What is most likely to happen, especially after the warehouse has had a chance to get started, is that hybrid combinations of these approaches will begin to make a lot of sense. For example, Figure 5.20 shows a new application that uses of a lot of previously collected data, a little bit of new data, and an entirely new access mechanism.

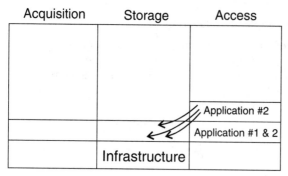

Acquisition	Storage	Access
		Application #2
		Application #1 & 2
	Infrastructure	

Figure 5.18 Access-only applications.

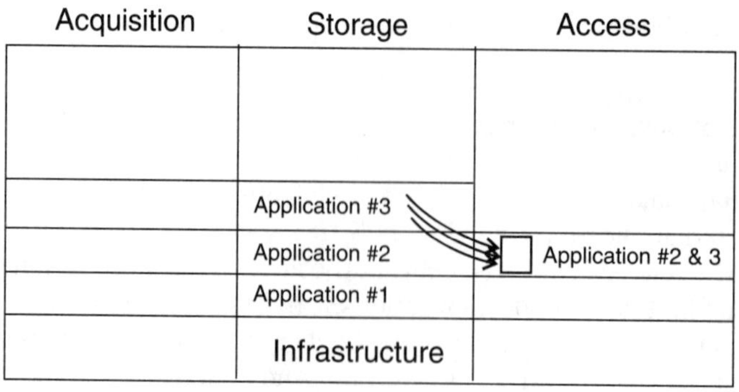

Acquisition	Storage	Access
	Application #3	
	Application #2	Application #2 & 3
	Application #1	
	Infrastructure	

Figure 5.19 Data-only applications.

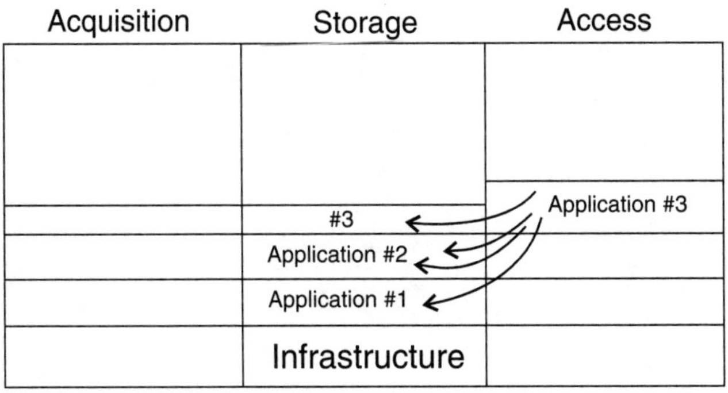

Figure 5.20 A hybrid application.

6

Application Development and the Data Disciplines

No matter how you look at it, a data warehouse is first, foremost, and always only as good as the data that it holds. It should come as no surprise then that the development of an effective data warehouse depends on the existence of an extensive and well-thought-out discipline for approaching how that warehouse should be laid out.

As I have cited previously, the systems-development life cycle has failed to meet the needs of modern systems developers in the vast majority of cases. In its place, I propose the following data-warehouse development life cycle.

Before we actually begin to unveil this approach, we will begin by explaining that it is not our intention to propose the following discipline as the solution to the problems of systems development in all situations. Far from it. Different kinds of systems require different approaches. Indeed, it is the failure to recognize this that dooms the "one size fits all" systems-development life cycle to failure. No, our approach is a very specific one and should be utilized only in those situations where our assumptions and specified preconditions have been met. It would be disastrous to try to make use of this approach to assist in the design of OLTP, object-oriented, or client/server applications.

The Approach

The process that we specify for development takes into account the idiosyncrasies and diverse requirements that each of the three components of the warehouse (acquisition, storage, and access) demand. Each of these components involves a different set of variables, different kinds of objectives, and a different kind of approach. Our development approach also recognizes that the key to the development of a successful warehouse is the integration of the data across these three components. The process therefore involves that you traverse these three domains many times.

At the same time, it is critical that whatever solution you develop be integrated across the different layers of the system (data disciplines and infrastructure); therefore, the approach also demands that you start at the top layer (data identification) and drive downward through the data discipline, operational infrastructure, and physical infrastructure process at the same time. (See Figure 6.1.)

An Iterative Process

While it would be possible to develop a complete data-warehouse system by going through this series of steps only one time, the realities of business environments demand that you actually go through them at least twice. The first time will be during the development of the overall warehouse strategy and plan. During the execution of these phases, it will be critical that you gather fundamental information from each of the data disciplines, operational infrastructure, and physical infrastructure layers. During this pass through the methodology, it will be your objective to identify key requirements, validate key assumptions, and develop preliminary estimates regarding the size, capacity, capabilities, and viability of the systems being proposed. The end product of this first pass will be estimates for the cost

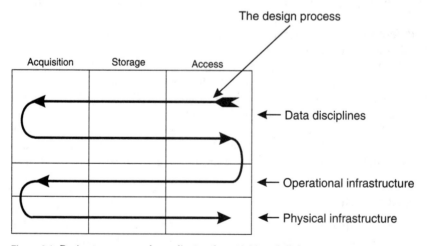

Figure 6.1 Design traverses and coordinates the activities of all three components.

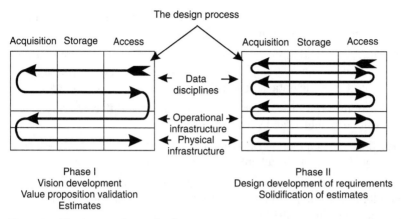

Figure 6.2 The data-warehouse development process.

and development time for each of the value propositions and a validation of the feasibility of the solution proposed.

After the solidification and approval of these value propositions, the warehouse-development team will use the intelligence and documentation created by the project-development team and use that as the starting point for a second, more detailed pass through the same process. (See Figure 6.2.)

Application Development and the Data Disciplines

Given this basic understanding of how the data disciplines fit into the overall framework of systems development, we are ready to begin a more formal definition of each of the steps. We have identified the process of application development as consisting of the following steps:

1. Solution development

2. Validation and estimation of the solution

3. Development of a plan of execution

4. Actual system development

To perform these steps effectively, you will need to make use of the following series of data disciplines. These include:

1. Solution development—A more detailed version of the vision-development process

2. Data identification—Identification of the data that the solution will require

3. Data sourcing—Identification of the legacy or external sources of data that will meet the requirements specified

4. Data-integrity validation—Validation of the sources of data, guaranteeing that the sources actually will be able to provide the information required and that the data is in a usable form

5. Data synchronization—Determination of how the different sources of data will be synchronized with each other

6. Back-flush development—Determination of how corrected and cleansed data is going to be fed back into the legacy systems

7. Data-storage architecture development—Determination of the nature and identity of each of the transitory data stores that will hold the data as it moves from acquisition area to the user terminal

8. Data-transformation mapping—Determination of the specific transformations the data will go through as it moves from the legacy system to the user terminal

9. Data-metrics gathering—Collection of quantitative information about the data and its transformation, its access, and any timing issues involved

10. Data modeling—Development of a formal data model for the data

11. Database design—Development of a physical design for the database

As we proceed through the definitions of each, it will be important for you to keep in mind several things.

First, remember that each phase of the process must be executed in the order prescribed if the process is to be managed efficiently and if the complexity and potential for design chaos are to be reduced. This technique has been developed based on feedback received from hundreds of data analysts and data-warehouse developers who have found that, as difficult as it might be sometimes, this sequence makes the most sense.

Second, remember that judgment must be exercised in the application of these phases. In some cases, it will be possible to "shortcut" a phase because the information required is easily accessible and trivial. However, there are certain key deliverables that each phase describes, and these deliverables must be at hand if the rest of the process is to work.

The imposition of this kind of discipline in this order might cause the experienced practitioner to be concerned or even perplexed. On the one hand, the logical order dictated seems to make perfect sense from a logical perspective.

On the other hand, the traditional approach to data modeling and design would seem to dictate that this approach is somehow out of synch. Our response to this is that all of the components of successful data modeling and database design effort, as they are traditionally described, are included within our definition of a data discipline. The difference is in the order in which steps are carried out and the emphasis upon which you place your energies.

The traditional modeling and design approach emphasizes logical data modeling and the development of good, third normal form, entity-relationship-based databases that meet a set of theoretical criteria for soundness. The emphasis of our approach is upon the tactical delivery of the information that is needed. In reality, as any DBA or data analyst will tell you, the developers of every system end up having to make these kinds of compromises during the late stages of systems development anyway. No matter how hard the data modeler and DBA try, the reality of system-performance requirements will demand that this tactical, impending delivery directive will take precedence over theoretical considerations at some point. All we have done with our approach is recognize the reality of the situation and build it into our approach.

Roles and Responsibilities

Another source of confusion during the execution of any kind of vision development or analysis-and-design process is the lack of understanding on people's parts about who should be responsible for what part of the process. In chapter 2, we stated that there were two things that contributed the most to the breakdown of the SDLC and the failure of projects.

The first was complexity overload, attempts made by people to try to take on more complexity than they could possibly work through. Our solution to that problem was to break the system down into a collection of discrete value propositions and to form our approach around the minimization of scope based upon those propositions.

The second was the problem of responsibility ambiguity—one that arises when no one is exactly sure of who is responsible for what. In chapter 5, we outlined the different areas of decision making that would be required to develop and deliver those visions, and we considered the appropriate allocation of responsibility to the management, operational, and systems areas. At this point, we will undertake to provide the same kind of allocation of responsibilities for the data disciplines. The only significant difference between the participation profiles of the three groups in the vision development phase, versus their participation in the execution of the data disciplines and infrastructure development, is that the role of management is greatly reduced. By the time you get to these phases, the vision and direction set by management should be clear, and the operational and systems people should be able to carry the process out.

Although we have yet to provide a lot of detail about each of these steps, we will begin by identifying the level that each participating area will play in the process. We will specify three types of participants in the data discipline development process: operational personnel (the user of the system), legacy systems support personnel (the technical and business people responsible for the maintenance and execution of Legacy and external data sources), and the systems-development personnel (the people driving the warehouse development process). (See Table 6.1.)

Applicability to the Components of the Warehouse

Another perspective that can help you understand what the objectives of each of these phases will be is to have a clear understanding of how each step applies to each of the components of the warehouse. Table 6.2 provides this perspective.

TABLE 6.1 The Data Disciplines: Participation Levels

Step	Description	Legacy support	Operational	Developers
1	Solution development	—	Heavy	Medium
2	Data identification	—	Medium	Heavy
3	Data sourcing	Heavy	Light	Medium
4	Data integrity validation	Light	Medium	Heavy
5	Data synchronization	Light	—	Heavy
6	Backflush development	Heavy	—	Heavy
7	Data storage architecture development	—	—	Heavy
8	Data transformation mapping	—	—	Heavy
9	Data metrics gathering	Light	Light	Heavy
10	Data modeling	—	Light	Heavy
11	Database design	—	—	Heavy

TABLE 6.2 The Data Disciplines: Warehouse Components Involved

Step	Description	Acquisition	Storage	Access
1	Solution development	—	—	Heavy
2	Data identification	—	—	Heavy
3	Data sourcing	Heavy	—	Light
4	Data integrity validation	Heavy	—	Light
5	Data synchronization	Heavy	Light	—
6	Backflush development	Heavy	—	—
7	Data storage architecture development	—	Heavy	Medium
8	Data transformation mapping	Heavy	Heavy	Heavy
9	Data metrics gathering	Heavy	Heavy	Heavy
10	Data modeling	—	Heavy	—
11	Database design	—	Heavy	—

Skills and Experience Levels

The levels of commitment considered in Table 6.1 assume a certain caliber of person or people involved throughout the process. Our assumptions regarding the type of person providing support in each area are as follows:

- Operational personnel—Familiarity with the day-to-day operations in the business area for which the value proposition is being developed. This includes the related procedures, work flows, existing computer systems, and interfaces with other operational areas.

- Legacy and external data source support personnel—Familiarity with the targeted source systems. Specific knowledge about the systems themselves, their operational business area interfaces, and computer system characteristics. Personnel familiar with both the business functionality and the inner workings of the computer systems. Access to the database and file layout information and the ability to quickly extract data from those systems, analyze it, and explain it.

- Systems-development personnel—The skills required to fill this role are very diverse. It is not uncommon to have a team of specialists working within this area. Specialized skill requirements include:
  ~Data analysis
  ~Business analysis
  ~Data modeling
  ~Database design
  ~Computer-systems analysis and modeling

It will be our assumption that the people assigned to work on this project will have the previously defined skill sets with a concomitant level of experience to make their assignment reasonable.

The First Pass Through the Phases

We said that the process of bringing the design of a specific warehouse to completion was going to require that you go through these phases at least twice. The first pass will be very cursory in nature and will occur during the vision-development process. During this pass, the objective will be to identify all of the critical success factors and resolve all of the critical unknowns. The deliverables from this pass will include cost estimates, time estimates, resource estimates for the infrastructure, preliminary hardware and software selections, and high-level metrics about the performance characteristics of the system.

The second time through the process occurs after the project has been approved. You go through the phases this time to conduct what traditionally has been described as the analysis and design phases. During this pass, your objective will be to generate a complete set of specifications for the construction of the warehouse application.

We will carry you through a set of the fundamental steps and issues involved for each pass.

The solution-development phase

The first time that you go through the solution-development phase, all you have is a general idea about what it is that people think the system can accomplish. It will be your role at that time to turn this soft concept into some kind of tangible solution. After identifying what the business people would like to accomplish, it will be your job to make this vision a little more tangible. The steps to follow during the first pass through this phase are:

1. Define how the system will work in business terms.

2. Define what the system actually will do.

3. Define how this system is going to change/improve the way things are done today.

4. Turn the solution to the problem into a series of screens.

5. Determine if there are any existing applications or tools that can ease the delivery of this solution.

6. If such a tool exists, use it as your template.

The participation of experts in whatever business area the analyst happens to be working in can be extremely helpful during this phase of the process. It is at this time that people need to seriously consider exactly what it is that they want to accomplish and how things can be done better and more intelligently.

The solution-development process is a very creative, very spontaneous endeavor. It often is helpful during this phase to consider how other companies are solving these same kinds of problems. It also can be helpful to get an idea of the capabilities that different kinds of data-mining products can provide. When completed, the team should have a pretty good idea about what they would like the system to deliver and how.

After this has been accomplished, you then can begin to develop the more specific systems aspects. The second time that you go through the solution-development phase, you develop a high-level model of what the system will do. This usually is documented in the form of a series of screen layouts. At this point, you need to decide whether the system is going to be developed based on a "custom application" where a series of code is written specifically for the application or if a package or software product can get the job done.

After making the create-versus-buy decision, you are ready to begin the process of data identification.

The data-identification process

The starting point for the definition of any kind of data-warehousing initiative must be with the identification of the data that the users want to see. No other approach makes any sense. Only when you know what people want to see at the end of the process can you hope to be sure that the rest of the system is going to meet those demands. If you were to try to identify the source of a great amount of the confusion and chaos that typifies the failure of the vast majority of data-warehousing initiatives today, you would find that disregard for this basic premise is at the source.

Provided that you have a good basic understanding of the screens that the system should have and the functions that they are to perform, you can begin to identify the data that will drive the process. The steps that you will follow include:

1. Define what each of the screens (or reports) is supposed to accomplish.
2. Define each of the critical data elements that these screens must have.
3. Generate a list of data elements by screen and provide a brief definition of what each of these elements should contain.
4. Generate a list of candidate sources for each of these data elements.

The process of gathering this information can be formal or informal depending upon the size, scope, and nature of the project being developed.

The first time through, you will concentrate simply on establishing the correct number and types of screens and on identifying all of the critical data elements required.

Data sourcing

During the first two phases of this process, you worked extensively with the operational users of the system. At this point, you are ready to approach the legacy and external data sources and begin the process of finding the required data.

During the data-sourcing step, you will take the list of proposed sources for the required data and validate that the data actually can be found where you think it might. This process usually is more difficult than it seems. The key phrase for a person participating in this process is the motto for the state of Missouri: "Show me." No matter how adamant people are about whether the data that you are looking for can be found or not, the analyst must insist that samples of it be extracted from the legacy systems where they should be located. These extractions need not be dumps of the entire database or file, but they must include some kind of random sampling.

Therefore the sourcing process has the following steps:

1. Identify the candidate source of data (from the data-identification process).

2. Validate with the legacy/external data-source expert that the candidate source is both likely to hold the information and the best potential source of it.

Verifying this second criterion actually is more difficult than the first. When you begin looking for the sources of data for your system, it is possible that the identified source is not the original source of the information but actually is a copy from someplace else. Wherever possible, you want to load your warehouse with sources of information, not copies.

In those situations where better and more accurate sources of the information can be found in other systems, the analyst must play detective and backtrack the data to its original source. Luckily, many systems have developed "Master Files" that contain the "real" values that you are looking for.

After the source has been validated as the best one, the analyst then asks to see two things:

- Copies of the data layouts for the targeted source files
- Sample extractions of data from each of the files

It then falls to the analyst to verify that the data specified by the users actually is the data that is found in the file.

Data-integrity validation

After the data has been properly sourced, the analyst must begin the process of validating its integrity. There are several kinds of integrity that you must be concerned with. They fall under the general categories of identity integrity and population integrity.

The steps involved in the process are:

1. Identify the sources of identity-integrity violation.

2. Identify the sources of population-integrity violation.

3. Develop the approach to be used to rectify these violations.

4. Identify the programs and storage files necessary to execute.

Identity integrity. We use the term *identity integrity* to describe whether or not the data that has been sourced actually describes the information that the user wants. While, in most cases, everyone will concur with the gross meaning of a term, the more subtle meaning of the term might cause it to be something other than what the user intended.

For example, during the development of a large data warehouse for a manufacturing concern, I became embroiled in what I will call "The Great Sales Volume Debate." It seems that the marketing group had asked for a field called "Sales Volume" to appear on their reports. I traced the field back to the legacy that was supposed to hold the "Sales Volume" number and found, much to the chagrin of the users, that the sales volume being reported was the real volume of sales for each product but was adjusted for returns and was stated in terms of retail prices, not in terms of the discounted dollars actually collected from high-volume customers. This caused the number "Sales Volume" to be greatly skewed and made their statistical-analysis program useless. They needed unadjusted, fully discounted volume numbers, *not* the adjusted numbers that they were getting.

We eventually were able to develop the means to get the users the numbers that they needed, but it was a painful and time-intensive process and one that no one had included in the project plan.

There actually are many ways that the identity of the data in the source systems can turn out to be inaccurate or inappropriate for the users of the system. It is the job of the analyst, during the integrity-validation phase, to identify those problems and rectify them.

Population integrity. The second kind of problem occurs, not because the data is inappropriate to the user's needs, but because the way that it is stored is not always up to standards. Often, only a small percentage of the data stored in a legacy system is accurate or stored correctly. As legacy systems get larger and more complex, they begin to play more and more tricks with the stored data. Problems with the population of the source file can take many forms. The two biggest are format problems and incomplete sets.

Data-format problems. In the most blatant cases of polluted data, the information in the source file is not stored in the kind of field that the system can read. In the perfect world, every field of a file or database will be defined as having a certain data type (character, numeric, binary, etc.) and a certain size (2 bytes, 10 bytes, etc.). Each of these storage areas is like a predefined "bucket" into which that data element can be stored. Unfortunately, ingenious programmers often have found ways to put the wrong kinds of data into the wrong places. So, lo and behold, when you dump out your customer file and look at the phone numbers, you might find that your list of numeric phone number values is peppered with little areas of text (messages like "no phone number," "XXXXX," or even a long list of little smiley faces that you cannot read).

There are only two things you can do when the data file that was identified as a source of information has data elements that are unusable. You can either fix the errant fields or eliminate the records from your population.

The first solution, the repair of the data, will require that special data-reformatting programs be written to identify the bad records and take whatever corrective action is required. These corrective actions might include looking up the accurate values in another file, substituting a default value, or deriving the correct value based upon other values that are available.

The second solution, eliminating the errant data, requires the creation of what are known as *purge programs*. Purge programs scan through the available data file and simply delete those records that do not meet the established standards.

Incomplete sets of data. The other big problem that you can have with a given population of data is that it might not hold the entire set of information for which you are looking. For example, you might have identified a Customer Master File that holds 1 million records. There, you would assume that your company has about 1 million customers. However, when you dump out the file, you find that only 500,000 of the records actually are complete. The other 500,000 records hold old, outdated, and incomplete sets of information. As in the other cases, it is the job of the analyst to discover these data-population deficiencies and develop a means for reconciling them with the needs of the new system.

Incomplete sets of data present an entirely different kind of problem. Usually, the solution to these problems is to create *merge programs*. Merge programs identify several different source files, each of which holds a different part of the entire population that you want to include in the warehouse file. The merge programs read in the records from all of these sources and merge them into one cohesive, complete file.

During integrity validation, it is the job of the analyst to identify exactly how bad or good the real data is and to develop a plan for reconciling the problems that are found.

Data synchronization

After you have developed solutions to any integrity or population anomaly problems within the source file, your next challenge will be to examine the problems associated with synchronization. Not only must the data in each file be accurate and have the integrity that you require, but you also need to be concerned with synchronizing that information with the other disparate sources of information that it will need to work with. There are two major categories of synchronization issues: referential-integrity issues and timing issues.

The steps involved in the data-synchronization process include:

1. Identify sources of referential-integrity violation.
2. Identify the sources of timing issues.
3. Develop an approach to rectify the violations and issues.
4. Identify the programs and storage files required to execute the solution.

Referential integrity. The term *referential integrity* is used to describe the integrity of a given data element in its relationship to other data elements. There are three types of referential integrity with which you should be concerned: utilization integrity, population standardization, and interfile integrity.

Utilization integrity. A lack of utilization integrity occurs when the data being provided to the users is not in a form that they can use. For example, the users might need to have all numeric values shown in the standard dollars-and-cents two-decimal-places format, but the data provided might be stored rounded off to the nearest dollar. In this case, some kind of conversion or recomputation of values will need to take place to make the numbers usable.

Population standardization. The second condition that might occur is that the values stored in a given field might be accurate but are stored in several different forms. This is what is known as the classic "code-table problem." For example, the field definition for the "State" where a customer is located might be stored in many forms. For example, the state of New York might be stored as NY, N.Y., New York, and New Yrk. To be usable, you need to standardize this field so that New York always appears the same way all of the time.

Interfile standardization. After you have resolved the utility and population referential-integrity issues, you then must check that the standardization applied to the information in one file is applied equally to the corresponding fields found in other files that this file will be related to.

For example, you might have standardized the "State" field in your customer file, but how is "State" stored in the Sales History file with which you are going to need to relate at a later point? The scope of your referential-integrity concerns reaches across the entire collection of data sources that you intend to include.

Solutions to referential-integrity problems. Unfortunately, the process of resolving referential-integrity problems is a painstaking one. In each case, you will need to employ a combination of data-reformatting programs and merge/purge programs before you can be sure that all of the data is going to be usable.

Synchronization issues

Not only must you address the referential integrity of the source data, you also must be concerned about all of the other ways that the data being brought into the warehouse is going to synchronize with all of the other data. We have isolated the three key areas of synchronization that you need to be involved with: key, timing, and historical synchronization.

Key synchronization. Whenever you deal with the merging of multiple files from different sources of data, you inadvertently will run into problems with keys. Keys are the technique that computer systems use to uniquely identify the individual records within a population of data, and it is the keys that drive these systems.

For example, a customer-information system inadvertently will have a key called Customer_Id or Customer_Number, which uniquely identifies each customer. For each major population of data within a system (customers, products, distributors, employees, etc.), you will find at least one key, if not a vast assortment of conflicting ones, to identify them.

There actually are three kinds of problems that you will run into with keys: redundant identification, hierarchy, and cross-system alignment.

Redundant identification. The first kind of problem occurs when the users of a system abuse the key structure and use that key to identify the same thing over and over again. For example, a customer system might have two, three, or a dozen keys, each pointing to the exact same company.

This problem occurs when different people are allowed to make use of the system and create company records at different times. In these situations, different groups of users will think that different company records are the only ones applicable to the company in question. When you are asked to make copies of these records and pull them into your warehouse, you are going to have to figure out a way to recombine all of these company records into one that is consolidated, then provide it with one key to identify it.

Hierarchy. The second kind of problem occurs when systems need to keep track of hierarchies of things. Hierarchies occur in just about every kind of system. You can have hierarchies of customers (parent corporation, subsidiaries, branch offices, etc.), hierarchies of products (groceries, produce, meat, dairy), or hierarchies of people (corporation, division, department, etc.).

The problem with hierarchies is that it is very difficult to develop a scheme for keying them that works well in many situations. Usually, the legacy systems involved will have a less than adequate structure in place, with a resulting amount of confusion about how exactly the data should be identified. These contradictory and confusing key structures usually occur because different people would like to see the data identified according to different criteria at different times.

For example, a hierarchy of corporations will have to be changed at least quarterly if it is going to reflect the changes in corporate structures prevalent in today's business environment. In the same manner, human-resource hierarchies, which reflect the almost daily shifting of the corporation's internal structure, are a common source of concern. Inevitably, wherever you have a hierarchy, you have the problems associated with the constant need to shift that hierarchy around, and it is the key structure that usually defines this arrangement.

Cross-system alignment. The final and biggest challenge to the person attempting to develop a warehouse and synchronize the data will be to reconcile those situations where different systems make use of different keying schemes. One system might identify customers with a seven digit number; another might utilize a code with eight characters and two numbers. Somehow, you must figure out how to get all of the information going into the system to hold the same keys, while at the same time making it possible to refer back to the sources of data when required.

Solving key synchronization problems. The development of key-synchronization solutions usually requires that some pretty extensive work be done, and the solutions are never eloquent. There are two principal approaches that you can take. You can drive the system off of one of the sets of keys provided and superimpose that key upon the others, or you can create an entirely new key structure unique to the warehouse.

Declaring a system to be the owner of the keys. One way that you can force the resolution of incompatible keys is to figure out which of the existing systems has the best key structure for what you are trying to do and impose it on the other systems. This approach works well only when the base system is clearly the biggest and most appropriate. In these situations, you then can use it as the core of a series of merge/purge/data reformatting steps that transpose the new key over the old, while turning the existing key into an ancillary, informational field.

The start-over approach. An even uglier solution is developed when it is clear that none of the legacy system's key structures is appropriate. In those cases, you create a brand-new key structure and impose it on all of the legacy systems data.

Reference-able conversion. Whereas cleaning up data fields with inappropriate or inaccurate information does not require that you allow for the ability of users to get back to what the original value of the field was, you do not have that same luxury where keys are concerned. It is critical that, whenever you rekey data, you provide the means for users to go back to the legacy systems and see where the tagged values originated. Somehow, the converted data must be made reference-able. This usually is accomplished using one of two techniques.

One approach is to store the old key and a tag indicating which source system the data came from on the record that goes into the warehouse. That way, the user knows what kind of data he or she is looking at. The other thing that can be done is to create cross-reference tables that point new warehouse keys back to the old source systems keys to which they refer. Depending on the requirements of the system, one or both of these techniques can be employed.

Timing and history issues. The final type of synchronization that you must worry about has to do with the timeliness of the data being transferred. You must keep in mind that the data within the warehouse is coming from many different sources and that each of those sources has its own timing characteristics. There are several types of timing issues of which you must be aware.

The series of steps that you will go through to analyze and resolve time issues will be the following:

1. Determine the collection rate of each source system.

2. Identify any processing lags that might affect the timeliness of the information.

3. Determine the warehouse refresh rate and technique that will meet the needs of the users while recognizing the realities of the data sources.

4. Identify the programs and storage files necessary to execute the synchronization.

Collection rate: Core transactions. The first thing that you need to understand about the data being fed into the warehouse is the rate at which the information is collected. Many legacy systems collect information on a real-time basis. In other words, as soon as something happens, the system is changed to reflect it. This kind of collection rate is the most common in core legacy systems like Sales, Accounting, and Warehouse Control.

Unfortunately, even the best system in the world cannot capture every event exactly as it happens. For example, systems that keep track of sales by mail usually will update the sales information only once a day after all of the incoming mail for the day has had a chance to accumulate.

Other times, the core legacy systems that track transactions will be dependent on other systems for the information, and these systems might make use of a regularly scheduled upload program to update the core system on a periodic basis. For example, at one company where I was working, the phone sales system kept track of all of the phone sales for a given day, but that information was uploaded to the main systems only on a nightly refresh cycle.

In other cases, the information required might come from an external source, like mailing lists, Dun and Bradstreet financial reports, etc. In these cases, the data available could be days, weeks, or even months old before it can be accessed.

Processing and derived data. Another whole class of data-timing problems can be found when you start trying to make use of data that is derived or calculated on a periodic basis. The classical case for this kind of data is the typical production control system and the generation of WIP (Work In Progress) files.

In a typical manufacturing process, there are hundreds or even thousands of different variables that must be taken into account to keep track of the process and make sure that everything is running efficiently. The amount of computing that must occur to develop these evaluations requires an incredible amount of computer power and also requires that everything in the plant be synchronized to a particular point in time.

The vast majority of manufacturing organizations today simply cannot afford to synch up and recalculate all of these variables on a real-time basis. Instead, they develop a WIP file that notes where everything was at the last synch point. This usually is done on a weekly basis, but some organizations have gotten it down to a daily cycle. If the users of the warehouse require any of this kind of WIP information, then they will to have to deal with this time lag.

Warehouse refresh rate. After you have developed an understanding of the timing characteristics of each of the data sources, the next challenge will be to figure out at what rate and by what method the warehouse will be refreshed.

Warehouse refresh techniques. There actually are three fundamental ways that the warehouse can be refreshed; however, in practice, a hybrid combination of these often is used.

The easiest and most common way to refresh warehouse data simply is to get rid of the copy of the data that currently resides in the warehouse and completely replace it with a new copy. This technique, which is called *periodic complete refresh*, greatly simplifies the workings of the warehouse and allows everyone to have an immediate and good understanding of exactly what they are looking at.

To figure out how timely the information in a particular table is, the user only needs to find out the last time that it was refreshed from the source.

The complete refresh solution might be easy, but it is anything but inexpensive. The fact of the matter is that it takes a lot of time and a lot of computing power to dump and reload database files, and few systems can afford the luxury of waiting that long or using all of that computer power just because the approach is easy.

Very large data warehouses can include tables that hold hundreds of millions or even billions of records, and it can take a very long time to load all of that data up. Typical load times for very large databases are measured in days and weeks, not hours. Few organizations can afford the expense or the time delay that these approaches entail.

The store-and-forward/update-in-place technique. To help ameliorate some of the problems imposed by the complete refresh approach, many warehouses are built to make use of the store-and-forward/update-in-place approach. To utilize this approach, the warehouse developers devise some kind of technique that will allow them to keep track of the changes that occur to the legacy system and store information about those changes in a hold file. After these changes have been accumulated for a specified amount of time (an hour, day, week, etc.), the file then is used to drive an update-in-place program, which goes through the warehouse and brings the records back up-to-date.

There are two techniques that can be used to create these store-and-forward files. The first technique involves making changes to the legacy system that updates the data in question. All programs making changes to the desired data are identified, and each of them is modified so that, whenever they make changes to the legacy system, they send a copy of those changes to the store-and-forward hold file.

The second technique for the creation of store-and-forward files is for the managers of the acquisition process to keep a copy of the legacy system data after it has been loaded the first time. When it comes time to create the new store-and-forward file, a new copy of the legacy system data is made. The copy of the new legacy file is run through a program that compares it, record by record, with the old legacy file. Any changed records then are copied to the store-and-forward file for processing.

The store-and-forward approach allows the users of the warehouse to have the best of both worlds: large volumes of data available on demand with a periodic update to that data to keep it timely.

Real time. In some situations, even the store-and-forward approach to warehousing is not good enough. Sometimes people require that the warehouse be updated immediately to reflect changes in the core systems. In these cases, real-time update-in-place programs are used to coordinate source and warehouse files.

The value of time. Timing issues are critical to the success of any data-warehousing endeavor. However, it also is critical that the designers of the warehouse and the users of the system understand that the timeliness of data comes with a cost. In general, the more up-to-date you need the warehouse to be, the more expensive it will be to build and maintain. When going through the process of understanding each of the value propositions that drive your warehouse-development process, it will be critical that the cost of the timeliness of the data be included in your value assumptions and cost estimates.

Back-flush development

After you have figured out all of the different ways that the data is going to have to be transformed, modified, merged, purged, and retrofitted to be placed into a form that is suitable for the warehouse to use, you are ready to take a step back and figure out what kinds of back-flush mechanisms might be required. The steps in the process are straightforward:

1. Identify the back-flush requirements.
2. Gather the requirements from legacy systems managers.
3. Develop back-flush mechanisms.
4. Identify the programs and data storage files necessary to execute the back flush.

Identifying back-flush requirements. The only way to identify whether or not back-flush capabilities are going to be required is to ask the people in charge of the legacy systems whether they want it or not. If they do not, then there is no problem. If they do, then it will be the responsibility of those areas to specify exactly what kind of data they want fed back into the legacy systems and to specify the method in which this feedback will be accomplished.

Developing back-flush mechanisms. In the vast majority of cases, the back-flush requirement specification simply will be for the data-acquisition process to export an additional, specially formatted file that the legacy system then can read in to upgrade its current information.

When determining how this mechanism will work, the designer must be sensitive to all of the same issues that were important when considering data for warehouse loading. Timing, synchronization, sanitation, keys . . . all of these issues will be as important to the legacy system as they are to the warehouse.

Data-storage architecture development

After you have been provided with all of this information, you are ready to begin the process of figuring out how the warehouse storage area will look and how the data will move from the acquisitions component up to the user's terminal.

Up until now, we have been referring to the data-storage component of the warehouse as a big, open area into which a lot of different data tables are to be placed. At this point, we will get a little more explicit about what kinds of tables the storage area will hold.

Types of storage area tables

In general, your storage area is going to hold several different types of tables. These include:

- Core (entity) tables
- Legacy system reflection tables
- Code tables
- Bridge/cross-reference tables
- Merge tables
- Subset tables
- Summarization tables
- History tables

We will begin this discussion by considering the purpose and nature of each of these types of tables.

Core (entity) tables. *Core*, or *entity*, *tables* are the foundation of any kind of database system. These are the tables that are developed based upon the execution of sound data-modeling principles like normalization and entity-relationship modeling. A core table usually is defined as holding all of the information that pertains to an object of interest within your population of data. A core table in your warehouse environment often will be based upon a master file in a legacy system or an entity object within your entity-relationship diagram.

A list of core tables that a system might hold would include:

- Customer tables—One record for each customer
- Parts table—One record for each part number
- Vendor table—One record for each company that provides the company with goods and services
- Employee table—One record for each employee of the company

Role. Core tables are the heart and soul of the data warehouse. Most data warehouse processing will be totally dependent on the existence of a core table to help drive the processing.

Characteristics. Core tables usually are the source of the vast majority of the keying and hierarchy problems that systems developers face. Usually they also are extremely large in nature, but users tend to rely upon them heavily for a lot of uses. This means that access must be easy to use and provide fast, subsecond response. This combination of characteristics makes core tables the most difficult to design.

Location. Core tables are found only in the main storage area of the warehouse, never in a workspace area.

Legacy system reflection tables. *Reflection tables* are tables that hold copies of legacy systems or externally provided source data. Their structure and layout usually mirror the structure and layout of the place the data came from.

Role. Reflection tables often are used to hold detail or history information for analytical or investigative purposes.

When used for investigative and reference purposes, it is important to the users that the data be stored and displayed in the same way that the legacy systems display it. By providing the information in this way, it will be possible for users to investigate anomalies that are found in the system. This often is helpful in the resolution of problems with customers, in the investigation of problems, and in the verification of findings.

When used to support analytical processing, the user requires that the data be in its original state so that the analytical tools that are being applied against it will have the best chance possible of working with the real values.

Characteristics. Reflection tables tend to be extremely large; they usually are larger than the corresponding core tables. Luckily, the nature of the processing against the tables, for the most part, is in terms of one record at a time. Therefore, performance tends not to be a problem.

Location. Reflection tables typically are found in the main storage area of the warehouse.

Code tables. A *code table* is a table that holds information about each of the codified values used within the system.

Role. Code tables are provided to users to give them the ability to look up information about the different codes that might be found in other tables. For example, a State_Code_Table will hold all of the abbreviations for states (IL, NY, CA, etc.) with translations into full state names (Illinois, New York, California, etc.) along with any other important information about those states.

Characteristics. Code tables tend to be small and easy to use. They typically present no processing or design challenges.

Location. Because of their importance, code tables always are found in the main storage area.

Bridge/cross-reference tables. *Bridge/cross-reference tables* are tables that hold values that are used to relate two other tables to each other. For example, your Customer table has information about who the customer is, and your Product table will hold information about the different products that they can purchase. To relate these two tables, you need a bridge table. In this case, a likely candidate for the bridge might be the Sales table. The Sales table will relate customers to the products that they purchase.

Another good example of a bridge table occurs when building a system to educational environments. In this case, you will have a core table for teachers and another one for students. To see which teachers are associated with which students, you need a Class table.

Role. Bridge tables make it possible to relate two tables (especially core tables) to each other when they cannot do so on their own.

Characteristics. In general, bridge tables tend to be at least as large as the core tables that they relate. All of the performance concerns associated with core tables apply to the bridge tables as well.

Location. Bridge tables usually are found in the main storage area, but they also could be located in the workspace areas under certain conditions.

Merge tables. Sometimes, for the sake of efficiency or ease of access, you will combine collections of tables into merged supersets of the data that they hold.

Role. Merge tables make it easier for users to access combined collections of data from disparate tables.

Characteristics. Merge tables can be very large, or small, depending upon the reason that they are developed.

Location. Merge tables are most frequently found in the workspace area.

Subset tables. To work effectively or efficiently, a great many of the data-mining tools require that the system cut down the amount of data that it needs to deal with. In these cases, a copy of the subset of data that the system needs is copied down into a smaller table, specifically tailored to meet the demands of the product. Subsets usually are mode core tables, reflection tables, and merge tables, but the other types can be subsetted as well.

Role. Subset tables greatly reduce the amount of data that the users or the data-mining tools need to deal with, making the process of investigation or analysis easier to do or to improve performance.

Characteristics. Subset tables tend to be significantly smaller than most other types of tables on the system.

Location. They usually are found in the workspace area, although main storage area subset tables might be developed.

Summarization (roll-up) tables. *Summarization* or *"roll-up"* tables hold summarized or condensed versions of the data found within the other tables on the system. The design and construction of roll-up tables could be the subject of a book in and of itself. What is critical to the development of these tables is a good understanding of the different keys and codes that will drive the users' access to the table and the volumes of data that must be managed.

Role. Summarization tables allow users of the system to presummarize large volumes of information up into more usable, more informative forms. The technique is extremely common when making use of many kinds of analytical or holistic types of solutions.

Characteristics. These tables are dramatically smaller then the main tables from which they are derived, and they are much more rigidly defined.

Location. Summarization tables are equally likely to appear in the main storage and the work areas.

History tables. The last type of table to consider within your system is the *history table*. History tables hold snapshots of how things looked in the past. There actually are a couple types of history tables to be considered, including:

- Cumulative history
- Snapshot histories

There also are several ways that they can be developed:

- Direct conversion from legacy systems
- Accumulation from the warehouse
- Update from the warehouse

Cumulative history tables hold a record of all of the different changes that have been made to each of the records of a given table. For the most part, your main storage area tables will contain the latest view of things being monitored, and your cumulative history table will contain a collection of all of the changes. In this kind of environment, there will be sets of tables: the main, real table in the warehouse and a single history table that holds the changes.

Snapshot history tables freeze a table, or collection of tables, as of a given point in time, then make a copy of that table over to a completely new table where changes will no longer be made. With this approach, you will end up with many tables: the main, real table and a collection of snapshot tables, each reflecting the status of the table at a different point in time. Snapshot tables often are developed on a yearly, monthly, or sometimes weekly basis.

Role. History tables are created to provide users with the ability to do historical analysis of different characteristics of the business environment or to allow for historical investigative work.

Characteristics. Historical tables, by their very nature, are extremely large and infrequently accessed. The cumulative tables often are more difficult for users to work with, but the snapshot types of tables tend to take up vast amounts of disk storage.

Location. Historical tables are always found in the main storage area.

Managing the synchronization and timing of tables in storage

While the synchronization and timing of data in the acquisition component of the warehouse is the most complex, there are just as many problems and concerns to consider when developing plans for managing the data within the storage component as well. The problem is simplified by the more rigidly defined database environment and the fact that a lot of these issues already will have been resolved before the data ever enters the warehouse, but you still must be concerned about the timing involved, especially in the utilization of summarization and subset types of tables.

Steps in the storage-architecture development process

The process that you go through to develop your architecture proceeds as follows:

1. Identify all of the different types and forms of data that users will require to meet the needs of their solution.

2. Identify all of the different sources of data and the staged files that will be available for loading into the warehouse.

3. Identify each of the core, reflection, code, bridge, and history tables that will be required to meet the users' requirements.

4. Examine each of the types of access that they will make. Also, when performance or ease of access appears to be a constraining factor, intercede with the insertion of summary, subset, and merge tables. The objective should be to try to do everything without the need of these intermediary types of tables.

5. Identify and describe each of the programs or processes that will be required to load all of the tables, and make these transformations.

Data-transformation mapping

After you have figured out the basic layout for the storage area of the warehouse, you will be ready to take a step back and put together a diagram of how the entire data-transformation process (the process of transforming external and legacy data into usable warehouse data) will flow. The process of diagramming these transformations will be critical because, until you attempt to put it all together, there will be no way for you to know if you have taken everything into account. Data-transformation mapping is as much a diagramming exercise as it is an analytical exercise.

A data-transformation map is made up of the following components:

- A list of all of the screens and data elements identified during the data identification phase

- A list of each of the legacy and external source systems that have been identified as the legitimate sources of that data

- A list of each of the transitioning and sanitation steps that each legacy system file will have to be put through

- A list of each of the transformation programs (reformat, merge, purge, etc.) that the data will be subjected to (including the specifications for each of the programs)

- A list of each of the tables that the storage area will contain (including their names, types, etc.)

- A diagram that illustrates this transformation process

Figure 6.3 shows a simple transformation diagram for a single source file. Obviously, the actual collection of transformation diagrams will be a lot more complicated than this simple example, but it will be critical that you somehow capture this process in a graphical form so that everyone involved in the process will be able to understand exactly how their data fits into the big picture.

Data-metrics gathering

Only after you have assembled your complete set of data-transformation information and validated its accuracy will you be ready to seriously approach the process of gathering data metrics. *Data metrics* consists of all the information necessary for you to make decisions about the sizing and capacity requirements of the system itself. You actually are going to need to have three types of metrics to develop good and meaningful estimates:

- User metrics
- Data volumes
- Access-rate and processing estimates

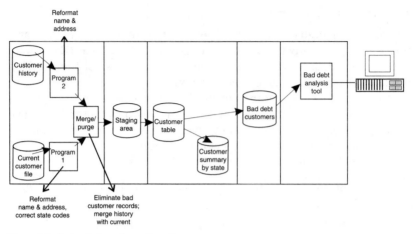

Figure 6.3 A simple transformation diagram.

User metrics. Included in your definition of user metrics is all that information about the users of the system that will be needed so that you can make reasonable estimates about the performance requirements of the system.

The steps involved in the collection of user metrics include the following:

1. Identification of the complete population of users (number, categories, locations, etc.)

2. Identification of the types of access that each category of users will need (simple, complex, work area read/write, etc.)

3. Identification of the data stores that each category of user will be pursuing

4. Identification of the rate at which each type of access against each data store will be executed

The process of collecting this information probably is most easily done at the same time that the data-identification process is going on. Throughout the process, it will be critical that the analyst assist the users in the development of this information. At each stage of the process, it is going to be necessary for users and analysts to estimate and project what they think the answer to many of the questions will be. Obviously, there is no way to know exactly what will happen until the system is completed. However, your intention in gathering this information is not to come up with a 100%-accurate answer but only to provide yourself with some kind of rough estimate as to what the performance characteristics of the system are.

It is amazing how many people will go through the process of computer systems development without even asking questions about how many users the system ultimately will have. Frequently, the answer will be "Who knows?" or "It depends?" Unfortunately, there is no way that you can come up with a good estimate of the effort and resources that will be required without some kind of best guess estimate of this most rudimentary form of information.

Clearly, it will not be enough for you to simply know how many people will be using the system. In addition to the raw number of users, you will need to come up with an approach that allows you to categorize this population of users according to several variables.

At a minimum, you need to identify system users in terms of:

- How many different types of users there will be. The nature of this categorization depends upon the system, but it usually turns out to be a segregation by the user's job description (marketing, management, clerical, etc.) or by the function (order taking, troubleshooting, etc.).

- What the principal types of access will be, and how frequently the users of each type make use of that access.

Access can be typified by the product that the users will utilize to gain access to information (spreadsheets, query managers, multidimensional databases etc.) or by the type of query that they will perform (simple, complex, read, write, update, delete, etc.).

Activity rates usually are measured in execution per minute, hour, day, week, or month, depending upon the nature of the activity. For example, an extremely active system might be used every other minute, while a sophisticated trend-analysis system might be utilized once a month.

Not only do you need to know the rate and nature of these transactions, but you also would like to have some idea about which tables in the warehouse these queries will be pursuing.

Where are each of the users going to be physically located? All in the same building? Different floors? Different states? Different countries? The analyst responsible for collecting this information usually will find that the screen layouts developed during data identification will provide the best means of driving and clarifying the entire process.

Data-volume estimates. After you have completed the collection of user metrics, you can turn to the development of estimates for the volumes of data that will be included in the system. This usually is a relatively straightforward and trivial exercise in mathematics.

Obtain legacy system metrics. Begin by gathering the volume statistics that are available about each of the legacy system and externally obtained data sources that will feed into the data acquisition process. You then can use this information to derive the volumes that you should experience with the rest of the tables in the systems.

Compute acquisition area file sizes. By combining the volume information available about each of the legacy system files and tracing it through the data-transformation diagrams that you developed, it should be possible to derive the volume estimates for the rest of the data within the system.

As each legacy system file proceeds through each of the cleansing, merging, and purging steps, you can make assumptions about what percentages of data will be included or excluded from the final calculations. By the time you have traced these files through, you should have developed relatively accurate size estimates for every file and table within the system.

In the development of these estimates, it is important that the analyst take the following points into account.

The volume estimates for legacy system data and all of the transitory files up to the staging area can be estimated in a simple, straightforward manner, because it is our assumption that these will be flat files. In other words, the volume requirement for a file that is made up of 100 records where each record is 25 bytes long would be 2500 bytes for the entire file ($25 \times 100 = 2500$).

You should not include the volumes of legacy system files in your final disk estimates because this disk area is not part of the warehouse system.

You must be sure to include the space required for all staging file areas. This includes the required disk space to stage data that has been removed from the legacy system before it enters the acquisition process and the staged data that is ready for loading into the warehouse itself.

Transitory disk space need not be estimated as the sum total of all of the files in each data loading sequence. In most cases, these files will be short-lived (some might exist for only a few minutes). However, it is critical that you estimate enough space to allow for problems to occur during the loading process. Usually, I choose a reasonable pad to be a percentage of the total disk space that could be required (50%?).

Database table volume estimates must be based on a number much higher than that required to house flat file data. I usually apply a multiplier to develop these estimates as well. This is because relational database tables use a lot more room to store data than flat files do. Relational database space estimates must include an adjustment for record overhead (each record needs room to store information about the data that it holds), dead space (relational databases leave unused areas in-between records for performance and management reasons), indexes, and overall system overhead. Multipliers in the range from 2.5 to 10 have been used to effectively estimate this space (i.e., take the amount of space that would be required to store the data in a flat file and multiply by the multiplier to get the real volume estimate).

Do not forget to develop estimates for the work area data (calculate these the same way that you calculated normal database table volumes).

Usually, the volume estimates for the system are summarized in a table having the following column headings:

- Table or file name
- Number of records
- Size of an average record
- Computed volume estimate

Estimating computer processing requirements. Once you have collected the user and volume metrics information, you will be in a position to develop some rudimentary processing requirements. Unfortunately, of all of the estimation techniques that you will employ, this one will be the least accurate and least scientific. The reason is that there really is no way to accurately derive the processing requirements that a group of users is going to put on the system without some pretty specific information about the kinds of queries that they are going to be executing. In the world of relational databases, the most subtle changes in the SQL commands that you execute and the table designs that you settle upon can result in drastic differences in the performance demands that will be put on the system. This fact leaves you with only two options for trying to develop these estimates:

- Attempt to derive the system requirements based upon the performance of similar types of systems
- Run benchmarks

Benchmarking. Ultimately, when you are working with relational database technology and you need to have a fairly accurate idea about what the performance is going to be like for a given collection of hardware, software, data, and user requirements, the best thing to do is to build a benchmark system and test it. A *benchmark system* is a database that simulates all of the critical assumptions that you have about the environment (volumes of data, transaction types, etc.) and allows you to establish for yourself what the real performance will be.

A benchmarking approach is expensive and time consuming; however, if you have any serious concerns about the viability of the system that you are putting together, it is a good idea to create one.

In a typical benchmarking situation, you identify the biggest and most complicated queries that the system will be expected to support. You then identify the source of data that will allow you to test those queries and load it into the database in its original form (you do not bother with the data-preparation and sanitation steps).

After loading the high volumes of required data, you then run test queries against it. In the most severe cases, programs are written that simulate the execution of dozens or even hundreds of queries in succession to try to attain the same activity level as the one anticipated for the system.

When the programs are finished, the designers of the system will have a very good idea as to whether the prescribed hardware and software will get the job done or not.

Comparing requirements against other systems. The other approach to developing these kinds of estimates is a lot less expensive but also is less accurate. When taking this approach, you identify the type of system load that the applications will put on the database, then try to find a similar system to compare it with. Sometimes the vendors of hardware or database software products can be of assistance in this exercise.

The fallback solution is to make use of published statistics, like those provided by the TPC (Transaction Processing Council). This group sponsors well-regulated, benchmark tests that are run against combinations of hardware and database software. The results of these tests are published in tables, which then can be used as references for people trying to derive the performance requirements of their own systems. The results of the TPC tests are available for a fee, are often given away by hardware or database software vendors, or can even be accessed via the Internet.

Unfortunately, the TPC has a severely limited set of tests that they run (TPC A, B, C, and D), and the tests are run only for the prescribed table layouts and volumes. However, the reports can be very insightful and can help the designer zero in on clearly acceptable and unacceptable types of solutions. (See the appendix for more information on the TPC.)

By the time you have finished collecting your metrics, you should be in a position to develop some reasonable estimates as to the types of hardware and software the system will require.

Data modeling

After you have developed the rest of the detail about how the overall data warehouse is going to work, you are ready to begin the modeling step. The term *data modeling* has been used to refer to all kinds of different processes, but we will use the term to describe the process of mapping all of the data identified by the users and all of the data provided by the legacy systems into one cohesive, comprehensive collection of data element groupings and definitions.

The data-modeling process will go through the following steps:

1. Identify all of the user-defined data.
2. Identify all of the legacy system-provided data.

3. Identify all of the storage area tables that have been specified.

4. For each storage area table, identify and document each of the data elements that users will require and associate it with the appropriate table.

5. For each of the user data elements, identify and document the source of information from among the acquisition area staged files.

6. Provide definitions for all elements.

Data modeling is an incredibly detailed process that usually involves many hours of research, reconciliation, and documentation; however, without it, the developers of the system leave themselves open to error and misunderstanding and without the most critical input necessary for the database design process.

At this point, many of the advocates of traditional data modeling might feel that our approach has slighted this critical aspect of systems design. We certainly have recommended that it occur at a different point in time within the framework of overall systems development. In response to them, all that can be said is that, if you want to start off the process of data discipline with the development of logical data models, then go ahead. Their existence can only help everyone understand the entire process that we have just laid out.

The other response to this concern is that it has been our intention from the outset to limit the scope of what people are looking at to those that are narrowly defined by a specific value proposition. It is our hope that the process of narrowing this scope has made it unnecessary to get involved in sophisticated and complex data-modeling exercises.

The only problem with this super-imposition of traditional data modeling over our data warehouse development approach is that it might tend to defocus people from the task at hand. It certainly has been known to frustrate, infuriate, and confuse users who could care less about third normal forms and the correct placement of foreign keys.

Those types of discussion are best left to the technicians' meeting rooms. The emphasis for the users, the warehouse developers, and the legacy systems experts needs to be focused on the task at hand: delivering important information to the users as quickly and efficiently as possible.

Database design

The final step in the data-discipline process is the design of the actual physical database. During this step, database administrators can be provided with all of the information that has been collected up until this point and be asked to develop the actual physical layouts that each of the proposed tables will have, in addition to the development of indexing schemes, storage approaches, backup/recovery procedures, and the tuning of SQL access queries.

The process of database design therefore will involve the following steps:

1. Identification of all of the previously specified tables in the storage and work areas (see the data-modeling step).

2. Population of these tables with all data elements (see the data-modeling step).

3. Development of a physical key structure for each table. (Physical keys are not exactly the same thing as the logical keys that you have been specifying up until now.)

4. Development of an indexing structure for each table.

5. Validation of these structures against the user access requirements.

6. Development of physical database layouts (schemes or DDL).

7. Development of backup/recovery, history accumulation, and other utility functions.

When the process of database design is complete, the developers of the system will have everything that they need to begin construction of the real data-warehousing application.

Summary and Observations

To any person who has never been through the process of data-warehouse development before, this chapter might seem a bit overwhelming. Indeed, the process of reconciling all of the issues involved with the data within the data warehouse is extremely complicated and detail-oriented. To any person that has been through the process, these steps undoubtedly will seem familiar. No one has ever been through the process of developing a warehouse application without going through each and every one of these steps.

The biggest difference in the approach, as we have specified it here, is that you recognize these idiosyncrasies and complication from the outset and attempt to build your solution around them. This approach is in direct contradiction to the traditionally accepted beliefs about how the warehouse should be developed.

According to the traditional model, you begin by defining the databases, then you try to apply those database designs to the user requirements, then you try to find all the data that was specified in a legacy system source file. In other words, the traditional approach takes a highly optimistic stand. In general, it assumes that, if you do a really good job on database design, then user requirements and legacy system sources simply are going to fall into place. It also assumes that developers are going to be given enough time to do a good job.

Years and years of experience with hundreds of systems have proven otherwise.

My approach is decidedly pessimistic. It assumes the worst. It assumes that users will be unclear about where data will come from. It assumes that the people in charge of the legacy systems are not aware of what data their systems contain. It assumes that preliminary data models will be bad ones, not perfect ones. It also assumes that people are going to be in a hurry to develop these systems and that everyone is going to be expected to put things together as quickly as possible, regardless of how well it is done or how usable it will be in the future.

In other words, this approach assumes that you are going to have to develop a system with less than optimum resources, in less time than is reasonable, and in an environment that is far from stable or well understood. Our approach assumes an environment similar to most of the business environments that we deal with today.

In the next chapter, we will continue with our diagnosis of the different layers of the warehouse application-development process by proceeding to take the information that you have gathered from the application of the data disciplines to the warehouse and apply that information to help you solve the problems with the development of an operational and physical infrastructure.

The Operational Infrastructure

Now that you have a much better idea about how the warehouse is going to look and of the process that you will need to go through to put it together, you now are ready to explore, in the same level of detail, the infrastructure that will be required to support it.

You might recall that we said that the infrastructure would be made up of two layers: an operational layer, which is concerned with the management and efficiency of the warehouse's operation, and the physical infrastructure, which consists of all of the physical hardware and software components with which it will run.

The Operational Infrastructure

In chapter 5, we introduced the concept of the operational layer and said that it included the feedback mechanisms, data disciplines, management software, procedures, and support staff necessary to make the warehouse a viable entity. In chapter 6, we invested a significant amount of time developing an understanding of the data disciplines involved in warehouse construction and maintenance and in the specification of feedback mechanisms.

We have yet to consider the other aspects of the operational infrastructure: staff, procedures, and management software. We will delay our consideration of staffing until later.

Management Software

It should be quite clear from the discussion up until this point that a warehouse can be a very complicated thing. A typical warehouse can involve the coordination of the activities of dozens or even hundreds of people and hundreds or even thousands of source files. Experience has shown repeatedly that, if you do not approach the management of this extremely complex environment with the same kind of rigor and discipline that we have been applying to the rest of the process, all of your efforts will be wasted. It does no one any good to spend hundreds of hours and millions of dollars on the development of a data warehouse that is unmanageable, confusing, and intransigent.

Management Challenges in the Warehouse Environment

When you approach the issue of managing the warehouse environment, you are faced with certain paradoxical challenges.

Stability versus flexibility

On the one hand, you want to make the environment easy to manage. Many times, after the initial burst of energy around the construction of the warehouse is through, the people responsible for managing it have found themselves left with a hodgepodge—a disorganized, incredibly complex, and highly unmanageable warehouse disaster area—that they then are asked to contend with. If the warehouse is to be useful and cost effective, then it must be easy to control. On the other hand, one of the big benefits that the warehouse offers is the ability of the users and of application developers to change things quickly and to develop new types of applications "on the fly."

Unfortunately, these objectives can be contradictory. On the one hand, a stable management environment is most easily and most cost effectively attained by locking down the characteristics and functions that the warehouse can perform. By limiting the functionality and by limiting the flexibility, you make management easier. On the other hand, a flexible environment demands that you establish the ways and means to allow the hectic rate of business change to drive the rate at which the warehouse itself changes.

Ease of use versus flexibility and power

The second dichotomy that you need to be concerned about revolves around the user and the way in which the warehouse makes itself available. On the one hand, the users of the system want the system to be easy to use. They want the complexities and idiosyncrasies of the warehouse to be transparent to them. All they want to do is "push a button" and let the warehouse do the rest. On the other hand, users want the warehouse to be powerful and flexible. They do not want to have to make any commitments about what they might want the warehouse to be able to do at some future date. They want the ability to change the way that the warehouse works at any time to get the new kinds of information that they want.

These objectives also are contradictory. You cannot make the system work at the push of a button, while at the same time making it possible to change what the button does on the spur of the moment. In both cases, some kind of compromise must be reached.

Therefore, you are faced with two related infrastructure-management problems when you build a warehouse: issues about user interface and issues about overall warehouse management.

User Interfaces and the Warehouse

Before you can address the issues about overall warehouse management, you first must decide upon what the interface with the users is going to look like.

The process of determining how complex or simple that interface will be depends upon a number of variables, including:

- The nature of the users' relationship with the data (the users' data-utilization profile)
  ~The nature of the data mining tools that will be used
  ~The nature of any customized applications that will be used

- The size and complexity of the overall environment

- The availability and allocation of computer resources

- The availability of support resources

The users' data utilization profile

The first thing that you need to consider when exploring the nature of the users' relationship with the data is establishing a good idea of the users' data-utilization profile. The data-utilization profile gives you a good idea about exactly what kinds of things the user will be doing with the data. Armed with this information, you can begin to put together an idea of how best to meet that user's data access needs.

The data-utilization profile is a snapshot that provides you with all of the critical data-access requirements that the users will have for the data that they are working with. This profile is made up of the following:

- Information about the different types of access that the user will perform

- Information about the timing requirements for that data

Types of user access. To understand the different types of access that a user might need to have, you need to consider his or her activities from several perspectives:

- The type of activity performed
- The population of the data being accessed

Types of access activity. You can categorize the users' types of access activity into the following (Figure 7.1):

- Simple look-up
- Simple search
- Relational search
- CRUD
- Data chains

To help illustrate each of these activity types, we will make use of a simple example. We will assume that the user has access to a population of customer information, information about sales, information about products, and some demographic information about the areas in which those users reside (Figure 7.2).

The information in each of these tables can be related to the others through the relationships shown on the diagram (a line indicates a relationship). As illustrated by the diagram, demographics records are related to customers via their zip code, customers are related to sales via the customer number, and sales are related to products via the product number.

Simple look-up. The easiest kind of access to manage in a relational database environment is the simple query. When executing a simple look-up query, the user simply asks for the information from one of the targeted tables making use of one of the keys to that table.

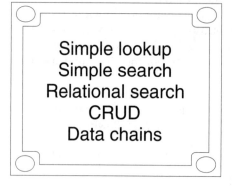

Simple lookup
Simple search
Relational search
CRUD
Data chains

Figure 7.1 Types of access activity.

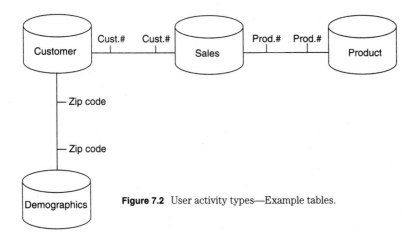

Figure 7.2 User activity types—Example tables.

For example, you might want to look up a certain customer record, by name or by customer number. The relational database will be able to do this in almost any situation without placing too much strain on the system or on the user.

Simple look-up queries form the foundation of the vast majority of systems, especially of the holistic and operational varieties.

Simple search. In a simple search operation, the user might not know the customer's name or number but will know some subset of information about the customer. The search might ask to see all records for customers in the state of Texas, or it might ask to see all products that are the color "blue" and cost more than $25.

These access types also occur frequently within almost any warehouse environment, and they can be used for simple information gathering (as in the case of the simple look-up operations). However, the more important aspect of the simple-search operation is that it often is utilized as the first in a series or "chain" of operations that might be required for more complex processing.

Relational search. The next example of access activity is the relational search. When doing a relational search, the user wants to know something about the relationship between things: for example, which customers have purchased more than $200 worth of products in the last three months, or what kinds of products (product table) that people (customer table) with large homes (information from the demographics table) purchase (sales table) most often.

To execute this kind of query, the keys of all four of these tables must be related to each other.

Relational searches also can be used to answer direct user questions and to serve as part of a processing chain.

CRUD. The next type of simple access is the acronym CRUD. CRUD stands for "Create, Read, Update, and Delete" and indicates that the user needs not only to find certain records, but also to make changes to them as well.

CRUD access is the more difficult type of access to deal with because the imposition of create, update, and delete capabilities on your warehouse makes it extremely difficult to manage and maintain. You went through a lot of trouble to get the warehouse to be accurate, synchronized, sanitized, and ready to use; however, if you now allow users to make changes to the warehouse without the imposition of controls, then you will quickly breach the integrity of the warehouse and greatly curtail its usefulness.

You will have to impose an especially rigid set of constraints around this kind of access, and it should be limited whenever possible.

Data chains. If you could simply categorize all of the different types of data access by the previous approaches, your job of managing the data environment for users would be quite simple. Unfortunately, an increasingly large percentage of the operations that users require involve the development of *data chains*.

Data chains are created when users need to perform a series of operations against a population of data to get it into a usable form. Data chains address a number of problems faced by the modern user of data.

In many situations, the user needs to perform so many different kinds of subset, search, and relational operations against the data to get it into the form that he or she wants that it would be impossible for he or she to perform all of those operations through the execution of one query.

For example, a user might want to:

1. Identify all customers in the state of Florida.

2. Associate those records with the demographics for the state.

3. Eliminate from the collection all customers who already have purchased over $1000 of product.

4. Get a list of all of the products that the remaining customers have purchased.

5. Take a look at the profit margin received on these purchases.

While it theoretically might be possible to get this information through the execution of one large, complex query, it is unlikely that many users would be able to develop it, and more importantly, it also is unlikely that the system would be able to execute it in a reasonable amount of time.

By breaking down complicated problems like the previous one into more manageable steps, the user is able to do highly sophisticated types of analysis in a relatively short amount of time. (See Figure 7.3.)

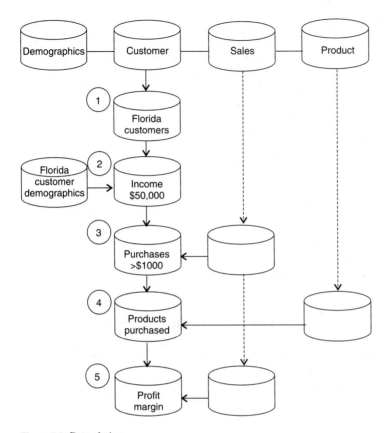

Figure 7.3 Data chains.

Data chains are the most common form of access in a typical warehouse environment, and they often are required to do a wide assortment of modern data analysis tasks. They usually are required for the:

- Preloading of data-mining tools
- Execution of complex analysis operations
- Creation of subsets of data that the user can access for his or her own processing purposes or the preparation of reports

The population of the data being accessed. As if the amount of complexity that the different types of access present were not enough, there is another very important aspect of data-accessing characteristics that must be taken into account. The thing to keep in mind at this point is that the way that you approach these different types of access is going to vary, depending upon the nature of the population of the data being accessed.

Volume versus performance trade-offs. One of the major characteristics of the data warehouse that we talked about in chapter 1 was that data warehouses typically involve the housing and distribution of incredibly high volumes of data. It is the ability of modern database technologies to work with these volumes that has contributed to the popularity and feasibility of data-warehouse solutions. Unfortunately, the fact that a database can manage billions of records does not mean that it is a good idea to do queries against such a large population.

As you move up the continuum of access types from simple look-up, to simple search, to relational search, to CRUD access, you also move down the continuum of database performance capabilities. In general, the bigger a database gets, the harder it is to get it to do the operations that we have just discussed.

For example, if you were to create a data warehouse where the population of records was relatively low (populations of data in the hundreds, thousands, or even hundreds of thousands of records), it would be possible to place a lot of the burden for processing on the database itself. (See Figure 7.4.)

In this kind of environment, you could design the system so that the vast majority of access requirements could be driven by good query writing. This also would eliminate the need for a lot of data chains; however, as the sizes of the populations of data increase, the flexibility of the system becomes curtailed. As the size increases, you will need to cut back on the types of access that you allow directly against the database and replace those accesses with a combination of data chains and accesses. (See Figure 7.5.)

In effect, what you will discover is that, when the volumes of data get higher and as the complexity of the users' data manipulations tasks get greater, you end up using data chains to bring the volume of the population that the user is accessing down to a level where the system can manage the query activity and where the user can more easily understand what is going on. In effect, you break the access process down into a series of intermediary steps. (See Figure 7.6.)

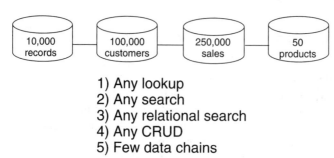

1) Any lookup
2) Any search
3) Any relational search
4) Any CRUD
5) Few data chains

Figure 7.4 Low-volume population.

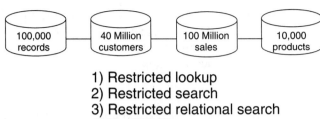

1) Restricted lookup
2) Restricted search
3) Restricted relational search
4) No CRUD
5) Heavy use of data chains

Figure 7.5 High-volume population.

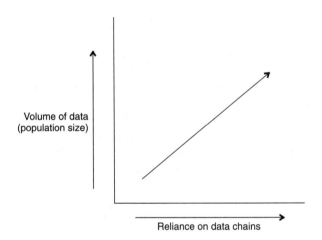

Figure 7.6 The volume/data chain trade-off.

This realization comes as a mixed blessing. The good news is that, as soon as you recognize this capability and the fact that you can "trade" volume and complexity for data chains, you realize that:

- There really are almost no physical restrictions on the size of your warehouse. The amount a database or a collection of databases can hold is the only limitation on how large your warehouse can become.

- You have a built-in escape clause that you can use whenever performance or complexity begins to be a problem. When it begins to look like the volumes of data that you are working on are going to place undue strain on your hardware or that the complexity of the processing is going to put a strain on the users, then you simply can back up and reapproach the problem through the application of data chains.

The bad news is that this built-in flexibility (the ability to switch from direct to data chain access) also makes the environment much less stable and less manageable and makes use of more disk storage and CPU resources.

What it boils down to is that direct access requires very little operational infrastructure support while data chaining requires a lot.

Timing and availability. The other thing that helps you to understand the composition of each user's data-utilization profile has to do with the timing and availability required of the data. There actually are three aspects of timing that you need be concerned with:

- The timeliness of the data itself
- The timing of the data-preparation process
- The timing of the actual delivery of data

The timeliness of the data. One of the most important things that users need to know about the data that they are working with has to do with the timeliness of the data itself. To do a meaningful analysis of data, users need to know for what time period each piece of data is valid.

What you can easily forget when you begin looking at this process from the user's perspective is that the data held within the warehouse is data that has been pulled from several sources and mixed together into a single, apparently homogeneous collection. In reality, when you mix that data from a lot of different sources, you also tend to mix the time frames for which that data is valid.

For example, in a typical customer data warehouse, you could end up combining customer information from several source systems. In this case, the timeliness of the customer data could very well be different, depending upon where the customer data came from.

If your customer table holds information from a customer-service system that is refreshed in the warehouse on a weekly basis, an accounts-receivable system that is updated on a daily basis, and an externally provided credit-rating source that is obtained and loaded on a monthly basis, you can end up with a pretty convoluted picture of that customer's status.

When a person gets a call from the customer complaining about something and you check in the warehouse to figure out what the problem is, you could end up with three different pieces of information, each of which tells you something different about what really is going on.

The same kinds of timeliness issues are important for performing analytical work with the data. Statistical analysis, trending, and forecasting are meaningful only when the people preparing the statistical models understand for which time frames the data applies. For example, a person performing trend analysis between bad debt over a three-month period will get very poor results if he or she fails to realize that the most recent month's data failed to get loaded for some reason and that he or she actually had run this month's analysis against last month's results.

Regularly scheduled versus on demand. The second characteristic of data-timing requirements has to do with how frequently or regularly users need to have access to data. In many cases, it can be worked out so that the warehouse managers can make the refresh or construction a regularly scheduled event. For example, you could promise to have the new sales and marketing data loaded by the fifth of every month.

Regularly scheduled data refresh and construction is easy to manage and easy for users to work with and schedule for. Unfortunately, there are many situations where setting up regularly scheduled jobs is not good enough. Sometimes users need to have data preparation done on an as-needed basis. These situations usually occur when the nature of the data that needs to be generated is so volatile from one time period to the next that there is no way for the managers of the warehouse to anticipate when it will need to be delivered.

Immediate versus delayed. The last aspect of timing has to do with how soon the users need the data after they request it. In the ideal world, the users could have anything they wanted as soon as it was available. Unfortunately, this is not always possible or even desirable. In many situations, the users can live with a situation where they request data at one point in time, then wait for it for anywhere from several minutes to several days. By structuring their work in a way that allows them to wait for the data to be delivered, the managers of the warehouse can "batch" up the requests and provide a more efficiently run warehouse.

Managing timing and access issues. Therefore, you will find yourself in the position of needing to make decisions about a lot of variables before you are able to develop a data-accessing profile that will meet the needs of the users and the warehouse managers.

The users' requirements for data are going to involve access to different sources of data, different types of access, and different kinds of timing requirements. This combination of factors can lead to the development of terribly complex and confusing solutions.

Who is responsible for what? The first challenge that you face when you decide to implement a data-access solution is to figure out who should be responsible for doing what part of the process. There are only three alternatives:

- The managers of the warehouse themselves will be responsible for the construction of all of the accessible data stores, and the users will be limited to making queries against those stores.

- The managers can provide a base set of tables, and the users can develop their own chains and workspace data sets "on the fly."
- Some combination of the previous two approaches.

You might recall that the list of table types in the warehouse included:

- Core (entity) tables
- Legacy system reflection tables
- Code tables
- Bridge/cross-reference tables
- Merge tables
- Subset tables
- Summarization tables
- History tables

Of these tables, the baseline functionality that must be guaranteed by the warehouse management team in any situation is that they provide support for all core, reflection, code, bridge, and history tables. The other types of tables (merge, summarization, and subset) fall into the area of negotiated functionality. In some situations, it will be the responsibility of the warehouse managers to generate them; in other cases, the users will build the tables themselves.

In general, we will refer to the basic set of tables (core, reflection, code, bridge, and history) that are managed by the warehouse as the *baseline tables*, and we will refer to the rest as *derived tables*.

As far as construction is concerned, you can assume that the baseline tables are built from within the acquisition area of the warehouse and that the data that they contain is loaded directly from the staging area into the storage area. You also can assume that any of the derived tables will be built through the construction of data chains.

At the one extreme are those cases where the warehouse managers are going to build the data chains. In these cases, the process for the end user is quite simple. The end users, or people responsible for the building of custom applications or the integration of data-mining tools, simply provide the warehouse managers with the specifications for what the end product of the data-chaining process should look like. It then falls to the warehouse managers to deliver what was requested.

For example, to develop data for preloading into a multidimensional database product, the specifications will be for a series of tables, each with an assortment of interconnecting key structures. The responsibility then will fall to the data-warehouse management team to figure out how those tables should be derived.

In another case, the end users might require access to a particular subset of data in a list selection and scoring software package. In this case, the parameters for the prescored set of data is provided as a specification that the warehouse then will need to fulfill.

The advantage of this approach for the end users is that they never need worry about how the data gets formatted, developed, or delivered. The process is transparent to them. They simply tell the warehouse team what they want, one time, and the rest is taken care of. When the user turns on the data-mining tool, everything is preloaded exactly the way that they need it.

This approach also provides the managers of the warehouse with many advantages. They need worry about this process of data generation only one time. They can write specific "data-chaining" sequences of jobs or stored procedures and then turn them into regular jobs that run themselves on a periodic basis. This kind of solution will work only when you have a predetermined type of access against a predefined set of data and the updating of the data stores can be scheduled.

In other situations, this kind of arrangement will not work. In these cases, you will need to develop a mechanism that makes it easy to the user to do some of this work themselves.

The user workbench environment.   At some point, the complexity with which the end users are going to have to deal will demand that you provide some kind of management environment software to simplify the process of dealing with the warehouse: as soon as you decide that the managers of the warehouse are not going to have full and absolute responsibility for the delivery of everything to the doorstep of the users; as soon as you decide to provide for any kind of flexibility or on-demand delivery capabilities; as soon as you find that the end users are going to have to stay aware of the time subtleties of the data within the warehouse itself; as soon as you realize that the entire process of acquisition, staging, storing, chaining, and delivering the data is not always going to happen without some kinds of delays or glitches in the process. You then are going to realize that this kind of software will be critical.

We now will look at some environments where this kind of software was put into place.

One organization that installed a warehouse with this kind of facility ran into problems with data timing. The warehouse that I built was for a major banking institution, and it was loaded up with data from over 25 different systems. Each of these accounting systems had a different "close date," which meant that, at no time, could the warehouse ever be completely in synch as far as timing went. I needed to provide end users with a screen that let them see how timely each set of data was and when the next refresh of that data was scheduled. The system also could be used to inform system users when problems occurred in the acquisition process. When source tapes failed to arrive at the data center or when batch jobs failed to run, users were notified so that they could anticipate when the right data would be available.

Organizations that have implemented data warehouses without this kind of facility have found that the warehouse support staff ends up spending a large amount of their time running around answering users' questions about timeliness and readiness.

Data-extraction scheduling. Assuming that you will allow the users to develop their own data chains in some kind of *ad hoc* manner, you are faced with the challenge of how to make that process as painless as possible.

The easiest solution is to train users in the use of the SQL-DDL language, allowing them to run create, delete, and update table commands and giving them the ability to actually build and load the tables themselves. While this certainly is the easiest for the systems managers, it can get a bit hard on the users.

The compromise solution is to create or purchase a software package that makes the process of data extraction, table construction, and table loading a menu-driven process. There are several products available in the marketplace today that provide users with this kind of flexibility. It also is a capability that can be found built into many data-mining products. The answer for many organizations has been to develop their own customized software to drive the process. In all cases, this provision allows system managers to ameliorate the risks of giving users *carte blanche* access to system resources, while at the same time making the whole process easier for users.

Many organizations that have found themselves needing to provide end users with the ability to create *ad hoc* requests for data extractions or to develop their own on-demand data chains have created software that allows the users to specify the extraction or data chain steps and turns the steps into a batch job request that is run overnight (or when computer resources are available). This kind of facility gives the users the kind of flexibility that they want while allowing systems managers to protect the resources of the system and balance work load demands.

By the time you are done examining the end users' data-utilization profile, you should be in the position to specify exactly what kind of user workbench environment will be the most appropriate.

The warehouse manager's workbench. It should come as no surprise that the managers of the warehouse probably are going to find this kind of environment useful in the execution of their jobs as well. As the size and complexity of the warehouse increases, it becomes exponentially more difficult to keep track of everything that is going on. A workbench application like this might be optional for end users, but it is critical for the managers of the warehouse.

Relationship to the storage and work space areas. Before you can begin to consider the issues of workbench construction, there is one additional aspect of the management process that you should consider and that has to do with the locations at which each of the steps in a data-chaining process will take place and where each of the derived data sets will be stored.

It can safely be assumed that those tables that you have defined as the base population of tables within the warehouse are going to reside in the warehouse storage area. These tables are loaded, managed, and controlled by the warehouse management team. However, when it comes to the derived tables, you are going to find that you have several options for the storage of that data. Derived warehouse data can be stored in three places. It can be stored in the:

- Warehouse storage area along with the base tables

- Work space area in between the users and the storage area

- Users' own computer disk storage areas on their PC or workstation hard disk or floppy

Your decision to place this data in one of these three locations is going to depend upon:

- How much data there is

- Who will be responsible for managing it

- The types of access that will be used against it

(See Figure 7.7.) In general, you should store data within the warehouse storage area only when:

- It is generated on a regularly scheduled basis

- It is under the full control of the warehouse management team

- It is to be shared by more than one user

- No create, update, or deletes of the data are going to occur (except for rare exceptions)

You will want to store data within the user's workstation disk space only when:

- It is to be used exclusively by that user

- It is of a low enough volume as to not strain the user's workstation resources

- It does not require the utilization of feedback mechanisms except those of the most rudimentary nature

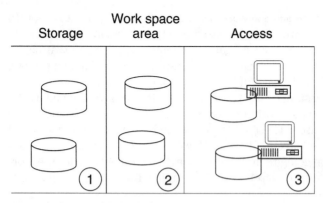

Figure 7.7 Storage of derived data.

Any data whose definition falls between the two extremes of the previous two options will land up being stored within the workspace area. These include:

- Data sets that require that feedback mechanisms be put in place to feed back changes into the warehouse itself
- Volumes of data that are so great that they cannot be managed on the user's own disk area
- Data that must be updated and shared between users

The purpose of the workspace area is to serve as the intermediary no-man's-land where the definition of responsibility and management for the data is not as clearly defined as it is in the other two areas.

We will continue with a more in-depth examination of the issues of data placement and physical management in chapter 8.

Specifications for the workbench systems. The reality of a workbench system that end users and warehouse managers can use to make the data warehouse easier to work with is going to depend in no small part on the size, complexity, and importance of the warehouse itself. If the applications being added to the warehouse are small and simple and if the number of data sets being managed is minimal, there is no reason to invest heavily in sophisticated management software. On the other hand, as the system grows in complexity and size, the need for the software gets greater.

Warehouse-management software falls into two major categories: scheduling and status reporting. A typical application might include one, some, or all of these features to varying degrees. At this point, we simply will describe one way that products of this nature could be developed, drawing upon our experience with systems that have been developed in the past to meet the same needs. At the same time, we realize that new applications of this type are being developed all of the time and that there is a range of products available in the marketplace today that perform some, if not all, of these functions.

Status-reporting capabilities. Obviously, what will be needed for warehouse managers and users is some way of finding out the status of the data being loaded into the warehouse at any given point in time. To do these, you are going to need to build a special set of tables within your infrastructure. (See Figure 7.8.)

These tables, which we will call the *infrastructure tracking tables*, will be physically located within the warehouse storage area. However, their purpose will be to hold status information about every major event that has occurred within the warehouse environment. By storing all of this information in this table, it will become a trivial matter to develop a set of screens that allow users and warehouse managers to check on status at any time.

Tracking the acquisition process. The first thing that you will want to keep track of is all the activities that occur within the acquisition area of the warehouse. You might recall that a typical data-extraction and -loading sequence can be made up of a long series of data cleansing, formatting, merge, and purge processes. It is going to be critical that you put some kind of mechanism in place that keeps track of all these steps.

In a lot of cases, the users of the system will not need to have any kind of access or familiarity with any of the steps; however, for the managers of the warehouse, the availability of a centrally defined and controlled repository that holds a history and current status of these operations is going to make the job of managing the environment many times easier. (See Figure 7.9.)

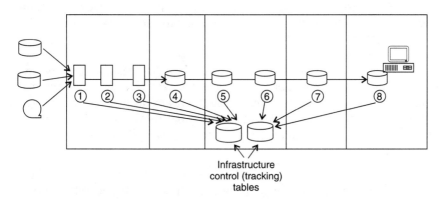

Infrastructure
control (tracking)
tables

Figure 7.8 Infrastructure tracking tables.

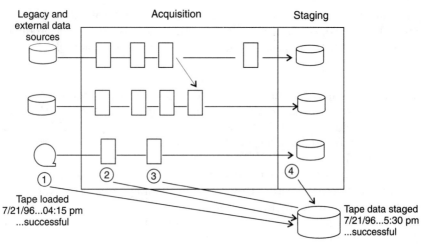

Figure 7.9 Tracking the acquisition process.

Tracking the loading of storage tables. The next event that you are going to want to keep track of is the loading of the core, reflection, code, bridge, and history tables. These tables, you might recall, make up the foundation of the overall warehouse environment and typically are loaded on a periodic basis.

By using the same control and management tables to keep track of load activity, the warehouse will be able to inform the warehouse managers and the end users about when each of these tables was last successfully loaded. (See Figure 7.10.)

Tracking the propagation of derived tables. Of course, the most difficult type of data-loading activity to track involves those tables that are derived for use by the end users. Up until this point, your system simply has been tracking whether regularly scheduled events have been successfully completed or not. In this case, you want to be able to keep track of not just the regularly scheduled derivation activities, but also the *ad hoc*, on-demand, and other unscheduled data extraction activities as well.

In this case, the existence of a software product that manages the extraction and data-chaining process itself will be key (see the next section). Without this kind of software to manage the users' *ad hoc* activities, there would be no way to keep track of exactly what they were doing with the data and how many computer resources they actually were using. (See Figure 7.11.)

Tracking the history of access to all tables. You might recall from chapter 4 that we said that the best way to measure how well the warehouse was functioning was in terms of the "turns" or levels of data activity that occurred within it. All of the warehousing activity in the world will be a waste of effort if nobody actually uses the data that is propagated.

From a management perspective, you have an even more immediate need for this kind of "turning" information. If the manager of the warehouse is going to take his or her job seriously, then he or she is going to need to be constantly monitoring the activity level of users against the different data sets. If it turns out that a data set is accessed only infrequently, then that data set might be a candidate for removal from the warehouse and placement in some other kind of environment. The managers of the warehouse should constantly be looking for better ways to make optimum use of the disk space and CPU power that they are commissioned to manage.

The only way to do this kind of activity tracking is to have some kind of history of the different types of access that the users are using against the

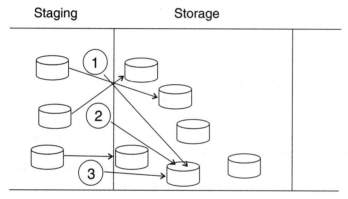

Figure 7.10 Tracking storage area activity.

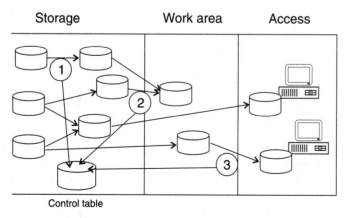

Figure 7.11 Tracking the propagation of derived data.

warehouse tables. While, in the worst case, the managers of the warehouse might need to figure out some way to capture and store this kind of information on their own, in most cases, the database software that you choose to run the warehouse will have this kind of end-user activity logging built right into the product.

All the managers of the warehouse need do is figure out how the user activity logging facilities work, engage them, and make use of the reports provided.

Scheduling. In addition to providing people with information about what has happened within the warehouse, it also can be advantageous to make use of the same mechanism to keep track of what is supposed to or going to happen. You will want to build this mechanism on top of the tracking mechanisms that you already have put into place to get as much consistency and integration of the two types of system as possible.

The types of scheduling systems that you might want to put into place will include systems that:

- Keep track of when activities are supposed to occur
- Provide facilities for the construction and execution of data manipulation events for scheduling or for immediate execution

Activity scheduling. Having information available about when different events within the warehouse have occurred provides you with valuable information. However, it will be even more valuable if you also know when these things were supposed to occur or the next time they are going to occur.

To make this kind of information available, you will need a complementary set of control and management tables to exist in parallel with the tracking tables that you have just defined. Into these tables, the managers of the warehouse will place information about when each of the data transformation events is supposed to occur.

For each activity within the warehouse—from extraction to merge/purge, to staging, to the loading of derived tables—you should be able to record the targeted dates and times when you anticipate each event to happen. By placing this scheduling information into the system, you can create a mechanism that allows you to predict warehouse activity, to anticipate problems, and to get a better overall picture of whatever you happen to be looking at.

This scheduled activity information will especially be valuable to end users who depend upon certain events occurring to plan their business activities.

Building data-chain specifications. The last facility that you want to build for your operational infrastructure will be the system that allows end users to develop their own data chains.

Customized data chain construction will allow end users to:

- Build their own input data sets for loading into data-mining tools
- Develop complex sets of data for utilization with their query-and-analysis tools
- Build source data sets for operational applications
- Create personal, transient copies of data for their own processing needs

By providing end users with a predefined set of screens that make this kind of activity possible, the managers of the system help to bridge the gap between system manageability and flexibility and between system user friendliness and technical complexity. It allows the system managers to give the end users the flexibility that they want, while defining a structure within which they can operate, making system management and system use easier.

Specifications for the tables. In a typical system designed to track and schedule warehouse activity, the following tables can serve as examples of a minimal set of data. The tables will include:

- Data-identity table—Holds information about each file, table, and data set within the warehouse environment.
- Data-transformation table—Holds information about the process of converting data from one data set to the next.

The data-identity table. The data-identity table holds one record for each data set and table within the warehouse environment. It holds information that includes:

- The name of the data set of table
- Its physical location
- Its minimum, maximum, and current size
- Its current status (loaded, empty, corrupted, available, etc.)

The data-transformation table. The data-transformation table holds process information for moving data from one data set to the next. The information it holds includes:

- The name of the source data set
- The name of the target data set
- The activity that is supposed to or has occurred (copy, merge, extract, etc.)
- The name of the program or stored procedure that performs the activity
- The outcome of the last execution
- The next scheduled execution

Obviously, as the scope and complexity of the system varies and as you try to use the system to do more and more work, the nature and complexity of these tables will increase. However, even this bare minimum of data capture can be of immense value to systems managers and users.

Tying the tables into the warehouse. While the capabilities that we have just described will provide an incredible amount of "value added" to the overall warehouse environment, ironically the cost to implement this kind of facility is minimal. All you need to do to build the foundation for this type of system is to create the tables to hold the data in the storage area. You then build a step into each data extraction, formatting and loading the job that makes an entry in the corresponding tracking table.

It is easy and straightforward to do this, as long as you build it into your understanding of how the warehouse is going to be managed. If you try to ignore the building of this capability until after a large amount of the warehouse infrastructure already is in place, then the cost will be much greater.

Main menu screen functionality. The main menu screen defines the principal areas of workbench functionality. It includes menu items that allow the user to look at the process of data transformation:

- Data extract and preparation—The status of data as it moves from legacy systems to the staging area
- Data loading—The loading of staged data into the warehouse
- Data chains—The movement of data from the base warehouse tables into their derived forms

It includes other items that allow the user to look at the status of individual data sets and tables:

- Data-set view—Allows the user to check the status of a given data set or table
- The ability to build data chains
- Data-chain construction and scheduling

Individual screens underneath this menu then can be designed to carry the user through the different processes and views of the warehouse's activity.

Conclusions

In this chapter, we have concentrated on the workings of the operational infrastructure of the warehouse. It consists of the identification and placement of data sets, the provision of mechanisms to allow for different types of user access, and the development of mechanisms that can ease the tracking and management of the overall warehousing process.

In the next chapter, we will complete our view of the warehousing environment by examining the physical infrastructure of the warehouse.

Chapter

8

The Physical Infrastructure

At this point, you might be uttering a sigh of relief:

> Finally! He's is going to tell me what I really wanted to know about the warehouse. I don't want to know about business issues, management approaches, data disciplines, and operational infrastructures. All I really want to know is which computers I should buy to build the warehouse. Just tell me what to use, and I'll figure the rest out myself.

Unfortunately, it just doesn't work that way. The last thing that I'm going to do is tell you about the one right way to build a warehouse infrastructure.

I'm not going to withhold this information out of some kind of perverted desire to torture you. On the contrary, I would like nothing better than to simply say "Buy two of these, one of these, and tie them together this way, and everything else will work itself out." Unfortunately, I cannot. The issues around physical infrastructure decision-making are the most complex in the warehousing world and require you to take many variables into account.

It might seem, based upon the amount of time that we have spent on all the business, organizational, data discipline, and operational characteristics of the warehouse, that the physical infrastructure is the least important aspect of the system. Nothing could be further from the truth. However, to have an intelligent discussion about that physical infrastructure, we needed to establish all of these other warehouse characteristics to have a framework within which the discussions could be held.

A warehouse is a diverse and complex thing, and the physical infrastructure upon which it runs will be the most complex aspect of all.

As soon as you begin entertaining issues about what kinds of hardware, software, and networking environments you should use to build the warehouse, you get into a quagmire of conflicting needs and demands. We will use the framework that we have presented up until this point to guide you through the process of making intelligent infrastructure decisions.

Problems with Physical Infrastructures

The fact of the matter is that, as soon as you begin talking upon physical infrastructures, you get into a whole range of issues and debates that, in the past, have proven to greatly curtail, and even destroy, some very well-grounded warehouse development efforts. The problems fall under several categories:

- Investment in existing infrastructure
- Tool drivers
- Territorial imperatives
- Religious debates
- Organizational history
- Vendor-promoted misconceptions about ease of use and low-cost solutions
- Integration, management, and performance problems

We will consider each of these issues before proceeding with the investigation.

Investment in existing infrastructure

The first problem that you run into when you begin discussing what the best physical infrastructure for the warehouse should be is the problem presented by current investment in different existing physical infrastructures.

This problem is best understood by referring back to the earlier discussions about the history of data processing within the business environment and the way in which different systems, and their correspondingly diverse physical infrastructures, might have propagated themselves across the enterprise.

In each business, you are likely to find several types of physical infrastructures, each vying for organizational supremacy in the environment. For different organizations, at different times, these battle zones might be different; however, in general, "turf battles" of this nature are quite common.

In the olden days of data processing, the battle lines for physical-infrastructure turf were pretty cleanly drawn. At the center was the infamous IBM mainframe environment. These computers were the unchallenged kings of the business data-processing environment. Even today, the functioning of most major corporations is highly dependent upon IBM mainframe processing to survive and thrive.

Other players in the marketplace tended to specialize in niches for which the IBM mainframe was ill-suited. Departmental-level processing was handled by Xerox, Wang, IBM-System 36, 38, AS/400, and DEC. Specialized large applications and government work were handled by Burroughs and Sperry. Specialized scientific and engineering were handled by Hewlett-Packard and SUN. In general, these systems hardly ever competed with each other, because each met specific business needs.

In those days, turf battles (at least in the mainframe environment) centered on the propagation of database-management system software. IBM's IMS, IDMS, Supra, Model 204, and a range of other major contenders all vied for ownership of the mainframe database marketplace.

However, as the computer evolved, the battlefield changed significantly. Scientific workstations by Sun and Hewlett-Packard began to challenge the supremacy of the mainframe. The personal computer became a standard fixture on every desktop in the world. Soon, the nicely drawn, well-organized battle lines became blurred. With the corresponding improvements in network technology, the propagation of LANs, and the designation of "client/server" technology as the approach of the future, the environment became a free-for-all. Suddenly every vendor became a potential provider of every kind of data-processing needs.

People began considering PCs with LANs or PCs working with UNIX-based servers as potential replacement environments for the formerly dependable mainframe. All of a sudden, every decision about every computer system turned into an overwhelming debate about infrastructure, future directions, and long-term hardware/software planning.

The problem with the selection of any kind of a physical infrastructure decision is clear. Every time you invest in hardware, software, or network architecture, you make a commitment not only as an immediate solution to an immediate problem. When you make these decisions, you limit people's choices in the future. These decisions are limited because you cannot afford to tear out the old systems every time you bring in a new system, and you cannot afford to retrain people every time a new, fancy solution comes along.

Unfortunately, as we discussed earlier, there is simply no way to make the "right decision" about infrastructure and be assured that the decision will hold up as the technology continues to expand and evolve.

There have been dozens of documented cases of organizations stymied by precisely these kinds of issues.

Over the past 10 years, many organizations have tried to eliminate their mainframe computers and replace them with UNIX servers or even distributed PC-based LANs. In general, these efforts have failed. No matter how hard they have tried, it has proved to be an almost insurmountable task to try to replace the efficiencies and incredible organizational and procedural investments that typical mainframe environments represent.

Others have tried to hold steadfastly to the mainframe-only processing approach. These organizations, for the most part, have found themselves deluged in a flood of PC-, LAN-, and server-based initiatives that have created havoc within the overall data-processing environment.

Therefore, the challenge is to come up with some kind of approach that allows you to leverage the current investment that the organization has while, at the same time, making it possible to take advantage of the new potential benefits that new infrastructure approaches might present.

The investment that an organization will have in an existing infrastructure will not be trivial. Included in your understanding of this investment is investment in the:

- Hardware and software itself
- Development of roles, responsibilities, and procedures for the management of this environment
- Skills and experience level of users and support personnel

Any consideration of the construction of a new system must take these costs into account, either as a cost already paid that developers can capitalize on or as a cost to be suffered if it is determined that the new physical infrastructure is going to require radical changes to the existing environment.

Tool drivers

As if the straightforward questions about which hardware and software to use would not be complicated enough, we are reluctantly forced to take even more variables into account before continuing the discussion.

The second problem that you encounter when trying to determine an optimal physical infrastructure becomes evident when you start to look at the specialized data-mining tools and warehouse-infrastructure management tools that promise to ease some of the overall development effort required to construct the warehouse. Unfortunately, new tools and approaches usually run on new types of infrastructures. Therefore, you are going to have to take the needs of these solutions into account as part of your physical infrastructure decision-making process. If you find that you need a data-mining tool that only runs on a Silicon Graphics workstation, then you are going to have to include these workstations, their cost, and their connectivity costs into your overall physical architecture plan.

If you decide that you need a product like InfoPump, which makes it possible for you to preschedule and premanage the data-acquisition process using a set of easy-to-use menus, then the physical requirements of that solution must be included. There is no way around it. New tools bring with them a set of environmental factors that need to be included in your plans.

Territorial imperatives

Another more insidious form of physical-infrastructure decision making occurs on the organizational level. For every specified physical infrastructure that is supported by an organization, there are groups of people who are heavily invested in that solution. Any attempt to choose infrastructure alternatives that differ from their chosen power base is going to create a great deal of dissension and controversy.

These territorial imperatives can take two forms: one on the systems support side and one on the business user side.

Systems territories. The territory defined by different groups of systems-support organizations is clear and straightforward. A typical corporation has mainframe support, UNIX support, and PC/LAN support departments in some form or another. The decision to choose one of these environments to support the new warehouse is a decision to promise more work, a bigger budget, bigger staff, and assured survival for whoever the "winning" environment happens to be. The tendency of individuals to promote their own infrastructure approach and to discount and undermine the approaches that others propose should be expected and anticipated during the physical infrastructure development process.

The fact of the matter is that all of the physical infrastructures could very well be appropriate choices to solve some, or all, of the warehouse's needs. The problem is that no project can afford to get hung up too long on the resolution of these issues. Your approach must minimize the chances of this kind of controversy occurring.

Business area territory. The users of systems that are based upon different types of platforms will have an almost equal vehemence in their attempts to defend whatever their infrastructure of choice might happen to be. Different groups of users within the organization are going to have experience with different assortments of tools and platforms. Some might work heavily with their own PCs and enjoy a great deal of autonomy from centralized data processing. Others might be comfortable using mainframe-based applications that provide them with "push button" ease of use that they have come to expect.

When you begin making physical infrastructure and software recommendations, there is a good chance that you are going to threaten their way of doing things. The designers of the infrastructure need to take these territorial issues into account just as much as the systems issues.

Religious debates

Perhaps the most frustrating kinds of issues to combat when trying to make sound infrastructure decisions come from the area that we call *religious debates*. These debates are often, but not always, founded within the territorial imperatives of different groups of users and tend to promote blanket solutions as the only answer to any physical infrastructure issue. These "religions" fall under the heading of "mainframe good; everything else bad," "client/server," "object oriented," or the most devastating of all: "just leave everything the way it is" or "just change everything and start over."

Your response to these issues must fall back upon the basic premise upon which your whole approach is based. The developers of the warehouse are not out to solve the physical infrastructure problems of the universe, or even the corporation. The objective is to deliver usable applications in a cost-effective manner, period. If the proposed solution can do that, great. If it can't, then it is immaterial.

Organizational history

Once you have cleared the territorial and religious issues around infrastructure development, you often will run into problems that involve the performance history of the people being asked to participate in warehouse construction. Whether the platform that you decide to use for the development of the warehouse is a mainframe, a UNIX server, or a PC, if the users of existing systems within the organization have had a history of bad experiences with the people slated to build and manage the system, then the project will be in serious jeopardy before you even get started.

A typical situation occurs when a mainframe support group begins to advocate a mainframe-based warehouse solution. Users might find that the value proposition holds considerable merit and might even find that they need the new warehousing application to survive. Yet, if that same mainframe support group has failed at their last three attempts to deliver other types of applications or if that same system is forcing users to wait weeks or even months to deliver badly needed enhancements to existing systems, then the users will be far from enthusiastic about the new initiative being built within that group's sphere of influence.

Many times, it is dissatisfaction not with the mainframe technology, but with the mainframe support organization that causes people to promote alternative platforms for new systems. On the other hand, within some organizations, the failure of previously attempted "client/server" initiatives might cause people to favor the "old standby' mainframe approach.

Vendor-promoted misconceptions about ease of use and low-cost solutions

When it comes to developing a physical infrastructure plan, another source of challenges is the influence that the vendors of different sets of products bring into the equation. Unfortunately, the vendors of different types of products tend to present users, managers, and systems personnel with pictures of how their products work that are in many ways too optimistic. The job of the vendor is to present their product in the best light possible. This includes telling you how easy it is to use, how inexpensive it will be to run, and how transparent its operation will be to everyone. Unfortunately, in their exuberance to paint a rosy picture of their product, vendors tend to overlook the consequences and assumptions that go into these claims.

In some cases, your challenge simply will be to be aware of the realities involved and to separate those from the misconceptions. In other cases, these claims can undermine your efforts to develop a robust, sound, and cost-effective overall warehouse solution. This is especially true in those cases where data-mining tools claim to be able to handle all of the warehouse management for you and in those cases of warehouse-management products that provide some, but not all, of the functionality that you require.

In these cases, the solution is to develop an understanding of the individual products as they fit within the warehouse template that you have been developing. The process of checking the claimed functionality against your logical understanding of what the warehouse must be able to provide can help the physical infrastructure developer from making mistakes in tool selection that can create problems down the road.

Integration, performance, and management problems

Finally, and of the biggest concern for the physical infrastructure developer, is to choose infrastructure components that are going to make the integration of the different parts of the warehouse, the performance of the warehouse overall, and the management of the environment as efficient and friendly as possible.

A solution that involves the utilization of 5 operating systems, 15 platforms, and 3 networks might meet the needs of all of the different political and financial groups within the organization, but it certainly will create a nightmare environment for the managers of the system.

On the other hand, an overly dictatorial and simplistic architecture might meet the minimum needs of the organization and be incredibly easy to build and manage, but it can leave the users short of the potential benefits that might be enjoyed with a more robust type of solution.

So as you can see, deciding upon the appropriate physical infrastructure is much more than the simple process of picking the best tool for the job. It involves people, investments, history, and expectations. It can never be a purely technical decision but will always be influenced by politics and feelings in addition to the simple costs and capabilities that you would like it to include.

Imperatives

Therefore, the imperatives for your physical infrastructure development process must be:

- To keep the approach as modular as possible. You want to create an environment where you can plug and unplug different parts of the application so that different parts can respond to different kinds of efficiencies whenever possible.

- To leverage as much of the existing physical infrastructure, both in terms of physical plant (the physical hardware, software, etc.) and the people investment (skills, aptitudes, and experience), as possible.

At the same time, you must bring as many appropriate and cost-effective new solutions to bear on the problem as possible. This is not an easy task.

Platforms

Therefore, the first and biggest discussion that you will have around physical infrastructures will be that of choosing the physical platforms for the warehouse. Under the term *platform*, we include definitions for all of the hardware, database software, the operating system, and network software components that will make up the system.

The single-platform solution

We will begin our examination of the different kinds of physical infrastructures and their corresponding strengths and weaknesses by starting with the simplest case: the single platform architecture. (See Figure 8.1.)

It might come as a shock to some readers, but a single-platform infrastructure for a data warehouse is not only allowable and feasible, but it often is the best option available to system developers. Long before the vendors of UNIX-based database products and PC-based data-mining tools came along, people were successfully building and deploying warehouses by making use of existing technologies.

A single-platform solution can be built using existing corporation mainframe technologies, mini-computers, or even UNIX-based servers. However,

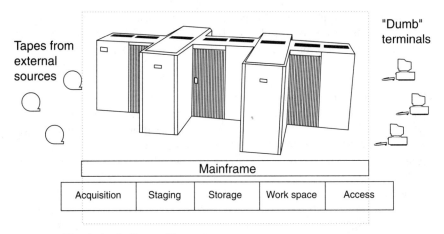

Figure 8.1 The single-platform architecture.

the feasibility of the solution depends upon several factors. In the single platform-based warehouse, all operations in the acquisition, storage, and access components occur from within the framework of the same technology.

Obviously, if this kind of solution is going to work, then your first assumption will have to be that all of the legacy systems that feed the warehouse already reside on the same warehouse. Your next assumption will be that the platform in question will be big enough and powerful enough to handle managing all of the data that the storage component needs to deal with.

Your final assumption will be that this same environment can support the management of end-user data-mining and data-access applications.

There are many situations where this solution will be both economically and organizationally the best solution possible.

A single-platform solution greatly reduces the risk and expense of system construction and makes the issues involved in system design and support a lot less cumbersome. One of the first approaches that we take when asked to evaluate platform alternatives is to see if there isn't some way to make a single-platform approach work. Unfortunately, there are many factors at work that can serve to make this a less-than-optimal approach. For any number of reasons, the single platform might prove to be inadequate or undesirable. The issues that will contra-indicate this kind of solution are discussed in the following sections.

Capacity. In many situations, the existing platform environment might not be in a condition suitable for the installation of a new major implementation. In a lot of cases, the existing legacy environment already might be stretched to capacity, making it impossible to upgrade the hardware and software to the state required for warehouse support.

Even if the physical capacity exists (CPU and disk space), the environment itself might be so complex or the support staff so overworked that they cannot envision making the changes necessary to support this kind of effort.

Competence. Even if the existing legacy-system environment could be retrofitted to meet the demands of the warehouse, it might be that the support staff is ill-equipped to build and support it. Unfortunately, legacy-system environments tend to be based upon older, and sometimes outdated, technologies. Technologies that require specialized skills that are not readily available.

One organization was considering the development of an extremely large, super-data warehouse. The only hardware that seemed capable of meeting the processing needs was a Cray-type supercomputer. However, after considerable research into the possibilities, the organization had to abandon the project. Even though the capacity was there, it was discovered that there would be no way to hire or train a staff large enough to develop the system.

A technological solution that cannot be implemented by making use of readily available and reasonably priced technical support is as infeasible a solution as one where the technology itself cannot be attained.

Availability of data-mining tools. One of the biggest driving forces prompting people to consider warehousing solutions is the existence of high-powered, low-cost data-mining applications. These tools make it possible for users to perform analysis and data-manipulation tasks that previously were available only within the most rigidly defined academic environments. Unfortunately, hardly any of these tools runs on legacy-system environments. Oh, there is a smattering of UNIX-, mainframe-, and mini-computer-based applications here and there; however, in general, the vast majority of the products run on Windows, OS/2, Macintosh, and X-Term environments.

Disparate legacy data sources. Another precondition that can make the single platform an untenable solution occurs in those environments where legacy systems exist across a wide variety of platforms. A typical corporate environment can include many mainframe computers, a collection of specialized mini- and UNIX computers, and an assortment of PC-based operations. With these many different sources to deal with, a single-platform approach becomes untenable.

Strategic platform directions. Many organizations today have established strategic platform directions that dictate which platforms can or cannot be used for new systems development. Corporations that make these kinds of declarations have been accepting that diverse and incompatible platforms cannot be immediately eliminated. By choosing these directions, the corporate directors hope to encourage the atrophy of old systems and encourage the development of new ones. In these environments, the strategic direction chosen must bear influence on the platform decision-making process.

Separating the legacy environments

So, probably the first thing that you will have to figure out for your physical infrastructure is how to incorporate disparate legacy system platforms into the environment. (See Figure 8.2.)

When you to try to incorporate this data into your overall warehousing environment, you are going to have to make some decisions. It is a given that the extraction of data from each of these legacy systems will occur on the platforms where those systems exist. However, what about all of the other steps of the acquisition process? Where will you develop and execute the data-cleansing programs and the data-synchronization routines? Will you attempt to do those on the existing legacy platforms as well?

More importantly, how will you manage the merge/purge kinds of processing that need to occur, especially when the two files that need to be merged exist on different systems? How do you decide which one to run it on?

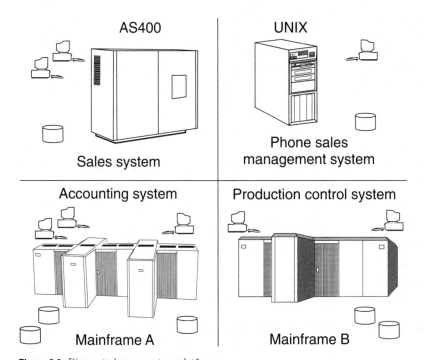

Figure 8.2 Disparate legacy system platforms.

In many cases, you will realize that it is going to be necessary to establish an additional legacy systems neutral location where the majority of the data preparation work will occur.

Platform allocation for the acquisition component

When trying to decide which platforms to use to do the different parts of the acquisition process, several issues will help drive the decision-making process.

First of all, you need to be aware of the capacity available on each of those legacy systems. If a system already is strapped for capacity (disk and CPU), then there will be little hope of using it to do anything except to provide you with the initial extract file.

Secondly, you have to make allocation decisions based upon the availability of resources that can work in each of the targeted environments. Many times, especially with smaller platforms, the organization will have limited or no in-house staff capable of developing the required programs. In these cases, the data will have to be moved to an environment where people who can work with the data are available.

On the other hand, some legacy system environments might have ample capacity and ample resources. In some situations, these environments also can be equipped with software that makes the development of data-cleansing and -formatting programs easy and cost-effective. In these cases, it might make sense to port all of the data to that platform and allow it to function as the main acquisitions-component platform.

In some situations, warehouse developers have opted to create a new, neutral environment where extracted data can be ported and manipulated. This kind of solution has several advantages:

- The environment can be optimized for data-transformation operations. It can be equipped with tools that make data cleansing and formatting easy.

- The environment can be staffed with people that specialize in the use of these types of tools.

- It makes the overall process of managing data acquisition easier to do, easier to manage, and easier to track.

In most cases, organizations end up developing a solution that involves a combination of these approaches. (See Figure 8.3.)

In all cases, it will be critical for the developers of the acquisition component facilities to keep several things in mind.

The need to make use of infrastructure control tables to track the process.

The more complex the acquisition component gets on a physical infrastructure level, the more important it will be to be sure that the centrally defined

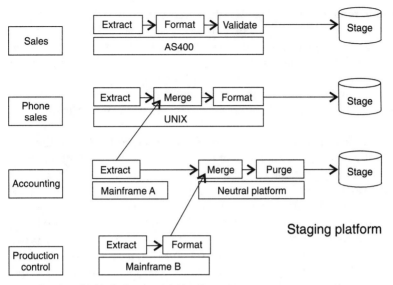

Figure 8.3 A multiple-platform acquisition component.

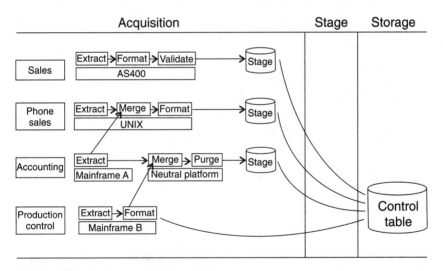

Figure 8.4 Keeping the control table updated.

infrastructure control and tracking tables are being utilized. This kind of centrally defined source of information about each step in the process will make it possible to manage an otherwise unmanageable environment. (See Figure 8.4.)

The need to reduce complexity. Many organizations have found themselves swamped in incredible amounts of complexity and poor coordination when these kinds of multiplatform solutions develop. You can easily end up relying upon dozens of programmers in dozens of environments to each perform a part of the overall data-conversion task. Yet because they are so scattered and are working in such different environments, it can become an incredible task just to keep them coordinated and working in the same direction.

The need to guarantee the integrity of data transformations. One of the side effects of the increased complexity of multiplatform solutions for the acquisition component is that the integrity of the data, as it goes through each of the transformation steps, can become compromised. You distribute the task across so many different environments and involve so many different people that it becomes easy to lose the meaning of the data being manipulated.

In addition to the more subtle form of data-integrity compromise, a problem occurs on the physical level when you cross so many different technological boundaries. Different platforms store data in different ways, and they are not always compatible with one another. You not only need to worry about the logical integrity of the data as it moves through the acquisition process, but also must assure its physical integrity as well. As you can see, your nice, simple, physical-infrastructure decision-making process now has been made a lot more complicated. (See Figure 8.5.)

At this point, what will be critical for the developers of the data warehouse to understand is that, while the development of the acquisition component might involve disparate platforms and most certainly will involve getting support from a wide variety of organizational units, the overall responsibility for the integrity and efficiency of the acquisition operations, as an overall process, still rests on the shoulders of the warehouse developers.

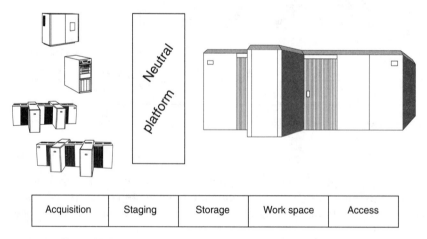

| Acquisition | Staging | Storage | Work space | Access |

Figure 8.5 Physical infrastructure with multiple legacy platforms.

Data-Transportation Issues (Acquisition)

Up until this point, we have been talking about the movement of data between programs and between platforms as if it were a trivial process, and in some situations, it is. In a single-platform environment, there is very little overhead or expense associated with the movement of data from one process to the next.

However, as soon as you begin to talk about moving data (the data created by one program to be read by another program) or information (the tracking records for your infrastructure control table) from one platform to another, you create a whole new set of problems and concerns.

Moving data from one platform to another

The fact of the matter is that—depending upon the platform that you are moving data from, the platform you are moving it to, and the network connectivity established between them—this process can be very easy or extremely difficult. There are four major categories of interplatform connections that you will need to consider:

- Real-time network connections
- Data ports
- Shared disk
- Tape transfer

It is important to note that these same interplatform connectivity issues will pertain to the access and work-area component platforms as well as the acquisition platforms.

Real-time network connections. The most intimate kind of connection that you can establish between two platforms is where a process or program running on one of the platforms can make use of resources on the other. This is the type of functionality provided by many types of client/server or crossplatform manipulation products. Depending upon how the hardware has been set up, it can be made possible for programs on one of the platforms to read from and write to disk spaces on the other computers. In many cases, these same connects can allow those programs to actually execute programs and schedule events on the other platform as well. This tight coupling of platforms usually is available between different platforms of the same type. For example, crossplatform mainframe processes have long been feasible. However, the ability to do this kind of crossplatform activity when the platforms are of different types is much rarer.

The recent popularity of client/server technology and the propagation of TCP/IP as an industry standard network protocol have made this kind of interplatform work a lot easier to develop. Unfortunately, even when this capability is present, it might not be configured to operate at the volumes and rate that are required for your purposes. At a minimum, this kind of tight coupling will make it feasible for your data-transformation processes to update a remotely defined infrastructure control table. (See Figure 8.6.)

Data ports. A second kind of interplatform connectivity is made possible via the creation of data ports. *Data ports* are intersystem mechanisms that make it possible for utility programs on one system to send massive amounts of data to the other system at a high rate of speed and of reasonable volume.

Data ports, like real-time connections, require that each platform involved in the process be especially configured to handle the transfer, including the presence of special hardware, special software, and sufficient network capacity to handle the anticipated loads. (See Figure 8.7.)

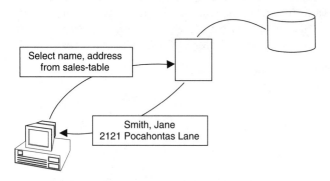

Figure 8.6 Real-time network connections.

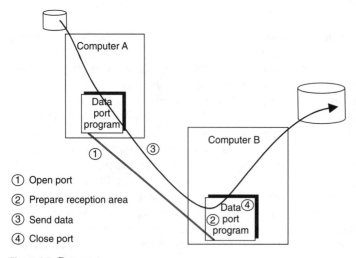

Figure 8.7 Data ports.

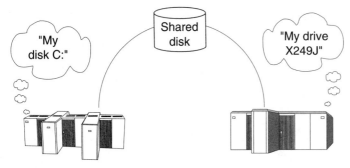

Figure 8.8 Shared disk.

Shared disk. Another way that the transfer of data can be handled is through the use of shared disks. Under a shared disk configuration, a neutrally defined disk storage area is set up so that each platform recognizes it as its own. By convincing both systems that the disk space is its own, it is possible for programmers on the first system to write data to this neutral area, which programmers on the second system then can read.

The biggest differences between the shared-disk and data-port solutions have to do with speed and ease of use. Access to a shared disk typically is very fast, as fast as any intraplatform read/write operation. On the other hand, data-port transfer rates usually are much lower.

It also is much easier to make use of shared disk. In a shared-disk environment, each programmer treats the data set as just another native data set. No special jobs, procedures, or machinations must be executed. Just read the data, and write it again.

Data porting, on the other hand, requires the scheduling and execution of data-porting software, and it can get complicated. (See Figure 8.8.)

Manual media transfer. Finally, when all else fails, you can always fall back on the way to move data between platforms that always works: manual media transfer. Under this arrangement, the programmer on the first platform writes the data to an external media, like a tape or a floppy disk. After this, the media is transferred to the new platform where another programmer reads the data in. (See Figure 8.9.)

While manual media transfer is not pretty, it is reliable and inexpensive. In those situations where no other connectivity is available, it becomes the only alternative.

Using and choosing data-transportation options. The development of a data-transportation approach to tie the platforms within your legacy system environment together is a critical one. The first step in making this determination is to find out what capabilities already are in place, and verify that they can handle the anticipated volumes and rates.

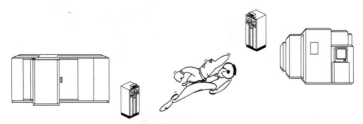

Figure 8.9 Manual media to media transfer (tape).

	Cost	Timing
Real time	High	Immediate
Data port	Medium	Internal speed
Shared disk	Low	Program bound
Manual media	Low	Human bound

Figure 8.10 Data-transportation options.

The decision to make use of one approach over another will have several consequences:

- Platform cost—The more tightly you couple two platforms, the more expensive the networking solution.

- Timing—As you move down the scale from real-time to manual data transportation, you increase the time delay. Part of your infrastructure decision will have to be based upon whether or not the proposed coupling technique will meet your timing requirements.

- Development cost—The more complicated the linkage between the systems, the more costly the development. Probably the least expensive solution in the majority of cases is a shared-disk approach. Data ports are cumbersome to work with, and real-time connections are complex to execute and also are resource intensive. (See Figure 8.10.)

Supporting data transportation

You really have two sets of concerns when it comes to figuring out how to configure your physical infrastructure from a data-transportation perspective. The first and biggest set of issues revolves around how to transform data from its raw, extracted form into the staged form required for warehouse loading. For these cases, the optimum solution is a shared disk, followed by data-porting options. Real time and manual transfer are feasible only as last resorts. The first because it is so resource intensive, and the second because it can cause significant time delays and requires manual intervention to work.

Supporting the Infrastructure Control Tables

On the other hand, you have just about the opposite set of preferences when it comes to figuring out how to keep your infrastructure control tables up-to-date. Ideally, each program that performs one of your data-transformation steps could include within it an SQL "call" to the control tables located within the storage area. This way, the control table could be kept up-to-date and up-to-the-minute.

If this is not possible, the only other option would be for these programs to write information about the successful completion of each step to a special file, which then could be transported to the storage area and loaded up into the control table via a special update program. In these cases, the file would get moved via either shared disk, port, or manual means. (See Figures 8.11 and 8.12.)

Adding User Workstations

Of course, not only do you need to worry about dealing with disparate platforms on the acquisitions side of the warehouse, but in most situations, you are going to have to figure out how to deal with a vast assortment of user workstation platforms as well.

While it is possible to build a data warehouse by making use of whatever "native" user terminal interface that the legacy system might happen to provide, you usually will be faced with a wide variety of users, each of whom have their own preferences for separate user workstations.

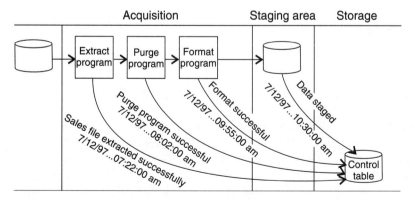

Figure 8.11 Direct update of control tables, using Direct SQL.

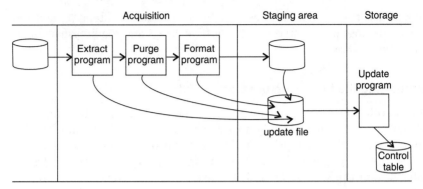

Figure 8.12 Indirect update of control tables by writing to a hold file.

By far, the most common form of user workstation in the business environment today is the personal computer, running with Windows and DOS as the operating system environment. Also popular in different areas will be personal computers with OS/2, Macintosh computers, and UNIX X-Terminals. One of your challenges is going to be to get these diverse platforms to fit within your infrastructure as well. (See Figure 8.13.)

Workstation selection

It is in the area of workstation selection that you get into some of the biggest "turf battles" over infrastructure. The problem is that, for a given population of users, you are going to find that there is an investment in technology and approach that is not easily abandoned. Different users are going to want to see different infrastructures put into place.

We already have reviewed many of the issues that are going to have an influence on what types of workstations that you choose. The issues involve the existing investment in:

- Hardware
- Software
- Networking infrastructure
- Management and support staff

Users' familiarity with existing technologies. In addition to the preference that people have for the protection of their existing investments, the battle for a workstation environment also can become the means for groups to advocate their solutions over others. For example, in one manufacturing organization where I worked, there were two groups of people. The first group consisted of engineers. These people were familiar with UNIX and C and were very comfortable maintaining a "hands on" technically intimate relationship with their environment. They felt that fancy graphics and user-friendly interfaces were a waste of good computing power. Their preference was UNIX-based scientific workstations as the access mechanism of choice. Another equally avid group was made up of the management and clerical staff. For them, there was no question about what the user interface should be. They were comfortable with a Windows-based personal computer environment. They had no desire to learn about the joys of FTP, grep-ing, and other technical details. They wanted a transparent environment that allowed them to work on the computer with ease and comfort.

In the worst cases, advocacy for different kinds of workstation solutions can become not-too-clever ploys designed to gain the users the type of workstation environment that they really want, regardless of the particular application under consideration.

For many organizations, the size, power, and capabilities of the workstation at your desk serve as a corporate status symbol. The bigger your PC, the more memory it has, and the more disk drive space attached represents more power, prestige, and worth in the corporate environment. In organizations like this, you will find users "shopping for solutions" that get them the workstations that they really want.

Getting something for nothing.   Whenever you get into these complex situations where large numbers of people have disparate demands about what the workstation environment should look like, you usually can get down to the issues about the real value of the alternatives being considered if you take a discerning look at the budgeting process. Everybody would like to see a solution provided that gives them the most benefit for the least cost, and this pertains to workstation selection as much as anything else.

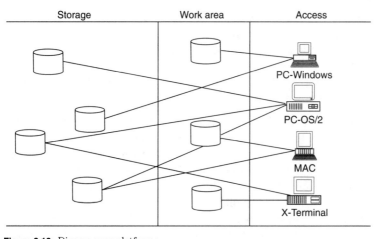

Figure 8.13 Diverse user platforms.

The problems come when it is unclear about who exactly is going to pay for the workstations as a part of the ultimate solution. Workstation expenditures are not always part of an overall systems development budget, especially if there already is some kind of infrastructure in place. In these cases, the question becomes:

> Do we modify our solution to make use of the existing infrastructure, or do we propose a solution that includes a large financial investment on the hardware/software/network side to get a more robust set of tools delivered into the user's hands?

If you choose the former and simply "make do" with what you have, does it undermine the overall objectives of the system? On the other hand, if you choose the latter, who is going to underwrite the additional expense?

Many times, users will advocate and support powerful and sophisticated workstation alternatives, as long as they are going to get some new and, from their perspectives, "free" toys to play with. When the solutions become plainer and less friendly, they often lose interest.

Ultimately, the solution to choose one workstation alternative over another is going to boil down to the same issues that you have faced at every other step of the process. When making these decisions, you must weigh the benefits against the costs, and if a justification for the cost cannot be found, then the solution should be abandoned for a more economically sound approach. There is never anything "free" in the systems-development environment and workstation environments can be extremely expensive.

On the other hand, some organizations already have invested heavily in robust, well-run workstation-type infrastructures. In these cases, the decision-making process is much easier. Your objective in these cases simply is to figure out how to best leverage what already is in place.

Terminal illness.   Some organizations have not had such an easy time of developing workstation infrastructure approaches. Within these types of organizations, it is not uncommon to find end users with two, three, or more terminals at their desks, each tying into a different system. In these cases, it will be imperative that, if at all possible, you try to simplify the environment and either leverage what is there or somehow replace it.

Diversion from objectives.   Unfortunately, as soon as you begin to get into this area, it becomes very easy to get diverted from your main objective, which is to develop and deliver low-cost data-warehouse applications. Issues regarding whether to use personal computers, dumb terminals, or UNIX workstations represents your first level of controversy. After that is resolved, the next issues will revolve around operating systems (Windows versus Windows NT versus OS/2 or SUN versus HP versus SCO UNIX). Then you will need to argue about windowing environments (Windows,

OS/2, Motif, OpenLook, etc.). Then you will need to argue about network protocols (NOVELL, TCP/IP, MS-NET, etc.).

There is no easy way to resolve these issues, and the developer of a data-warehouse solution is going to have to get involved in the controversy if he or she is going to be able to deliver the data to the user. My only recommendation is that the project team that is working on the warehouse concentrate only on those issues having to do with the delivery of the applications at hand.

The study. One of the biggest sabotages of warehouse projects in this department happens when the issues about infrastructure are raised and someone suddenly says, " These decisions are too all encompassing and too important to be made in hurried manner." A committee will be assigned to study the problems and make recommendations at a later date.

Unfortunately, as well-meaning as this solution might be, the decision to wait for a study before proceeding with warehouse development is a decision to postpone the warehouse indefinitely. At best, committees take several weeks or months to make their decisions, and even if the organization was ready to act on those recommendations immediately, it could take months or years to implement the recommendations. Ultimately, the warehouse project will never get started.

Taking a proactive, profit-driven approach. The only way to function in an environment like this is to concentrate on the value propositions at hand and to figure out how to deliver them as well as possible given the current environment. If the value propositions that you are dealing with are financially sound and of strategic importance to the business, then the case can, and should, be made for the development of immediate compromises that allow the project to move forward.

At no time, however, should the developers of the warehouse allow the workstation decision-making process to be put on hold while the rest of system developments continue. The mistaken belief in this case is that the workstation decision is a trivial and/or secondary one and that, after everything else has been finished, the workstation simply can be tacked on the end.

Taking this approach is a good way to guarantee the failure of your project. Just as you must constantly synchronize all of the data-discipline activities across all components of the warehouse, so too must you coordinate physical-infrastructure activities. Failure to do so can seriously jeopardize the entire process.

Workstation decision making

Given that the environment that you are working in might or might not force you to contend with a collection of nontechnical issues, you nonetheless do have some specific things that you can base physical access-component decision making on.

Tool and product availability. In most cases, the single biggest driver towards preference for one type of workstation platform over another is type of platform required to support the selected data-mining tools. Almost every data-mining tool and programming language works only in specific platform environments. The limits of the selected tool set are going to define the limits of the platform options that are available.

In addition to the availability of specific tools for a given platform is the availability of different programming languages, graphical user interfaces, and windowing environments. The customized portions of the workstation environment will have to be written using some kind of language or product, and these too have platform limitations.

Workstation disk storage area. Less clear is the requirement that you develop for disk space on the workstation. Should your solution involve the extraction of small amounts of data onto the users' workstation, you will have to be sure that those workstations have the disk space available.

Disk space availability is nowhere near the problem that it used to be. In the past, personal computers were severely limited in the amount of disk space that they could handle, but it now is possible to attach several gigabytes of storage for a very low cost. It also is much easier to upgrade this disk space than it used to be.

When deciding about what kind of disk storage capacity you will want the workstation to have, it will be important to remember that you always have other options. You can always think in terms of trying to figure out how to leverage work area disk space or even storage area disk space to supplement the workstation's own capabilities.

Workstation processing power. Another capacity to consider is the computer processing power that the workstation will need to have. Just as with disk space, there is a way that you can trade off workstation power with the power that the work area and storage area platforms can provide.

For example, if the user needs to create a data chain, which requires that a number of data-reading, -manipulating, and -writing processes occur, that functionality can be built into the workstation itself or can be off-loaded onto the bigger work area and storage platforms through the use of stored procedures and remote applications.

Workstation network and data-transport capabilities. The thorniest set of issues around workstations can be found in the area of connectivity. How will the workstation be connected to the warehouse? In the perfect world, the workstations will have connections that allow for real-time, shared-disk, and data-porting capabilities. In the real world, you might be forced to settle for less. At a minimum, each workstation must provide for real-time access via remote SQL capabilities.

The simple establishment of a connection between the workstation and the warehouse is not enough to guarantee success. You also must be concerned about the capacity that this linkage will support. A real-time connection between the warehouse and the workstation that provides for a 10-minute response time is not going to be very functional in most cases. Your workstation networking decisions therefore must include a robustness that will support the anticipated loads.

Remote access to the warehouse. It is becoming increasingly popular for developers to come up with data-warehousing solutions that provide for remote access to the warehouse. This remote access usually takes the form of a dial-in capability that allows sales people, customer-support personnel, and managers to make use of phone lines, radio linkages, or cellular networks to allow the user to get at the warehouse from anywhere at any time.

The capacity and network capability issues that we have considered up until this point take on an added importance when this is the type of environment being envisioned.

Homogeneous solutions. One of your principal drivers in any data-warehousing construction exercise is to try, at all costs, to minimize the complexity of the solution being developed. This is especially true in the area of workstations and connectivity. The more different types of user environments that you need to support, the more complex the corresponding physical infrastructure, operational infrastructure, and application characteristics become. The conflicting drives—one force driving you to simplify the architecture at all costs, one demanding that you minimize the expense, and another dictating that you maximize the flexibility and diversity of the solution for the users—leaves you with very difficult decisions to make.

Decision making

Therefore, your process of determining the best workstation (data access) physical infrastructure consists of the following decision points:

- Determine requirements—At this stage, you will want to identify each of the data-mining tools that are required in the environment and the workstation capacity that will be required. (This will include requirements for disk space, CPU power, and connectivity.)

- Evaluate current environment—Based upon these requirements, you then will want to turn to the environment itself and develop an inventory of exactly what kind of existing infrastructure is available.

- Develop compromises—Finally comes the hard part, where you compare the lists and develop a "gap analysis" that analyzes where the existing infrastructure falls short and specifies the cost/benefits involved in the upgrading/modifying of those situations.

Separating the storage area. So far, you have considered the issues involved in the utilization of multiple platforms for the support of the acquisitions component of the warehouse and for the access component. In some situations, this level of platform dispersion will be enough.

In some cases, however, you also will need to consider the possibility that the storage area and the corresponding staging and work areas also might be placed on multiple platforms.

While there are a lot of reasons for you to prefer that the storage area of the warehouse be a single-platform solution, there can be extenuating circumstances that make this impossible or undesirable. The reasons for choosing a multiple storage area configuration can have to do either with:

- Leveraging of existing platforms
- Establishment of scalability

Leveraging existing platforms. By far, the most common situation that people find themselves in is that there is an existing platform infrastructure already in place that can be used to easily meet some of the needs for the warehouse but that, for many reasons, the same platform might not have enough excess capacity available to use it for the delivery of the complete storage solution.

For example, an organization might have an existing mainframe environment within which some of the warehouse storage can be managed, but constraints within that environment make it impossible to use it for the complete solution. These constraints might come from disk space limitations, the financial inability to cost justify CPU upgrades, or the technical inability to upgrade the existing platform any higher. In these situations, it will be possible to complement the existing platform with another one, which then can be utilized to support the rest of the warehouse's storage needs.

Homogeneous versus heterogeneous solutions. When the decision is made to "split" the storage area across platforms, you introduce another set of complexity and management issues. Where will the control tables reside? How will the organization manage to coordinate the activities on each of the platforms? How will the organization provide technical support for both environments equally well?

These problems are not trivial and their solutions are very expensive. The decision to support different types of platforms at the heart of the warehouse is a decision to double the technical support staff and to more than double the complexity of the technical solution and corresponding management software.

Regardless of these problems, the multiplatform warehouse storage area is not only feasible, but it also can be incredibly cost-effective as well. If the people involved in the process of designing and managing the solution are aware of the complexities, costs, and risks involved and are able to address them effectively, then the solution is a viable one. (See Figure 8.14.)

Partitioning warehouse storage. When you begin looking at ways to keep different sections of the warehouse's storage on different platforms, you must address the issue of storage area partitioning. *Partitioning* is the term used to describe the process of breaking a database up into logical blocks. There are several partitioning approaches that will make sense.

Subject-area platforms. The first and most logical approach to separating different populations of data onto different platforms is to partition the data based on subject area. The term *subject area* is used to describe a logical grouping of data tables into logical/functional clusters.

For example, a typical data warehouse might have subject areas called Customer_Information, Product_Information, and Sales_History_Information. In this case, you might decide to keep Customer_Information and Sales_History_Information on one platform and place Product_Information on another.

User-access partitioning. Another good way to partition data is by who will use it. If it is possible to separate different collections of data that

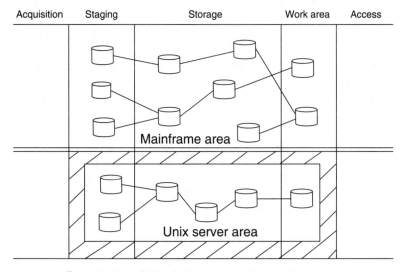

Figure 8.14 Example of a multiple-platform storage area.

different groups of users will need access to, then you can identify a "natural" breaking point for the partitioning decision.

History platforms. In many situations, it makes a lot of sense to store historical information on a different platform than the main warehouse storage. Historical data usually is accessed a lot less frequently than storage tables, and it usually involves extremely high volumes of data as well. Separating historical data out to a separate platform might be done even if the existing platform could handle it because, by separating it out, you make it possible to optimize each environment for the type of processing it will require.

Associating data from disparate platforms. While at first glance the decision to partition data across multiple platforms might seem like a very good idea, there are several reasons why it should be avoided. Along with the already considered complexity and management overhead, you also must determine how to allow users to associate data when part of it is on one platform and the other part is on a different platform.

Multidatabase joins. The principal means that users have to associate data from different tables will be via the SQL JOIN command. When an SQL command identifies data from two different tables, the database system takes care of finding it and associating it for the user.

Unfortunately, when you store data on multiple platforms, you make it difficult or even impossible for the system to provide that functionality depending upon the hardware platforms involved, the database software that each one will be running, and the network capabilities present.

In the best case, the decision to split the storage area across multiple CPUs will involve storing each of these partitions of data on a similar hardware platform running a similar database product. In these cases, there is a good chance that the selected database product will be able to take care of the crossplatform joining of data automatically.

For example, in the IBM mainframe environment, multiple mainframe-based DB2 databases can be forced to function as one logical database from the users' perspective through the use of the built-in distributed database capabilities. This facility ties each DB2 database on each mainframe to all of the other databases on the other mainframes. When the system is presented with an SQL command, it figures out where the data is and takes care of the crossplatform activities transparently.

In the same way, the major vendors of UNIX-based database products (Sybase, Informix, and Oracle) also have built-in crossplatform capabilities.

In those situations where the two platforms and databases involved are not totally synchronized, there still are some ways to make it usable. These techniques include:

- The use of middleware—*Middleware* is the name given to third-party software (software not provided by the hardware vendor or database vendor) that makes it possible to tie disparate systems together so that they function as one system from the user's perspective. Middleware can make two different hardware/database platforms look like one to the user.

- The construction of data chains—Another approach that users can take in this kind of environment is to construct data chains that extract the required data from each of the hardware environments and place the resulting sets into the work area. The users then can do their crosstable manipulation from that area. The execution of this type of approach assumes that data extraction and transportation linkages exist between the user workstation, the work area, and all storage area platforms.

- The replication of data—Probably the least popular of the solutions to this problem is for the managers of the warehouse to actually make copies of key data and store them on both platforms of the warehouse. In this case, the complexity and waste of disk resources can be quite limiting. However, in some situations, it provides the most viable solution.

When the multiple-platform replication approach is taken, it will be critical for developers to:

- Ascertain that no other approaches are viable

- Determine if the database products include any replication facilities that can make the job easier

- Determine that the data being replicated is the minimum required to get the job done

Upward scalability. The other reason for advocating a multiple-platform solution for the warehouse storage area was the need to establish scalability. *Scalability* is the built-in ability of the system to grow bigger or smaller as the demands for system resources change. To understand how the selection of a multiple-platform solution can provide you with a foundation for scalable solutions, you need to understand something about the ways in which computers can be upgraded.

Families of computers. When you first buy a computer system, you buy it with certain operational assumptions in mind. Based upon those assumptions, you will specify a certain amount of memory, processing power, and disk space. As your needs change, however, you are going to want to upgrade these decisions.

In the olden days of data processing, this upgrade process was a pretty expensive and complicated process. Now, for the most part, upgrading is accomplished through the simple replacement of chips or cards in the machine. Therefore, your first level of upgradeability is the ability to bump up the capacity of the given platform to whatever maximum it can handle.

Once you have maxed out the upgradeability of a given machine, your next option will be to go back to the manufacturer and see what "family" or "line" of computers your machine belongs to. Most manufacturers provide an upgrade migration path that makes it easy to switch from a lower-capacity machine to a higher one within the same family line. (See Figure 8.15.)

Why upgrade along the family line? The next question that someone might have is: "Why upgrade along the family line at all? Why not simply upgrade by changing to a different line of computers or by buying a bigger computer made by a different manufacturer?"

The answer to this question is simple. Every time you change the platform on which your databases and applications run, you must undergo the time and expense involved in converting it to the new environment. Despite the claims of "open systems" and "industry-wide compatibility," the fact of the matter is that any attempt to change platforms outside of the vendor-provided migration path is going to cost you big in the conversion department.

Therefore, your problem, when it comes to choosing platforms for the warehouse, is: "How do I choose a platform that will be big enough or upgradeable enough to anticipate all of my future needs?" The answer to this question is that you cannot.

Making platform decisions today is going to have consequences tomorrow, and the architects of the warehousing solution need to make these decisions based upon some expectations about how big the system might ultimately get.

Distributed architectures. An alternative approach to the direct upgrade of the warehouse-storage platform is to assume from the outset that the warehouse is going to be made up of multiple platforms. By choosing the archi-

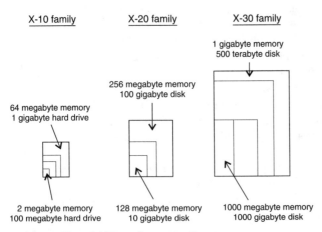

X-10 family   X-20 family   X-30 family

1 gigabyte memory
500 terabyte disk

256 megabyte memory
100 gigabyte disk

64 megabyte memory
1 gigabyte hard drive

2 megabyte memory
100 megabyte hard drive

128 megabyte memory
10 gigabyte disk

1000 megabyte memory
1000 gigabyte disk

Figure 8.15 Upgradability and computer lines.

tect and the warehouse around a multiple platform solution, you guarantee that it can be scaled up to however big you might happen to need it. Under this plan, you upgrade the system by adding more platforms.

Required characteristics for a multiple-platform warehouse. If you are going to choose to go with a multiple-platform architecture from the outset, then you are going to need to understand and make decisions about all of the problems that you considered earlier. How will the user effect multiplatform joins? How will you keep complexity to a minimum?

At this time, there are several vendors of hardware/database software solutions that make it possible to tie the systems together so that they function as one system from the users' perspective. While these products still are relatively new, their presence makes it feasible to consider basing a long-term architecture on this kind of multiplatform approach.

Separating the staging area. Your decisions about whether or not you want to partition the storage area notwithstanding, there also might be reasons to separate out the staging area from the main storage platform. The staging area, after all, is mostly an area used to simply hold data before it is loaded into the storage area. While it certainly is the most convenient to stage data on whatever storage platform it happens to be loading, it also is feasible to make use of the legacy platforms or acquisition platforms to hold the data.

What will be critical when deciding whether to stage data on the storage platform or not is to be sure that whatever alternative you consider, it will be easy and fast for the storage area to access and copy the data over.

The ideal situation is one where the staging area is made up of shared disk space that both the acquisition and storage platforms share. When this is not possible, it will be imperative that some kind of high-capacity data-porting capabilities exist.

Separating the workspace area. The only area of the warehouse that you have yet to consider for its own platforms is the workspace area. Here too, you might find good reasons to give this area its own platform to work from. The decision of whether or not to place the work area of the warehouse on a platform separate from the storage area is going to depend upon several things.

Your first consideration will be disk capacity. If the storage area is constrained for space, then the use of a separate platform for the work area certainly will be called for.

Of more pressing need, however, will be for you to consider exactly how much processing power is going to be associated with this area. If the environment that you are building is going to require that a large amount of processing be done (creating data chains, executing those chains, performing other kinds of reformatting or rearranging of data), then the CPU requirements of the storage area might well exceed those for the warehouse itself.

In general, the entire suite of issues revolving around the storage and transition of data from the storage area to the user can be viewed as having several alternative approaches, each of which makes use of the idiosyncrasies and capacities built into the storage, work area, and access areas.

Any nonbaseline data (all of the derived tables and data chains) can be constructed and stored within the storage area, the work area, on the user's own workstation, or making use of some combination of the three. (See Figure 8.16.)

In some situations, the users' need for customized data chains, and the storage of massive amounts of personal or limited share data, makes the need for dedicated work area platforms a necessity. In other situations, the users' needs can be met without the existence of any kind of work area at all. The creative utilization of the work area can greatly enhance the functionality and flexibility of the overall warehouse environment.

Tying in the work area. As soon as you decide to make the work area a separate platform, you once again greatly increase your complexity. A separate work-area platform must provide compatibility with the storage area and be able to function as an extension of that area, and it also must have all of the tie-ins to the access-area workstations.

Platform selection. Having completed the review of the different components of the warehouse and their relationships to platforms, you now can begin to consider the issues involved in selecting those platforms.

Before you risk making the mistake that so many theorists make in this area, let's begin by considering what people actually are doing today and planning to do in the future.

Sources of data. Recently, an independent survey was taken of a sampling of large corporate organizations regarding the issue of data warehous-

Scenario 1

	Storage	Work area	Access
Data storage:	80%	0%	20%
CPU:	90%	0%	10%

Scenario 2

	Storage	Work area	Access
Data storage:	50%	40%	10%
CPU:	60%	30%	10%

Scenario 3

	Storage	Work area	Access
Data storage:	40%	60%	0%
CPU:	60%	35%	5%

Figure 8.16 Leveraging the Storage, Work Area and Access Area platforms.

ing and future plans. That survey yielded some interesting results. The first question asked was: "What technologies (platforms) house the legacy system data that you anticipate loading into your warehouse?"

Their response:

- 25% of the data will come from mainframe DB2 systems.
- 21% will come from mainframe VSAM files.
- 33% will come from other mainframe sources.
- 21% will come from other sources.

In other words, the vast majority of legacy system environments will be mainframe based.

Target platforms. In the same survey, individuals were asked which platforms they intended to use for the storage component of the warehouse.

Their response:

- Over 50% plan on using UNIX-based client/server databases like Oracle, Informix, and Sybase.
- Over 25% plan on using DB2.
- The rest will make use of other technologies.

While these statistics do little to answer specific questions about what one should do in a given situation, it does provide some direction in terms of which way the industry seems to be going.

First of all, if you are planning on designing the acquisition component of your warehouse, then you will almost inevitably need to base that portion of the system in a mainframe environment. Because most of the data will be coming from mainframes, it will make sense to build your acquisitions component with that technology.

Second of all, when it comes to the platform for the storage component, you probably are going to have to make some tough decisions about:

- Whether to build it in a mainframe DB2 environment
- If you are going to build it in the UNIX environment, which UNIX database to go with

Both of these decisions are difficult but are critical to the success of the warehouse.

As far as helping you to make those individual decisions, all I can say is that we have spent this chapter clearly examining each of the issues and considerations that should be taken into account when making platform and infrastructure decisions. There is no way to make the process of weighing these issues any easier than to assure you that everyone must go through the process and to say that there is never only one right answer to any of the questions and that compromises are going to have to be made.

Conclusions

This marks the end of the process of examining each of the different layers and components that make up the data warehouse. We have defined them, analyzed them, and considered the trade-offs involved in making decisions in each of these areas.

Armed with this more intimate knowledge about the warehouse's makeup and structure, you now are ready to return to the issues of management, construction approaches, and cost-estimating techniques.

9

A Model for Overall Warehouse Planning

Equipped with a more detailed understanding of exactly what is going to be involved in the construction and running of the warehouse, you now are ready to return to the issue of how you are going to manage the overall warehouse-construction process.

So far, we have identified that your process will consist of two major phases: The first has to do with developing a common understanding of what the warehouse will be and a set of requirements for how it will be built. We call this the *overall warehouse-development project*. The second phase consists of the construction of a series of autonomous, value-based applications, each to be placed within the subsequent warehouse environment. (See Figure 9.1.)

The Overall Warehouse-Development Project

We then proceeded to define some of the individual steps within the warehouse development process. These included:

- Vision development
- Validation and estimation
- Warehouse planning
- Infrastructure development

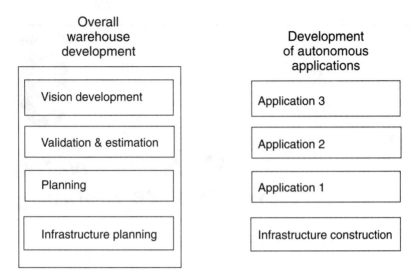

Figure 9.1 The two major phases of warehouse development.

Each of these steps in the process plays a critical role in the development of the overall warehouse solution, and none of the steps can be skipped or taken out of order. (See Figure 9.2.) Later, we will consider some of the ways in which variations to our proposed approach can be worked into the plan. For now, however, we will continue to describe the process as it would be executed in the ideal environment.

We'll begin by developing some understanding of what should happen within each of these steps and what the outputs from each should be.

Vision development

The objective of the vision-development step is to assist the organization in developing a consistent, realistic, and meaningful consensus about what the warehouse will be. The process that you will go through to develop that consensus will vary with the situation and environment, but the end result must be a vision statement, describing the warehouse's scope, intent, and characteristics and, most importantly, must include a collection of specific value propositions, each of which defines an autonomous, value-added function that the warehouse can deliver.

Therefore, the output of the process is:

- A meaningful definition of the warehouse
- Consensus

- A collection of well-defined and well-documented value propositions, each of which can be used as the starting point for the execution of a warehouse application development project

See Figure 9.3.

Validation and estimation

Using these value propositions as input and armed with the advocacy of all management, operational, and systems personnel that the solutions are desirable and valuable, your next step is to validate and estimate their costs.

At this stage, each of your value propositions will be little more than rough outlines of how people think things could work. During the validation step, you apply some rigor to them and ascertain whether they are financially, organizationally, and technically feasible. Most importantly, you will need to determine whether the proposed solutions actually will be financially feasible or not. When we say *financially feasible*, we mean that you must validate that:

- The organization can afford to build them
- The value that they will deliver will be greater than or at least equal to the cost

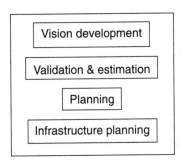

Figure 9.2 Steps in the overall warehouse development.

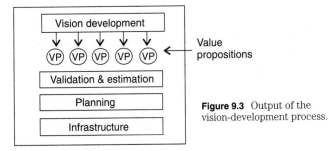

Figure 9.3 Output of the vision-development process.

When you attempt to validate these assumptions, you might encounter situations where there is no way to know whether they are feasible or not, unless you develop some good estimates as to the effort it will take to develop them and as to the technical resources that will be required to deliver them. Therefore, you will need to conduct the validation and estimation processes in tandem, each one feeding information to the other.

The output of the validation-and-estimation process will ensure that you have ascertained with a high degree of confidence that both the overall warehouse proposed and the individual applications therein can be delivered on time, on budget, and with the subsequent delivery of value to the organization. The physical deliverable is both a set of greatly enhanced value propositions, which now include a set of requirements for the applications to be built, and a set of specifications for the infrastructure of the warehouse itself. (See Figure 9.4.)

Planning

Once the feasibility of the overall warehouse and of the individual value propositions has been determined, you then can turn to the development of a plan to deliver the overall solution to the organization. The end product of the planning process will be several things:

- An overall plan for the construction of the warehouse
- Budget, timing, and delivery deadlines for each application
- A plan and budget for the construction of a physical and operational infrastructure

Infrastructure development

Once the plan has been proposed and accepted, you will want to develop the actual physical infrastructure that will support it. (See Figure 9.5.)

Variations

While it certainly would be your objective to see all warehousing projects proceed according to the structure in a nice, organized, serial series of steps to be executed, the reality is that, for a lot of different reasons, you are going to have to get creative in the way that you approach these projects in the real world.

The steps, phases, and processes that we have been describing are each critical components of a successful warehouse implementation, but the realities of business, finance, technology, and the corporate environment are going to force you to vary your plans to meet the needs of the situation.

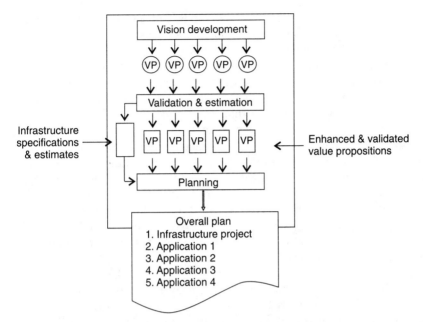

Figure 9.4 Validation, estimation, and planning.

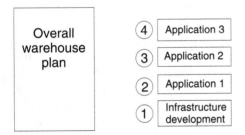

Figure 9.5 Execution of the warehouse plan.

When you look at this progression of steps and develop an understanding for exactly what is supposed to happen during each phase, it is clear that this is the order in which things should be done.

Variations under vision development

Obviously, you need to begin with a good vision of exactly what it is you are trying to build. During the process of vision development, you assemble that picture and enlist the aid and participation of all the parties that will benefit from the endeavor. Only through a rigorous and formally defined process of vision development can the builders of the warehouse hope to prevent all of the organizational misunderstandings and infighting that sabotage projects after development has begun.

We also have established that the objective of the vision development process should be the definition of tactically applicable value propositions. By basing your overall project plan on specific, attainable, and immediately beneficial pieces, you guarantee that the entire warehousing project will yield maximum benefit to the organization.

Unfortunately, sometimes, the environment that you are working in will not support this kind of overall vision-development initiative. Sometimes, upper management opts not to participate in the process, feeling that these are technical or operational issues and not worthy of their attention.

Other times, the environment is so laced with animosity and negativity based upon the history of relationships within the organization that you will be forced to function without the benefit of participation from people that would seem to be key to your success.

The question that you must answer when trying to work within situations like this is: "What is the definition of a minimally acceptable vision-development process?" Assuming that you cannot enlist the participation of everyone needed to do a good job, where do you draw the line and say that you have involved enough people?

The answer to this question really is pretty straightforward. The success of your warehousing project and of our vision development efforts must be viewed in terms of its scope and breadth. If the warehouse that you are developing is being proposed as a major corporate undertaking, if it is being put forward as a major strategic direction for the entire computer systems development area, if it is being proposed to involve the collection and dissemination across all organizational units of the corporation, then the vision-development phase must involve all of the key upper-management executives and the key management staff from each of the operational areas. There simply is no way around it. The budget requirements for a project of this size and the participation required from the people at all levels of management will be so high that, if you fail to get their participation during vision development, there is no way that you can expect them to "buy in" to the project at the later, more painful, and more expensive phases.

In a sense, the vision-development project is a thermometer, which allows the sponsors of the project to test the water—to see if the project will gain acceptance or not.

Many times data-warehousing initiatives are sponsored by the data-processing organization. In these cases, the ability or inability of the group to present the concept of the warehouse in the kinds of business terms that operational and upper-management personnel will respond to will be a good acid test of the overall approach. If your warehouse initiative is one based upon technical sophistication and upon the simplification of the operational data-processing environment, then who will care other than data-processing people? If on the other hand, the warehouse is presented and perceived as the means to quickly deliver valuable capabilities into the hands of operational and managerial personnel, then the reception will be much warmer.

Limiting scope

Within many organizations, it will not make sense to approach warehousing projects in such a grandiose manner. If the receptivity on the part of upper management or certain operational areas is not there, then the proponents of the approach will need to lower their sights a little bit and come at the problem from a much humbler perspective.

In these cases, the developers of the warehouse will need to identify specific operational areas within the organization that have needs that the data warehouse can meet and have the predisposition to get involved in the process. By limiting the initial scope of the vision-development process to include only those areas that will benefit immediately from the effort, the project advocates greatly increase their chances of success.

The long-term strategy might be to roll out a limited scope project to prove to people what the warehousing concept can accomplish, then to approach the more grandiose overall corporate direction.

The single-application warehouse

At the low end of the scope spectrum are those situations where it is decided to build only one specific, discrete application, making use of the warehousing approach, in the hopes that the results will gain the interest and trust of a bigger group of users.

In all cases, what is critical is that you define the scope of the project (in terms of the operational groups to be supported and the functional areas to be addressed), then ensure that the vision development process is executed for that group. Vision development is not an optional step.

Variations in application development

The second area where you already have developed a well-defined set of steps to follow is in the area of application development. Chapter 3 laid out the progression of steps that you will need to go through to deliver an application in the most efficient way possible. The data-discipline process does not correspond too well with the accepted industry practice of using data-driven design and data modeling as the core of systems development. It probably most closely aligns with a general understanding of the RAD approach (rapid application development). RAD, like our data disciplines, advocates the streamlined, minimalist focusing of your efforts on the delivery of small, tactical relevant applications in the shortest time possible.

The fact that the "old-school," data-driven approaches were conceived over 20 years ago and were developed specifically to support the development of databased, online transaction processing systems is immaterial. The fact is that it simply is "the way things are done" for many organizations.

Recognizing this fact, we allow for the variation of our data-discipline approach. We do this for two reasons.

First, we do it to take advantage of whatever work organizations might have done already that might make the process of application development easier. Existing enterprise models, data models, and data analysis certainly cannot hurt the effort, and they actually can contribute greatly, as long as they accept the shift in focus that you require, namely, the shift towards the more practical, tactical, and immediate needs of the users of the warehouse as opposed to the more general overall needs of the organization as a whole.

Second, we will incorporate the data-driven approaches to help increase the comfort level of the people involved in the development process and to leverage existing skills as much as possible.

Data-Driven Data Disciplines

My proposal for the blending of the traditional data-driven approach and our newly proposed data-discipline approach will involve starting with the data models. Under this variation, we will add several data-modeling steps to the beginning of the procedure:

1. Identify the data required to support each value proposition.
2. Develop subject-area models to support each value proposition.
3. Develop an inventory of principal entities for each subject area.
4. Develop an integrated key structure for each.
5. Consolidate subject-area models into a overall warehouse model.
6. Instigate the previously detailed data-discipline process.

After this data analysis has been completed, you then can proceed with the previously described steps.

There actually are some advantages to this kind of approach, and in some cases, you might decide to append this process to your project plan whether the people involved require it or not. By doing this kind of data-modeling work up front, you certainly will make the rest of the application-development process easier. The development of these subject area and entity models can only serve to help people understand the business areas that they are working with, and the early attack of key issues certainly will prevent problems in the future. We also will identify an additional place where this kind of preliminary research and set-up work can be helpful when we consider the validation and estimation processes.

While the developers of a warehouse application do not absolutely require this kind of preliminary data-modeling effort, it certainly can be helpful. If data-modeling work that pertains to the application already has been done, it should be leveraged wherever possible.

At this point, we want to emphasize that the level of data-modeling activity that we propose at the beginning of this process is very rudimentary and shallow in nature. Under no circumstances should any warehouse-development resources be spent in the development of detailed entity-attribution processes. There is no way that the appropriate identification of specific data elements for the warehouse can occur without a great deal of information about the data-mining tools being utilized and the needs of the users taken into account.

It is here—in the area of when, where, and how detailed data attribution should occur—that we vehemently resist the premature application of data-modeling efforts. Experience with hundreds of data-modeling projects has proven one thing beyond a shadow of a doubt: People that go off and develop attribution information, without knowledge of the applications that will use it, end up going through the process twice—once on their own and again when the needs of the application become known. While there certainly is some small amount of benefit that can be gained from the research and development effort done ahead of time, the amount of information that can be carried forward usually is minimal.

This usually is not due to the abilities of the people doing the modeling; it simply is a function of the very specific needs for data that most applications have and the realities of where data actually is going to come from. The development of a theoretically sound database schema that doesn't hold the information in the form that users want it is useless, as is a schema that identifies data that cannot be located.

Other than the subject that we have just considered, there really are no other places in the data-discipline process where you can get away with much variation. Any attempt to shortcut or skip these steps is going to result in a major disconnect in the ultimate delivery of the application.

The blending of steps

So far, we have considered variation in the vision development and the application development processes, but we have said nothing about making changes to the validation and planning or the infrastructure-development steps. That is because it is in these areas that the most drastic, and often fatal, kinds of variations occur. It also is because we have yet to actually describe the validation and planning steps in any kind of detail.

We have postponed our discussion of these processes for several reasons, but the biggest is that, until you describe the rest of the environment within which you would be working, it would be too difficult to explain how it fits in. The other reason is that the variations that can be, and often are, utilized can make the whole discussion very confusing.

The biggest temptation in the development of any large, expensive, and complicated system like this is to look for shortcuts and ways to leverage the efforts of one stage to make the next easier. We will address each of these temptations.

Other variations within application development

Of course, our consideration of ways in which the application development process can be varied does little to address the vast majority of variations that people traditionally apply to the process. The assumptions that we make when we talk about application development are that:

- The organization has gone through the vision-development process, and the application has been defined as being tied to a specific, narrowly defined value proposition.
- The system has been carried through the corresponding validation and estimation steps.
- The physical and operational infrastructures already are in place.
- The application developers can concentrate on the task of building this one focused application.

The real variation in the process that you need to worry about are those cases where people fail to carry their project through these steps, in this order. What is more typical of the application-development process is that people try to accomplish vision development, validation, estimation, and infrastructure development at the same time that they are doing the development of the application itself. These attempts to cut corners invariably lead to complexity, confusion, waste, and in some cases utter failure.

However, we live in a real world, and there are good reasons for trying to blend these steps together. In chapter 10, we will consider some of these situations and see how you can include this kind of variability into your planning process without allowing it to get out of hand.

Shortcuts

Unfortunately, there is absolutely no such thing as a shortcut when it comes to warehouse development. There certainly are a large number of people claiming to know how to do shortcuts. There are even vendors of products that claim to be able to sell you shortcuts. However, the reality has been proven again and again that shortcuts have only three potential outcomes:

- They cause you to underestimate or skip key steps in the process.

- They cause you to underestimate the cost and level of effort necessary to complete the project.

- They build "traps" into your project that can and will be "sprung" by someone, somewhere along the line.

Types of shortcuts

Shortcuts in validation. There all kinds of ways that people delude themselves into thinking that there is a way to get around the work that must be done to do a good job of warehouse development. In the area of validation, people often try to minimize or dismiss problems found in the business area.

Developing an understanding of the business issues. Many times, people assume that, if the business solution sounds like it makes sense, everyone simply will agree and go along with it. It is critical that all operational areas involved have the opportunity to truly understand what the solution proposes and validate that it can be done. Many times, organizational issues, budgeting constraints, time factors, or business procedures can invalidate otherwise sound business plans.

Developing strong advocacy and support from operational and management areas. The second area where developers get themselves into trouble is to minimize the need to have advocacy from the operational and management areas. *The solution is so good*, they think, *that surely everyone will go along with us. We'll just get started, and they'll see the light.* This is the kind of thinking that gets projects in trouble.

Validating the existence of the required data. A critical business assumption that must be addressed is the assumption that all of the data that is needed can be found somewhere. Somehow, these assumptions must be validated.

Validating the effectiveness of a data-mining tool. Another situation where business users can set themselves up occurs when people become enamored with data-mining tools before finding out the details about how they work, what it will take to make them work, and what it will take for the users to make use of them.

Validating that the proposed technical solution actually will work. It is appalling how many computer systems projects get proposed and budgeted, where the technical staff has no way of knowing whether the proposed solution actually can work or not. Assumptions about the volumes of data to be handled, the capacity of the hardware, the nature of the network environment, and the validity of vendor claims have created a great many situations where projects were undertaken only to be abandoned late in the process because somebody's assumptions were incorrect.

Validating the technical solution proposed can be delivered on time or on budget. The other place where technical assumptions usually are far out of touch with reality comes in the area of the estimation of the person effort required to bring a system to completion. The data-processing industry is notorious for the underestimation of timing and the overestimation of the abilities of staff to work with complex new technological approaches.

All in all, the validation process that we will be defining shortly must be followed vigorously if the rest of the planning and execution process is going to be valid.

Shortcuts in estimation. Right in line with the use of shortcut assumptions to skip timely validation steps is the slip-shod manner in which most organizations perform the estimation process. This process involves developing estimates for hardware, software, systems development, user participation, and overall budget dollars as well as timing.

We also will spend a significant amount of time analyzing the estimation process in greater detail in chapter 10.

Shortcuts in planning. The process that many people go through when planning systems development projects actually is quite amazing. Some spend no more than 15 minutes discussing what to do next, then tell everyone to get started! Others spend days and weeks in the creation of Gantt charts and project plans that ultimately turn into nothing more than footnotes to the real systems-development process.

Somehow, you need to define a project-planning mechanism that prevents people from skipping this step, while avoiding becoming a career unto itself.

By providing everyone with a physical and organizational framework for the development of a warehouse, you already have taken some big steps in this direction. In this chapter and the next, we will complete the picture and provide a more comprehensive approach to the process.

Shortcuts in data disciplines. We already have spent a considerable amount of time documenting and explaining the many ways that people try to get around having to do the tedious process of data identification, sourcing, mapping, and synchronization. As with the other phases of the development process, any attempts to avoid these steps simply lead to problems in the future.

Shortcuts in infrastructure development. Of all of the areas of shortcutting, the tales and woes of organizations that have underestimated the complexity and expense of infrastructure development are the most legion of all. In case after case, people have dismissed infrastructure development as a trivial or automatic process and have paid the price.

Major variations. Given the premise that there are a lot of bad reasons for trying to shortcut the warehouse-development process and given that, by allowing shortcuts and variations to occur, you often can get into trouble, you nonetheless must accept that reality does not always correspond with your wishes. Therefore, you must establish some criteria for determining what kinds of variations should be permissible and under what conditions they should be allowed.

The variances that we have been considering up until now are relatively minor in nature and will not change your overall plan to any great degree. The overall sequence of events for the warehouse development that we have laid out as the perfect execution plan would be as follows (Figure 9.6):

- Overall warehouse development:
  1. Vision development
  2. Validation and estimation of the warehouse
  3. Planning for the overall warehouse
  4. Development of the infrastructure

- Project approval:
  5. Project approval and budgeting

- System development:
  6. Construction of the infrastructure
  7. Construction of individual applications

There are three major areas of variance in this proposed approach that you are going to have to deal with head-on. While it is clear that there are certain steps that simply cannot be skipped if you are going to succeed, in the following areas, there is a strong likelihood that, if you cannot come up with some kind of alternative solution, you are going to condemn the project to budgetary obscurity before you even get started.

Attempts to minimize the planning costs and time: Variance in the overall warehouse development project. Many of the examples cited previously were examples of ways in which people attempt to shortcut critical planning and estimating steps to move the project forward. While we cannot condone the skipping of these steps or any attempts to execute them in a different order, we realize

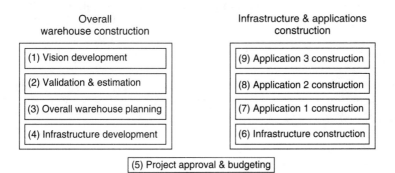

Figure 9.6 "Normal" sequence of events.

that there might be times when the formal execution of these steps would be redundant. Many times, you will find that different people already have accomplished a lot of the objectives of the planning and estimation steps.

For example, in some organizations, there already might have been a great deal of thought and planning put into the development of a warehouse vision. You also might find that certain value propositions are so simple, easy to do, and so clear-cut that very little work needs to be done to accumulate and document them.

In other cases, validation and estimation might be trivial processes because the proposed solutions are so easy to deliver and involve no exceptional volumes of data, system complexities, or problems with source-data identification. For example, a system that is designed to pull data from a purchased list and provide *ad hoc* access to it will be relatively easy to turn into a proposition, and the requirements determination process will be practically completed before you start.

Basically, the criteria for the minimization of any of the steps in the process will be simple: You can skip the work involved, but you cannot skip the deliverables. Each step in the process has a set of documented deliverables that communicates things about the system to the readers and developers of the system. Failure to spend a lot of time analyzing is not a problem. Failure to thoroughly document assumptions and gain consensus among all of the parties involved is a sure road to ruin.

The need to ameliorate the up front infrastructure costs: Variance in infrastructure development (incremental infrastructure building). The second area where there will be a lot of resistance to the approach proposed is our insistence that the infrastructure, both physical and operational, be put into place before the development of actual applications begins. The accepted way of building systems is to develop the infrastructure while you develop the application. Actually, this is the perceived truth, not the reality. The reality is that, when the systems-development life-cycle methodologies and procedures were being developed, there were no major infrastructure issues to deal with. Applications were built on platforms that were stable and that had known parameters for capacity, management, and development. The problem these days is that the builders of applications try to minimize the tremendous amount of work involved in the establishment of these new infrastructure environments.

If you are unable to get the funding for infrastructure development up front, then your only other option is to proceed with a scalable infrastructure architecture and attempt to build it up over time.

This approach actually can be not as bad as it first might seem if it is handled correctly:

- Scale up the storage component by making use of scalable database/ platform architectures, such as distributed database mechanisms and middleware.

- Scale up the access component by rolling out the physical terminal and network components only to users that need them at each stage.

- Scale up the acquisitions component by continuing to upgrade the acquisitions platforms and capability as the size of the component grows.

In all three cases, it is essential that you determine how to scale the infrastructures development so that applications gaining the enhancement are paying only for what they need.

You can greatly enhance your chances of making use of a scalability approach to infrastructure development if you determine the following at the outset:

- The current, intermediate, and ultimate makeup of the acquisition, storage, and access components.

- Wherever possible, dictate hardware, software, standards, and procedures compatibility at the outset.

- Keep long-range objectives in mind while building each layer of the system.

The long-term efficiency of the effort can be reduced by this approach, and the complexity certainly will be increased, but adherence to goals, objectives, and decisions made at the beginning of the process will greatly enhance the chance for final success. (See Figures 9.7 and 9.8.)

The need to resolve validation or estimation problems: Proof of concept projects, prototypes and benchmarks. By far, the most challenging situation that requires you to vary your approach is when you are unable to validate or estimate the overall construction effort due to insufficient information. There are several ways this occurs. You might be unsure:

- About how the end users need the final application to function.

- That proposed hardware or software can handle the volumes, access rates, or complexity of processing.

- About what the development effort for a proposed application actually will be. This is prevalent when many untested technology or business assumptions are in play.

- That the proposed solution actually can work.

- That the desired data can be located.

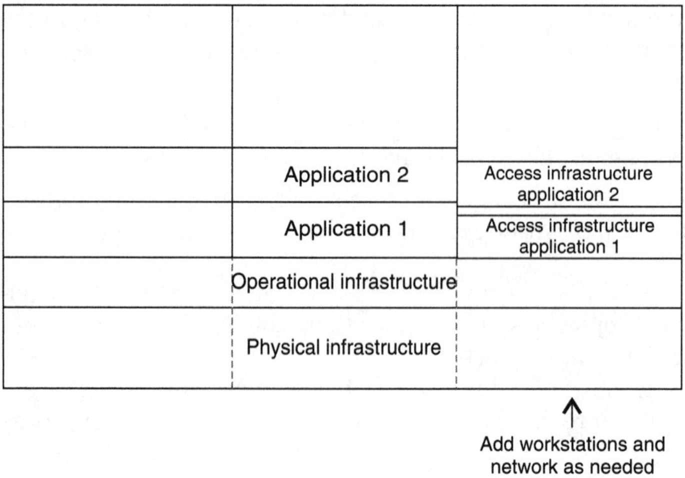

	Application 2	Access infrastructure application 2
	Application 1	Access infrastructure application 1
	Operational infrastructure	
	Physical infrastructure	

↑
Add workstations and
network as needed

Figure 9.7 Scalable infrastructure (access component).

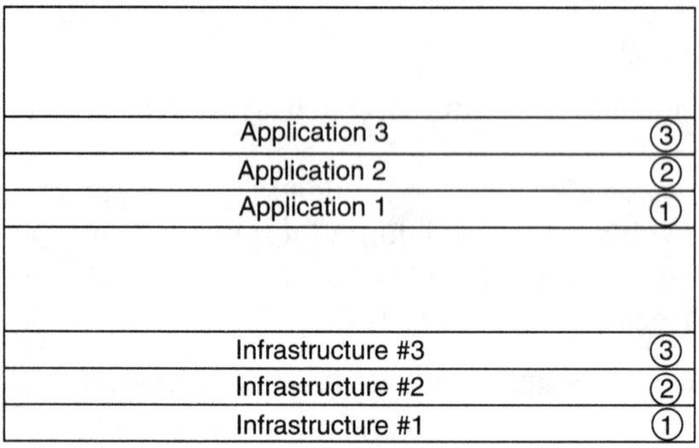

Application 3	③
Application 2	②
Application 1	①
Infrastructure #3	③
Infrastructure #2	②
Infrastructure #1	①

Figure 9.8 Scalable overall infrastructure.

When these kinds of situations occur, you have only two choices:

- Make up some numbers and blindly proceed with the rest of your development steps, hoping that somehow your guesses are good.
- Create nonconventional development techniques to help resolve these problems for the good of the overall project.

While all of the techniques that we are about to consider can provide great value to the overall warehouse development effort, it is important to establish several ground rules for their use at the outset. The problem is that these solutions tend to become real projects in the minds of the people who sponsor them. When this happens and you attempt to skip all intermediate steps and just start construction, you usually end up with trouble. Because the utilization of these techniques is expensive and time-consuming and because they yield no real value in and of themselves, there is a strong tendency to pretend that they are more than they really are, just to get them approved.

It also is critical that you minimize fantasies about leveraging the work that you can count on from the execution of these kinds of alternative approaches. You should not be deluded into thinking that a heavy investment in benchmarks and prototypes or proof of concept projects will drastically reduce the cost of real systems development. The way that these projects often are sold is that the development work can be reused in the ultimate system. This kind of double-think causes nothing but inaccuracy and disappointment. If you knew what was going to happen when you instigated a benchmark, prototype, pilot, or proof-of-concept project, then you would not start them in the first place; you simply would begin with normal construction. You sponsor projects of this type when you need to discover things about the system that you do not already know. These projects are not simple assumption validations; they are experiments and fact-finding missions that provide you with the information to successfully estimate and build the real system.

When these kinds of projects are worked into your project plan, they need to be identified as separate projects in your overall project plan. You should not replace any real projects (infrastructure or application) with these alternatives, and you should not drastically reduce your estimates of the effort that subsequent projects will take.

Even more importantly, if the point of the project is to determine the ultimate development effort, then you need to make it clear that no estimates of overall effort will be forthcoming until after they are completed.

For each of the alternative approaches, we will consider:

- What they are
- What they should be used for
- What their deliverables should be

Benchmarks. A *benchmark project* is designed to ascertain whether a targeted combination of hardware and software can meet the anticipated workload created by a warehouse system. Benchmarks are narrow in scope and are utilized to test assumptions about the ability of a proposed system to perform well under anticipated conditions. They usually are associated with the storage component of the warehouse.

You should make use of a benchmark whenever you are unsure of the capabilities of the hardware or software that you propose. They most often are used to validate:

- The ability of the database storage area to support the volumes and loads anticipated

- The ability of the access component networking structure to handle anticipated traffic

The deliverable from the process should be an identification of suitable hardware and software for the subsequent project and accurate cost estimates for each.

Prototypes. Prototypes usually are proposed to resolve questions about whether analysts are unsure about the assumptions that have been made regarding how the system should work or behave. A *prototype* is a scaled-down working model of the real thing. Therefore, prototypes usually consist of mockups of the screens that the ultimate system will utilize, loaded in small samples of the types of data that it will manage. These usually are associated with the access component of the warehouse.

Therefore, a prototype has an entirely different objective than a benchmark. While a benchmark answers questions about technical capacity of the overall warehouse environment, prototypes answer questions about functional and operational feasibility of a specific application. Because a prototype is a mockup and not a real system, it can be instrumental in helping people visualize solutions.

Under no circumstances should people assume that the screens and functionalities of a prototype are investments in the ultimate application. The shortcut methods used to develop these components quickly make them usable only as guidelines for the real thing.

When an artist makes a miniature prototype of a sculpture or when an engineer makes a prototype of a bridge, he or she does not try to use those prototypes as part of the real objects. He or she simply uses them as examples of how the real objects should look and behave.

In summary, the output of a prototype process is a collection of screens with a minimal functionality.

Proof-of-concept projects. *Proof-of-concept projects* are defined to help substantiate a collection of assumptions that have been made about systems development that cannot be validated without more hard proof. Proof-of-concept projects usually are much larger than benchmark or prototype efforts and actually begin to work with at least some of the components of the real warehouse environment.

A proof-of-concept project often will be a combination benchmark and prototyping effort, but it also can be developed to test even larger feasibility issues. For example, you cannot ascertain how difficult it will be to identify data in source systems and transport it through cleansing, formatting, staging, loading, and access with either a benchmark or a prototype. The biggest difference between them is that the other two test singular components of functionalities of the warehouse, while a proof-of-concept project tests end-to-end functionalities.

When you begin talking about proof-of-concept projects, you enter an area where it can become exceedingly difficult to avoid the "and then we can leverage it all to minimize construction costs" trap. Proof-of-concept projects are stripped-down versions of real applications, developed in a manner that allows developers to test critical assumptions awaiting validation. For example, you might develop a proof-of-concept project to validate whether the keys for the data required by a data-mining application can be identified and exported to the access area.

You also might develop a proof-of-concept project to validate your ability to interconnect a collection of legacy, warehouse, and access components. In all cases, the output of a proof-of-concept project is a set of loosely defined working code that performs some key functions required of the warehouse, but without all the detail to make it truly usable.

Adding alternative projects to your planning process. As you can see, based upon the objectives for each of these types of projects, they need to be included at a different point in our project execution process.

The benchmark tests, because they are executed to test the overall ability of the warehouse to perform, need to be executed as a part of the validation and estimation process for the overall warehouse project. (See Figure 9.9.)

However, pilot and proof-of-concept projects have to do with the validation of assumptions about specific applications. They should be executed only after the overall warehouse plan has been approved and after the infrastructure has been developed. Then they can be developed, and you can learn from them before discarding them. (See Figure 9.10.)

Pilot projects. A *pilot project* is designed to deliver a fully functional part of an overall application. As such, it will be treated and developed as any other application would, except that its scope has been drastically reduced. The deliverable from a pilot project is a fully functional part of an application.

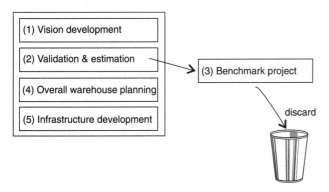

Figure 9.9 Adding benchmarks to the plan.

Unlike the other types of projects considered, the pilot project is not discarded. A pilot project is nothing more than a scaled-down component of an overall application. Therefore, when planning for its utilization, you include it as part of the cost of developing the application it "pilots" for. (See Figure 9.11.)

Rapid application development. The last type of variance to application development that we will consider is a relatively new approach to development called *RAD*, or *rapid application development*. Under RAD, developers approach application development as an iterative process, where they move quickly between prototyping, construction, delivery, and back again. The cycle is repeated until the application is complete. RAD has strength to it and approaches some of the problems that we have been addressing in the same manner.

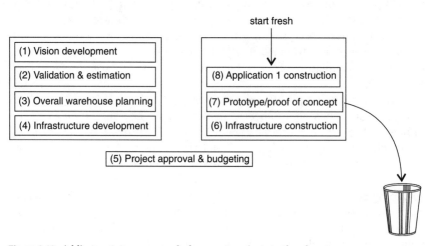

Figure 9.10 Adding prototype or proof-of-concept projects to the plan.

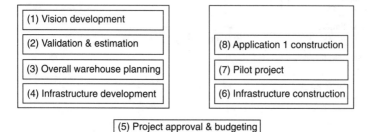

Figure 9.11 Adding a pilot project to the plan.

Experience has shown that the RAD approach will work well, if and only if, the infrastructure environment is stable and the objectives of the development effort are clearly defined. There should be no disharmony between the approach that we propose and a RAD approach, as long as all aspects of the data disciplines that we have identified are considered in the process.

Conclusions

Throughout this chapter, we have concentrated on presenting the reader with an overview of some of the challenges involved in the planning of the overall warehouse and some of the ways that variations can and will occur. In subsequent chapters, we will be zeroing in on the vision development, validation, and estimation steps in more detail. We then will be able to return to a more in-depth discussion of the planning, management, staffing, and budgeting processes.

10

Vision, Value, and Focus
The Vision Development Phase

We are ready to start formally defining the first of the phases: vision development. In chapter 5, we presented a diagram that provided a picture of what the vision-development process should look like, and we began the process of fleshing out the details of how the process would work. We now are ready to complete this picture so that you can come to a full understanding of how this process can work. (See Figure 10.1.)

The Vision-Development Process: An Overview

You can break down the vision-development process into the following two stages:

- Start with the collection of the different ideas and visions that each of the individuals involved in the warehouse development process might hold.

- Then analyze this collection and distill from it a collection of specific, well-defined value propositions.

After this is completed, you can proceed with the validation, estimation, and planning steps, which will allow you to assemble and organize these value propositions into a strategy for warehouse deployment.

This approach starts at the earliest phases of a proposed warehouse's life cycle. The assumption is that, for any given organization that is in the process of considering a warehouse, the people involved in all areas of the business,

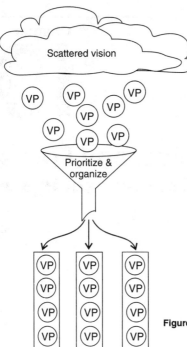

Figure 10.1 The vision-development process.

management, operations, and systems perceive the warehouse in a different way. Each will approach the project making a different set of assumptions about what the warehouse is supposed to do and how it will be cost justified.

Getting a Clearer Picture of the Warehouse

Your first job is to talk to the people involved in all areas of the business who are interested in using the warehouse to help them determine what they would like to see the warehouse provide and how they view its potential value. The process of collecting and analyzing these proposals can be very informative.

My experience, based on conducting hundreds of interviews of this type, has enabled me to identify certain thought patterns that most people apply to the warehousing issue.

Specific phases of the vision-development and the validation-and-planning processes

We will call this process of gathering up everyone's visions and developing a common vision of the warehouse the *vision-development process*. We will call the process of validating the practicality of these approaches and the development of estimates for delivery and the development of plans the *validation-and-planning process.* These processes can be conducted by an internal computer systems group, an operational area, or an outside consulting firm that specializes in this kind of activity. No matter who does it, the process involves interviewing all of the people who might be involved in the warehouse-development process.

The vision-development steps include:

1. Collecting the visions—Your first task is to interview everyone who has expressed an interest in the warehouse (or anyone that you suspect might benefit from the warehouse) and determine their vision of how the warehouse could help them.

2. Evaluating the visions—Your next step is to evaluate each of these visions for their scope, focus, and hardness or softness. During this phase, you will begin to understand what each vision really is about and what the underlying objectives might be.

3. Decomposing the visions—After evaluating each vision, you begin the process of decomposition. During this phase, you will attempt to break the larger, less-focused, and broader-scoped visions into a collection of smaller, more tangible ones. Any large vision should be able to be decomposed into a collection of smaller ones.

4. Verify the decomposition—After decomposing the visions, you can return to the people who originally provided them to ensure that the decompositions and valuations make sense and that the solutions defined are practical and desirable.

5. Recruiting of sponsors—After the verification stage, you are left with a collection of well-defined, narrowly scoped candidate applications. You can take each of these candidate applications and identify the business areas that would be willing to sponsor them. In the vast majority of cases, the identification of sponsors is easy. However, the willingness of the sponsors to lay claim to them might be more difficult. Once a sponsor has been identified, the candidate application becomes a proposition for systems development.

6. Determination of hard benefits—The first thing that the sponsor of the application will be asked to do is verify and assign hard benefits to the effort. In other words, the sponsor is asked to state that, should this application be delivered, the following benefits would accrue.

After you have determined the benefits associated with these propositions, you are ready to begin validating them and developing a plan. This includes:

1. Determination of reasonableness and cost estimates—After the assignment of hard benefits, the evaluation team needs to develop rough estimates of the cost of delivering the solution for each proposition.

2. Development of formal value-proposition statements—By combining your hard benefits estimate with cost estimates, you can define value propositions. A value proposition proposes that a certain type of system should be developed. It further details the cost of delivery and what the benefits of the effort will be.

3. Consolidation of value propositions—After the solidification of each of your value propositions, you can look at all of the value propositions that have been developed and determine the overlap, consolidation, integration, or sequencing requirements that you might have. Remember, warehouse applications must be developed either autonomously, or serially.

4. Development of deployment strategy—Finally, an overall strategy for warehouse development is assembled.

Roles and Responsibilities

If the previously described process is going to be successful, you have to make assumptions about the various roles of the different participants in the process, along with a corresponding set of expectations about the level of their commitment. To successfully implement this process, you are going to need the participation of individuals from three groups:

- Management
- The operational area being considered
- Systems

The first question that anyone would ask when getting ready to set up a team to tackle this process will naturally be, "Who is responsible for driving this process?" As we have noted previously, one of the biggest sources of problems in the development of requirements for systems is that no one seems sure of their role.

Therefore, you will propose an allocation of resources that seems most logical. If the situation at hand forces some variance of this proposal, it certainly does not mean that the project will fail. This allocation simply makes the most sense for the majority of cases.

Because it makes the most sense that the computer systems area (or specialized consultants) will drive the process, then it will fall upon them to be responsible for ensuring that everyone else is aware of what is expected of them.

Allocation of roles by steps

I have prepared Table 10.1 to indicate whose participation should be required for each step and what their level of commitment should be.

TABLE 10.1 Vision-Development Participation

Step	Description	Management	Operational	Systems
	Vision development			
1	Collecting the visions	Light	Medium	Heavy
2	Evaluating the visions	—	—	Heavy
3	Decomposing the visions	Light	Medium	Heavy
4	Verify the decomposition	—	Light	Heavy
5	Recruiting of sponsors	Light	Medium	Heavy
6	Determination of hard benefits	—	Heavy	Heavy
	Validation and planning			
7	Determination of reasonableness and cost estimates	—	Medium	Heavy
8	Development of value propositions	—	Light	Heavy
9	Consolidation of value propositions	—	—	Heavy
10	Development of deployment strategy	Light	Medium	Heavy

TABLE 10.2 Development Rules

Rule number	Description
1	*Contiguity*—Each application must include an acquisition, storage, and access component.
2	*Business focus and decomposition*—Each application must be based upon a specific value proposition.
3	*Serial development of dependent applications*—Applications that are dependent upon the components of another application must be developed one at a time.
4	*Parallel development for autonomous applications*—It is permissible to build applications simultaneously, as long as they have no dependencies.

Correspondence to the application rules

In chapter 5, we introduced the concept of the data-warehouse "application." We said the data warehouse, like the real-world warehouse to which we compared it, was nothing more than an empty framework, which you could utilize to store and access data. We further stated that you needed to segregate the different inventories of data within that warehouse into discrete applications. We then proceeded to propose a series of rules about how those applications were going to be defined. (See Table 10.2.)

It is critical that the individuals involved in the process of vision development are aware of the previously mentioned rules and their consequences for the overall vision identification and analysis process. In addition to these general directives, we also defined certain characteristics that you must require each of these value propositions to include. (See Table 10.3.)

TABLE 10.3 Value-Proposition Rules

2a	Every value proposition must be based upon a specific business need.
2b	Every value proposition must have a single, responsible business sponsor.
2c	Each value proposition must define a tangible benefit to the sponsoring organization.

Correspondence to the real warehouse decision-making process

Before you try to begin the development of a warehouse plan, you need to interview all of the parties who have stood up and said, "I think it would be a good idea." There is a big difference between a person saying that it sounds like a good idea and someone saying, "If you could provide me with this functionality for this cost, we could deliver this benefit."

After you get past the initial flush of excitement and enthusiasm for a warehousing project, you often find that there is little substance behind the apparent momentum.

Wouldn't it be lovely?   By far, the most common response that you get from people when discussing data-warehousing solutions is that there are an almost infinite number of "neat things" that they could do if the warehouse were in place. For example, I was helping a manufacturing company to create a customer-information warehouse. This system was designed to reconcile all of the different names, addresses, and customer information into one central location.

People's immediate responses to this project were overwhelmingly positive. Yes, having this information in an accurate, usable, easy-to-access form would be fantastic. Everyone thought that it would be a good idea, and the project was approved.

Unfortunately, when I was well into the project, people started to ask, "What will we do with this information now that we have it?" When this question was asked, the answers were far from what they expected, and the project was abandoned.

The problem was that I asked the wrong question! Everyone thinks that something is a good idea if:

- It provides them with something that they do not have.

- It doesn't cost them anything.

It is a very different story when they are made aware of the costs of those benefits.

The question that I should have asked at the onset of the project was not "Would you like to have . . .?" but rather "How would you make use of . . .?" If the latter question were asked, I could have determined the real value of the effort.

Great for somebody else. When you ask people the "How would you make use of . . .?" question, the next thing that they usually say is that they would like to have it because it would be nice to have. However, more importantly, some other department would benefit greatly from such a marvelous tool. This "somebody else's solution" diversion enables these individuals to defocus from their own operational environment and envision the warehouse as somebody else's problem.

In one case, I was called in to help a large financial institution with their data-warehousing plans. The sponsors of the project were convinced that everyone thought it was a good idea. I agreed to help them with this "visioning phase." A team of four analysts spent five days each interviewing dozens of business area advocates for the warehousing solution.

Unfortunately, by the time they finished, not one business person had stood up and said, "If you were to provide me with this solution, it would yield this benefit." Everyone wanted it, but everyone thought someone else could use it. No one was willing to take ownership of it.

Costs of solutions. When you begin the process of validating people's assumptions about what the warehouse will provide, there is an overriding tendency towards optimism. What people do not realize is that everything has a cost and that most things that involve a warehouse involve a lot of costs in a lot of areas.

Financial costs. The easiest thing for people to accept about the construction of a warehouse, or a specific warehouse application, is that some kind of financial investment is going to have to be made. Unfortunately, the concept of the warehouse usually is presented in such a way that people are led to believe that the vast benefits of the warehouse will greatly outweigh those physical costs or that somehow someone else is going to pay for it.

Time costs. Another cost that many operational and management areas overlook is the time that the development of a warehouse will require. The systems staff paints a picture of what the warehouse will do and asks for funding. In many cases, the operational and management areas will assume that, once the funding is approved, their cost is covered. The reality is that management and operational personnel need to invest a significant amount of their time in the project, in addition to the funds that they have allocated, if the project is ever to succeed. This touches again on our requirement that systems, operational, and management personnel all understand their roles in the ongoing process.

The cost of change. Though there have been many cases where the managers of the project had enough foresight to ensure that everyone was aware of the required time investment, it is the rare organization that considers the organizational and procedural impacts that a warehousing project will entail.

The naiveté with which some people enter these projects is unbelievable. They are going to spend millions of dollars. They are going to invest a large amount of time. Yet they hardly ever think about how the existence of these new systems is going to change the way that people do their jobs. Will certain jobs be eliminated? Will certain functions become redundant? Will certain computer systems become obsolete? Many is the project where those questions have not been asked until after the new system has been completed. Then everyone scrambles to figure out the answers to these questions.

The real value of solutions. Besides falling short in their understanding of what the warehouse initiative is going to cost, it also is quite common to fail miserably at determining what the value will be. The objective of our approach is to always tie costs to specific benefits and vice versa.

Value, Vision, and Focus

Ultimately, whenever you begin to take a look at these kinds of issues, you end up needing to deal with questions about value, vision, and focus. If you want to create a framework for the diagnosis of these varieties of costs, benefits, and different operational units' perspectives on the project, you are going to have to be able to understand it all within a common context.

Vision

One of the definitions of the word *vision* in the dictionary reads as follows: "The act or power of anticipating that which will or may come to be; foresight." It is critical that the developers, sponsors, and users of any system, especially a data-warehouse system, have an accurate and shared vision of exactly what that warehouse is supposed to be. This shared vision is what allows everyone to understand exactly what the system is going to look like when it is complete. The development of a comprehensive vision guarantees that what you are building will have value.

Coupled with your desire to get everyone to share the same vision is the need to get people to identify the focus that the system should address. *Focus* is described as a central point of attraction, attention, or activity. While the vision of the system allows people to picture what it will be like, a clear focus allows them to see exactly how their actions will fit into that vision.

When you step into an organization where the idea of a data warehouse has been bantered about for any length of time, you inadvertently step into a veritable quagmire of seemingly contradictory and extremely diverse visions. The management group might harbor visions of a data warehouse as the solution to a broad range of strategic business problems. The systems staff might see the approach as a way to reduce the cost of systems maintenance or to deploy systems more quickly. The marketing group might see it as an incredibly complicated and expensive way to accomplish some specific, narrowly focused tactical program that they are trying to put together.

Types of vision. There are many different kinds and levels of vision and focus that you must deal with when you begin considering warehousing solutions. You need to understand some of the differences before you can undertake to help people sort through them all.

A hierarchy of visions. When you step into a typical business environment and start asking people what their vision for the business is and how the vision of a warehouse fits in, you will find that these images fall into several categories.

Focus of the vision. First of all, every vision that a person holds assumes a particular focus, which usually is, but not always, related to their role within the organization. Some visions are applicable to the overall organization, while others apply to specific business areas.

Ask a CFO (Chief Financial Officer) about her or his vision, and you will hear things in terms of the current profitability of the company, long-term debt, dividends, and stock splits. To the CFO, a data warehouse looks like a big expense, and he or she will be looking for some big revenues or cost reductions to justify its existence.

Ask a marketing manager about her or his vision, and you will hear things about market shares, gross margins, and corporate posture. This person has a decidedly customer and sales orientation, and his or her vision will involve making changes in those areas.

Ask a production manager about her or his vision, and she or he will talk about the cost of production, downtime on the line, and operational efficiencies.

Ask a computer systems manager, and you will hear about disparate operating systems, production and development backlogs, and the need to make the environment more manageable and less complex.

Scope of the vision. The second thing that every vision will have is a scope. Some visions call for small changes in narrowly defined areas, and others call from broad, sweeping revolutions across the entire organization.

One warehousing project might involve the creation of a warehouse that holds copies of data from only two files, which then allows end users to make use of an *ad hoc* query tool to analyze it. This project would affect few other systems and only a small population of users. Another warehousing effort, like one that I built for a major financial institution, might involve the integration of data from dozens or even hundreds of disparate file sources and the consolidation and delivery of that data to hundreds or even thousands of users in support of their daily decision making. Clearly the latter would entail a much larger scope.

Hard and soft benefits. Not only will a vision have a specific scope and focus, but it also will have a certain hardness or softness associated with it. Soft visions speak in less concrete terms about less tangible kinds of results, while hard visions speak to specific objectives and initiatives occurring within specific time frames.

Corporate culture and vision. It is important to bear in mind, when you evaluate the different visions of people within the organization, that different corporate cultures view the visioning process differently. In some organizations, visions are very direct, concrete things. In these corporations the visions tend to be very hard in nature. In other organizations, it is a taboo to speak of visions in anything but the most general of terms. These organizations tend to proliferate the soft visions.

Not only do different corporations have their own sets of rules and taboos about the vision-development process, different business disciplines (i.e., marketing, production, systems, management, etc.) also have their own formulas. Your job, in the evaluation of these disparate visions, will be to proceed without violating any of these cultural directives.

Getting a perspective on visioning. Clearly, visioning can be done in many different ways. It is very important for you, as you begin to move through this world of different kinds of visions, to establish, clearly in your own minds, what kind of visions apply to the warehouse development effort.

Strategic corporate visioning

The process that we will call *strategic long-range corporate vision development* is at the highest level of the visioning hierarchy. While it is not within the scope of this book to spend much time on this process, it is important that you understand it and its implications for your objectives.

Strategic long-range corporate vision development is the process by which the people in charge of the corporation set the long-term direction. There are several different ways that this process is approached, depending upon the industry that the company is in and the company's current situation.

In general, strategic visioning at this level is a three-step process.

First, the visionaries look outward from the corporation and try to develop an understanding of the current and future environment in which the corporation will have to exist. Among the focuses of these kinds of studies are: marketing and the future economic environment, the competitive environment, the legal and legislative environment, the impending financial environment, emerging technology and process improvement options, raw materials and source of supply analysis, etc.

During these studies, the planners develop a business perspective on how to survive and thrive in the future. After this is determined, the planners take an inward look at the business. They identify areas where changes are needed and recommend changes of direction for different groups and operations. In general, they set the direction for the operational units and tell people what is important and what is not. The final step of this process will be to take the information gained and develop a set of strategic initiatives. They will set goals and objectives for the organization as a whole and for individual groups to meet.

Reduced to more practical terms, in a very real sense, the annual budgeting-and-forecasting cycle that most businesses go through is a modified version of this strategic-visioning process. In many cases, the vision espoused by the budgets that are approved is far more accurate a corporate vision than any kind of "vision statement" could ever be. In summary, where the corporation has decided to put the money is where they have placed their priorities.

Clearly, there is no role for the data warehouse at this level of vision development. A data warehouse is a tool that the business can use to help accomplish the objectives that have been established. The data warehouse might make it possible for people to develop solutions that otherwise would not be possible. However, within the context of the discussions here, the process of vision development that we have been discussing does not apply. (See Figure 10.2.)

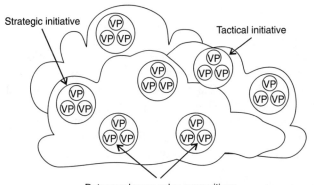

Figure 10.2 The visioning hierarchy.

Focused strategic initiatives. One of the outcomes of the corporate vision-development process should be a collection of strategic initiatives. These are goals that strategic planners believe different areas of the business should meet. These initiatives can be large in scope or narrow; however, in most cases, they will require the utilization of computer systems to make them a reality. It is here that data warehousing can play a vital role, and it is within the context of one of these strategic initiatives that your warehousing vision-development process should begin.

In general, there are three kinds of strategic initiatives that organizations will undertake:

- Improvement of existing operational efficiency
- Redesign of operational approaches
- Creation of new operational approaches

We will consider what is involved in each of these and how a data warehouse could contribute to its success.

Improvement of existing operational efficiency. Developing strategies and approaches that help make each of the corporation's organizational units more efficient represents the "classical" approach to corporate computer systems planning. Indeed, the history of computer systems deployment is a history of business people identifying ways that the computerization of certain tasks can enable them to be executed at increasingly higher levels of efficiency.

A data-warehousing approach can be of assistance in the development of some of these types of solutions. In these cases, the opportunity for improvement is made possible by the availability of new kinds of data-processing tools. These tools require a data warehouse to function effectively. For example, the production-control department might realize that, if much of the currently available information was placed in a common data-storage area, a lot of new operational efficiencies could be figured out, making use of statistical analysis tools. In these cases, a small, tactically focused warehousing application provides an easy, cost-effective solution.

In many cases, a data warehouse will not represent the best possible solution for certain types of problems. A data warehouse is not an operational system. It is not built to handle the kinds of processing that a traditional OLTP (online transaction processing) system is meant to handle. For example, an airline reservation system or a cash station management system is a poor application of a warehousing approach. These applications are better addressed with different kinds of architectural solutions.

Redesign of operational approaches. Over the years, corporations continually have invested in the improvement of each of their organizational unit's efficiencies. In many cases, the introduction of new tools and approaches offers very little real value to those operations. However, what is becoming increasingly important is the development of applications that cross traditional organizational boundaries and allow businesses to coordinate and analyze the end-to-end operations that drive the business. Often, these initiatives are known as *business process re-engineering initiatives*. These applications represent an area that the data warehouse can effectively address.

By their very nature, business re-engineering initiatives involve attempting to preserve existing legacy system functionality wherever possible, while adding on new kinds of cross-system integration of information. These projects represent some of the best applications of data-warehousing techniques today.

Creation of new operational approaches. Sometimes the planners decide that what is needed is an entirely new kind of business unit or functionality. In these cases, a combination of data warehousing and traditional OLTP, operationally based applications, will offer the best solution.

It is important for anyone attempting to run the data-warehousing vision-development project to clearly understand the type of initiative that the warehouse will address and the clear application of the rules that we have set out for when the warehouse is, or is not, a good solution.

Determining Whether You Need a Data Warehouse or Not

While going through the process of inventorying and validating each person's vision of the warehouse, you automatically will accomplish one of your major business objectives for this phase: determining whether the warehouse is a good idea or not.

Before undertaking a project of this kind, I always warn the client that there is a distinct possibility that the end result of my analysis might be that a data warehouse is not a good idea. This can be for many reasons.

Among some of the biggest "show stoppers" that I have uncovered in the past are:

Infrastructure challenges (physical infrastructure). In many cases, the corporation's computer systems infrastructure will not support the deployment of the technology required to make the system feasible. For example, in some organizations, I have found a great demand for PC-based data-mining tools to be integrated with mainframe-based data. In some cases, it would be very easy to bring that data together but be cost-prohibitive to put the personal computer and networking infrastructure in place. In these situations, the infrastructure challenges make the system cost-prohibitive.

Infrastructure challenges (operational infrastructure). In other cases, I have found that the physical deployment of the warehousing solutions would be possible, but that the organization could not figure out any way to provide the kind of operational support required to make the warehouse feasible. Building a data warehouse entails more than the simple installation of a database server and loading it with data. If ongoing operational support is not going to be available, then a data-warehousing solution is not going to be feasible. Organizations that try to build "self-managing" warehouses end up either failing miserably or turning their end users into systems managers.

Legacy data intransigence. Sometimes everything about the data warehouse seems feasible until you take a close look at your legacy sources of data. Sometimes you find out that very little of the data that you need actually exists, or it exists in a form that is not usable. The intransigence of legacy data easily can make a warehousing project infeasible.

Lack of sufficient demand. Many times your analysis of the different visions that people hold for the warehouse are so limited in their scope that there simply is no reason to deploy a warehouse solution to solve the problems. If you are not looking to build a warehouse to figure out how to share large amounts of data from diverse sources for access by diverse groups of users, many times you are better off building a simple integrated, single-data application, as opposed to a full-scale warehouse implementation.

Data warehouse as redundant step. In some situations, the inclusion of a warehouse architecture in a systems-development plan turns out to be redundant. If the warehouse that you are envisioning requires a very high turnover rate (where a large percentage of the data is fully refreshed on a very frequent basis), does not require history retention, or has very few turns (data is refreshed once a quarter or once a year), then there is a good chance that warehousing is too complex a solution for a much simpler set of problems. Many times I find that developers are better off simply bypassing the warehouse and loading legacy system data directly into data-mining tools. If there is no reason to put things into the warehouse, then you should not use it.

Lack of cost justification. The most heartbreaking of all reasons to not use a warehouse is in cases where the need for a warehousing approach shows great merit but the estimated costs far outweigh the benefits. In those cases, sponsors of the initiative must either give up on the project or start over again looking to generate more interest in other business areas that might help to leverage the overall solution.

Developing criteria for the valuation of the warehouse

The second business objective for your vision-development project is to determine at the very outset of the project what kinds of valuations or scales will be used to assess the effectiveness of the warehouse. Different organizations have different criteria for measuring an initiative's success. When an organization decides to build a real warehouse, it is because they have determined that there is some kind of a need in terms of inventory management. The criteria for the success of this real warehouse might be something like:

- Elimination of the overstocking of merchandise at the retail level
- Ability to stockpile inventory so that production can attain higher levels of productivity
- Speeding up of the movement of merchandise through the system

or any number of other criteria. In the same way, your overall warehousing initiative needs to be associated with the same kinds of valuations.

Will you consider the warehouse a success if you are able to develop 10 new systems that otherwise would not be achievable? What if you can justify the creation of only 2 new systems? Then is the warehouse a bad idea? Are you looking at a situation where the warehouse is being put into place to relieve the data management burdens of nondata-processing personnel? If so, how do you place a value on this kind of effort?

In one organization, I found that managers, clerical personnel, and engineers were all spending more than 20% of their time loading and unloading spreadsheets, formatting queries, and managing data in general. In this environment, it was getting to the point where people found that they were having less time to do their real work, because more and more of their time was spent identifying and moving data around. For this organization, the data warehouse was the solution to a very large data-management problem that was not associated with any specific business objective but that dealt with the effective and efficient use of time.

Decomposing the visions

Equipped with this new insight, you are ready to return to your vision development process. So far, you have begun the process of collecting the visions from different advocates of the warehouse solution, and you have applied some analysis and understanding to the different visions that people have espoused. After you begin to apply much of this discipline to the different visions that people have stated, you now must execute the most difficult part of the process: the decomposition of these visions into their least common denominators.

We already have observed that different visions are going to be stated in terms of varying degrees of scope, focus, and tangibility (hard versus soft). You must try to break each of these down into smaller, more manageable pieces.

Examples of visions. The following sections present a sampling of the kind of "mixed bag" of visions that typically can occur during this process.

CEO: Corporate-level vision. "I would like to see this warehouse make it possible for us to reduce our net operating costs by 3%. I don't care how that happens, but the board of directors has made that our number-one priority for this year.

"This company already has a good reputation as the most friendly, most approachable vendor in our industry. I am looking for ways to increase our level of service to our customers while maintaining our current profit margins."

Marketing manager: Marketing-level vision. "Our company is moving in the direction of one-to-one marketing. We want to have a personal relationship with each of our customers. To do that, we need to have access to all of the information that we can get our hands on about those customers. We've got the information. We've got the sales history, returns records, and credit ratings, but we can't get at it. We need all of that information in the same place at the same time."

MIS manager: Information systems vision. "Our organization currently is suffering from a nine-month production backlog, and our users have had enough. I need a way to deliver these new types of data-mining applications more quickly and at less cost than I am able to deliver anything today."

Production manager vision. "We need a system to help us track products as they move through our factory. Right now, we have dozens of systems, but none of them talk to each other. Somehow we need to integrate this information so that we can identify production problems faster and respond more quickly to changes in conditions."

Testing engineer vision. "I need the information in this file ported to a relational database so that I can use my statistical analysis package against it."

Secretary vision. "I could save three hours of work every week if this information for this status-report spreadsheet was centrally located. Right now, I have to get seven different printouts and key all of the information back into the system. It just seems silly! All of the information already is in the computer, so why can't we just leave it in there and move it around a little."

Turning visions into candidate applications

Obviously, each of these visions of how to use the data warehouse has a different scope, level, and hard/softness factor. Your challenge is to figure out how to break them down.

Fracture lines: The visions decomposition process. There are several approaches that have proven to be effective aids in the vision-decomposition process. In general, the process is similar to those employed to decompose data models or process models or those used in many of the business process re-engineering types of analysis.

Organizational decomposition: Find the owner (departments, roles, and responsibilities). One criterion that can help you to decompose a large vision is to break the vision down into the pieces of the solution that belong to different organizational units or individuals.

For example, a large vision usually will require the cooperative efforts of many different departments. Marketing, accounting, production control, and management might all need to do something to make it work. In this case, your first cut at decomposition will be to figure out what each of these areas needs to do as their contribution to the ultimate solution.

At the next level down, you find that different areas within the department have different roles to play. Marketing might consist of a direct mail, phone solicitation, direct sales, and catalog areas. Production control will include inventory management, process engineering, and maintenance. You can continue breaking the vision down along these organizational lines, all the way down to the individual person, if you must.

Functional (process) decomposition: What are the steps in the process? The functional decomposition process is used frequently in the development of specifications for computer systems or in the execution of business process re-engineering exercises. These approaches go under many names, but they include things like brown-paper analysis, functional decomposition, task analysis, process-flow engineering, and a wide variety of others.

While many of these approaches might end up being too formal and involved, the general process is the same: break down the big processes into smaller ones.

Financial decomposition: How is the cost allocated? Another good clue to figuring out how a vision might be broken down into smaller pieces is to apply some financial criteria to your analysis. How is money involved in the process, and how does it move from one part to the next?

Syntactic decomposition: Verbs and nouns. Another technique for reaching a quick answer is to apply the verb-and-noun rule. Write a description of the vision so that everything about it is clearly defined, then start to figure out where each of the verbs and nouns are in the sentences. Each verb and noun is fully decomposed or can be broken down into smaller verbs. When the verbs and nouns can no longer be broken down, you will have isolated the full population of discrete candidate applications.

For example, if you were to take the MIS manager vision:

> Our organization currently is suffering from a nine-month production backlog, and our users have had enough. I need a way to deliver these new types of

data-mining applications much faster and for considerably less cost then I am able to deliver anything today.

You would find the nouns:

- Organization
- Production backlog
- Users
- Data-mining applications

Break each one down by going back to the MIS manager and getting more detail about what is specifically meant by each phrase. Table 10.4 shows how each of these nouns was decomposed.

This very general vision could be decomposed into a collection of candidate applications for each of the areas listed (marketing, accounts payable, management, and production control) using each of the tools listed (SAS, SPSS, and Excel). In likelihood, the real candidate application probably has something to do with some specific needs of the marketing area (because they show up three times in the list). In this case, you probably would decide to go back to the marketing group and determine what really is needed.

If you apply the same technique to an already decomposed vision, you should get the same result as you started with. For example, the testing engineer vision (Table 10.5):

> I need the information in this file ported to a relational database so that I can use my statistical analysis package against it.

When you have completed the decomposition process, your end result is no longer a collection of unrelated visions but now is a list of candidate warehouse applications.

TABLE 10.4 Diagnosing Nouns to Detail a Value Proposition

Noun	Breakdown
Organization	Marketing, accounts payable, and management
Production backlog	Marketing and production-control applications
Users	Marketing users
Data-mining products	SAS, SPSS, and Excel

TABLE 10.5 Diagnosing Nouns: Engineering Case

Noun	Breakdown
We	A group of three engineers in the same department
Information in this file	A specific set of data is identified
Relational database	The place to which they want the data ported
Statistical-analysis package	Lotus spreadsheet

Verifying the decompositions. After you have applied the decomposition techniques that seem to make the most sense, you need to find out if the decompositions still make sense. There are several criteria that you apply to validate this decomposition:

- Does each candidate application make sense as an autonomous project?
- Will it involve aspects of acquisition, storage, and access?
- If it does not include all three, are there other candidate applications that include what this application needs?
- Do the candidate applications seem to make sense from a business perspective?

In many cases, you will have to go back to the people that you interviewed and validate that your understanding of the original problem and your subsequent breakdown were accurate.

Rejection criteria. As a part of this process, you also will develop a list of rejected candidates. Candidate applications will be rejected for many reasons, including:

- The application does not make sense for a warehouse application. Perhaps it could be pursued as an independent project. Sometimes the candidate application might not even require the use of any computer facilities at all.
- The candidate application will obviously cost a lot more than the value it will bring. This will include those "pet projects" that some people harbor, where the value delivered will be much lower than other solutions might provide.

For example, one vice president that I approached wanted me to integrate 12 different reports that he had to review into one report. While I certainly could have developed a warehouse to do this, this executive would be the only user of the system. In this case, it would be considerably more cost-effective to hire part-time office help to do these basic tasks than go through the trouble of engineering a warehouse solution.

Recruiting of Sponsors

Now that you have collected the visions, evaluated them, decomposed them, and verified their practicality and applicability, you are ready to begin the process of finding business-area sponsors for each.

Until now, you should (at least theoretically) have been able to conduct your investigation without regard for the politics, organizational, and environmental constraints that you might encounter. It is at this point that you attack these problems head-on. Remember that some of the biggest problems that you face when trying to develop a warehouse are problems in the areas of focus, ownership, and economic return on investment. The assignment of a sponsor to each of these initiatives will provide you with the means to eliminate many of those problems.

The Roles of the Sponsor

When you begin looking for a person or organizational unit to sponsor each value proposition, you are looking for someone to take responsibility for several things. You need a person or organizational unit that:

- Is interested in what the value proposition has to offer and sees a lot of benefit for him- or herself and his or her group.

- Has a vested interest in the successful and timely completion of the application.

- Is willing to take responsibility for the benefits that the value proposition is supposed to deliver.

- Is willing to take responsibility and provide leadership in the resolution of the many different data-identification and -delivery problems that you are going to encounter.

- Is willing to provide the business expertise necessary to pull the application together.

- Is able to provide a solid cost justification for the premise of the proposition.

It is during the stage of sponsor recruitment that you find out whether the value propositions that you have been working with have any real value or not. It is not uncommon to come up with a long list of impressive candidate applications only to find that, although they would clearly provide benefit to the company, no one is willing to take ownership for them. In many cases, the issue of ownership is straightforward. For example, a tactical application that enhances the capabilities of the human resources department can clearly be sponsored only by that department. In other cases, especially in those situations where the candidate application crosses organizational lines, it can be very difficult to figure out who would most appropriately handle the benefits.

You might think, "Why make such a big deal about the sponsor-recruiting process? Surely, if a value proposition shows the potential for big savings or big process improvements, everybody will jump on it." Unfortunately, that is not the case. You must remember that the candidate applications elicit several different kinds of consequences. Certainly they will offer some value to the company; however, what is unclear until you begin the sponsor-recruitment process is exactly what kinds of hidden costs might be involved.

In some cases, I have found that value propositions actually frighten or threaten people. They are afraid that, if they admit that the assumptions of the value proposition are correct, it reflects badly on them. The thinking goes that, if these people could identify a way for us to improve our processes, we must not be doing our job. Although this kind of paranoid thinking is far from accurate, it still appears from time to time. Another situation that can sabotage the best of value propositions is when the value propositions in question open up issues of political discord. This kind of discord can take two forms:

- Interoperational unit rivalry
- Operational versus systems animosity

Interoperational unit rivalry

We already have alluded a bit to this type of rivalry. In general, this happens when different organizational units feel that the value proposition, benefits, and improvements are something that they should enjoy. In some situations, you actually can run into people trying to set things up so that another group absorbs the cost while their group enjoys the benefit. It is important to remember that any change to the typical corporate business environment is going to represent a chance for all of the political agendas to come out. Many a project has been sabotaged by this kind of maneuvering.

Operational versus systems animosity

Another kind of rivalry manifests itself in value propositions between the operational units that need the system and the computer systems support department. In some organizations, the relationship between the two groups is so strained that no systems project can be considered without taking all of the historical baggage into account. This animosity usually takes the form of some kind of power play. The operational people might feel resentment because they have been forced to live with a long history of ignored requests for system enhancements and long wait times for new systems. The thinking of these individuals might be "Why should I work on this value proposition with you, when you have been unable to meet even the simplest of my requests in the past?" or "How can you have budget money for this when you don't have it for my other projects?"

In the worst cases, the proactive advocacy of a data-warehousing solution by the systems area is interpreted as a political come-on—a way to raise budget dollars for systems or a way to shift focus from the other problems in the systems area. There are even organizations where the systems area maintains a not-so-well-hidden agenda that views the building of a data warehouse as a means for systems to wrest control from independent user areas. This will force everyone to abdicate their data and their systems options for the sake of a single, monolithic, centrally (I/S) managed data warehouse.

A necessary step

Despite all of the problems that recruitment of sponsors is going to create, it is a critical step in the process. Resolving the political, organizational, and budgetary issues that appear when you begin looking for sponsors is critical to the success of the project. Many times, enthusiastic advocates of data-warehousing solutions have "pushed through" the projects by gaining higher-level corporate sponsorship and attempting to bypass the "in the trenches" political and organizational in-fighting.

While this might seem like a solution, it really only postpones the turf battle. It is better to get all political and territorial issues resolved before the warehousing project begins than to allow those issues to fester under the surface, waiting for the chance to explode on the scene, invalidating most, if not all, of the work that has been done.

Do not create corporate-sponsored or I/S-sponsored value-proposition initiatives

For these reasons, I strongly recommend that people not try to get support for individual warehousing value-proposition initiatives from upper management. I also have found that I/S-sponsored value propositions usually fail.

Certainly, you need to have I/S and upper-management support for the overall data-warehousing process and project, but this support is for the warehouse itself. Individual applications must have individual business-area sponsors if they are going to succeed.

Determination of Hard Benefits

After you have successfully identified a sponsor for your value proposition, your next step is to work with that sponsor to develop an idea of the potential hard benefits associated with this proposition. Until now, your assessment of benefits has been very high level and general in nature. You need to get specific about what this value proposition is going to deliver.

The nature of the benefits that you intend to associate with a given value proposition and the way that it is presented will be the key to the overall success of the project. The single biggest factor providing focus for the people associated with the project is a clear understanding of which benefits the application is being asked to deliver.

Benefits and focus

While, at face value, the previous sentence might seem to be overly strong or dramatic, when you get down to the nitty-gritty of systems development, a common understanding of the drivers of the system will ease the process greatly. Few people realize the volume of issues that appear while you are in the process of addressing the thousands of details that make up a modern application. Time and time again, programmers, analysts, and users are going to be forced to make hard decisions and compromises about what they should and should not do. In a large number of the cases, a clear understanding of the potential benefits will provide them with an answer.

There actually are several different ways that the benefits of a system can be determined. Probably the most commonly mentioned justification for a system is explained in terms of some kind of savings. There are many ways that savings can be calculated and rationalized.

Time savings. Sometimes the data warehouse provides no additional functionality at all. What it does provide in these situations is the ability to do certain kinds of operations more quickly, saving time. I built a data warehouse for a grocery wholesaler. The buyers for this origination were spending an inordinate amount of time pulling together information about each of the products that they were managing. Each buyer spent over half his or her time simply plowing through a vast assortment of reports and online systems, making redundant phone calls to suppliers and retail outlets, just to figure out how each of their products was doing. In this case, the data warehouse simply provided the same information in less time. The direct benefit of this system was calculated as a percentage of the buyers' time.

Ripple effects when time savings are concerned. When you save someone the time needed to perform a task, you create more value than simply the amount of time that they spend. You also create a whole range of dependent benefits.

When a professional who is paid to do a certain kind of job ends up spending a lot of time doing trivial and redundant data-processing tasks, they not only lose time, they also become defocused. By saving the time, you also increase the overall effectiveness of each person, because they have more time to do their real job.

Another chain-reaction benefit to time savings occurs when the timeliness of a given operation is critical. For example, not only were the buyers in the grocery example able to spend less time investigating their product groups, they also got their analysis done much more quickly. In a business where making decisions quickly is critical, the chain-reaction value can be great. For example, what good is it to find out that you had a load of lettuce sitting on the loading dock for four days when it gets spoiled after two?

When calculating the benefits that this kind of process improvement can have, you must take these dependent benefits into account as well.

Money savings. Another way that people appraise the value of an initiative is to look at the amount of money it is going to save. In many situations, the value proposition has some straightforward savings associated with it. For example, at one large financial institution where I installed a warehouse, I was able to justify the elimination of over 30 redundant clerical positions. Other systems that I have installed have resulted in the reduction of scrap, speeding up of the assembly process, and elimination of redundant processes. All of these translated easily into hard savings.

Computer-resource savings. Sometimes some of the benefits of the warehouse can be attributed to savings in the computer-systems area: reduced disk utilization, reduced CPU costs, and sometimes even the elimination of redundant systems. All of these can add up to respectable savings. For a large brokerage firm, I installed a system that made it possible for brokers to handle twice as many transactions a day, more accurately and more comfortably than they could before (meaning that each broker could do twice as much business).

Revenue generation. A data warehouse often provides an organization with the ability to generate revenue in ways that were not possible previously. For example, a clear revenue benefit can be provided by the installation of a marketing data warehouse to provide the company with the ability to run direct-marketing and phone-solicitation departments that it previously could not service.

Profitability improvement and efficiency of operations. The ability to integrate information from a variety of disparate sources often provides companies with creative ways to improve overall profitability. Many of the "third-generation" data-warehousing solutions that I built provided companies with the ability to manage their processes in ways never before possible. For example, studies with many different manufacturing companies have shown that a data warehouse provides the perfect means to integrate manufacturing processes.

Hidden benefits. Occasionally, companies find that, with the implementation of data-warehousing solutions, they have created benefits that they had not anticipated.

   Accuracy. These have included incredible improvements in the accuracy of existing systems with concomitant improvement in the overall decision-making process.

Fraud detection. In some rare situations, the developers of data warehouses have uncovered cases of computer systems-related fraud that remained undetected because of the quagmire of conflicting data systems that auditors needed to wallow through.

Redundant processes. It is not uncommon for a warehousing initiative to uncover systems and departments whose functionality is being duplicated in other operational areas. By mapping the data out, these processes can be identified and reduced.

Marketing values. The benefit that a warehousing application can provide need not be limited to the operational and financial kinds of benefits that we have been discussing. In many cases, warehousing applications provide companies with the ability to accomplish things in the less explicit area of marketing position improvement. Increased market share, retained market share, improved customer relationships, one-to-one marketing posture, and more profitable marketing initiatives are common applications of the warehousing approach.

Data-Mining Tools and Benefits

Although we will be spending a considerable amount of time talking about data mining and the access component of the warehouse in later chapters, it makes sense at this point to introduce a few of the fundamental concepts associated with data mining and value propositions. First of all, it is important that you realize that, when we are talking about the data warehouse and value propositions, it is only in one small area of the warehouse that those payoffs can be realized. (See Figure 10.3.)

The pay-off zone for a data warehouse consists of all of those data-mining applications within the access component. When you examine the realm of

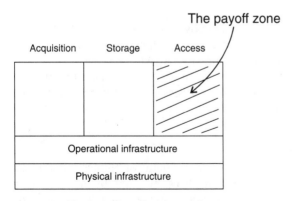

Figure 10.3 The "payoff zone" of the warehouse.

products and applications that function within this pay-off zone, you find that the applications that operate in this area are one of three types:

- Holistic solutions
- Analytical solutions
- Operational systems

Holistic solutions

Many applications for the data warehouse involve the development of holistic solutions. We include in our definition of *holistic applications* any kind of system that allows people to get a more comprehensive, more accurate view of some aspect of the business. For example, a holistic customer application will make the full extent of the history and characteristics of a given customer available to the user. From one screen, the user can see a history of all of the sales made to that customer, a listing of all of his or her service calls and complaints, a history of all marketing materials sent to them, and all promotions run in their geographical area.

On the other hand, a holistic production-control application will provide the engineer with all of the information available about the progress of a given lot of materials through the manufacturing process, the status of the material at each phase of manufacturing, the results of different tests applied to that lot, and related information about each of the components that went into that lot.

A wholesale or retail organization's holistic application might track the movement of goods, along with the associated costs as product moves from manufacturer to warehouse to sales floor. The system also can provide cross-reference sales information, comparing different lots of like material in different stores.

Analytical solutions

The second type of applications provided by data mining fall under the category of *analytical solutions*. These products allow users to analyze collections of data in ways not possible previously. With analytical solutions, users can identify trends, make more accurate predictions, and optimize decisions about pricing, scheduling, and process control by applying the insights that the analytical products provide.

Operational systems

Although we have stated several times that a data warehouse itself could not function as an operational system, we also stated that, by making use of feedback mechanisms and the work area, it would be possible to stack operational systems on top of the warehouse. These systems typically are dependent upon the warehouse for the bulk of their usable data, but they also can be considered to be functioning as independent of the system itself.

Each of these types of solutions offers a different kind of benefit to the sponsoring organization, and your definition of the value proposition needs to take all of them into account.

Determination of Reasonableness and Cost Estimates

After you have developed a comprehensive definition of what the benefits of the proposed application will be, you need to come up with some estimates of what it is going to cost to deliver those solutions. To say that cost estimation is an art more than a science would be a gross understatement. Clearly, there is no way to accurately estimate system costs without a great deal of information about the system itself.

Unfortunately, few organizations can afford to do exhaustive cost estimating before actually trying to get approval for projects. Your best alternative is to develop a discipline for estimating warehousing costs that will at least minimize the risks of running into problems. This estimation process will take a worst-case-scenario approach. You will assume that everything involved in the process will be at the extreme end of the range, thereby minimizing your risk of underestimating the costs. This phase of the vision-development process is the most time and resource intensive of all the steps. During this phase, you need to determine things like:

- Where will the data come from?
- Who will use the information and how?
- What will it take to deliver the data?
- Systems integration issues (hardware, network, application software, and tools)

and a score of other issues.

My approach to developing these estimates will be fourfold. First, you will develop physical infrastructure estimates of exactly how much disk space and computer power you estimate will be required to support the system. Second, you will develop estimates of what kind of operational support will be required and how long it will take to put that operational support in place. Third, you will examine the nature and complexity of the data analysis and delivery effort, developing estimates for how many people and how long it will take to develop the application data stores. Fourth, you will analyze the data-access and data-mining requirements and develop estimates for the activity required to bring that into existence. Then, you will put these estimates together for the development of a full application plan and cost estimate.

Before we can provide a comprehensive approach to this process, we are going to need to examine the physical, operational, data-discipline, and data-mining characteristics of the system in a lot more detail. We have covered these issues in chapters 7, 8, and 9.

Development of value propositions

After you have succeeded in gaining sponsors, developed a benefits statement, and derived your estimated costs, you will be ready to create your official value propositions. These value propositions must explicitly summarize each of the steps that you experienced in developing them and summarize for management, the operational sponsoring areas, and the systems area exactly what is to be done and why.

Categories of value propositions

Throughout this chapter, we have referred to many of the different ways that visions and value propositions could be categorized and cataloged. While there indeed is a vast assortment of these propositions, you should be able to categorize any value proposition based upon several distinct parameters.

The industry category/discipline value-proposition grid

What you will find, when you actually begin to isolate the individual value propositions that different companies develop, is that patterns begin to occur. In general, all of the value propositions for a given business discipline area (marketing, production control, etc.) tend to share a lot of the same characteristics across all industries, and the value propositions for related industries tend to be similar. Basically, what this tells you is that value propositions are significantly dependent upon the industry that the company happens to be in and upon the business discipline to which it is related. (See Table 10.6.)

As you go through the process of understanding more and more of these industry- and discipline-driven value propositions, you should be able to develop an understanding of the pattern that underlies them all.

Consolidation of value propositions

Once you have formalized your understanding of each of the value propositions that you have collected, you are ready to begin the consolidation process. You have several objectives for this consolidation process:

- You want to develop some estimates for the overall size of the fully implemented data warehouse.

- You need to be able to begin to develop cost and time estimates for the overall effort.

- You want to begin organizing and prioritizing the value propositions and grouping them into different phases of development.

With this information in place, you should be ready to develop a full-blown warehouse-deployment strategy.

Sizing the warehouse. The process of warehouse sizing involves little more than simply adding up all of the sizing estimates from each of the value propositions that you have successfully produced. The net result of this process will be full disk estimates, computer CPU estimates, and all of the

TABLE 10.6 Industry/Discipline Cross Sections

Industry—category discipline	Manufacturing				Retail				Financial services				Telecommunications			
	Automotive	Computers	Consumer goods	Industrial goods	Department stores	Clothing	Grocery	Direct marketing	Banking	Investments	Real estate	Insurance	Cellular	Telephone local	Long distance	Satellite
Marketing																
Production control																
Accounting																
Logistics and support																
Customer service																
Human resources																

other kinds of physical and operational infrastructure issues that you have captured.

Developing overall cost and timing estimates. However, the development of overall cost estimates is a slightly more complicated process. The sum total of the estimates for each of the value propositions will not be the same as for the real development plan. Your actual, full-systems costs might be higher or lower depending upon your deployment strategy. At this stage of the process, however, you need to summarize the estimates from each of the value propositions and use that information as input to your deployment strategy and ultimate costing model.

Organizing and prioritizing the value propositions. After you have developed your overall system estimates, your next step is to figure out how best to deploy each of the proposed applications. Obviously, the more value propositions that you intend to implement and the more interdependency that you have between them, the more complicated the process becomes. When you begin to organize the value propositions, you probably will want to develop several different groupings to look for efficiencies.

Value-proposition grouping strategies. One way to group value propositions is by sponsoring organization. Under this mode of operation, you group all of the same business area's propositions into the same phase or cluster of applications. Another way is to group them in the order of priority. Which ones have the most strategic importance?

Yet another way that this process can be approached is to prioritize them by cost/benefit ratio. The value propositions with the best payback get done sooner.

In some cases, the propositions might need to be grouped by infrastructure requirements. Some might require a very large investment in workstations and network implementation, while others might require little or no investment in that area.

In all cases, you must consider the dependency between applications. In some cases, there might be several value propositions with very little inherent value in and of themselves, but a great many other value propositions depend upon the existence of those propositions to succeed. In general, what you want to accomplish through the grouping process is to come up with a logical sequence of events that allows you to group propositions in a manner that maximizes:

- Physical and operational infrastructure costs
- Serial dependencies
- Business priorities

Limited investment to start. In some cases, the organization might decide to take a piecemeal approach to value-proposition roll-out. In these situations, the organization bypasses the development of an overall roll-out plan and opts instead simply to take on one or two of the most promising propositions and use them as pilot, proof-of-concept applications.

Development of a deployment strategy. Given your value-proposition deployment plan, you are ready to put the full-blown warehousing plan together. During this process you will need to:

- Select the architecture (platforms, network configuration, etc.)
- Develop a high-level architectural specifications document
- Determine the location
- Report on high-level cost estimates
- Report on the prioritization of all of the value propositions

In the next few chapters, we will take a closer look at the data disciplines that drive the actual process of application development, after which I will show you how the output of the data discipline process can be used to drive the development of your infrastructure. With that complete, we will develop a case study involving several value propositions and begin considering some of the lowest-level detail of how the warehouse actually is going to be created.

Chapter

11

Validation and Estimation

While you know that cases of shortcutting are legion in the history of data-processing systems development, this knowledge does little to help you in organizing your project to prevent falling into the same traps. Actually, you are faced with another paradox when it comes to this issue. Experience has shown that the dedication of a large number of resources to the analysis-and-design process usually ends up with little to show for it. On the other hand, the simple advocacy of a "just build it and we'll figure out the details later" is just as dangerous. You must figure out where the middle ground lies.

When you look at all of these different problems and consider them as a whole, you can come up with some fundamental conclusions. Underlying all of them is one of two factors. The developers of the system failed to:

- Validate the assumptions that they made about what the system would or could do.

- Develop accurate estimates of what it would take to bring the project to completion.

Obviously, there is a serious overlap between validation and estimation issues; you cannot accomplish one without the other. For the rest of this chapter, however, we will concentrate on the validation process and will spend the next chapter on the topic of estimation and project planning.

Levels of Validation Effort

You actually have several places within your framework for systems development where you must deal with validation issues. The first is at the highest level, during the development of the overall warehouse plan. Validation at this level is concerned only with the viability of the solutions proposed at the highest level. When validating at this stage, you will be only minimally concerned with specific technical and business issues but will concentrate instead on the feasibility of the overall warehouse's objectives.

The other place where validation will need to occur is in each of the applications that are going to be developed. This level of validation takes a lot more technical detail into account and actually is an important part of the application development process.

Validation and Assumptions

The first concept that you must understand is systems assumptions. The objective of the validation step is to examine each of the assumptions that have gone into the development of the systems vision and determine whether they are valid or not. There are several things that make assumptions tricky. First, whenever dealing with a large systems project, there are a lot of assumptions that people make. Secondly, different people can make different assumptions. Thirdly, when different people make different assumptions, there is no way to know if they are in agreement. Because everybody is assuming, nobody sees any need to talk about it. The fact that people are making different kinds of assumptions is not a bad thing in and of itself. It certainly is possible for things to work out as long as the disparity between the assumptions is not too great. A much bigger problem arises when special kinds of assumptions occur. Two categories of problem-causing assumptions occur when people:

- Make the assumption that somebody else understands it or has taken responsibility for it.

- Fail to communicate the confidence level associated with the assumption, assuming somebody else is taking care of it.

This is an obvious consequence when people begin to make assumptions. You assume that everything has been taken into consideration when it really hasn't. The cases of misplaced assumptions occur frequently throughout the systems-development process. The problems associated with this condition tend to get worse as the project continues. Usually, the revelation that something has been missed occurs slowly over time, as people begin to realize that there is a problem. Usually, by that time, it is too late.

The Confidence Level of an Assumption

The other thing about assumptions is that there usually are levels of risk associated with each assumption that you make. You assume that the sun will rise in the morning with a high confidence level. You assume that users can learn how to use a new data-mining tool with less confidence. As the risks associated with your assumptions grow, it is imperative that those risks be identified and addressed during the validation phase. Those who go into the development process while harboring serious doubts about the viability of a solution are setting themselves up for failure.

Your objective should be to enter infrastructure development and applications development with an exceedingly high level of confidence (at least 80%). It is the job of the validation process to ensure that is exactly what happens.

The Validation Process

Therefore, the validation process has several things it needs to accomplish. It must:

- Be systematic and thorough, thereby guaranteeing that all of the important assumptions have been identified and documented. One of the biggest objectives of the validation process is to make sure that everything important has been considered and reviewed by everyone involved in the process.
- Evaluate and minimize the risk associated with systems development. Another important function of this process will be to clearly flag those areas where the risk is higher than acceptable and to develop mechanisms that will minimize that risk.

When it comes to identifying assumptions and minimizing risk, there is something else that you are going to have to do during validation. The only way that you can evaluate what the assumptions mean, and the risk associated with each one, is to gain some assurance that you truly understand how it is going to be executed (definability) and that the effort required for development can be accurately estimated (estimability).

You also must remember that, in the area of risk, you really have several types of risk to worry about. You must be concerned with:

- Functional feasibility—Whether the proposed solution can work. This applies to both business/operational functionality and technical functionality. For example:
  ~Is it possible to get the marketing department to change the way they do things to make use of this system? (Business/operational functionality)

~Can you build a system that can handle these volumes of data and deliver it to the users in a reasonable time frame? (Technical functionality)

- Delivery feasibility—Can the solution actually produce the results that you want? For example, if the system is put in place, do you really believe that sales revenue will increase by 25%?

- Developmental feasibility—Can the solution be developed on time and on budget? Does the proposed development staff have the expertise, experience, tools, budget, and management structure to actually complete the system?

It is a common occurrence for people to dismiss different capabilities or functionalities as doable, when they really have no idea about how it will be done. They simply assume that somehow, someone will figure it out.

In general, therefore, you want the validation process to answer the following questions about each aspect of the warehouse solution:

- Is it feasible? Are the assumptions valid?

- Is it definable? Can you define each of the steps involved in its development and operation?

- Can it be estimated accurately? Is it defined well enough so that you can generate relatively accurate estimates as to effort level, time tables, and other costs?

- What are the risks? For those situations where the risks are high, can you identify them and minimize them before committing significant resources to the project?

A Systematic Approach to Validation

Because you want your approach to be thorough and systematic, you should make use of the warehouse framework that we have been defining throughout this book as the starting point for the process. We will envision the warehouse with its three components and multiple layers and consider the validation process from two perspectives: validation as it relates to the overall warehouse project and validation of the individual applications. (See Figure 11.1.)

Notice that, in addition to the basic framework itself, we have added two things. First, extending from the data-access area, we have shown the different grouping of users within operational clusters. It is our assumption that each application has been designed to meet the needs of a different operational group, and the risks and feasibilities associated with these business operations also must be included in the analysis.

Functional
legacy
systems

User
operational
areas

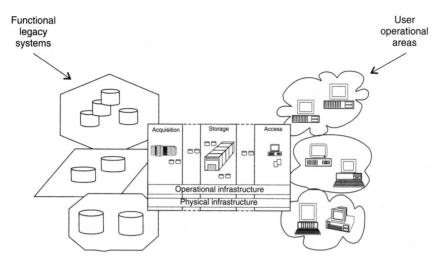

Figure 11.1 The warehouse framework.

At the other end of the warehouse, we have included the different functional legacy-systems areas. These areas also have an impact on the validation process. There are two kinds of validation that you need to consider. The first type occurs when you are developing your initial vision of the overall warehouse; this occurs in those situations where the warehousing project is going to have a very wide scope and involve the implementation of several applications. When the warehouse infrastructure under consideration is large, this will be a process all by itself. The other kind of validation to take into account is the validation of each of the applications that are going to be implemented.

Validation of the overall warehouse

When you begin wrestling with the issues of overall warehouse validation, you must take a decidedly "big-picture" perspective. From this view, you are not concerned with the minute validity of individual value propositions and their assumptions but with the overall warehouse approach as a viable solution.

Overall operational validity

When you consider the operational validity of the data warehouse, the question that you need to answer is "Do I have a high degree of confidence based upon what I know about the different value propositions that were proposed for utilization within the warehouse to believe that investment in a warehouse is justified?" In other words, has the vision-development process convinced you that the warehouse is a good idea?

While it certainly would be nice to know all of the details about how each of the proposed value propositions is going to be executed, it really is not essential that you validate each of them at this stage. All you really need to do is validate that:

- Each value proposition has merit (shows the potential for providing value).

- Each value proposition exhibits at least *prima facie* evidence of being feasible, definable, and estimable.

- The value propositions represent no major risks in their assumptions.

- The warehouse solutions provided will be able to be operationally integrated into the existing business areas.

See Figure 11.2.

At this level, therefore, the process of validating the operational assumptions for the warehouse is almost completely business and organizationally based. If the preponderance of evidence indicates that the different groups involved see a value in the warehouse, can envision themselves making use of it, and are willing to propose benefits in hard terms, then the warehouse certainly is validated from this perspective.

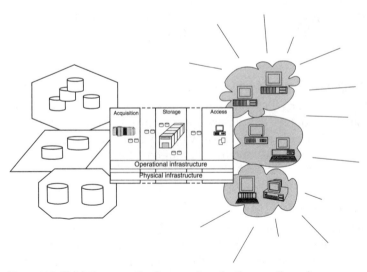

Figure 11.2 Validating operational assumptions for the overall warehouse.

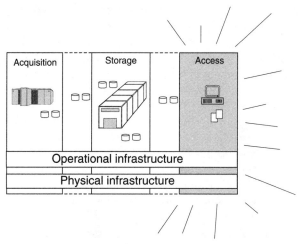

Figure 11.3 Validating access-component assumptions.

Validating data-access assumptions

There are many things that we can do to validate these assumptions and many perspectives to consider. (See Figure 11.3.)

Viability of access assumptions. Your first and most basic assumption about the data-access component of the overall warehouse is that all users will be able to gain access and make use of the warehouse through the use of their existing workstations, terminals, and supporting network infrastructure or that the organization will be able to afford and/or cost justify making that possible.

The only way that you can hope to validate this assumption is by developing an inventory of all proposed future users of the warehouse and ascertaining whether that capability exists or not. If it does exist, then you simply need to validate that the anticipated work loads will be attainable by the system. If it doesn't, then you need to figure out what it will take to bring these workstations up to the required level and determine whether doing so is going to be cost effective.

Obviously, there is a significant amount of overlap between ascertaining the validity of this component and developing the corresponding estimates of cost involved.

Utilization assumptions. Your second assumption will be that those users have the ability and desire to make use of the different data-mining and data-access mechanisms envisioned or that the ability and desire can be developed.

It is a serious mistake to make that assumption just because the developers of the system or the managers within the organization think that a solution will be capitalized on by the users without verifying this fact firsthand. I will never forget the experience I had as a fledgling system designer for a manufacturing company. I was given the mission of implementing a change to the existing loading dock tracking software to include some new functionalities. After six months of effort, the new solution was implemented. It was beautiful, sophisticated, and met all of the requirements. Everyone at the home office thought it was great. Unfortunately, when we implemented the change out in the factories, we ran into a serious problem. It was too complicated for people. The solution confused them and frustrated them. Finally, they actually got the union involved, and my eloquent solution was replaced with a much simpler, more user-friendly solution.

At another organization, many years later, we made the same mistake. We assumed that the terms Windows and user-friendly were synonymous, so we proceeded to develop a beautiful user interface for the warehouse. It had icons and menus, and everything was driven by the mouse. Unfortunately, the user community was comfortable with their old 3270 menu-driven screens. The supposedly "user-friendly" interface was intimidating and frightening. We ended up needing to add three months to the project schedule to give everyone a chance to become trained and comfortable with the new approach.

The previous two examples represent minor changes to the system when compared to the changes in operational procedures and user interfaces that most sophisticated data-mining efforts entail. As a consequence of this, it will be crucial that this aspect be evaluated and your assumptions about user acceptance validated before proceeding.

Validating storage-component assumptions. To validate these assumptions, there are several steps that we must go through, depending on the aspect being considered. (See Figure 11.4.)

Platform viability. The next evaluation that you need to perform is for the storage component. Your principal assumption about the feasibility and costs of building the storage component is that the platform in which you choose to house the storage component can store the volumes of data that the warehouse eventually will hold and will be able to provide end users with timely access.

This is another area where the traditional approach to data processing really is stuck. According to the rote method of database design, the only way to know whether a database can handle the data that you expect it to is to develop detailed models of all of the data and volume estimates for each

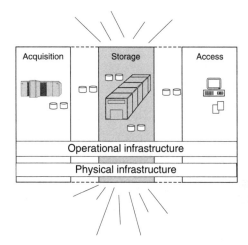

Figure 11.4 Validating storage assumptions.

one. You then can determine all of the different ways that people are going to access it. In other words, you must practically complete building the system before you can develop estimates!

While it is very difficult to argue with the premise that the best and most accurate estimates can be developed when you have as much information as possible about what you expect the warehouse to do, it also is not feasible in most situations. Therefore, the issues of estimation and validation for the storage component are going to have to be managed through some kind of compromise solution.

While it is not possible to validate the viability of the selected platform without information about volumes and access rates, it is possible to develop high-level estimates of these things without the benefit of all of the detail. In this case, you will assure the viability and develop your capacity estimates through the use of generalization and approximation techniques, which we will detail in the next chapter.

In this case, as in all cases of validation having to do with warehouse capabilities from a physical perspective, you will rely heavily upon the estimation process to provide you with your validation.

Validating acquisition-component assumptions. The final component of your warehouse is the acquisitions area. (See Figure 11.5.) The acquisitions area is responsible for taking care of the process of extracting data from legacy systems, preparing it and staging it for loading into the warehouse. Your principal assumption about the warehouse in this regard will be that it is possible to perform each of the acquisition processes in a reasonable amount of time.

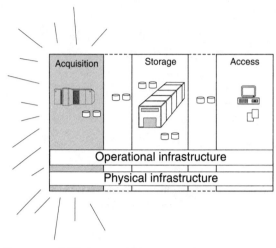

Figure 11.5 Validating acquisition assumptions.

Data sourcing and mapping viability. Some of the biggest assumptions that people make about acquisition are that:

- The data that they are looking for exists.
- The data can be easily extracted.
- The data can be used within the warehouse.
- There are resources available who understand the legacy system or externally defined data and who can assist in the process of understanding it and working with it.

Let's consider some of the ways that these assumptions can be invalidated.

Data existence. As I have mentioned on several previous occasions, people often make assumptions about exactly what data is available and where it can be found. In too many cases, these assumptions are discovered to be invalid.

While the principal area of concern is when you talk about validation of the existence of data for individual applications on a much higher level, you need to get some assurance of the likelihood that the data that you are seeking exists on the system in the early stages of overall warehouse development.

The validation of data existence at this level can easily be accomplished by determining exactly what types of data users will expect and where they think it can be found, before talking with the people responsible for the management of those systems for verification.

Data extraction. Another assumption that we will make is that the data can be obtained from the sources provided. Unfortunately, this is not always the case. Sometimes legacy systems are so complicated, backlogged with work, or making use of so many resources already that it is determined that the data simply cannot be provided. If this kind of issue can arise, it must be identified at this time.

Data utilization. One of the most frustrating things that can happen is when users identify desired data and the data is located, but the owners of the data are not willing or able to allow the data to be used. An interesting case occurred recently in which a government organization tried to make use of another governmental agency's lists to help track down traffic violators. A person apprehended through this new system argued that the transference of the list from one agency to another was a violation of his right to privacy, and the agency was forbidden to use the information again.

In addition to those cases where the ability to use data has been legislated away, there are cases where the organization owning the data simply does not want to share it (as is common in the case of mailing lists, where one organization does not want another to use their list because of the impact it would have on the recipients of the mail) or want to sell it for more money than the requesting organization is willing to pay (as in the case of purchased or rented lists).

When any source of data that is critical to the operation of the warehouse is owned or managed by a group other then the one building the system, then the validity of your assumptions about utilization must be addressed.

Data understanding. Another place where people's assumptions fall short occurs when you assume that there are people available to help you understand what the data is, how it works, and what it means. Unfortunately, in today's lean, mean data-processing organizations, you often find legacy systems that have been left to "run themselves." The staff that understood the system has long since retired or moved on to other jobs. If you make assumptions about the availability of these resources, then you had better get some assurance that, when the time comes, assistance will be there.

Validating application-development assumptions from the overall perspective

In general, most of your assumptions about application development will be made in regard to the development of each application. However, you will need to make certain assumptions about how the overall process is going to be managed and run.

From the perspective of the overall warehousing project these assumptions need to be stated, and assurances need to be gained from all parties involved that these procedures will be followed. It would be an incredible waste to go through the entire process of vision development, validation, estimation, and infrastructure development only to find that there is no commitment to the prescribed methodology.

Validating operational-infrastructure assumptions

You also will find yourself making assumptions about the operational infrastructure that will support warehouse operations. Each individual will be counting on this infrastructure to make using the warehouse easier. At the same time, you don't want to build more robustness into this layer than is necessary. To validate your assumptions in this regard, you need only to develop a general understanding of how it will work, develop a rough estimate of what it will cost to develop, and reach concurrence from all participants that this functionality is desirable and reasonable. (See Figure 11.6.)

Validating physical-infrastructure assumptions

The final area where you will need to perform serious technical validation is the physical infrastructure. While the viability of the data-identification process and the ability of the platforms to support their designated functions will have been validated in previous steps, you also must develop assurances that the overall infrastructure can handle all of the different operations envisioned.

Data-transport assumptions. While your evaluation of the acquisition, storage, and access layers weighed the ability of each component to accomplish its objectives, you have yet to examine whether the infrastructure will be able to handle all of the different kinds of data transport that it must support. How will data move from legacy systems to the acquisitions area? How will acquisitions processing be managed? How will data move from the acquisitions area to the storage area? What about the staging and work area components?

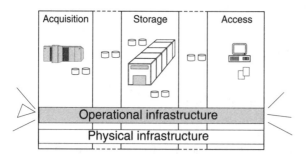

Figure 11.6 Validating operations-infrastructure assumptions.

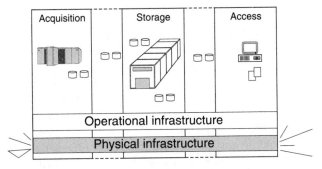

Figure 11.7 Validating physical-infrastructure assumptions.

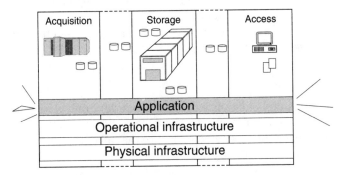

Figure 11.8 Validating individual application assumptions.

The assumption that the networking and other kinds of data-transport mechanisms will be in place to move data from the legacy system to the access area must be validated. Many times people have discovered too late that major changes to platforms and networking arrangements must be made to support the initiative. (See Figure 11.7.)

Data-storage and -location assumptions. The other place where assumptions can leave you short occurs when people dismiss the process of storing, processing, and moving data through acquisition. If a series of programs must be run that need to read and write from a progression of multimillion-row files, it is essential that enough disk space be available to make that progression doable.

Application validation. While the previous validation steps will help you to gain some assurance that the overall warehouse will be a success, you also must apply those criteria, and some additional ones, when validating each of the individual applications. (See Figure 11.8.)

Validating the operational/business assumptions

Before beginning the development of an application, you are going to need to validate that the business assumptions upon which it is based are valid. It is one thing to say that a new application sounds like a good idea, and it is another to say that you hope certain things will happen when the application is complete, but it is an entirely different matter to be sure that the assumptions represented are reasonable. For example, one group proposed that, by having access to different types of purchased list and historical sales information, they would be able to improve marketing efforts by over 25%. Their assumption was that more ready access to the information would result in better decision making. Unfortunately, after suffering great expense, when the system was finally activated, it was discovered that the actual quality of the decision making was worse than it had been under the older and more disciplined methods of data analysis.

Somehow, for each value proposition that you consider, you need to gain some assurance that the assumptions are accurate.

Validating data assumptions

While at the higher level of validation you were concerned only with the general question of whether data would be available or not, when you get down to the specific application, you need to ensure that all of the data that is required to get the job done will be available. The steps that we outlined earlier—about validating the data aspects of the access, storage, and acquisitions components—must be applied to a far greater level of detail when you find yourself focusing on an individual application.

Validating technical-performance assumptions

In the same manner, you also must apply a great deal more rigor to the validation of the technical assumptions made for each application. Hopefully, in the process of validating the technical assumptions for the overall project, you already have addressed whatever an individual application might need. If not, then it will have to be addressed at this time.

Checklists. To assist you in the process of validation at both the overall and individual application level, I have found that it can be helpful to maintain several checklists. Because the major objectives of the validation process are to identify all of the assumptions that have gone into the development of the solution, to ascertain the validity of each, and to be sure that the nature of those assumptions and the risk associated with each are communicated to everyone involved, the following lists have proved to be instrumental.

Validation checklists. The validation checklist shown in Table 11.1 summarizes the validation issues that we have identified so far. It should be used as a minimum starting point in assuring that all aspects of the warehouse's development are being explored and to ensure that there are no hidden, high-risk assumptions.

Critical-assumptions checklists. In addition to the maintenance of the validation checklist, it also is standard practice on projects of this nature to maintain a list of the critical assumptions that people have made about the project. The critical-assumptions list serves as a way to highlight areas of concern and then should be used as the means to guarantee that everyone involved in the process understands what is being developed.

The estimation process. Many aspects of the validation cannot be developed without a significant amount of specific information about exactly what the proposed warehouse is supposed to be able to do. The development of this information is referred to as the *estimation process*. Because estimation and validation are so closely related, you can almost consider them to be two parts of the same process. However, when you talk about estimation, you need to realize several things about the process.

First, when you begin talking about estimation in this environment, you must realize that there actually are several kinds of estimates with which you need to concern yourself. Secondly, you need to develop a better understanding of the estimation process itself.

Estimating warehouse development. There actually are four kinds of estimates that you need to develop in a typical warehouse development environment, and several more as you need to propose benchmark, prototype, and proof-of-concept projects.

The major areas where estimation is done are:

- The time and effort required to develop the warehouse plan—The effort required to perform the vision development, validation-and-estimation, planning, and infrastructure development steps.

- The time and effort required to build the overall warehouse itself—This is the output of the validation-and-estimation step.

- The time and effort required to build the infrastructure—One of the outputs of the infrastructure-development step.

- The time and effort required to develop each individual application, and additional estimates for benchmark, proof-of-concept, and prototype-development efforts.

See Figure 11.9.

TABLE 11.1 Validating Assumptions

Area to be validated	Assumption to be validated	Comment
Value propositions		
	Has merit	The value proposition will provide real value to the organization.
	Feasible	The solution can be executed.
	Definable	We can figure out how it will be done.
	Estimable	We can estimate what it will cost.
	Low risk	There is a low risk factor.
	Can be integrated into operational environment	The solution will integrate with other operations in the business.
Data access		
	Users will have ready access	Workstations and network are in place (or the cost has been factored in).
	Users can utilize the solution	Users will be able to use the delivered tools.
Storage		
	Platform can handle volumes	The database can operate with these volumes of data.
	Platform can handle access rates	The database can support the proposed number of users and number of transactions.
	Platform will fit in the environment and be supported	The platform will be supported by organizational support staff.
Acquisition		
	Data exists	The needed data can be located.
	Data can be readily extracted	It will be easy to extract data from legacy systems.
	Data will be in a usable form	The data will be usable (it will not require an inordinate amount of effort to cleanse it and prepare it for access).
	Expertise and support available for legacy systems	Staff familiar with legacy systems will be available.
Application development		
	Staff will be available	Staffing levels will be sufficient.
	Staff will be competent	The staff will know the technology, application, and approach being used.
	Staff will be dedicated	Staff will be allocated sufficient time to give good support.
Operational infrastructure		
	Solution is understood	Do we understand what the operational infrastructure will do and not do?

Area to be validated	Assumption to be validated	Comment
	Solution is communicated to all	Has it been communicated to all?
	Solution will be budgeted and executed	Have sufficient resources been allocated for the development of the operational infrastructure?
Physical infrastructure		
	Data transport mechanisms are in place	Data ports, shared disks, and network connections between all components and legacy systems exist and are of sufficient capacity.
	Data storage areas will be available	Sufficient storage area has been allocated for the overall process.

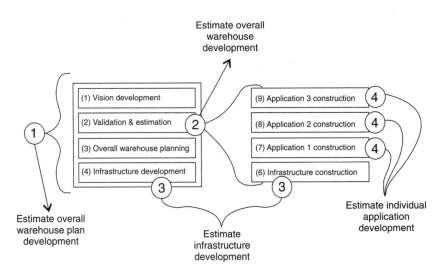

Figure 11.9 Areas of warehouse-development estimates.

Before we can begin to take a look at the requirements for developing each of these estimates, we need to take a step back and consider the process of estimating itself. An *estimate* is a discipline that you follow that enables you to develop a reasonable idea about what is required to accomplish different tasks. In a very real sense, an estimate is a qualified guess. Because an estimate is nothing more than a guess, then how in the world are you going to determine whether it is accurate?

You cannot estimate what you cannot define! Of course, one of the biggest assumptions that we will make before going any further in the discussion of the estimation process is that the managers of the project have set out to eliminate as many inestimable factors as possible. All of the estimation effort in the world is wasted if you proceed with the execution of a project plan that includes large inexplicable gaps.

For this reason, we have thoroughly defined the warehouse-development process and demanded that things be done in certain ways and in a certain order. It also is for this reason that you have completed the validation phase. The main purpose of the validation phase is to identify those places in the project plan where it is not possible to develop estimates and take actions before estimation begins to make their development possible. A couple examples of how these "black holes" in a project plan can cause the rest of the project's estimates to be invalid should help illustrate our point.

Database-access and -scalability assumptions. One of the "black holes" that has scuttled many a warehousing project can be found in the area of database accessibility and response times. When making decisions about whether a database can support the volumes of data and access requirements that they think the warehouse is going to need, most inexperienced developers assume that there is a straightforward trade-off between the amount of data that the database can handle and the ability of that database to support it. This assumption can be viewed in terms of a graph, showing the gradual decline in system performance as a direct function of the increase in data volumes. (See Figure 11.10.)

Unfortunately, these assumptions have proven to be wrong. In reality, as the volume of data increases, all databases hit break points where performance drops off drastically for no apparent reason. (See Figure 11.11.)

This step-function curve drastically changes your assumptions about what a database can handle. What is even more frustrating is that unique combinations of hardware, memory, disk devices, database software, data

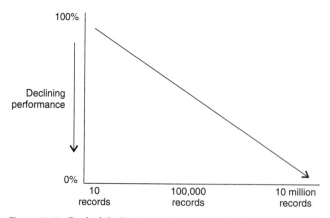

Figure 11.10 Gradual decline in performance as the database volume increases.

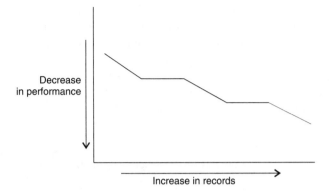

Figure 11.11 Step function decline in database performance.

volumes, and application access all force these step functions to occur at apparently different and random points along the curve. Often the only way to know if a database can handle a projected work load is to try it. This represents a significant drawback to your ability to estimate costs and development times in a warehouse environment of high data volumes, and it is impossible for you to develop estimates without a mechanism for making that determination.

Software-connectivity assumptions. Another type of "black hole" can occur in the utilization of unique combinations of software, hardware, and networking environments. Unfortunately, most environments combine a vast assortment of nonstandardized network and software arrangements that hamper your ability to confidently estimate how well something will work.

There have been many situations where the end users have selected a data-mining tool, and the development team proceeded to execute the project plan that would deliver the application. Much later in the process, people realized that the chosen software product would not work in the targeted environment and that the cost of making the product usable was not acceptable. This kind of misfire can wreak terrible chaos on the overall project plan. When it is discovered that the tool might not work, the entire development effort must be halted while the problem is investigated, causing serious backlogs in the project plan. When it is discovered that a different tool must be used, the project must be relaunched, taking the new tool and its idiosyncrasies into account.

Therefore, our assumption will be that the developers of your estimates have done everything possible to eliminate risk, stabilize the infrastructure, and validate assumptions about the system before attempting to develop estimates. Our approach to estimation will assume that these things will not occur or will be appropriately addressed if they do occur.

Sources of input into the estimation process

Experience and history. Ideally, one of the most reliable sources about how long something is going to take or how much it is going to cost is to find someone who has done it before. Get this person to use his or her knowledge to help develop your approximations. Unfortunately, in most cases, the systems being developed are so unique that there is little experience that people can draw upon to help in the process. When estimation based on experience falls short, you must try to do the job by other means.

Existing systems inventory. The second source of potentially helpful information is to look at existing systems within the organization that perform equivalent or related functions. Developers of estimates often will get their best information about transaction rates, user characteristics, data volumes, and activity levels by examining these characteristics for existing systems and using that information to develop the estimates for the new system.

Models. The final source of information for your estimates will be models. Models and methodologies are formally or informally defined techniques and approaches that people have used in the past that try to simulate the behavior or characteristics of the system on a conceptual level, allowing you to apply mathematical techniques in developing meaningful estimates.

Perhaps the best known of the estimation modeling techniques is *function-point analysis*. Under function-point analysis, the estimator examines the functionalities that the system is expected to perform and translates those into function points. The function points then can be added up, and algorithms applied, to derive estimates of development times and levels of activity.

Derivation, extrapolation, and multipliers. The key mechanisms in the estimation process are derivation, extrapolation, and the use of multipliers. *Derivation* and *extrapolation* are mathematical processes that take a given set of information and apply mathematical processes to them to project the ultimate size, shape, or duration of something. In less-sophisticated situations, the estimator will develop simple multipliers, allowing them to derive the expected requirements that a system might have.

Confidence levels and costs of estimates. Before we consider the estimation process, there are two more prerequisites: the confidence level of the estimate and the cost. Confidence level is much more then the simple assignment of a probability to an estimate. There actually are several components to it. In the simplest case, we might say that we are 99.9% confident that the sun will rise tomorrow. What is assumed in this statement is that there is a 0.1% chance that it will not. In this situation, there are only two choices (either the sun rises or it doesn't), so a one-dimensional confidence level is acceptable. However, what if we were to say that we are 80% confident that the sun would rise between 6 A.M. and 7 A.M., meaning that there also is a chance that it will rise before 6 A.M. or after 7 A.M. In this situation, there is more than a simple binary (yes/no or on/off) choice. In cases like this, it is typical to express probabilities as a function of a curve. (See Figure 11.12.)

This figure shows a typical probabilities curve. It tells you that, while the greatest probability is that the sun will rise within a half hour of 6:30 (the center line of the curve), there is an 80% chance that it will be between 6 A.M. and 7 A.M. (the left and right quartiles), a 10% chance that it will be before 6 A.M., and a 10% chance that it will be after 7 A.M. By exploring and reporting probabilities in this way, you are able to communicate a lot more about what the real probabilities are.

The perfect estimate.   Let's just say that it will be our objective to develop the perfect estimate. An estimate with a 100% confidence level and absolutely no risk or variance. (See Figure 11.13.)

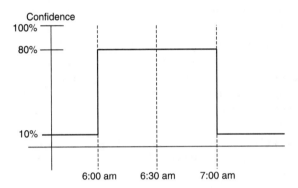

Figure 11.12 Probability chart for the sun rising.

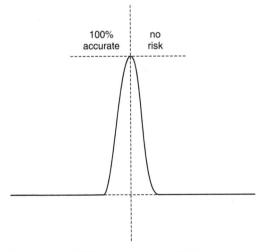

Figure 11.13 A 100% accurate cost estimate.

No problem. How did we do it? We simply finished the project and wrote down everything it took to get it done. Obviously, if you had to finish the project before you could estimate its cost, you would not need estimates in the first place. However, this revelation tells you two very important things about the estimation process. First of all, what is clear is the more of the project that you have completed, the better and more accurate your estimates will be. (See Figure 11.14.)

The conclusion that you can draw from this is that the longer you can postpone the estimation process and the more you can find out about what you want to do before you start, the better the estimation will be. The second thing that you learn from this relationship between estimates and percentage of completion has to do with the cost of the estimate. Of course, the estimate will be extremely accurate, but the cost of that estimate will be very high. It will be the cost of doing the entire project. This establishes the second relationship: the one between estimate accuracy and cost. (See Figure 11.15.)

Generally, the more you spend on estimation, the more accurate the estimate will be. This relationship between cost and accuracy is not always valid. It certainly is possible to spend a lot of time and money on the development of estimates that are of a minimal value. This presents the third characteristic of an estimate to consider: its value.

The value of an estimate. For every given estimating situation, you must weigh the cost (in time and money) to develop that estimate against the accuracy that the estimate will give you (including its ranges of confidence

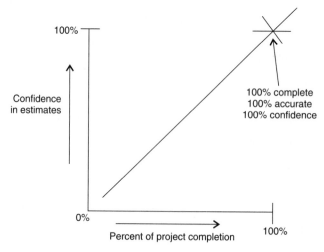

Figure 11.14 Accuracy and confidence increase as more of the project gets completed.

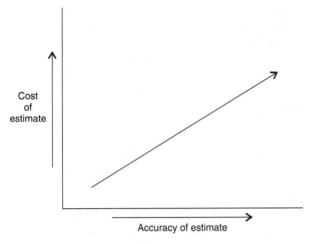

Figure 11.15 Relationship between the cost of an estimate and its accuracy.

levels) and the ultimate value it will provide. While it certainly would be nice to have extremely accurate estimates, there are many situations where the information is not worth the price. There have been many situations where organizations have spent unbelievable amounts of time and money in their attempts to determine whether a given platform or database product could handle the anticipated work loads. In many of these cases, the organizations have dedicated so much time and effort to the estimation process that they found it would have been less expensive to simply build the infernal system and try it from the beginning.

Overcoming the need to overestimate things. Because there has been such an abysmal history of systems failure in the past, many people have started to try to compensate by overestimating. Our objective is to take an approach that attempts to balance the extremes.

While we already have identified the parts of the overall development process that require estimation, we have yet to consider the types of estimates that you will need to develop. There are several:

- Wall-time estimate—Estimate of the time that it will take to complete a task or project. This estimate answers the question "When will it be done?"

- CPU-time estimate—Estimate the amount of time that people will have to spend on the execution of the tasks. This estimate answers the question "How many hours will how many people actually spend working on this task or project?"

- Hardware/software estimate—Estimate the sizes, types, costs, and capacities of the physical resources that will go into the construction of the system. These estimates answer the question "How much will I need to spend on hardware and software to build this system?"

Of the five areas of estimation that we have defined for this approach, all require the first two types of estimates mentioned. Some require that hardware/software estimation be done.

Confidence levels and the areas of estimation. While you certainly would like all of your estimates to be as accurate as possible, it is important for you to keep the costs of that accuracy in mind and develop a criterion for their development that is appropriate to your objectives for the process. When making this evaluation, you want to stay cognizant of not only the costs and confidence levels of the estimates, but also of the consequences and risks involved in the creation of less-accurate estimates. For each area of estimation that you consider, you should begin by identifying the reason for developing the estimate and the overall objective of the estimation process.

Overall warehouse planning. The process of planning the overall warehouse involves no estimation of hardware and software whatsoever. It is entirely a thinking, writing, and communicating process. Therefore, the risks involved in the development of inaccurate estimates in this area are minimal. The big challenge in this area is to determine how to reconcile the differences between the wall time and the CPU time (actual activity time) involved.

The problem with estimating the planning process is that it involves investigating, interviewing, and consensus building. That means that the really important things happen when the managers, operational personnel, and systems people can get together and hammer things out. The second kind of time lag occurs when people need to find out "how things work" or what the capabilities of new components might be. Again, the people doing the planning are totally dependent on the availability of vendors, sales people, and people working on other systems to provide them with the information that they need.

The actual ratio of the time spent waiting to the time spent working in this environment can be great. At a minimum, you will need to assume at least a 50/50 ratio between the two, and it can easily turn into 25/75 ratio. In other words, you can assume that it will take a one-week effort to successfully complete vision development. However, the unavailability of key people and other inflexibilities in people's schedules can easily turn that one week into four weeks. Therefore, your estimates for the execution of this phase of the project must be based upon realistic expectations for the availability and dedication of the parties required. If enthusiasm is high and the resources are available, then a relatively tight estimate can be utilized. If part of the process is to educate people on something that they know nothing about or to work with people who are less than enthusiastic, then you will need to allocate more lag time. Estimates for the execution of this phase usually can be measured in weeks. Exceedingly large projects might reach the several-months range if resistance to the project or the complexity of the issues becomes very high.

Developing estimates for the overall warehouse-development effort. The second area where you are going to need to exercise good estimating practice is in the area of estimating the overall development effort (part of the general planning process).

The estimates developed during this phase must provide information about:

- The overall time that it will take to finish the warehouse.
- Some idea of the times required to complete each application (value proposition).
- The hardware, software, and network infrastructure required to support the warehouse.
- The effort required to deliver the systems (the people and time that they spend on each project).

Estimating the time and level of effort for the overall warehouse. There is no easy way to come up with these numbers, especially as early in the process as you are going to need them. There are several things that you should keep in mind before beginning the process. Somehow you need to develop an approach that allows you to determine the best possible overall appraisal of the effort without forcing yourself to actually design each of the systems. An approach that has proven effective in the past involves the following steps:

1. Identify each of the value propositions to be included within the scope.
2. Separate the applications into the different major categories of effort that they should entail.
3. Develop high-level estimates of the level of activity for each component of the warehouse (acquisition, storage, and access) by developing an understanding of the screens required, volumes of data required, access rates, and development effort for one of the projects from within each category.
4. Extrapolate the overall level of effort from these samples.

Categories of level of effort applications. While each warehouse application is going to be unique, it also is true that the different types of warehouse applications tend to cluster into the following different groupings. They can be categorized by:

- Acquisitions component size and complexity
- Storage component size and complexity
- Type of application

Acquisitions component size and complexity. In general, you can evaluate any data warehousing effort in the area of acquisitions activity as involving:

- No effort—For those cases where the acquisition of data will have been accomplished by the development of a previous application.
- Low effort—A low number of input files (1 to 5) and a low level of data transformation is required.
- Average effort—A medium number of input files (5 to 15) and a reasonable level of interfile coordination and synchronization requirements.
- High effort—A large number of files and a lot of complexity in the data-preparation process.

Storage component size and complexity. Storage component development activity is easily measured and estimated in simple terms. How many tables will there be? How big will they be? What kinds of access will they be required to support? Armed with this information, it should be a relatively straightforward task to develop good, rough estimates of this activity.

Type of application. Probably the most difficult thing to estimate at a very high level will be the effort required to deliver the applications portions of the system. Applications will be of the following types:

- Customized solutions, written using application programming languages and graphical user interfaces.
- Solutions that involve the direct linkage of data-mining tools to the warehouse storage area.
- Solutions that require the building of data chains and the feeding of the data from those chains into data-mining tools.

In cases where a data-chaining mechanism will be required, the development of that facility, the first time, will suffice to meet the needs of all future applications that require it. After you have ascertained the characteristics of each of the applications according to these criteria, you can pick the critical components to drive your estimation process and determine realistic development levels for those areas. When those estimates have been completed, you can use the information to extrapolate your final, overall development effort.

Not only must you include an estimate for the development of each of these applications, you also must provide a reasonable estimate of the effort required to establish the infrastructure. To do that and complete the estimates that you already have initiated, you are going to need some relatively dependable physical system estimates to drive the decision-making process.

Thoroughness in the area of physical and user requirements. Experience has repeatedly shown that, when you are developing estimates for the construction of warehouse environments that involve the use of user workstation and client server technologies, the number of technical and managerial issues that need to be addressed can be astronomical. The following checklists have been developed to assist people in ensuring that all the issues of personnel and technical capability have been addressed.

Technology inventory (master list). The first table provides a checklist that identifies the different kinds of hardware/software that need to be included in your estimates, with columns indicating the critical functions that must be performed in relationship to each other. For example, in the selection of hardware, you must allocate cost for the purchase of the item, leave time in the plan to allow for the time needed to make the proper selection, go through the process of installation, provide for ongoing development support, and provide for support of the hardware in the ultimate production environment. (See Table 11.2.)

Data architecture checklist. In the area of databases, you need to be sure that you have addressed all of the issues that have to do with the topology of the data architecture (size, volume, location, etc.) as well as the modeling, administration, and software-support issues. (See Table 11.3.)

Operational requirements inventory (master list). This next checklist can serve as a starting point to help you ensure that all of the operational information for validation and estimation has been collected. (See Table 11.4.)

Administrative issues checklist. The last checklist takes a cross section of the other issues and identifies key issues in the execution of administrative functions. (See Table 11.5.)

TABLE 11.2 Platform Checklist

Platform	Selection	Installation	Development support	Production support
Hardware				
CPU size				
Chip type				
Internal architecture				
Disk requirements				
Cost/maintenance				
Branding/dependability				
Operating system				
Topology/geography				
Utilities				
Full system				
Backup/recovery				
Disaster recovery				
Machine security				
Network				
Topology (Where & how)				
Hardware (Cabling, NIC...)				
Typology (Ethernet, token ring)				
Protocol (IPX, TCP/IP...)				
Network operating system (Novell, LAN Mgr...)				
Capacity				
Transaction rate				
Volumes				
Throughput				
Bandwidth				

TABLE 11.3 Physical-Infrastructure Checklist

Data	Estimate development	Ongoing support
Topology		
Sizing		
Volumes		
Access rates		
Location		
Logical data		
Models		
Dictionary/repository		
Database administration		
Database hardware		
Database middleware		
Database software		
Software		
Windows		
OS/2/Windows/X Windows		
Environments		
PowerBuilder		
SmallTalk (et al)		
etc.		
Languages		
C, C++, Basic		
Visual Basic, etc.		
Tools		
Word-processing tools		
Spreadsheet tools		
Graphics tools		
Personal databases		
Personal utilities		
Applications		
Custom-developed systems		

TABLE 11.3 Continued

Data	Estimate development	Ongoing support
Prepackaged systems		
E-mail, work flow, etc.		
Suites and families		
Application architecture		
What runs where?		
Business rule storage		

TABLE 11.4 Operational-Management Checklist

Operational	
Who will use the system?	
Users	
User departments	
User types	
User classes	
User functions	
Functional areas	
Where will the users be?	
Topology	
Geography	
When will they use the system?	
Timing	
Cycles	
Work patterns	
What will they do with the system?	
Functions	
Transaction types/classes	
Operation types/classes	
Application types/classes	
Desktop load types	
How often will they use the systems?	
Rates	
Temporal parameters	
Transactional drivers	

TABLE 11.5 Administrative and Development Checklist

Administrative		
Who will support....		
Selection		
Installation		
Development		
Ongoing support		
Backup/recovery		
Security		
Monitoring and tuning		
Troubleshooting		
How will we manage....		
Standards		
Procedures		
Policies		
Roles		
Responsibilities		
Developmental		
Design		
Methodology		
Case		
Models and tools		
SDLC		
Architecture		
Application		
System		
Project		
Environmental setup		
Version control		
Software migration		
Test, development, production migration		
Tool selection		
Staffing		
Training		

TABLE 11.5 Continued

Hiring/contracting		
Estimation		
Project plans		
Timelines		
Estimation procedures		

Chapter

12

Budgeting, Bidding, and Staffing

The last topics that we will consider in the overall warehouse construction are the budgeting, bidding, and staffing processes. While the framework that we have been describing up to this point certainly provides the reader with a lot of helpful structure, it is important that we include within this framework some understanding of the process of financing and managing it.

To Build or to Buy?

The first thing to consider when trying to decide how to finance the construction of a large-scale system is to determine whether you are going to build the entire data warehouse on your own or get some help. Outside assistance in data-warehouse construction can come from several sources, but the principal sources are hardware vendors, software vendors, and consultants.

Hardware vendors

There are many ways that you can use hardware vendors to help leverage your data-warehousing development efforts.

Bundled solutions. As data warehousing becomes a more popular alternative, innovative vendors of hardware products have begun to create "data-warehousing packages," which combine specially developed hardware arrangements combined with specifically designated software to offer the would-be data warehouser a "ready to use" solution.

These kinds of packaged solutions offer many advantages. The purchaser is assured of getting a well-coordinated collection of products. Many infrastructure and operational issues will have been worked out in advance. The big risk in these situations can be avoided if the person investigating the options ensures that he clearly understands the strengths and limitations of the package.

Hardware vendor-provided consulting. In addition to providing assistance with the technical aspects of the construction process, many hardware vendors have added consulting support services to their staffs to provide customers with a more complete solution. For the most part, these services should be considered in the same vein as "normal" consulting activities.

Software vendors

The second place where help in the warehouse construction process comes from is through the vendors of data-warehousing software products. There are several categories of products to consider.

Acquisition component products. This category includes all products designed to assist the developer of the warehouse in the process of analyzing, converting, and transporting data from legacy systems to the storage area. There are several types of products in this category.

Data movers. These products automate the process of moving data from one place to the next. By making use of a separate platform and network connectivity between the platforms, these products allow the user to input specifications for the data to be moved, where it is to be moved, and when. The product takes care of the rest. The Info-Pump is a good example of this kind of product.

Data analyzers. These products assist people in the process of understanding where their data is and what it means. They usually are tied in with existing data dictionaries and other types of repository support software but can save many days of analytical effort when used correctly.

Data cleaners. Software in this category actually makes it easier to clean up data. It uses special rules and routines to check for the validity, accuracy, and compliance level of each field within the database. Data cleaners often include adjustment software that cleans up the data automatically, after it is discovered.

At the most sophisticated end of the spectrum are the highly intelligent, specialized data-cleansing products like PostalSoft, which reads in name and address information and makes use of sophisticated soundex, postal standards, and merge/purge processing to clean up files for mailing.

At the more general-purpose end are products like Vality, which uses reference files and search criteria to validate and cleanse individual fields.

Storage component products

Databases. No data warehouse would be possible without a database management system software package to run it. These packages ultimately turn out to be the "heart and soul" of most data-warehouse applications.

Products in this area include the "big databases"; the most popular in the industry include DB2 on mainframes and Oracle, Informix, and Sybase in the UNIX arena. Also included are products that deal in specialized industries or in the delivery of specialized database services, like Red Brick and Ingres.

Data accelerators. As an adjunct to the normal database software, many people have begun purchasing accelerator products. These products work as add-ons to existing database technologies and make it possible for queries to be executed in a fraction of the time that a normal query would take. These products are especially important when databases get extremely large.

Repositories. Repository products provide a software-enabled framework that makes the management of the warehouse storage area easier. Repositories make use of special indexes and control tables that store metadata (information about the information in the warehouse). The utilization of a repository product can make management of the actual warehouse, the data extraction, and data chain-building processes easier.

Access component products

Data-mining products. The driving force behind many warehousing initiatives today is the ability to attach high-powered data-mining tools to it. In the closing chapters of this book, we will spend a significant amount of time considering the products in this category.

Middleware. All of the data-mining tools in the world are useless if you don't have a mechanism in place to make it possible for you to hook them up to the warehouse. While in some situations you will be able to make direct connections between user workstations and the warehouse, in many cases you will need the assistance that middleware products can bear to help make those connections inexpensive and user friendly.

Operational infrastructure products. The final category of products that can be purchased provides the ability to manage the entire operational layer of the warehouse. Several vendors of data-warehouse management packages include a variety of services and mechanisms that can provide the kind of operational support that we have described throughout this book.

Percentage of Budget Analysis

After you have determined the products to include in the development of your warehousing solution, your next step is to begin determining how to allocate the costs for each of the development steps. While the development of the hard numbers required to do this should be a product of the estimation process, there are some things about the overall ratio of costs allocated that can be helpful both in understanding the budgeting process and in validating that our estimates are accurate.

The easy warehouse: Budget analysis

We will begin our investigation of budget ratio analysis by considering the simplest and easiest kind of warehouse development case to help you develop an appreciation for the issues.

The simplest kind of data-warehousing solution that we could envision might be where a group of users has identified that the information on a list of potential customers (available from one of the legacy systems within the organization) contains information to which they would like to gain *ad hoc* access. Their intention is to perform *ad hoc* queries against the information in that file to investigate the different characteristics that the customers might display. No special data analysis or identification work will be required, and the users simply will accept the data as it is extracted from the system.

Therefore, assuming that the infrastructure (physical and operational) is in place, the process of delivering this warehouse solution requires that you read the file into the storage area, then provide the end users with a query tool to access it.

Your allocation of the expense for the delivery of this system might look something like this:

- Acquisition development—33%
- Storage development—33%
- Access development—33%

See Figure 12.1.

Sophisticated user analysis.   You now can begin to change the variables involved and see what kinds of impact it will have on this allocation. In the first case (where the acquisition, storage, and access components were all relatively simple), you saw that the percent of budget was allocated rather evenly. Now let's consider what happens when the end users decide that they still would like to use the same data but plan to be more sophisticated in their use of it. For example, they might decide to use a multidimensional

Figure 12.1 An "easy" warehouse—Percent of budget.

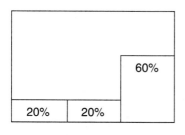

Figure 12.2 Sophisticated user access.

database or a neural net for better processing. In this case, your allocation of the funds for the project will be different, more like:

- Acquisition—20%
- Storage—20%
- Access—60%

See Figure 12.2.

Complicated input data. In a third case, we will assume that the users require only the simple access mechanism that we assumed in the first situation, but now the data that they want to see is much more difficult to get at. For example, it might require that you pull data from three or four different files. You also might need to merge, purge, and sanitize much of it before it can be loaded. In this case, the percentages would be reversed:

- Acquisition—60%
- Storage—20%
- Access—20%

See Figure 12.3.

Large volumes of data. In the last situation that we will consider, we will assume that the data to be used in the warehouse is easily attained and that the user's access will be simplistic. However, the volumes of data that you

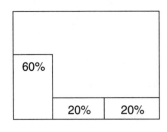

Figure 12.3 A complicated acquisition process.

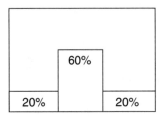

Figure 12.4 "Heavy" storage requirements.

need to work with are quite high, and the relationships between tables are made more complicated. In this case, your allocation of budget will become skewed at the center:

- Acquisition—20%
- Storage—60%
- Access—20%

See Figure 12.4.

By taking the total estimate of the requirements to develop the warehouse, breaking it out, and viewing it in this manner, you begin to gain some valuable insight into the real effort needed to develop the warehouse.

Reality checking

The first thing that you can do when you distribute the budget along these lines is determine how realistic the plans for the warehouse are. If the allocation of budget is skewed in one way or another, that might be a sign that someone has made an omission in the overall estimation process.

In general, unless there are some special circumstances or situations to be addressed, the ratios for allocation of the budget to the warehouse by component should show either:

- A lower storage component budget than the other two
- A clear pattern of ascent or descent from one component to the next

Storage component as lower percentage of budget. Probably the most common allocation of budget for a warehousing project follows this high-low-high kind of allocation. (See Figure 12.5.)

This pattern indicates that there is a high degree of activity required to find and prepare the data and a comparable level of activity in the preparation of data-mining solutions. In general, a high level of activity on the data acquisition side usually is accompanied by a high level of activity in rendering that data usable.

The storage-component development budget is much lower because the hard work is being done by the other two development areas. By recognizing this high-low-high pattern, you are not saying that the acquisition and access components will have the same percentages of budget but that they will both be higher than the storage component. (See Figure 12.6.)

Clear pattern of ascent or descent. Sometimes conditions are so extreme at one end of the warehouse that the pattern will resemble an incline or decline pattern. This can happen when the volume of work required to develop the acquisitions component is very high because of legacy system conditions, there is a corresponding simplicity on the access end, or vice versa. (See Figure 12.7.)

Using the Ratios as a Reality Check

By examining the ratio allocated to each component, you can get a reality check on how reasonable the development effort will be. For example, if you show a low acquisitions allocation but you know that the task is very complicated, you should question the developed estimates.

Figure 12.5. A "typical" high-low-high ratio pattern.

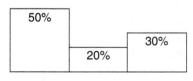 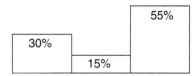

Figure 12.6 Variations in the high-low-high pattern.

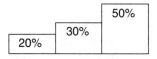

Figure 12.7 Incline and decline patterns.

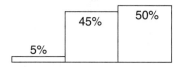

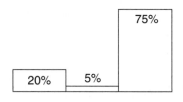

Figure 12.8 Radical variances—A warning signal.

Radical variance in the allocation of budget

You must be vigilant in looking for cases containing a radical variance in the allocation. If any component is being allocated a significantly lower percentage of resources than the others, that is a very good indication that something has been missed. (See Figure 12.8.)

Staffing and allocation ratios

Another useful insight that analysis of budget ratios can give you is to serve as a starting point for the development of staffing requirements. Clearly, your allocation of people to the job of developing the warehouse should correspond to the level of effort projected for each component.

It is amazing how individuals can develop plans and budgets, then simply throw personnel at the tasks involved, without really considering the requirements to get the job done.

When it comes to data warehousing, different organizations and different situations can bias people towards the over- or understaffing of key positions.

In an environment that is heavily database and data-oriented, there often is an overstaffing of the storage component development. In environments where working on legacy systems is considered as punishment duty, the allocation of resources to the acquisitions component tends to be de-emphasized and, as a consequence, greatly understaffed.

In environments where the focus is on the development of user-friendly solutions, we find an emphasis on the access component.

Before considering the specific skills and level of experience required for warehouse construction, it is critical that you ensure that the staffing approach is balanced. The best way to ensure that the balance is correct is to base it on these budget ratios.

Other understaffing dangers: Complete warehouse solutions. The one type of product or offering that should make the purchaser the most wary is the "complete" warehouse solution offering. These packages or offerings claim to provide buyers with everything that they need to run their own warehouse. Just buy their product and the rest is automatic. At least, that is the claim.

Unfortunately, the reality of the situation usually is far from that simple or straightforward. You can use the budget analysis ratios that we have just discussed to validate or disclaim the merit that a proposed "total" warehousing solution will have.

The first step in considering the purchase of a warehouse solution is to develop an understanding of what the product does and determine what percentages of the overall warehouse functionality it really will provide. For example, a good, broad-based solution might concentrate on the management of the storage component, while providing support for 505 of your acquisition needs and 50% of your access needs. (See Figure 12.9.)

Having developed this analysis, you then can start to estimate what the real warehouse solution is going to cost.

Allocation of percentages by layer. Another kind of ratio analysis that can be useful, both in the validation of estimates and in the development of

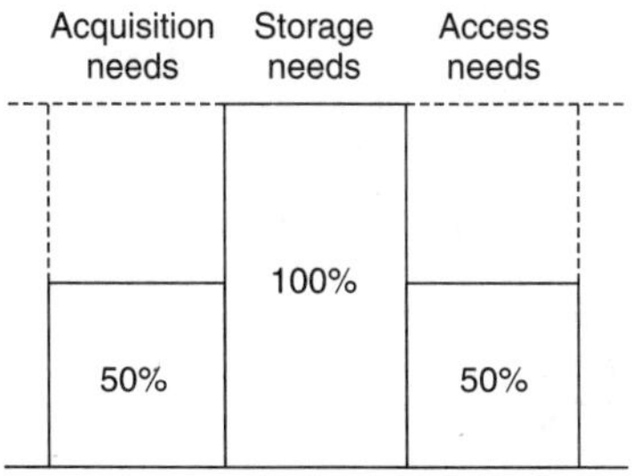

Figure 12.9 Percent of needs met by warehouse-package solution.

staffing requirements, is allocation by layers. You might recall that the warehouse consists of several layers: the physical infrastructure, the operational infrastructure, and each of the application layers. (See Figure 12.10.)

By determining how much of your overall budget is to be spent on physical hardware and software (versus operational software and applications software and databases), you can get a much better idea of what the project really is about.

Warning signs.   Some of the warning signs that your project is out of synch with your objectives will become apparent when the allocations across these layers become skewed.

The operational layer should always represent a small percentage of the overall budget but not so small that it is nonexistent.

If the cost of providing the infrastructure for a warehouse is significantly higher than the cost of the development of the solutions, there might be reason to suspect that the project is ill-proposed. (See Figure 12.11.) More importantly, when considering the purchase of packages and bundled hardware solutions, it is critical that you develop estimates for the activity needed to complete the warehouse after the vendors have left.

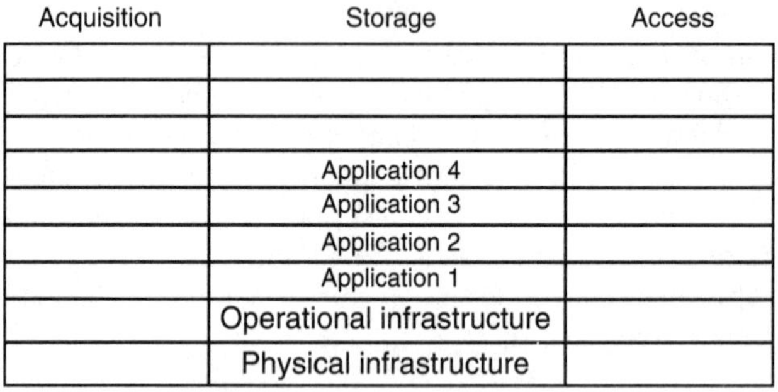

Acquisition	Storage	Access
	Application 4	
	Application 3	
	Application 2	
	Application 1	
	Operational infrastructure	
	Physical infrastructure	

Figure 12.10 Layers of the warehouse.

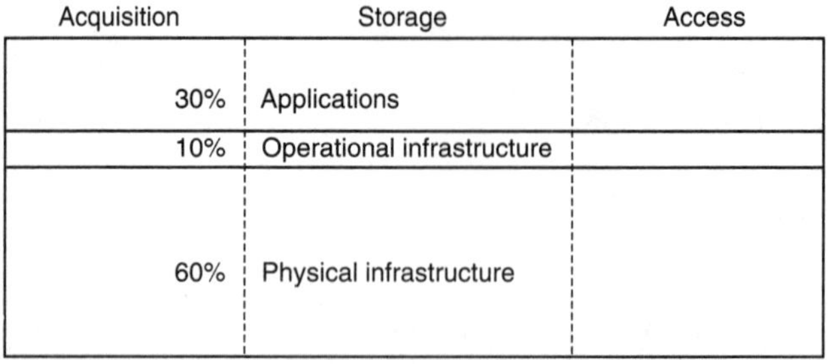

Acquisition		Storage		Access
	30%	Applications		
	10%	Operational infrastructure		
	60%	Physical infrastructure		

Figure 12.11 Over-budgeted physical infrastructure.

Acquisition	Storage	Access

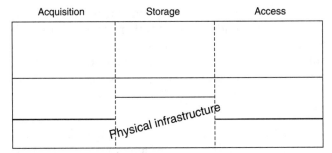

Figure 12.12 Ratio of physical infrastructure budget by component.

The hidden costs of warehouse development

Hopefully, the different forms of budget ratio analysis that we have considered will provide the prospective warehouse developer with a good idea of exactly what it is going to take to complete the system. In too many cases, people habitually underestimate the real level of effort required to identify, cleanse, synchronize, and load the data into the warehouse. This is especially true in those cases where the vendor offers a "complete" solution.

The danger in these situations comes when people allow the vendors to "guesstimate" the level of effort that the execution of the data disciplines is going to require. When these disciplines are estimated lightly, people discover all of the subsequent data integrity and synchronization problems too late in the process to do anything about them. Failure to budget adequately for data preparation and mapping is the principal source of most warehouse budget mistakes.

Physical infrastructure ratios across the components

The last kind of ratio that we will look at is the ratio of the overall physical infrastructure budget that has been allocated to each of the warehouse components. By developing these ratios, you have the final piece of information that you need for effective staff decision making. (See Figure 12.12.)

These ratios typically map out into two patterns. The physical-infrastructure requirements for the acquisitions component usually are pretty low. For the most part, people will try to leverage existing legacy systems platforms as much as possible to support them.

In a great number of cases, the allocation for the storage component will be the highest. In those cases, people intend to purchase separate dedicated platforms to support the activity. In other cases, the storage component will be managed via an existing platform. Obviously, in those cases, the ratio will be low.

The budget for the development of the access component can be nonexistent or the highest expense, depending upon whether or not the users already have workstations and network connections in place.

In all cases, your understanding of how these ratios play out will give you a good idea about how resources need to be deployed to carry out the plan.

Staffing Requirements

Provided with the information that you obtained from the estimates and each of the different types of ratios that we considered, you can turn your focus to ensuring that you have put a staff in place that is capable of delivering the warehouse on time and under-budget.

The size of the project

One of the first things that you need to do before making specific staffing decisions is to determine the size and scope of the overall project. This is essential because, the bigger the project, the more able you will be to identify specialized roles and responsibilities. Conversely, the smaller the project, the more you will be forced to blend these jobs and try to identify a few people with an incredibly rich set of experiences and capabilities.

We will begin our discussion of this topic assuming that the project is relatively large (more than 15 people working on it simultaneously) and that you therefore will be able to identify many specialized kinds of roles. As in our other considerations, we will attack the problem of staffing by starting with the data warehouse framework, considering the staff required to address the needs presented by each layer and each component of the system. (See Figure 12.13.)

Physical-infrastructure skills

As you might recall from chapter 8, there is an almost infinite variety of combinations of hardware, software, and networking components that can

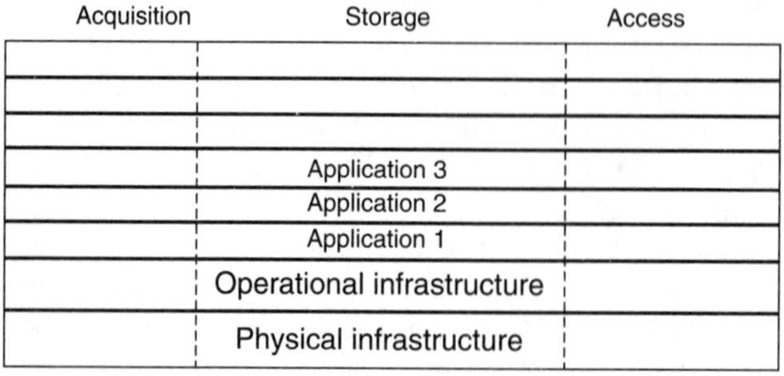

Acquisition	Storage	Access
	Application 3	
	Application 2	
	Application 1	
	Operational infrastructure	
	Physical infrastructure	

Figure 12.13 The warehouse framework.

be used to deliver a data-warehousing solution. Obviously, the staffing requirements are going to depend upon that particular combination.

However, experience has shown that certain types of skill sets will be required, regardless of the selected platforms. For every unique environment, platform, or tool set utilized, there should be resources available who understand what it takes to install and utilize them. In many cases, these support personnel already will be in place; however, if (and when) they are not, they will need to be identified. It is amazing how many people will bring in vast quantities of disparate products and simply forget that each of them will have to be supported in some way. The major categories of products that need to be supported will include:

- Hardware
- Operating system
- Network
- Windows environment
- Programming languages
- Database software
- Data-mining tools

Traditionally, this level of support was known as the *systems* or *internals level*. In the good old days of mainframe computers, there were extensive staffs to support each of these areas. In today's environment, this level of support often is overlooked, with disastrous consequences.

Operational-infrastructure skills

Luckily, in the area of the development and maintenance of the operational infrastructure, the skill requirements are relatively self-defining. To begin with, it is routinely accepted that the physical-infrastructure support will need to be in place if the operational infrastructure is going to function properly. In addition, the main skills required will be:

- Database management—The biggest requirement for the development of an operational infrastructure will be the presence of a database administrator who is able to design, build, and deliver the core control/tracking tables that drive the operational-infrastructure management process.

- Front-end development—The second need will be for a person able to program the end users' and warehouse manager's interface screens. These screens allow people to check on the status of different data feeds, files, and databases throughout the course of the warehouse's different load and utilization cycles.

- Network connectivity—If the legacy systems that are performing data extraction and preparation or the data chain-building and data-mining tools are located on platforms that are not already connected to the main storage area platform, then it will be critical that a person who is able to initiate those connections be available. If the legacy systems extraction programs are unable to update the control/tracking tables, then the operational infrastructure will be greatly hindered in its ability to manage.

- Native legacy system programming—The final skill required is the ability to place customized control/tracking table calls into the extraction programs themselves. These skills probably already will be part of the skill sets of the people writing and delivering the extraction and preparation programs.

Application-development skill requirements

The previous two areas that were covered represent only a very small portion of the overall allocation of staff to a data-warehousing project. The lion's share of this staff will be dedicated to the construction of warehouse applications themselves. We will separate the staffing requirements for this process into three major categories: management, operational, and technical support, then spend the majority of our time considering the required technical and analytical skills.

Management level of participation. While clearly the biggest draw of management's time during the process of warehouse development occurs earlier on in the process, during the vision-development and -planning phases, it is important that everyone understand that management must remain involved throughout the development of the project.

The most obvious level of management participation will be at the level of budget and project-status reporting. Management needs to stay apprised of the progress of the warehousing project on a weekly basis, at a minimum.

Not so obvious, however, will be the need to have management available to make policy and judgment decisions when the data-discipline process begins to uncover serious problems with the integrity and meaning of the data. Inevitably the data-discipline process will uncover many anomalies in the nature of the data within systems. While some of these anomalies might be trivial, occasionally a major revelation about the nature of the legacy systems, or about the way things get done, comes to light. This might change management's decisions about how the warehouse should be rolled out.

Operational level of participation. While management's role in the application development process might be minimal, the same is not true for the people who work within the different operational units that will be using or

Acquisition	Storage	Access
		Solution development
		Data identification
Data sourcing		Data sourcing
Data integrity validation		Data integrity validation
Data synchronization	Data synchronization	
Back flush development		
	Storage topology mapping	Storage topology mapping
Data transformation mapping	Data transformation mapping	Data transformation mapping
Data metrics gathering	Data metrics gathering	Data metrics gathering
	Data modeling	
	Database design	

Figure 12.14 Data disciplines.

feeding the warehouse. These individuals will need to have significant time allocated to assist the technical staff in the development of specific solutions.

As far as the skills required of these individuals, the biggest requirement will be that they are familiar with the business area for which the solution is being developed and also are familiar with the current *modus operandi* in that environment.

Unfortunately, the usual case is that the people best qualified to serve in the role for the warehousing team also are the most valuable people overall and consequently are least able to spend the required time. There is no easy answer to this problem. The right business people must be ready to spend the time on development if the system is going to work the right way the first time.

Technical skills for application development. The majority of the staff required for application development will come from the technical area. In general, we will consider the skills from the following general areas:

- Data-discipline and database skills
- Application-development skills
- Warehouse- and operational-support skills

Data-discipline and database skill sets. We already have talked a lot about the skills required to perform the data-discipline skills, but we will briefly review them again for consistency. Figure 12.14 shows the different specific steps involved in the data-discipline process and shows which of the three components they are the most concerned with.

What is important about the tasks specified in Figure 12.14 is that they represent a combination of skills. The position of a task in one of the three component areas (acquisition, storage, or access) implies:

- Technical familiarity with the platforms each of those respective components will be built within—For example, if the warehouse is going to be based upon a mainframe acquisitions component, UNIX-Informix storage component, and a Windows-based access component, then people involved in each of these areas will have to be technically competent in their respective areas in order to do their jobs.

- Business and operational familiarity with the processes being modeled and the solutions being developed—For example, those people involved in the access-component data-discipline tasks will need to be familiar with the business problems that the end users are trying to solve with a particular data-mining approach. While people involved in the acquisition-component efforts will need to understand the business functions that the legacy systems are delivering.

- A core set of skills involving data analysis, modeling, database administration, and systems analysis. This includes data modeling, data mapping, and the identification and documentation of key data characteristics.

All told, the problems faced by people trying to staff a data-warehousing project in the data-disciplines area can be extremely challenging and compromises often must be made.

Application-development skills. In the area of programming and application-development skills, the requirements are a little more straightforward and more easily specialized. You will need:

- Graphical user interface and windows programmers—People to develop user "front-end" solutions and to write the programs and jobs that move data through the warehouse.

- Data-mining specialists—People familiar with the process of installing data-mining tools, hooking them into the warehouse, and utilizing them.

- Batch/background job execution—Another set of personnel competent in the development of programs, often in the legacy system environments, who will be involved in the extraction, cleansing, and synchronization of that data.

Warehouse and operational support skills. The final area of staffing concerns in the operation of the warehouse is the designation and allocation of personnel who actually will run and manage the warehouse after it is built. A warehouse is an extremely complicated and mission-critical system, and there will need to be permanent staff assigned to its "care and feeding." These people will be responsible for ensuring that everything within the warehouse is working well, and they must be available when things go wrong.

The process of budgeting and staffing a warehousing project can be an extremely complicated and critical process.

The Bidding Process

Hopefully, by the time you get to this point in the book, it will become apparent that there are a variety of superior ways that the bidding process for warehouse development can be handled.

We have partitioned the entire process of warehouse development into a series of discrete phases, each of which should be executed in a serial order. By using this framework as a guideline, it should become easy to determine how to proceed.

The first and biggest revelation about the overall process should be that the development of a warehouse plan is a very different process than the process for developing and delivering specific solutions. In view of this, it might make sense in many situations to approach the development of the overall warehouse plan as one project and the delivery of each of the subsequent parts of the warehouse (physical infrastructure, operational infrastructure, and each application) as separate projects.

This makes great logical sense and, in many cases, will be the best way to proceed. Unfortunately, there will be times when the simplicity and linearity of the approach will need to be varied to take business or economic issues into account.

When Validation Fails!

The single biggest reason that you will find yourself needing to vary from your plans will occur when the execution of the validation process uncovers a number of issues that cannot be resolved without the investment of a significant amount of money in the development of prototypes, benchmarks, and proof-of-concept projects. When this occurs, you will have little choice but to vary your plans accordingly. The important things to keep in mind when you decide to vary from this ordered approach to the process are that:

- You clearly identify the purpose and deliverables expected from the special project being proposed.
- You do not overvalue the reuse value of the solution being developed.
- By no means do you allow the development of these validation projects to somehow make it possible for everyone to skip the rest of the steps involved in the process.

The execution of a proof-of-concept project does not eliminate the need for the validation of all of the other warehouse propositions nor does it eliminate the need to develop an infrastructure and propose an overall warehouse plan. It doesn't even eliminate the need to develop a plan for the real solution that the project has been designed to validate!

If the people preparing to put a warehouse project (or some phase of it) out for bid are aware of the many issues that we have identified and are familiar with the structure that we have proposed for its execution, then the bidding process should become considerably easier and more accurate.

13

Data Mining Is
What It's All About

At this point in the consideration of data warehousing, we are going to make an abrupt shift. Up until now, we have been concentrating on the issues, problems, and concerns that you might have when thinking about building and managing a data warehouse but have spent almost no time talking about *what to do* with it. More importantly, I have made some rather tall assumptions. I have assumed that you are fully aware of what *data-mining tools* are, how they work, and why all of our discussions about data warehousing would be next to pointless without them. So, let's correct this gross negligence.

What Is Data Mining Anyway?

The first problem is to come up with a meaningful definition that the majority of people will be able to accept. Just as the data-warehousing marketplace is rife with a plethora of contradictory and complementary definitions of the term, so too is the data-mining area.

There are people who have an extremely narrowly focused meaning who believe that data mining should be defined as a collection of end-user tools and/or applications that perform analytical and statistical analysis of a large pool of data. On the other hand, there are individuals who believe that any product that enables end users to access data directly from a database, without the benefit of customized application programs, also should be included.

We will address the data-mining subject to include the broadest and most liberal interpretation of the term. For our purposes, we will assume a data-mining tool to be any product that allows end users direct access and manipulation of data from within the data-warehousing environment without the intervention of customized programming activity.

Why the Fuss?

There is a dizzying array of data-mining tools available on the market today. Some of them are relatively new, offering end users capabilities that, until only recently, were considered to be impossible. Some of the products have been around for a long time but have undergone a recent face-lift. However, all of these products have several things in common.

They are PC or UNIX workstation based. While tools for data-mining operations and customized applications for data-mining functions have been around for a long time, the real hoopla about data mining today is a direct result of the widespread acceptance and popularity of personal computers and scientific workstations. As personal computers have continued to increase in power and decrease in price, the possibilities for desktop computation have skyrocketed. Personal computers not only make this kind of power affordable, but they make it extremely convenient as well.

Probably the most frightening thing about this trend is that we are just now only beginning to understand and exploit the vast potential it represents. Indeed, data warehousing on its own is practically a meaningless concept. It is only with the kind of power these desktop tools represent that we can begin to capitalize on the information that the warehouse provides.

They are Windows, or at least WIMP, driven. Although we can give some credit to the PC as a desktop computer for making this kind of activity possible, it is not that power in and of itself that makes it attractive. If that were the case, then we would all be busily programming our PCs, using COBOL or BASIC language, and looking at printed green bar reports at our homes and offices. No, it is the power and intuitive usefulness of the Windows-style environment that really makes data-mining tools work. With these 256-color, graphically pleasing, sound-card squawking WIMP interfaces (Windows, Icons, Menus, and Pointers), almost everyone now can get friendly with their computers.

They make it possible for end users to gain access to computer data directly. Most importantly, by delivering this power and ease of use directly to the user, it enables people to grab, manipulate, and report on vast accumulations of data. The client/server revolution has served its purpose. Suddenly it is possible for personal computers to be attached to disparate sources of data and to treat them as if they were on the same machine.

The Categorization of Data-Mining Tools

Given this decidedly broad-based definition of the subject and this very generalized observation about the products, we next have to develop a scheme to differentiate the various kinds of data-mining tools and approaches. Because the field is so broad and complex, we need to categorize these products according to several criteria. Our categorizations will include:

- The type of product
- The characteristics of the product
  ~Data-identification capabilities
  ~The media it uses to display results
  ~Formatting capabilities
  ~Specification management (the way people tell the product what to do)
  ~Execution management (the way execution and timing is controlled)
- The objectives (what you do with the product)
- Developmental participation (the roles of hardware, software, and grayware) in the delivery of information

Types of Products

The vast assortment of data-mining products can be broken down into the following general types:

- Query managers and report writers
- Spreadsheets
- Multidimensional databases
- Statistical-analysis tools
- Artificial intelligence and advanced analysis tools
- Graphical-display tools

Query managers and report writers

This group represents the biggest collection of different types of products and has the longest history of existence. From almost the earliest days of computers and databases, vendors have attempted to provide simple tools for end users to query for data and print out the results. In the prerelational database days, this category of products was represented by FOCUS, EASYTRIEVE, and RAMIS. These products allowed users to define data that they would like to see, then ran against the databases and files that stored the data. Then, with the relational databases came the introduction of products like QMF, ISQL, and a wide range of SQL-based query and reporting tools. These products were an improvement but still left a lot to be desired in terms of ease of use.

The query managers and report writers of today have come a long way since those days. Now it is possible to pull and generate these reports in a fraction of the time that it used to take and with a fraction of the effort. The same basic functionality, however, still holds true and still provides value.

Spreadsheets

The second most popular data-mining tool is the spreadsheet. Typified by Microsoft Excel and Lotus 1-2-3, these products perform a wide variety of analytical and reporting functions within one easy-to-use environment.

Multidimensional databases

The next generation of products actually turned out to be a combination of the first two. Multidimensional databases allow users to tie queries to spreadsheets in a way that executes many different kinds of sophisticated multidimensional analysis. While the typical spreadsheet is limited to a few dimensions, the multidimensional database greatly expands the capacity and, at the same time, works directly with database stored data. In chapter 14, we will explore this type of mining tool in more detail.

Statistical-analysis tools

Another of the "old timers" in the data-mining area are the statistical analysis tools, represented by products like SAS or SPSS. With these products, users can pull in data and perform sophisticated statistical-analysis operations, allowing them to compute regressions and clusters, display graphical relationships, and perform all manner of complex computation to gain new insight into the nature of the available information.

Like the query managers, the statistical-analysis tools have undergone a significant GUI (graphical user interface) face-lift over the past several years, making them more user-friendly and more intuitive than they were in the past. Chapter 15, "Statistical analysis," provides a more thorough consideration of this category.

Artificial intelligence and advanced analysis tools

While artificial intelligence and advanced analytical approaches have been around for some time, only recently has it become possible to bring their computational power down to the level of the typical end user. These products employ extremely complex algorithms and approaches to develop and refine new insights into previously collected data. In this category, we include neural nets and other advanced approaches. We have included subsequent chapters to consider neural nets in general and a look at working with specific neural network applications. Refer to chapters 16 and 17.

Graphical-display tools

Last but not least are the graphical display products. Many products in the previous categories include graphical display capabilities, but specialized graphics products can fit the bill in situations where really sophisticated graphical representation is desired. Chapter 19 provides more information about this category of product.

Characteristics of the Products

While understanding the basic focus of each of these product groups is helpful, categorizing them by that criterion alone provides far too little information to really appreciate what they are and how they work. There are several operational characteristics that all of these products share.

Data-identification capabilities

No matter what kind of data-mining tools you are talking about, they all must provide the users with some way to identify the specific data that they want to pull into the program for processing or display. Capabilities in this area are defined by the language that the product uses to "call" for the data and by the way the user codes that language gets.

Data-access languages or data-manipulation languages (DMLs) are either prerelational or relational. The prerelational languages consist of a broad range of proprietary languages. In general, each language is specific to a particular platform and a particular database product. Because of this, these languages are cumbersome, complex, and far from user-friendly.

The relational access language, SQL, put an end to all of that. Suddenly we had one common data-access language that could be used to access data from almost any platform or environment. SQL certainly has revolutionized data access. Although SQL still is far from being user-friendly, working with only one data-access language has simplified data-mining tools development. Without SQL, the vendors would need to build hundreds of customized user-access mechanisms into their products, making it impossible for them to support as many different sources of data as they do.

The second important aspect of data-access capabilities is the way that the user inputs the query specifications. At the low end of the continuum are products that allow you to input the raw SQL calls yourself. While this certainly is an improvement over earlier "manual" proprietary data-access language entry, it is far from optimum.

Some vendors stop at this level of ease of use; others provide the end user with query-building capabilities. These products have screens and menus to select and point and click from options to interactively "build" the queries. Those screens provide the user with metadata (data about the data). The user simply selects the desired information from the menus, and the system builds the SQL command automatically.

At the high end of this continuum, we find the business object generators. These products actually allow programmers or DBAs to preload already organized queries so that the end user needs to do little more than select the particular business object of interest.

Output media

After you have figured out which data you want the data-mining tool to give you, your next issue is to decide how you want that information displayed. Data-mining tools can provide output in several forms.

Printed. To this day printed output still represents the vast majority of data-processing output. Now we need to worry about things like PostScript, laser, plotted, or full-color printouts.

Green screen. Unfortunately, a large number of end users still are saddled with the old fashioned 3270-type green-and-black or amber-and-black two-tone screens. Although it is becoming rarer with each new release of personal computers, there still is a need; therefore, there are data-mining tools that can work in this mode.

Standard graphics. By far, the most common form of output for data-mining applications these days is the personal computer 256 (or higher) color screens.

Enhanced full graphics. In some cases, normal PC graphics will not provide the detail and depth that the graphical display requires, and special high resolution graphics terminals need to be called into play.

Formatting capabilities

After you have identified the data that you want to look at and have determined which media will display it, you have to figure out how it is going to look. There are a number of ways that data can be displayed.

Raw data format. The data is dumped out to the screen or paper exactly as it is stored in the file.

Tabular. This is the standard SQL output form with data organized in columns and rows and headings describing what data is in which column. This form of output also can include what is known as "control break" logic, which prints summary lines at different levels.

Spreadsheet form. It not only shows data in column and row form but also allows you to embed formulae and calculations into the structure of the output itself. This format makes it possible to include complex calculations within a simple framework. While the keys to tabular reporting are columns and rows, the key to spreadsheet type reporting is the *cell*. Each cell can contain a different calculation. While tabular reports can perform calculations only on complete columns or rows, the spreadsheet/cell-formatting approach allows you to refer to any cell anywhere on the screen and work with all of the data that is available.

Multidimensional databases. These tools take the power of data-access languages and build them into the column, row, and cell structure of the spreadsheet. With a multidimensional-display, tool cells can be tied not only to cells that are available but also to fields within the database itself, making it possible to add many more dimensions of computational capability from the same screen.

Visualization. Visualization is at the high end of the formatting capabilities. Many tools allow you to convert the formatted data into graphical displays.

Computation facilities

Some computational capabilities are inherent in the way that products format data. However, the category of computation facilities itself really is something different. Computation abilities are provided to the user through the following.

Columnar operations. The standard "control break" or SQL columnar functions perform summarization, addition, multiplication, and other operations on the available data on a column-by-column basis.

Cross-tab capabilities. They take the columnar operations one step further by enhancing the product so that it performs those same operations on the individual rows of data.

Spreadsheets. These provide the "cell math" approach that we already have talked about. Cell math greatly enhances the usefulness of the tool with the ability to compute any field on the screen.

Multidimensional spreadsheets. This is the approach used by multidimensional databases, making it possible to build "virtual spreadsheets" that are several layers deep.

Rule-driven or trigger-driven computation. With these facilities, you can prestore and pre-execute different kinds of computations.

Specification management

Putting the ability to go after data in the hands of the users presents a new problem. How will you manage the process of putting your specifications into the machine for what you want the system to do? In the traditional world, this was the programmer's job. He or she figured out what the program should do and how it would get done, then wrote the specifications using a programming language.

In the data-mining world, we open up a whole new range of possibilities. With the automation of metadata access and the development of query builders, report builders, and other forms of automated specification, it suddenly is possible to let end users "write" their own programs.

Execution management

Directly related to the way some data-mining tools allow end users to write and manage their own specifications is the way their execution is timed and managed. In the traditional I/S world, there are only two options:

- Batch jobs—Programs are scheduled to run on some kind of regular basis.
- Real-time/interactive—Hit a button, and the program runs.

Now other options are available. Users can schedule jobs to run at a certain time, to execute overnight, or to run over the next few hours.

At the high end of these capabilities are agents. *Agents* are software modules that sit out on the system and check for conditions. When the specified condition is found, they trigger the execution of a program or a report.

For example, an accountant might create an agent that monitors the balance of the corporate checking account. This agent will check the balance every hour and, if the amount drops to a certain level, will trigger the execution of a checking account audit and activity report, which is printed immediately and shows up on the accountant's desk.

By using agents to schedule work, the users' and the systems personnel's time and energy are optimized.

Objectives

Understanding how a data-mining tool works gives us one perspective on its usefulness. Another, more puzzling aspect is understanding how or why these tools are different from the traditional applications programs or simple query writers that we have used in the past. One of the easiest ways to develop an appreciation for these differences is to look at what the objectives are for using each of these types of programming tools or approaches.

All application development programs and data-mining tools fall into three operational categories. You use the application for any one or for a combination of these.

Data collection and retrieval. This is the traditional definition of an online transaction processing or legacy system or operational system. Data-mining tools apply very little, if at all, to this category.

Operational monitoring. This is the process of keeping tabs on your business operations and making effective decisions to correct or improve its workings. Clearly more than half of the data-mining tools, as we have defined them, fit into this category. They include query managers, report writers, spreadsheets, multidimensional databases, and visualization tools.

Exploration and discovery. This is the process of taking a look at your business with the objective of trying to discover new things about how it works or how to make it run more efficiently. It is in this category that we find the rest of the data-mining tools and the statistical analysis, artificial intelligence, neural net, advanced statistical analysis, and advanced visualization products. The "die hard" definers of data mining would say that only this category holds the "real" data-mining tools.

The operational monitoring cycle

Regardless of the technology or tools that are available, business people spend a considerable amount of their time monitoring and maintaining the business's activities. They proceed through three steps.

Step 1. First, there is the actual monitoring of activities and conditions. In the traditional I/S world of the 1960s, 1970s, and 1980s, the vast majority of monitoring was done through the use of printed, regularly scheduled reports. These reports allowed the business people to check on the status of whatever they happened to be responsible for. Consequently, dozens and even hundreds of printed reports—showing inventory levels, balance sheet amounts, and other types of activities—were created regularly. The problem was that people had to actually read all of those reports to make sure that things were running smoothly. The second problem was that, once the reports were written, it was difficult to turn them off. It had been so much trouble to get the report in the first place that it was a lot easier to just leave it running just in case it was ever needed again.

Data-mining tools have made the monitoring process many times easier. Now, through the use of the online tools, users can very easily check on whatever it is they want, whenever they want. More importantly, the use of agent technology makes it possible to have the system do the monitoring work for you. This eliminates the menial, tedious aspects of the monitoring process.

Step 2. During this process of monitoring, the business person eventually will discover a problem or strange situation. The next step then in the monitoring cycle is the investigation phase. During investigation, the users need to dig much more deeply into some aspect of the system's operations. They might need to take a look at historical, operational, and real-time transactional data. It is during this phase that the new data-mining technologies and data-warehousing approaches can make a significant difference. All sorts of information now can be accessed immediately, which in the past might have taken days, weeks, or even months to figure out.

Step 3. Finally, after discovering what went wrong, the business person makes adjustments to the organization to correct the problem. After that, it is back to the monitoring process.

The data-mining tools make the monitoring cycle easier, faster, and more efficient and, therefore, provide a significant improvement to the overall operational efficiency of the business people and the organization as a whole.

The exploration process

The exploration of data is a relatively new phenomenon in the business world, but it is a process that has been extremely popular in the scientific community for some time now. Data exploration entails assembling as much data as possible about a given problem area, then applying analytical criteria to it to discover new cause-and-effect relationships that can help better predict future activities.

For example, medical researchers use this technique when trying to figure out how a new disease works or how a plague spreads. Social scientists use the same approach to study attitudes and behaviors in different societies and cultures. Biologists, physicists, engineers, and psychologists all use this technique to help unravel the mysteries of how things work in the physical world.

This is not to say that the application of these same techniques has never been used in business. Underwriters in the insurance industry take a look at the statistical probabilities of how likely a person is to die within a given timeframe when deciding upon life-insurance rates. Banks have long attempted to use the same techniques to try and get a handle on who is most likely to default on a loan.

Three things have happened relatively recently.

First, business people have discovered that they own a vast wealth of information that often holds useful insights into predicting how to better run their operations or how to better predict the behavior of consumers. In effect, they are finding that they have a resource that they need only figure out how to tap.

Second, the increased ability to manage large amounts of data through a data warehouse makes it possible to get at the data in a convenient form. Let's face it, who would want to do statistical analysis on billions of records that can be accessed only via micro-fiche or tape?

Third, the sophistication, power, and ease of use of today's new generation of data-exploration tools make it economically and functionally feasible to do things that, in the past, required a team of statisticians and a support staff of dozens of clerks to execute.

We have dedicated a good portion of the rest of this book to offering you some different perspectives and explanations of how this data-exploration process is executed and used in practical business situations.

Developmental Participation

The last area of data-mining characteristics that we will consider is the developmental participation. It is only through understanding developmental participation and the roles of hardware, software, and grayware (the software in people's heads) that we truly can come to appreciate just how powerful the data-mining and data-warehousing concepts are.

Under the traditional mode of application development, end users gained access only through application programs written by inhouse programming staff or by the vendor of the application package.

In the process of writing this package, the developer sat down and figured out everything an end user might need to know. Usually, subject matter experts in the area that the application was designed to service (accounting, marketing, etc.) would be called upon to provide input to the process. End users were asked about the functionality that they were looking for. Any computational or statistical analysis that the system would provide was researched and built into the software.

The end result of this process was a piece of software that made most of the decisions for the user. It was an application that shielded the end user from needing to think about anything but whatever the application had decided. Not only were the business rules and mathematical characteristics of the system built in and automated, but the whole process of finding the requested information also was done for the user.

However, when you move into the world of data-mining tools, a large amount of that research, development, and other brainwork is no longer built into the system.

The provision of data-mining tools to the end user is both a blessing and a curse. On the one hand, the business person now is able to gain access to all sorts of data that was never before available, which he or she then can put through almost any kind of computational or statistical regimen imaginable. On the other hand, the flexibility and power that now is at the users' fingertips requires that they be able to understand the data that they are using, the statistical analysis processes that they invoke, and the systems that they are manipulating to a degree that was never before required.

We can break this analysis down into its component parts to help explain it better. You start with the "raw" application. Whether it is programmer-written or delivered data-mining tool, every application is made up of a series of logical and physical processing steps. (See Figure 13.1.)

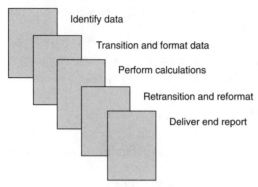

Identify data

Transition and format data

Perform calculations

Retransition and reformat

Deliver end report

Figure 13.1 An application is a combination of dozens/hundreds of processes.

In the traditional environment, all of those processes and steps were packaged by the programmer as one application program. (See Figure 13.2.)

In the data warehouse/data mining environment, you "break up" this "package" into pieces. The data-access and -identification functions, formally hardcoded into programs, now are managed by data-warehouse facilities, metadata managers, and data-mining tools.

The ability to access, manipulate, and format that data now is placed under the direct control of end users via the data-mining tools themselves. The brain power necessary for figuring out how to assemble these steps, and what to do with the data recovered, now must be provided by the end users themselves. (See Figure 13.3.)

Too often, people have undertaken to develop large-scale data-warehouse and data-mining projects without taking these facts into account. The end result has been disastrous. Data mining is not a replacement for application development. You cannot take your existing business processes, procedures, and staff and simply replace OLTP and legacy systems with warehouse/mining systems.

To capitalize on the capabilities that we are talking about requires that the end users themselves change the way that they view their jobs and develop a deeper understanding of the "bigger picture" of the problems that they are trying to solve. Without this kind of end-user paradigm shift, the effort to move into the data-warehouse/data-mining universe is a colossal waste of time and energy.

The Following Chapters

In the following chapters, I have taken a very different approach from the rest of the book. Each of these chapters has been designed to highlight and provide an in-depth discussion about data mining from a different perspective—specifically, from the perspective of each of the different types of tools being considered.

The area of data mining is very diverse, and the assumptions and paradigms that make sense for each are very different. To honor this diversity, I have invited several individuals—specialists in the different areas—to provide their insights and perspectives on the issues.

Additionally, I also have included some detailed explanations of how typical products of each of these categories are utilized. This should provide you reader with an understanding, not only of the issues and approaches, but also of the practical considerations when using products of each type.

As you are reading each of these chapters, it will be important to consider the different categorization and approach schemes that we have been discussing and see how each of the tools fit.

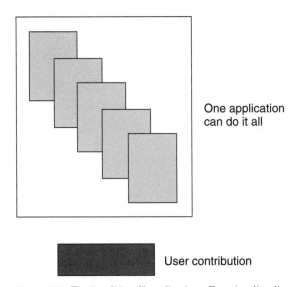

One application
can do it all

User contribution

Figure 13.2 The "traditional" application—Functionality distribution.

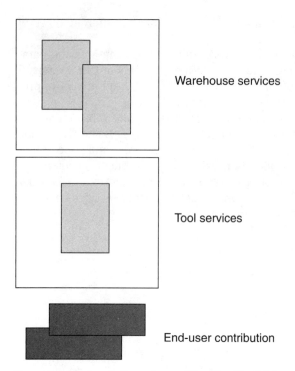

Warehouse services

Tool services

End-user contribution

Figure 13.3 The "perfect" warehouse—Functionality distribution.

Multidimensional Analysis of Warehoused Data

RICHARD TANLER
Chairman, Information Advantage Inc.
KAREN DROST
Marketing Manager, Information Advantage Inc.

In this chapter, we will begin to explore how the data warehouse is used to improve the timeliness and quality of the information available to decision makers. The goal of this chapter is to unravel the similar promises of decision-support systems, executive-information systems, and most recently, online analytic processing, or OLAP. Regardless of the label, each is designed to provide information to decision makers at the precise moment that critical decisions are being made. Data warehousing emphasizes the importance of creating a database that is organized for decision makers' use. Robust reporting and analytic systems are the warehouse-access tools that add value to the data delivered to the decision makers.

Virtually every form of data analysis and most forms of sophisticated data presentation (reporting and graphics) seek to reduce a large mass of raw data down to more easily understood concepts and relationships. Statistical data-analysis techniques turn raw data into mathematical functions. These mathematical functions are essential for developing predictive models. Data visualization works from the premise that a picture is worth a thousand words. Data visualization is the most efficient means of illustrating complex data relationships. Pattern-recognition software isolates the relationships that would not be easily discovered by the casual user. Pattern-recognition tools are extremely useful in market segmentation, which underlies database marketing. These approaches are explored in subsequent chapters.

Multidimensional analysis is tactical and therefore is used daily by a very large number of decision makers. The need for multidimensional analysis emanates from the rapid-fire management questioning sequence typical of day-to-day decision making. The first questions arise as a result of some observed business event or operating-performance issue. The questions increase in number and complexity as answers to previous questions are addressed. Multidimensional analysis tools provide answers to unstructured and unpredictable questions that arise every day in the course of business management.

Constrained Query versus Multidimensional Analysis

Relational database management systems provide a computer protocol, SQL, for writing data queries. SQL is a complex protocol, which by its nature, makes it virtually unusable by nontechnical users seeking a simple means of data access.

The SQL coding problem was quickly recognized. The first generation of PC-resident database-query tools allowed nontechnical users to structure database queries without writing computer code. The users are isolated from the complexity of writing SQL code but not from the complexity of the relational database design. A second generation of query tools adds a semantic layer that further masks the relational database from the user and allows the user to construct queries in terms more common to the user. The first generation of query tools provided virtually no computational capabilities. Data simply was retrieved, listed, and formatted into columns and rows. The second generation of tools supports some basic computational capabilities.

Query tools perform data retrieval based on constraints and answer questions like "How many employees are 35 years of age or older?" This type of query, the constrained query, produces a simple list of information.

Multidimensional analysis provides a very robust set of computational and data-navigation capabilities that are far beyond the features of even the most advanced query tool. Multidimensional analysis provides the analytic flexibility to answer questions like "How have advertising expenditures impacted sales?" This kind of question requires an analytic process. For this type of question, the answer is not, nor should it be, stored in the data warehouse but is *derived* from what is stored in the data warehouse.

It is nearly impossible to predict the data requests and the analysis path that a user will select to answer the question. Therefore, the multidimensional analysis tool must allow users to create reports that contain user-defined calculations and multiple layers of subtotaling on-the-fly. The user will navigate within the report (drill up/down/across) and change report parameters until an answer to the question emerges. Then more questions will be raised.

In summary, query tools simplify data retrieval of information stored in a data warehouse. Multidimensional analysis tools simplify the analytic requirements that underlie decision making by allowing on-the-fly calculations and summarization of information in the data warehouse. Ironically, many times it is what's *not* stored in the data warehouse that's most important to decision makers!

Dimensions, Facts, and Measures

The data warehouse stores *facts*, such as unit sales, price, occupancy, expenses, etc. In addition, calculated measures are created by specifying mathematical formulas. *Measures* are created from stored facts as well as from other measures. For example, the measure "volume change" is calculated by subtracting a prior period volume from the current period volume. This measure, when divided by the prior period volume, yields a second measure, "percent change."

Facts and measures change over time. Time is the one database *dimension* common to every data warehouse and is the most difficult for many analysis tools to handle because of the infinite number of possible time period combinations. Time periods can be days, weeks, months, accounting periods, or nonstandard time periods, such as the Christmas season or the current six weeks.

A single-dimension analysis would allow users to retrieve facts and calculated measures for one or more time periods, including totaling a group of periods. For example, assume that unit sales is a fact stored in the data warehouse each week. A user might want to compare the percent change in unit sales for the latest six weeks versus the prior six weeks. Assuming that a single unit sales fact is stored for each week, unit sales for each six-week summary period first would have to be totaled, then a volume change measure could be computed. From this, a percent change measure is calculated. Not too difficult, but seldom are data warehouses limited to a single dimension.

Additional database dimensions define the business characteristics that are unique to each enterprise. A package goods manufacturer will likely include product and market dimensions. Markets could include sales territories, distribution centers, and sales representatives. An insurance company would track customers as a key dimension. A retailer might include store and vendor. It is common for a database to contain 3 or 4 dimensions, and it is not uncommon to encounter 7 or more database dimensions.

The unique requirements of multidimensional analysis begin to emerge when a user requires subtotaling of facts and measures along multiple dimensions, *including* the time dimension. Many facts and most calculated measures are "nonadditive." These include facts like price, which must be computed at the time of the request using a weighted average function and percent change that must be computed on-the-fly at each level. (See Figure 14.1.)

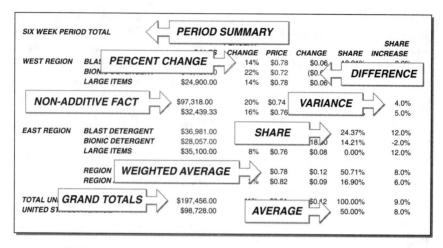

Figure 14.1 Multidimensional report.

As users of PC spreadsheets, we have become accustomed to a spatial model where formulas are defined by referencing cell location. A spreadsheet really has two dimensions: letters (A, B, C, etc.) and numbers (1, 2, 3, etc.). The specific value in a cell is unimportant in defining the formula; only the cell reference is important. We all know the problems encountered if a parenthesis is misplaced in a spreadsheet formula. A calculation error will occur without any warning and can be quickly proliferated if the computed cell is itself referenced in other formulas.

In one-way multidimensional analysis, software shares a similar concept with the spreadsheet. Rather than specifying cell locations in a spreadsheet to define a calculated measure, the location of data in the database is used in specifying the formula to compute a measure. In a spreadsheet, if prior period sales data is located in cell "A1" and current period sales are in "B1," then sales volume change is simply "A1-B1."

In the multidimensional database, the formula requires the location of two facts defined by the database dimensions. To compute sales volume change, we subtract prior period sales from current period sales for a given product and market set of dimensions. The power of multidimensional software is that the *formula* does not change regardless of what product, markets, or periods are specified. The user should be able to navigate any combination of dimensions while the logic to calculate the required measure is maintained.

It is important to note that, like the spreadsheet, multidimensional analysis tools should allow the use of calculated measures in the definition of other calculated measures. It is essential that users have the ability to create, share, and store calculations throughout the enterprise. This creation of highly complex business logic is the true power of multidimensional analysis.

Basic Features of Multidimensional Analysis Tools

In addition to providing the capability to define calculated measures by referencing the location of facts within the database dimensions, users expect to be able to drill down/up/across any dimension, pivot a report (alter the column/row formula), and change the constraints of any dimension, all the while maintaining the integrity of the computed measures and embedded subtotals. An example of a typical multidimensional analysis session will demonstrate the power of these tools.

The first report includes facts stored in the data warehouse (unit sales and unit price) for a series of products sold in the U.S. market. This data warehouse is limited to three dimensions for simplicity: period, product, and market. (See Figure 14.2.)

Next the user adds several subtotals along the product dimension. This creates the need to compute measures "on the fly" to satisfy the user request. Importantly, the subtotals are not derived by simply summing values. (See Figure 14.3.)

The user then drills down on the market dimension, displaying the sales regions within the total U.S. market definition. Embedded subtotals for products are maintained as the drilling logic is invoked. (See Figure 14.4.)

Next the user pivots the report format, displaying regions as column headings. (See Figure 14.5.)

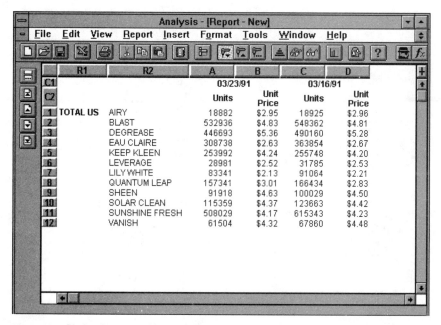

Figure 14.2 Listing facts stored in the data warehouse.

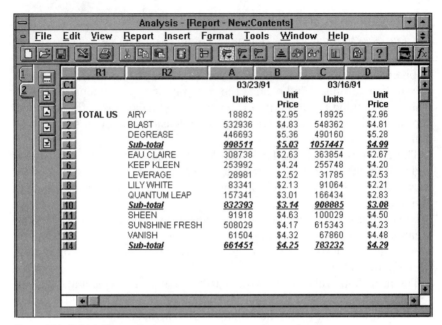

Figure 14.3 Subtotal by product.

			Units	Unit Price	Units	Unit Price
			03/23/91		03/16/91	
1	TOTAL US	AIRY	18882	$2.95	18925	$2.96
2		BLAST	532936	$4.83	548362	$4.81
3		DEGREASE	446693	$5.36	490160	$5.28
4		*Sub-total*	*998511*	*$5.03*	*1057447*	*$4.99*
5		EAU CLAIRE	308738	$2.63	363854	$2.67
6		KEEP KLEEN	253992	$4.24	255748	$4.20
7		LEVERAGE	28981	$2.52	31785	$2.53
8		LILY WHITE	83341	$2.13	91064	$2.21
9		QUANTUM LEAP	157341	$3.01	166434	$2.83
10		*Sub-total*	*832393*	*$3.14*	*908885*	*$3.08*
11		SHEEN	91918	$4.63	100029	$4.50
12		SUNSHINE FRESH	508029	$4.17	615343	$4.23
13		VANISH	61504	$4.32	67860	$4.48
14		*Sub-total*	*661451*	*$4.25*	*783232*	*$4.29*

			Units	Unit Price	Units	Unit Price
			03/23/91		03/16/91	
1	SOUTHERN REGION	AIRY	11322	$2.07	10363	$2.13
2		BLAST	210410	$4.54	225676	$4.78
3		DEGREASE	66761	$5.09	65670	$5.09
4		*Sub-total*	*288493*	*$4.57*	*301709*	*$4.76*
5		EAU CLAIRE	56962	$2.45	68804	$2.42
6		KEEP KLEEN	97028	$3.92	99552	$3.80
7		LEVERAGE	16929	$1.75	18538	$1.71
8		LILY WHITE	32142	$2.44	30138	$2.43
9		QUANTUM LEAP	82537	$2.89	84683	$2.83
10		*Sub-total*	*285598*	*$3.03*	*301715*	*$2.95*
11		SHEEN	28806	$3.99	30474	$4.19
12		SUNSHINE FRESH	94986	$3.93	98182	$4.02
13		VANISH	13847	$4.10	16949	$4.03
14		*Sub-total*	*137639*	*$3.96*	*145605*	*$4.06*
15	WESTERN REGION	AIRY	108	$5.44	132	$5.14
16		BLAST	147605	$4.82	143635	$4.84
17		DEGREASE	111935	$5.31	121211	$5.24
18		*Sub-total*	*259648*	*$5.03*	*264978*	*$5.02*

Figure 14.4 Drilling through the report.

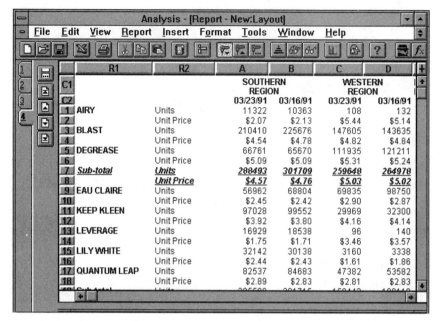

Figure 14.5 Pivoting the report.

Finally, the user requests that only period totals are shown, simplifying the report format. (See Figure 14.6.)

This example is a very simple form of multidimensional analysis. In addition to reporting in tabular form, the user expects to be able to portray data in a graphical format. Users need to define new, more complex calculated measures and create multiple hierarchies of subtotals. Users also expect to be able to report on data based on multiple exception criteria. For example, report only those product and region combinations where unit sales declined during the current month and where price remained unchanged.

The key differentiating characteristic of multidimensional tools is the extent to which the user can author and publish new calculations and filters as well as add subtotals easily to any analyses. The power of the spreadsheet is the ability to define a calculation or replicate the calculation down a row or across a column. The power of multidimensional analysis is enhanced with the ability to author calculations and filters based on database dimensions, distribute them across analyses, then share the analyses with a single user, workgroup, or the enterprise.

For simplicity, the examples used are limited to product, market, and period dimensions of a product manufacturer. The concepts are no different for a bank, insurance company, airline, or any other industry that must analyze data stored across many different dimensions. The examples also

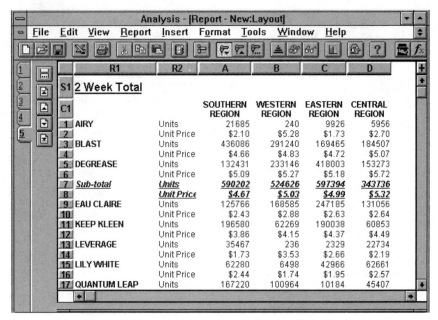

Figure 14.6 Period totals by region.

were limited to three dimensions. It is not unusual to have many more dimensions.

Advanced Features of Multidimensional Analysis

Multidimensional analysis is the essential tool for monitoring operating performance and at any point allowing every user to diagnose business issues. With respect to operating performance monitoring, routine analyses should be defined as agents that are triggered based on some event. In turn, an alert should be sent to only those users with a "need to know." Sophisticated trigger, agent, and alert technology allows the performance monitoring process to be automated and run continuously in the background leaving the user's PC available for other activities.

As data warehouses continue to grow and become very large, it is unreasonable to assume that users will have sufficient time to surf the data warehouse to analyze vast amounts of data while effectively monitoring operating performance. Productivity and success will depend on agents performing directed analyses on large data warehouses versus aimless data surfing through gigabytes of data. Some vendors are beginning to provide technology to automate the creation and routing of reports based on agent technology.

With respect to diagnostic capabilities, one aspect is sophisticated drilling (up/down/across dimensions) to isolate a problem. Another set of capabilities deals with the mathematical sophistication of the vendor's products. Multidimensional analysis tools will continue to provide more and more sophisticated mathematical- and statistical-analysis capabilities to describe relationships within and across dimensions. Time-series smoothing and currency-conversion algorithms are examples.

One of the most promising advanced features of multidimensional analysis is *interactive shared decision making* that results from workgroups sharing "live" analyses and collaborating to make the best decision. Decision making is a collaborative process that recognizes the importance of experience and ideas of various workgroup members in arriving at the most appropriate decision. Users need to share in the data-analysis process as a catalyst for decision making. In sharing analysis, each member of the workgroup should be able to receive a "live" report, add to the analysis, even set off in an entirely new direction, then distribute the report throughout the organization. "Live" analyses include not only text but also the calculations, assumptions, and logic that support the reports so that, when a report is shared, the recipient can retrieve it and become immediately productive.

The idea of collaboration in the decision-making process, supported by an ability to freely share information among users, is the next major milestone in the evolution of client/server computing. What Lotus Notes has done for the sharing of textual information must be duplicated in the sharing of numerical information. However, in this case, the information that is shared must be pointed directly back to the data warehouse and multidimensional logic used to create the analysis. In this way, reports are "live," not a text representation of the report.

The Database Link

Returning to the spreadsheet analogy, "A1," "B1," and "C3" are coordinates in a two-dimensional space. "A1" provides a row and column coordinate for data stored in the spreadsheet cell. The coordinate is used to locate cell contents (facts or measures derived via formula) that can be referenced in the creation of a formula. The numeric value contained in the cell is substituted for the coordinate used in specifying the formula when the spreadsheet logic is executed.

Database dimensions are much like the number and letter dimensions of the spreadsheet. Period, market, and product dimensions, in the simple example used thus far, allow for the definition of coordinates within the data warehouse. By constraining a combination of database dimensions (e.g., "where product = Blast" and "where market = Eastern Region"), facts are easily located within the data warehouse.

In multidimensional analysis, formulas are specified using database coordinates. The multidimensional software, like spreadsheet software, substitutes actual numeric values for the coordinates and manages the constant changing of coordinates as the user makes changes. In the spreadsheet, a user can change the value in a cell and compute all of the formulas. In multidimensional analysis, the user changes the constraints on one or more dimensions. For example, changing from "where market = Eastern Region" to "where market = Central Region." The problem in multidimensional analysis is complex because a data warehouse has many dimensions.

There are three ways that the leading software vendors have implemented multidimensional analytic capabilities:

- Proprietary multidimensional database management
- Relational/database logic repository
- Relational/metadata logic repository

Proprietary multidimensional database management systems

The most obvious solution for creating the logic for multidimensional analysis is to lock the database structure. By fixing the database structure, the logic to process multidimensional analysis can rely on a well-defined method of establishing data coordinates. The logic and the database are tightly linked.

The problem with this approach is that the data warehouse becomes a single vendor's proprietary database management system. Not truly an open data warehouse, the approach is best suited for so-called data marts created for departmental applications.

In addition, proprietary multidimensional databases introduce other issues, including database size limitations, an inability to incrementally load data, and a limited number of dimensions.

Relational database management systems

Most data warehouses will be built using a relational database management system as the foundation for an open system available to a range of reporting and analytic tools. The scalability of these products, sophistication of the database management tools, and performance gains that will result from parallel processing make relational databases the logical choice for data warehousing.

In developing multidimensional logic for relational database access, the vendor does not have the advantage of a fixed set of database coordinates, because each data warehouse will be designed to meet the larger enterprise set of requirements. One approach to providing multidimensional logic, employing relational databases, is to code the logic essentially *in* the data warehouse. This is conceptually similar to the approach in a spreadsheet where formulas are contained in the body of the spreadsheet. Relational database management systems provide some support for this approach, which often is referred to as *stored procedures*. In implementing this approach, the multidimensional analysis software vendor's contribution is in developing a user interface (PC resident) that can execute the logic stored within the relational database management tool upon user command.

The limitation of this approach is the same as the problem that is encountered within complex spreadsheet applications. Maintenance is critically important. In a rapidly changing data warehouse, maintenance can be overwhelming.

The alternative approach is to create a definition layer that defines dimensions and other important "data about data," or metadata. This approach partitions the logic for multidimensional analysis from the database and rejoins the two with metadata acting as the "glue." Importantly, metadata provides the database dimensions, dimension hierarchy, and data characteristics so that the multidimensional logic can create the SQL query (specifying coordinates of facts) to retrieve the numeric values. The numeric values then are substituted for the database coordinates in formulas. Metadata is a very sophisticated means of joining logic and multidimensional data structures and is the preferred means of providing powerful analysis capabilities in conjunction with relational database implementation of the data warehouse.

By authoring SQL queries on the fly, essentially defined by a combination of user requests and metadata rules, the multidimensional analysis engine should intelligently manage the data retrieval. From a maintenance standpoint, a single metadata change is all that is required when the data warehouse is updated or changed; all applications remain unchanged. To maximize the benefits of this approach, including improved performance and simplified user access, the database design must be carefully considered. (See Figure 14.7.)

Client/Server Architecture

As data warehouses become very large, there are architectural considerations regarding hardware sizing and network management. There are two issues related to scalability of the data warehouse: "How large will the data warehouse become?" and "How many users will be provided warehouse access?" Both of these issues must be considered within the context of what the users will find acceptable in terms of system response.

The relational database vendors combined with efforts by the hardware vendors have made substantial progress in managing very large databases. The problem will never be truly solved because the enterprise's ability to collect data will always outpace the vendor's ability to manage data. However, the gap has narrowed significantly.

The problem of supporting a large number of users, many of whom might be remote users with "thin client" laptops, is far more of a challenge. Much

	Database size	Relational database API	Performance scalability	Maintenance and support
Proprietary multidimensional database	Limited	Limited	Poor	Poor
Relational database Database logic repository	Unlimited	Open	Good	Poor
Relational database Metadata repository	Unlimited	Open	Excellent	Excellent

Figure 14.7 Approaches to dimensional analysis.

of the software developed for client/server systems was developed with a PC-centric view. At one time, it was deemed acceptable to store and retrieve data as well as perform all computations, formatting, and presentation on the PC itself. After all, there hasn't been that much data available or that many users demanding data access *until now*. The driving force behind data warehousing is a very large number of users demanding access to the data assets of the enterprise.

The alternative to a PC-centric development view is forced by the decision to warehouse data. The decision to build a data warehouse will establish, at minimum, a two-tier client/server architecture. Most vendors of multidimensional analysis tools for relational database access physically and/or logically partition the data from the presentation tier. The logical partitioning is accomplished with an application programming interface (API) such as ODBC. The physical partitioning occurs as a result of managing the presentation (user interface and result display) on the PC client and the data warehouse on a high performance server. In a two-tier architecture, any computational or rules-based logic can reside on either the server or the client but is not separated by any programming interface. In other words, the logic cannot be separated from the tier to which it is attached. (See Figure 14.8.)

A three-tier application development model separates the logic tier *logically* and perhaps *physically*. A three-tier client/server architecture is absolutely essential to deliver scalable client/server applications that address complex business issues. (See Figure 14.9.)

Multidimensional analysis tool vendors are realizing the shortcomings of the two-tiered approach and are just beginning to announce direction toward support for a three-tier architecture. Implementations vary widely from a true logical and optionally physical three-tier partitioning to hybrid distributed processing models. The distributed processing model merely off-loads some of the processing from the user's PC to another network server.

The benefits of a true three-tier architecture, which separates the data warehouse, logic, and presentation, are performance, flexibility, and scalability. Development can occur independently at the data, logic, and presentation layer, maximizing flexibility. Performance is improved as a result of applying the appropriate hardware solution for each tier. A three-tier architecture is *essential* for large data warehouse and large user community support.

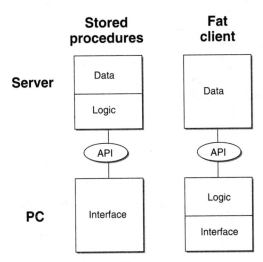

Figure 14.8 Two-tier architecture.

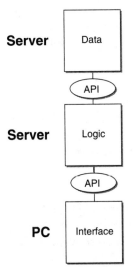

Figure 14.9 Three-tier architecture.

Previously, the advanced features of multidimensional analysis tools were discussed. Included were capabilities for automating analyses and workgroup collaboration. These capabilities require a high performance middle-tier server to support continuous background processing and communications.

Consolidating the Concepts

Multidimensional analysis provides a very powerful set of analytic capabilities that are required to respond to the rapid-fire questioning sequence that is the day-to-day business-analysis requirement. At a fundamental level, multidimensional analysis supports the *ad hoc* creation of calculated measures, warehouse navigation (drilling, pivoting, and aggregations), and presentation (formatting and exporting to a PC tools environment).

The following sections contain a checklist of the 15 keys that should be considered as *minimum* requirements when selecting a multidimensional analysis tool.

Multidimensional view

Users and developers should be provided with a dimensional view of the data warehouse that shields them from the complexities of the underlying data structures and query algorithms and that allows them to pose questions from their business perspective. Each dimension should define standard hierarchies, including multiple hierarchies within a single dimension.

Pivot/rotation

Users should be able to point-and-click to dynamically cast and recast dimensions into any report layout of columns, rows, and section breaks at any time. This capability allows users to view and present analytic results from an unlimited number of perspectives.

Intelligent drilling

Users should be able to dynamically explore their business at *any* level of detail by drilling down, drilling up, and skipping multiple hierarchy levels on *any* dimension at *any* time *without predefining drill paths*.

Cross-dimension calculations

Users should be able to dynamically create, save, and share simple and complex custom calculations *without writing stored procedures*. Calculations affecting one dimension should automatically operate correctly when applied across other dimensions during analysis.

Dynamic sets

Users should be able to dynamically create, save, and share custom item groupings and summaries across any dimension, such as test markets or products on promotion. Users should be able to define a hierarchy of custom groupings and immediately *drill up and down* through the hierarchy. This lets the user define and analyze unforeseen or temporary business occurrences when necessary.

Filters

Users should be able to define report content by dragging and dropping filters that constrain the data appearing on the report to items meeting a specific criterion. Filters associated with one dimension should be able to be combined with filters from other dimensions *at any time*. Users should be able to create, save, and share filters.

Decision groupware capabilities

Users should be able to create and share any decision support information object—such as reports, analyses, sets, calculations, filters, templates, intelligent agents, alerts, and triggers—across workgroups or the entire enterprise. To really be effective, groupware should contain *"live information."* For example, a member of a workgroup can create a report, perform their own analyses, and share the report with others in the group who receive an intelligent "live" report. The group members then can immediately drill, analyze, rerun, and resend the report. "Live" reports contain not only the text, but also the calculations and assumptions supporting the analyses. Simply sharing the text of the report *is not* decision groupware. In addition, shared information objects must incorporate appropriate security to prevent unauthorized access.

Collapsible browsing

Users should be able to define report content by quickly and flexibly browsing a list of all valid choices in the data warehouse and selecting from this list items to be included in the report. Available lists of items should "collapse" as users constrain on dimension attributes. For example, a 100,000 item listing of soft drinks might collapse down to 25 after the user selects "Diet, 12 oz., Can, Caffeine Free, Cherry, Cola." Users should be able to expand and collapse browse lists by pointing and clicking.

Flexible period definitions

Multidimensional analysis logic should support multiple noncontiguous periods, period ranges, period calculations, and period variables, including "most recent." Support for nonstandard time period analysis is critical (e.g., "Compare fiscal year 1993 to calendar year 1994"). Users should be able to create period calculations and define nonstandard time period analysis without storing it in advance.

Direct access to relational databases

Multidimensional analysis should be performed directly against standard RDBMSs without the need to extract and place data in a proprietary multi-dimensional environment. Systems must support any combination of relational databases required by the application including *simultaneous* access to multiple heterogeneous databases. Using relational databases, the flexibility and openness of your data warehouse will be maintained, and the many shortcomings of proprietary multidimensional database engines are eliminated *without sacrificing performance.*

Metadata

Metadata, a directory that describes the data warehouse to the application, *can* and *should* be used as more than a card catalog. It should be used as an architectural component that reduces development time and user-support requirements by providing a dynamic layer between the data ware-house and application logic. Metadata should transparently manage business rules to allow instant drill-up/drill-down, user created calculations, and custom groupings. *Changing the database structure should not require a change to the application.*

Sparse matrix schema support

Multidimensional analysis logic should support sparse matrix schemes. The database design *should not* require the storage of N/As or zeros where dimensions intersect but data doesn't exist (e.g., July sales of snow shovels in Phoenix). Products requiring the storage of nonexistent data points can cause the size of the database to explode by an order of magnitude.

Read and write

Users and applications should be able to read and write to the data ware-house. Many decision support applications require this capability, including forecasting, budgeting, and sales-force automation.

Query generation

The multidimensional analysis logic should dynamically generate efficient SQL at runtime based on user requests and applications requirements. This capability provides users with unlimited interactive exploration of the data warehouse.

Openness

Multidimensional analysis logic should be able to directly access standard local or distributed relational databases. Multidimensional logic should be accessible by any PC development and productivity tool.

Increasingly, advanced features are being added to support the automation of routine business-performance monitoring and communications at a collaborative level within and across workgroups. The multidimensional analysis tools should become aligned with the business management processes.

For enterprise deployment, which assumes a large data warehouse and a growing user community, a relational database management system is recommended for the management of the data warehouse. Multidimensional analysis tools that are designed to access the relational database *directly* must be evaluated carefully based on the manner in which the multidimensional logic is implemented. Using relational databases for multidimensional analysis has proven effective provided the calculations are performed *outside* of the database. Performance and maintenance issues must be carefully considered in addition to the robustness of the analytic capabilities.

Proven Three-Tier Client/Server Business-Analysis Tools

The first company to introduce a true three-tier business analysis application suite that performs multidimensional analysis *directly* against relational databases is Information Advantage. Information Advantage develops and markets DecisionSuite and AXSYS, which are the only proven three-tiered relational business analysis solutions and technology for data warehouses and data marts. DecisionSuite stretches beyond traditional decision support to meet the needs of the "decision-making majority"—the managers making the day-to-day decisions that shape the fate of your business. AXSYS is a software development technology that has been used in production environments since 1991 across industries as diverse as retail, insurance, telecommunications, government, and manufacturing. AXSYS technology provides the foundation for DecisionSuite.

As part of DecisionSuite, Information Advantage offers a server-resident multidimensional analysis engine that employs a metadata interface between the data and logic tiers. Using the most advanced trigger, agent and alert, server-resident background processing capabilities, users are presented information in business terms so that they can explore gigabytes of information without knowledge of database structures or SQL. The multidimensional analysis engine is continually evolving to meet today's user requirements.

DecisionSuite includes four integrated applications, each providing the appropriate level of functionality to users across the enterprise:

InfoAlert

InfoAlert delivers critical "live" information, reports, and alerts generated by co-workers and intelligent agents to busy professionals, turning data into action. Users are alerted to the latest opportunities and problems affecting their business by an infinite number of software agents that continually monitor, analyze, and filter gigabytes of information 24 hours a day, 7 days a week in the background. Drill up, down, across business dimensions any-where in the data warehouse, then pivot and export results with a spread-sheet hot-link.

NewsLine

NewsLine includes all of the functionality of InfoAlert plus the ability to view and modify all assumptions behind the analyses, including calculations and filters with complete security. Users drag and drop calculations and fil-ters to surf the entire data warehouse. NewsLine includes robust business charting and integrates with external applications, including operational systems, catalogs, and powerful GIS mapping systems. Draw attention to critical information with personalized annotations inserted into reports.

Analysis

Analysis provides all of the functionality of NewsLine plus allows power users to start with a *blank-sheet-of-paper*, then point-and-click to author and publish filters, calculations, calculation templates, reports, report tem-plates, distributed intelligent agents, triggers, and alerts as well as navigate the entire data warehouse—without calling IT. Alerts can be directed and broadcast as "live" interactive reports or as messages via e-mail, beeper, telephone, and the Internet. Users are presented information in business terms so that they can explore gigabytes of information without knowledge of database structures or SQL.

Workbench

Workbench allows DBAs and administrators to manage resources and secu-rity, as well as customize and distribute desktop profiles across the net-work. Developers can create more sophisticated intelligent agents, custom applications, and add-in functionality and can integrate with operational systems.

All Information Advantage products work with any relational database or combination of databases including: DB2, Informix, Oracle, Sybase, Red

Brick, and Tandem Non-Stop SQL. The logic portion of the software runs on Unix servers from IBM, Hewlett-Packard, Sun, AT&T, Unisys, and Silicon Graphics. The graphical user interface operates in a Windows environment on the PC.

DecisionSuite provides a graphical user interface and powerful multidimensional business analysis applications that make it easy for everyone in the enterprise to point-and-click to create and share "live" analyses regardless of user location. With automated analysis, detect and alert agents, workflow and desktop integration, business information objects, and collaborative decision making, users can work together to make more timely decisions through interactively exchanging "live" work. *Everyone* can make more informed decisions, identify trends and exceptions, draw comparisons, and share enterprise data *without* writing stored procedures. Information Advantage is established with a proven model that delivers the user answers through collaborative workgroup "live" information sharing.

Information Advantage is headquartered in Minneapolis, Minnesota and has direct sales operations in North America and Europe. The company complements its direct sales operations with affiliates world-wide and relationships with technology, consulting, and application partners.

15

Statistical Analysis

ELAN LONG
Director of Corporate Marketing, SPSS Inc.
DOUGLAS DOW
Director of Strategic Partnerships, SPSS Inc.

Data mining is uncovering the hidden meaning and relationships in the massive amounts of data stored in the data warehouse. In short, the value of the data warehouse lies in the information that can be derived from its data through the mining process. Successful mining of data relies on refining tools and techniques capable of rendering large quantities of data understandable and meaningful. Since its creation in the 18th century, statistics has served this purpose, providing the mathematical tools and analytic techniques for dealing with large amounts of data. Today, as we are confronted with increasingly large volumes of data, statistics is, more than ever, a critical component of the data-mining and refining toolkit that facilitates making effective business decisions.

What Is Statistics and Why Use It?

Way of thinking

Statistics is a general method of reasoning from data. It is a basic approach shared by people in today's society to draw conclusions and make decisions in business and in life. It lets us communicate effectively about a wide range of topics from sales performance to product quality to operational efficiency. Statistics is the way that we "reason effectively about data and chance in everyday life."[1] The goal of statistical analysis is to gain insight through numbers. We will consider four important aspects of statistics: developing good data, strategies for exploring data, drawing conclusions from the data, and presenting your results.

Because data from different sources can vary, the conclusions that you can draw from them are uncertain. For example, as you measure sales, attitudes, and characteristics, you will get different measures because people and things vary—or sometimes the measurement system itself introduces variation into the measures. Because you are making inferences from variable data, your conclusions have some uncertainty. David Moore, in his book *Statistics: Concepts and Controversies*, says:

> Statistics faces the variability and uncertainty of the world directly. Statistical reasoning can produce data whose usefulness is not destroyed by variation and uncertainty. It can analyze data to separate systematic patterns from the ever-present variation. It can form conclusions that, while not certain—nothing in the real world is certain—have only a little uncertainty. More important, statistical reasoning allows us to say just how uncertain our conclusions are.[2]

Producing data

You will have a wealth of data in the warehouse and available from outside sources. There are important concepts to consider in selecting the data that you actually use in your analysis. These concepts are: sampling, experimentation, and measurement. They are important because the efficiency and accuracy of your analysis—and therefore your ability to draw useful conclusions in a timely manner—are dependent on the quality of the data reflecting the business situation.

Sampling is based upon the idea that you can draw conclusions about an entire group of people or objects by examining part of the group. It is used to gain information about the group. With proper sampling, you do not need to look at every piece of information to draw reasonable conclusions. In regards to the data in a data warehouse, you will find that with certain types of analysis, you will prefer to obtain sample data rather than including every case in storage. You can get an accurate picture of your order-to-shipment turnaround by randomly selecting a subset of orders to analyze rather than pulling every order over the time period from the warehouse. Similarly, you can conduct a quarterly survey of employee satisfaction using sampling techniques and get good information with less time and expense (and annoyance to the employees) than polling each person each quarter.

---

[1]Moore, David S. 1991. *Statistics: Concepts and Controversies*, 3rd ed. New York, NY: W.H. Freeman and Company. p. xii.

[2]Ibid., p. xvii.

Experimentation is used to produce data when you are interested in cause-and-effect relationships rather than just collecting information. Experiments require that you impose change on the subject of the study to see the impact of the change. You look at explanatory and response variables (or fields) and try to isolate and understand the impact of a change in an explanatory variable on a response variable. For example, you might try altering the machining speed used in manufacturing parts to see if there is an impact on the number of defective parts or experiment with decreasing the time to preventive maintenance to see if machine failures also decrease.

With designed experiments, you can test a variety of explanatory factors in a group of experiments to see which will have the greatest impact on reaching the desired state of the response variables. For example, two materials are not bonding properly in the assembly process. Is the answer a change in one or both materials, the bonding agent, the bonding temperature or pressure, or the speed of the cool-down process? Because you need multiple measures to distinguish variability in measurement versus true change, testing one factor at a time could result in a very lengthy and expensive experimentation process. Statistical design of experiments lets you test multiple factors simultaneously and get the most informative results with the least number of experiments.

Understanding measurement is important for data analysis. You cannot draw valid conclusions if the data does not accurately represent what you assumed. Sometimes you can use something that you cannot measure as a proxy for what you really are interested in measuring, such as number of returns is equated to unhappy customers. It is possible that returns are caused by multiple factors and not all of them indicate problems. Understanding the measurement will improve your analysis. For example, are monthly sales numbers in the data warehouse gross shipments or net of returns? Does the organization measure and store both numbers or only the net numbers? Are they coded in one field or two different places?

Measurement is how you produce data in either observation or experimentation. Statistics deals with cases, variables, and values that are the individual objects being measured, the specific properties being measured, and the assigned number measuring the property in that object. You define a sales representative's performance in terms of sales, returns, pipeline value, and number of calls made. Each variable has a different measure. However, all measurement varies, and one goal of analysis is to understand if the measurement variation is random or biased in a specific direction.

Because much of this book is related to producing and storing data, we will note that understanding the data is essential to effective data mining. That means understanding the source of the data whether observation or experimentation as well as the meaning of the variable and its measuring system. To draw meaningful conclusions from the data, it actually must measure the characteristic that you are interested in understanding.

Exploring data

Exploring data is important for understanding the quality of the data in the warehouse and to begin looking for areas to mine for information. Exploring data will tell you if most of the observations are missing or will indicate if the measurements are suspect because of extreme variability. In effect, exploratory data analysis gives you a "feel" for the data and will help uncover possible directions the analysis can go. Just as the mining company explores the terrain looking for the place to put a mine with the highest likelihood of success, so too does the data miner need to gain a sense of where the key relationships are in the data. Probably equally important, exploring data will serve to highlight any problems inherent in the database in terms of inaccurate or missing data.

The first step in data analysis must be exploring it to see overall patterns and extreme exceptions to the patterns. This is best done by graphing the data and visually identifying the patterns and the number of exceptions. In exploring data, we typically look at each variable separately, starting with basic counts and percentages that tell us the number and proportion of measures at each level. Then we look at the distributions of the data using charts like histograms, dot plots, boxplots, line charts, and others. We also look at some measure of the data that describe various characteristics of the data in terms of average, variability, and distribution.

Descriptive statistics include the following measures:

- Mean—Arithmetic average of the values
- Median—The midpoint of values
- Mode—The most frequent value
- Percentiles—Breaking the numbers into groups by percentage of values above and below
- Variance—Average deviation of observations from the mean
- Standard deviation—The spread of values around the mean

Data exploration also will show you if there are a few extreme measures that are wildly inflating or deflating the measures of the variable. In cases like this, you will get more accurate information from your data by eliminating these extreme outliers before continuing with the analysis. They typically are reflective of data-entry errors or odd circumstances and will not reflect the true situation that you are trying to understand. You might want to investigate the source of the oddity; however, for statistical analysis, you can eliminate the cases from the sample without jeopardizing the quality of your analysis.

In data-mining applications, there often is a problem related to the sheer size of the data set being used. In addition to computer resource limitations, you might find that the vast number of interrelationships between data items can obscure the relationships that you are truly interested in. Statistical tools also can sample or summarize data to make it easier to work with. Random sampling allows you to create a smaller, more manageable working subset of the data from which statistically valid conclusions still can be drawn. Techniques like principal components or factor analysis allow you to reduce a data set to its underlying dimensions by grouping together fields that are very closely related into a single measure.

Exploring your data first will keep you from spending time and effort on unsupported analyses and will help prevent drawing conclusions that are not supported by your data. The goal of data exploration is to start you on a successful path towards full data mining and refining—drawing actionable conclusions from your data.

Drawing conclusions from data

Statistics is concerned with finding relationships between variables. Once you have mined to an area with an interesting relationship, statistics provides the additional tools to "refine" the data into an understanding of the strength of the relationship and the factors that cause the relationship. For example, order values and sales lead sources are interesting characteristics to measure and summarize. However, order value and sales lead source for the same order give you significantly more information than either measure alone. When you have the source and the value of orders linked, you can look for associations between the source and value that will lead you to evaluating higher promotion spending on the sources that bring the most high-value orders or possibly on the sources that bring the highest total revenue even if it is booked as smaller transactions in higher volume.

You begin by describing the association of two variables, usually with a table or chart. You also can indicate the strength of a straight-line relationship using a correlation coefficient. Then you begin to look for an explanation of the relationship. Does one characteristic cause the other? Does lead source cause order size? Does one measure predict another? Can you predict the average order size from the lead source? In some cases, a variable can predict another even though there is no cause-and-effect relationship between them.

Typical explanations for association between variables are causation, common response, or confounding. *Causation* means that changes in variable A cause changes in variable B, such as increased employment of temporary workers causes a change in salary expenses. *Common response* means that changes in both A and B are caused by changes in a third variable, C. For example, sales revenue generated and hours of customer contact are both influenced by length of tenure as a sales rep. *Confounding* describes the association when changes in B are caused both by changes in

A and by changes in the third variable, *C*. Sales revenue fluctuates from both changes in promotional spending and changes in the number of sales representatives available to follow up on leads and take orders.

It is not a simple leap to go from association of variables to causation. Causation can be concluded only with significant evidence. Without conducting properly designed experiments to demonstrate the causal link and eliminating any other possible explanations, statistics does not support concluding that associations are due to causation. However, statistics can help determine the likelihood that the relationship is coincidental. This is particularly useful when you want to explain an unusual occurrence, such as if you discovered that the sales for a product were generated by one salesperson. Are you missing the data on other sales? Does only one salesperson understand the product well enough to close orders? Is the market so small that the only customers are in one territory?

Strong relationships between variables are useful when you want to predict the value of one variable from others. If you can describe the relationship as a line or curve, then you have a formula for predicting certain values when the data exist for the other predictive variables. The basic technique used is *regression*, which fits a line between the data points in such a way that it minimizes the distance from the known data points to the line. Prediction does not depend on having causal relationships between variables. A high college grade point average does not cause high-quality job performance in a new employee. However, an employer might predict that the study skills, work ethic, and intelligence that resulted in high grades also will be reflected in the applicant's performance on the job once hired.

A special case of prediction is time-series analysis where the same characteristics are measured over time intervals. For instance, daily or monthly sales revenue could be predicted from past measures of revenue along with corresponding measures of inventory status, promotional dollars spent, available sales reps, etc. Similarly, past history of absenteeism does not cause an employee to miss work, but an employer interested in projecting a worker's available days can reasonably start from the worker's prior years' days worked.

Another special case of prediction is called *classification*. This technique is used when you want to predict membership in a group or category, rather than a specific number. In our database marketing example that follows, the company was predicting whether the account would respond or not respond to the new product offering based on attributes of the company and its previous purchases.

There are more advanced statistical techniques available to draw stronger conclusions or to tease out relationships that are not described by a straight-line. The fundamental principles are the same. Statistics is the method by which you describe relationships, draw conclusions, and state the level of uncertainty associated with your conclusions.

Some Practical Applications of Statistics in Business

Applications of statistics in data mining

Statistical analysis is the secret weapon of many successful businesses today. It is the essential tool for mining the data that you have, refining the data into useful information, and leading you to other data that you might want to acquire. Businesses that effectively employ statistical analysis can increase revenues, cut costs, improve operating efficiency, and improve customer satisfaction. They can more accurately identify problems and opportunities and understand their causes so that they can act more quickly to eliminate threats or to capitalize on opportunities.

One particularly rich and easily accessible solution for statistics in the data-mining area is represented by the products of SPSS, Inc. They have focused their business on developing statistical product and service solutions to bring the power of statistics to bear on the analytic problems emerging in today's marketplace.

About SPSS

SPSS supplies a complete range of data-analysis tools for data mining and refining, with a special emphasis on the end user and application developer. The richness of the product line is reflected in providing the most comprehensive set of statistical tools available. The benefits to the end user are threefold: The breadth of the line assures that you will have the right tool for the job when facing a wide variety of data analysis situations; the depth of the line provides a system that you won't outgrow; and availability on all major graphical user interface environments ensures short start-up time and continued ease of use. The additional benefit to the application developer is that the product line has been opened up so that proven and reliable pieces of the data-management and statistical toolkit now can be embedded as components in custom applications. Clearly, SPSS provides complete tools for data mining and refining.

SPSS, Inc. grew out of a practical application of statistical thinking. The original product was conceived in the late 1960s, growing out of an academic research project. Absorbed with trying to quantitatively understand the dynamics of how and why people vote, Norman Nie wanted to be able to tell the computer, in plain English, the type of analysis he wanted to do, without converting everything into FORTRAN code. In collaboration with Hadlai Hull, the core of the SPSS system was developed—software that made both the power of the computer and the power of statistics more accessible to the end user.

SPSS, Inc. is a comprehensive supplier of statistics. The company offers not only a complete range of software products, but comprehensive training programs and consulting services as well. From public course offerings focusing on topics such as market segmentation and customer satisfaction to customized training focusing on the customer's particular data analytic needs, SPSS provides instruction in the meaningful use of its products. SPSS consulting services cover a wide range of expertise in statistical analysis with particular emphasis in data mining and refining.

Variety of examples in all fields

SPSS's products have helped their clients solve problems in a variety of fields from customer satisfaction and database marketing to credit-risk analysis and sales-force productivity. In the remainder of this section, we will highlight cases in each of these areas. First, however, let's look at additional applications of data mining using statistics:

- Sales forecasting resulting in more efficient manufacturing planning
- Sales territory evaluation resulting in better coverage of sales opportunities
- Payable analysis resulting in more effective cash management
- Product-line performance resulting in rationalizing or expanding product offerings
- Employee-success analysis resulting in more effective recruiting of personnel
- Employee-satisfaction assessment resulting in reduced staff turnover
- Benefits analysis resulting in the most attractive and cost-effective plan offerings
- Promotions analysis resulting in more effective spending to generate business
- Customer-service analysis resulting in elimination of sources of errors and complaints
- Customer-support analysis resulting in most effective staffing levels to meet demand
- Customer-attrition analysis resulting in more effective revenue planning
- Customer-value analysis resulting in increased repeat business at lower cost

Customer satisfaction

IBM was experiencing a steady three-year decline in customer satisfaction. The company's management decided to focus on improving customer satisfaction and designated certain people as "Customer Satisfaction Advocates." Their job was to figure out what was wrong and how to fix it. One of the advocates used statistical tools to refine data to identify the key areas of opportunity and to measure improvement in customer satisfaction levels.

The advocate used two surveys to collect his data. One was a national blind survey, while the other was specific to his region and was developed in conjunction with other members of the IBM team. The advocate used statistics to identify patterns in the data, or to refine the data into nuggets of useful information. Using correlations, F-tests, regression, and other statistical techniques, he identified five specific traits of Technical Service that IBM customers in his region really cared about:

- Continuity of their relationship with IBM—Customers wanted to be able to count on their IBM team.

- Value of their investment—Customers wanted to know that they were getting the most value out of their hardware, software, manuals, training, support lines, etc.

- Technical support—Customers wanted reliable technical support that was there when needed and that provided useful, accurate information.

- Hardware service—Customers wanted to know that their hardware was the best, guaranteed, and with a warranty and that, if it needed to be fixed, IBM would fix it properly.

- Good company to do business with—Customers wanted to feel like IBM was taking care of them.

Based on this understanding of what was important to their customers, IBM was able to "manage by fact" and develop specific programs and initiatives that enhanced the five key areas of interest. They developed a custom application that was effectively a specialized customer database. The system, called QUEST, was installed in each IBM store or office in the region. Using the QUEST system, IBM managers could more easily tailor their service to key customer issues. They can look up a specific customer's service records, or they can look at how other reps in similar situations in other regions are solving customer problems. The system gives each business segment owner a unique customer satisfaction model. Each model provides:

- Unique predictors of customer satisfaction for the business segment

- Expected improvement

- Focused actions

- Forecasting methodology

In other words, it lets the business-unit manager identify factors that indicate whether a customer will be satisfied. Then it lets her identify what improvement is expected by the customers, set plans to focus on solving that problem, and finally measuring results of the program and forecasting the satisfaction of the customers based on their experiences with the company.

For example, "Red" customers in the territory with a "stripes" installed less than 12 months showed a statistically significantly lower customer satisfaction index when compared to other "Red" customers. The IBM business unit responsible for "Red" customers decided to focus on the delivery of technical support as the best, most targeted, most impact-potential opportunity. The result of the QUEST system and its ability to identify and focus attention on specific problems is that customer satisfaction has increased over three consecutive quarters. This was based on a logical, structured process using statistical analysis to highlight requirements for a highly targeted program.

Database marketing

Industrial components supplier RS Components of Corby, England planned to attack a new sector of its target market but needed to ensure that telesales effort was not wasted on no-hope prospects. RS Components' main business is the supply of electrical components. An opportunity was identified in mechanical parts and tools, for which it was expected many potential customers would be found within the existing user base.

To determine where the best prospects lay, the business development manager, Nigel Thompson, set the sales force a four-month task to approach the top 75% of their customer base. This exercise yielded a success rate of 11%—one solid prospect for each nine sites approached.

The remaining 25% of their customers were to be addressed with a telemarketing campaign. Because it was known that the previous exercise probably had creamed off the best prospects, some way had to be found to ensure that the telemarketing campaign targeted those remaining sites offering the best chance of live prospects.

During the initial exercise, the sales force had recorded a lot of information about those sites that had, and had not, yielded prospects, and these attributes were added to the customer database. Thompson decided to review this information to see if the characteristics of those sites that yielded prospects differed from those sites that did not. If they did, then the groups could be meaningfully segmented.

The attributes added to the customer database were:

- Industrial classification
- Size of company
- Geographical location
- Status of sales force assessment
- Transaction history

- Recency of last order
- Order value
- Products purchased

The database was queried using SPSS statistical-analysis software. The first step was to run some simple summary statistics to determine measures such as averages and ranges for each attribute. The process itself revealed some interesting facts about the customers that had not previously been measured. Of more interest, however, was determining which attributes were related to prospect yield. For example, did companies of a particular size yield more prospects than others? Identifying such relationships would enable RS Components to predict which companies in the remaining 25% were likely to yield prospects. They began exporting the data with crosstabulations (*crosstabulations* are counts of one variable against another) to get a feel for how different attributes interacted. However, it quickly became clear that, while this approach was useful in identifying the most significant attributes, they would miss something because there were potentially five million crosstabulation cells to examine.

Crosstabulations were limiting for two reasons. First, if there are numerous attributes, the number of crosstabulations required to investigate every possible relationship can be unmanageable. Secondly, crosstabulations do not take into account how attributes might interact. For example, it might be that geographical location is a significant predictor (e.g., sites in the South East yield more prospects than sites in other locations). It also could be that the size of company is an important predictor (e.g., companies with over 100 employees yield more prospects than other sites). However, what about sites with 100+ employees in the North West? Which is the most important predictor—geographic location or size of company? Is it the combination of the two that is important? SPSS CHAID analysis solves these problems by analyzing and ordering every possible combination of attributes. It then identifies which attribute is the most important predictor, which attributes have no predictive value, and how attributes combine or interact together to help in prediction.

SPSS CHAID segments a database into groups according to their prospect yield or whatever attribute you are trying to predict. Each group can be identified by a combination of attributes and ranked from best (e.g., the best group yielded 50% prospects and was made up of companies with the following characteristics . . .) to worst (0% prospect yield in companies with these characteristics . . .).

By applying this information back into the remaining 25% of the database, half the sites were identified as not being worth a telemarketing call. This in itself produced a cost saving of $80,000. Those that were called produced a success rate very close to the anticipated 15%—a better rate than had been achieved by the blanket approach to calling the top 75% of accounts who supposedly were the best targets. The company was highly encouraged by the results. They continue to use these techniques for further profiling and segmentation of the customer base and with similar success. SPSS and SPSS CHAID now are vital elements of RS Components' database marketing analysis.

Credit-risk analysis

Our example of the application of data-mining techniques to credit-risk analysis comes from the U.K. The banking industry has used statistical models widely for many years. Banks would like to make consistent, accurate, and efficient decisions about whether or not to extend credit to customers. Initially, the data was quite limited. However, because the industry practice is to justify and document credit decisions, there has grown a vast wealth of data and the problem has been how to store and harness it effectively for use in modeling and decision-making.

Estimates are that a bank might have roughly 1500 pieces of information per month for each customer. Because, in the U.K., they are required to keep information for six years, they could reasonably have 108,000 pieces of information per customer. If a large bank has 9 million customers, they will have roughly 1 billion pieces of customer information. Unfortunately, in most banks, there are no links between different accounts—such as credit card, checking, and savings accounts—for the same customer. Banks are beginning to assemble customer information in data warehouse form because they are recognizing the importance of understanding and managing the complete relationship with the customer as a whole.

One bank has worked extensively with a statistical modeling firm using SPSS to pull together the relevant information and develop a model for making credit decisions—consistently, accurately, and efficiently. A collections model was developed with a goal of understanding which customers are likely to go into default and when an effort should be made to collect against them.

Initially the collections model looked at all accounts that had reached a trigger point, usually the due date of an installment payment. The accounts were divided into good and bad, and a cutoff score was established, similar to the approach that banks use in scoring credit applications in the first place. This approach probably is the most widely used in the banking industry today. However, if we reflect on the situation further, we might begin to believe that this simple categorization of customers into "good" and "bad" is not accurate or useful enough, particularly when the measure of good and bad is a given level of delinquency.

There are many different patterns of behavior that can be expressed as levels of delinquency or movements between levels. Some customers will consistently fail to pay the credit card outstanding balance if the amount is small, so they might miss one or two months payments and then pay off the entire debt. An examination of past payment patterns revealed that there was no significant risk attached to customers in this group. Other customers might be consistently 30 days past due on their accounts. This group often contains customers that use their card for business purposes and face a built-in administrative delay in payment as a result of claiming the expense for reimbursement before paying off the card debt. Use of cluster analysis led to the identification of different customer groups based on their behavior patterns. Once the behavioral groups are defined, then the decision models were built to effectively separate the groups.

This analysis was based on the data set that described the customer's behavior only in terms of the amount owed at each time of billing. The question then arises whether we can identify when a customer will leave the group (i.e., change behavior). The state of the bank's data made it infeasible to analyze delinquent balances, but it was possible to construct a model for payment patterns. When the data on payment dates and amounts was incorporated into the data set, analysis showed a very strong and consistent pattern of payment behavior for customers. Once the pattern was breached, it appeared that the customer was much more likely to default. This was true whether or not the account was overdue before the behavior change.

The models used have evolved over a five-year period. The issues were a combination of data assembly and analysis. Data comes into play when better decision making is required. Often, useful and powerful pieces of information already are available to be retrieved from storage and used to understand the underlying situation. In this case, a huge amount of data on each customer (probably 95%) was of no interest. Creating an all-encompassing historical database from which to develop perfect decision models for customer management is unrealistic and unnecessary. Applying the techniques of exploration, mining, and refining with statistical tools allows good conclusions with known levels of uncertainty from a much smaller, simpler data solution.[3]

Sales and marketing productivity

A software company uses statistical analysis for data mining in sales-force productivity analysis. They combine data from their customer database, order-entry system, and telephone system to measure their effectiveness in generating prospects and closing orders. This approach grew out of a basic exploration of their customer database system and analysis of leads generated through promotional activities, such as advertising, direct mail, and

---

[3]Hoyland, Chris. 1995. Data Mining—Case Study. *Data Mining Conference.* London: July 11–12.

public relations programs. They quickly realized that they could generate leads much more easily than they could close them; leads piling up waiting for sales reps seemed to indicate a capacity problem in the sales group.

Further analysis found that there were two distinct patterns in the time to close an order. For a large number of orders, the time between the initial inquiry call and the order was one week or less, and the number of contacts with the prospect was small. For another group, the duration was substantially longer—three to six months in many cases—and there were many contacts with the prospect over time.

This led them to conclude that the first group of prospects required little "selling" by sales reps; they basically called to order or for some specific information required before placing an order. Their calls could be handled through a group of more junior sales representatives who had access to price sheets, product specifications, and delivery information. Thus the data mining led to establishment of an "order taking" group within the sales department that provided excellent customer service at lower cost to the company than processing simple orders through experienced sales representatives.

Regular analysis of measures across sales groups has led to more effective allocation of sales resources and identification of personnel-development opportunities. Call volumes were tracked by sales representatives.

Measuring the hours each rep spent on the phone indicated two opportunities for improvement. The sales systems required significant time by the rep to record information on their sales calls and even longer to actually enter an order in the system. Because reps were required to spend so much time off the phone on paperwork, it was difficult to evaluate when they were on essential but nonselling tasks and when they were not.

Improvements in the sales-information and order-taking processes and regular measurement—with known standards—of phone time at the individual rep level led to a significant increase in actual selling time available. Patterns became identified in the ramp-up for a new sales representative to reach average phone time levels, and representatives who have difficulty achieving expected call volumes can be identified easily without waiting for them to miss their sales quota further down the road. The early intervention with additional coaching and skills training has resulted in decreased sales rep turnover and in new reps reaching full productivity sooner and more consistently.

In addition, business units within the sales organization now can be compared on a quarterly basis. Each unit reports standard statistics on rep call volume and phone time, pipelines in expected revenue and number of active sales opportunities, and sources of leads. Sales management can quickly see if certain business units still are severely capacity-constrained and are losing business because of their inability to contact prospects quickly.

Business units with lower lead-to-rep ratios and close rates could shift resources either temporarily or permanently to units where the incremental revenue of an additional sales rep is significantly higher. Similarly, promotion dollars can be shifted to markets where the incremental return is highest and out of markets that are producing revenue for the company at a slower rate. This ability to capture opportunities by shifting resources to the highest performing areas is a significant advantage in today's competitive business environment.

Who Does the Data Mining and When?

End users are the best data miners

With flexible, easy-to-use statistical tools, the subject matter experts become the best data miners and refiners. In effect, who is better to explore customer characteristics than the marketing and sales personnel in the company? Who will spot trends appearing across the industry in the employee satisfaction levels of the company, if not the human resources professionals? The best data miners are those who have an understanding of interesting places to look for problems and opportunities: typically those people who love their professional area and have a vision of making the company more profitable, more nimble, more competitive.

SPSS software takes statistics beyond the realm of the statisticians and puts it in the hands of people who are interested in exploring, refining, understanding, and drawing conclusions. The result is that these professionals are no longer locked into turning spreadsheets inside out and upside down to subset and analyze data. They can pursue interesting ideas immediately. As long as they have access to the data—and to an accurate description of the source and measurement system used to collect or generate the data—they can mine for the new and interesting information that will change the organization.

Application developers deploy statistical tools in the organization

Application developers have an opportunity to build statistics into their programs to capitalize on the full potential of the stored data. SPSS provides a developer's kit that enables IT professionals or others to quickly link the SPSS data management, statistics, and graphing routines into their custom application. This means that, when the organization wants to look at the same relationships regularly and in consistent form, the most effective approach is building the application.

The SPSS Developer's Kit provides the option of including SPSS functionality in three ways:

- Completely hidden to the end user but performing statistical analysis in the background.
- Partially exposed where the user sees the SPSS dialog boxes, probably with the language of the organization or application substituted in for the

standard statistical terms but allowing the user to make selections that define exactly how the data is analyzed and presented.

- Fully exposed where the application provides SPSS access for *ad hoc* analysis or more sophisticated users.

The advantage of incorporating SPSS into your data mining applications is that you save massive programming and testing time by plugging in known routines rather than coding your own from scratch. You have the proven algorithms and usability of the leading end user statistical tool right at your end users' fingertips. You also have a powerful tool for prototyping reports, analyzing data, assessing the status of the data warehouse, etc.

Start mining immediately for your best payback

Your statistical tool should be one of the first things that you acquire when you begin your data warehouse. If you begin to work with the data immediately and have users mining for gold right from the start, you are likely to avoid some overbuilding and to substitute in data that has more value.

You cannot predict what you will find to explore once you start delving into the data. The techniques described are designed to look for interesting patterns and associations and then dig down into them to draw conclusions or make predictions. As in the case of the bank developing the credit-scoring application, there was a lot of data available, but the cost of bringing it all together was exorbitant and not justified. Instead, they began by building a simple model for predicting defaults and then making it more sophisticated over time. They could use it from the beginning, and they could identify areas of potential gold to dig into before making the investment in bringing together disparate data. Often the data that is easily available can approximate another measure of the same characteristic that is more costly to acquire or integrate. Keeping an eye on the payback is not completely at odds with developing good analyses and drawing actionable conclusions.

Ad hoc and periodic analysis are both important

You have seen examples of both *ad hoc* and periodic analysis in our data-mining applications. In many cases, *ad hoc* analysis leads to periodic reporting as it did with SPSS's investigation of sales rep productivity or the automotive company's customer satisfaction, loyalty, and profitability measures. Both approaches have value in the data-mining context. You cannot find the new exciting nuggets of information without some data exploration, asking questions, examining relationships, and so forth. However, to continuously improve the profitability and operations of the organization, the maxim "you get what you measure" always holds. If you don't put systems in place to measure and evaluate the associations that are important to your success, how will you know if you are succeeding? SPSS tools give you the flexibility and flow-of-consciousness operation to make *ad hoc* analysis both fun and productive. They also provide the features required to repeat the analysis every year, quarter, month, day, or hour—and to compare the results over time. Once you know what you are looking for, SPSS tools let you easily measure that the relationship still holds and/or how it is changing as a result of changes in other factors.

An Annotated Example: New Product Development

Here is a more thorough case study showing how SPSS works and can facilitate making effective business decisions.

A large financial services company was launching a new mutual fund. The marketing manager was interested in exploring who is most likely to buy this new fund or, more generally, what are the most important predictors of buying a mutual fund. The new fund was an extension of the company's most successful mutual fund: the Summit Fund, which invested in large, established companies. This new fund also would invest in the similar types of companies, yet it had a larger minimum deposit. It was believed that, by looking at the main predictors of purchasing the Summit Fund, the company would be able to explore how best to target customers for the new fund.

There were many factors believed to be important in buying a mutual fund: age, gender, marital status, region where the customer resides, and past sales history. The goal of this analysis was to determine which is the most important predictor of buying the Summit Fund or whether it is a combination of multiple factors that is important. The customer database that contained the three-year purchase history was accessed using SPSS software to profile the Summit Fund's buyer profile. As previously mentioned, it was believed that customers of the new fund would have a similar profile as the Summit customers because both funds invested conservatively. The first step was to explore the data with crosstabulations (*crosstabulations* are two-way counts of one variable against another) to see how the different predictive factors each relate to buying a mutual fund.

Initially three crosstabulations were set up to analyze the relationship between owning the Summit Fund and the marital status, gender, and age. Figures 15.1 through 15.3 highlight these analyses.

In Figure 15.1, you can see that there is a significant relationship between marital status and owning the Summit Fund. Interestingly, the married category is almost double the next highest group. Significantly, more men than women own the Summit Fund. (See Figure 15.2.) There are significant differences associated with age. Those aged 41 to 60 represent the highest percentage of those owning the Summit Fund. (See Figure 15.3.)

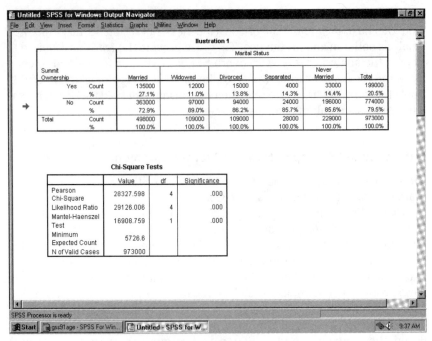

Figure 15.1 Summit Fund ownership by marital status.

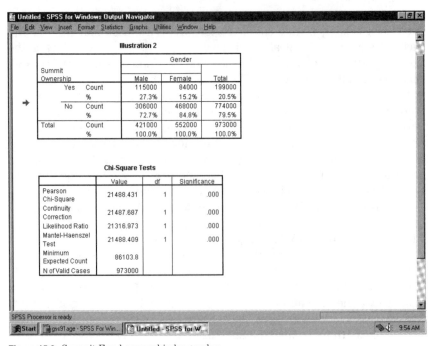

Figure 15.2 Summit Fund ownership by gender.

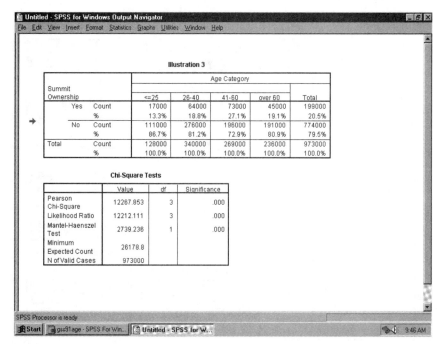

Figure 15.3 Summit Fund ownership by age.

Through this analysis of crosstabulations, three of the six predictor variables were examined and found to be highly significant. However, it became clear that, while this approach was useful in identifying the predictive factors, it would not take into account how these factors might interact with each other. The key questions posed were: Which of the three factors is the most important predictor? Which is the second most important predictor? By knowing this, the company can target the particular customer segment with the highest chances for success.

An SPSS CHAID analysis solves these problems. This is done automatically by first analyzing and ordering every possible combination of attributes and then identifying which factor is the most important predictor, which factors have no predictive value, and how factors combine or interact together to help predict.

The CHAID analysis is easily run (Figure 15.4) by first specifying the dependent variable (purchaser of the Summit Fund) and the predictor variables (marital status, gender, region, and age category).

CHAID immediately creates tree diagrams that show the interaction of these factors (Figure 15.5). This analysis shows that marital status is the single best predictor of being a Summit Fund customer. Of those who are married (M), 27.11% own a Summit Fund, while all the other marital status

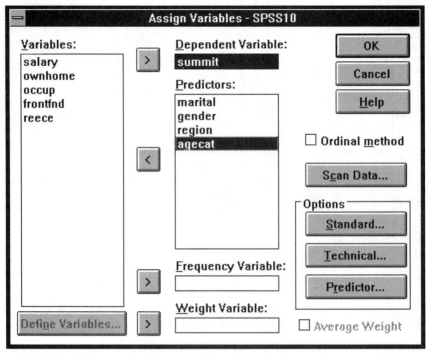

Figure 15.4 Assignment of dependent and predictor variables for Summit Fund ownership.

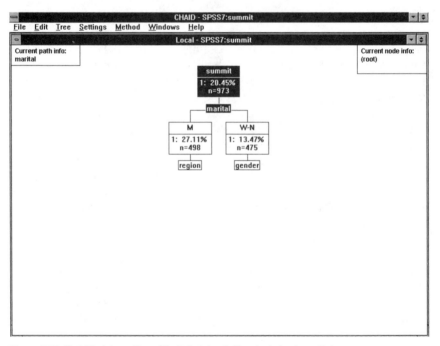

Figure 15.5 Variable interactions: Marital status is the single best predictor.

categories (widowed, divorced, separated, and never married) did not differ strongly from one category to another and were automatically combined into a single category. In this second group, 13.47% owned a Summit Fund. (See Figure 15.6.)

Going further down the tree diagram, the company realized that, for the married group, an additional predictive factor was region. In particular, the Central region tended to own the Summit fund. These findings were surprising for the marketing manager who believed that age would be the most important predictor because older customers had a tendency to purchase the more stable mutual funds that invested in large, established companies. Based on this analysis, the marketing manager was able to more effectively target the promotions of the new product by targeting married people who lived in the Central region. This analysis resulted in being able to target the groups that were twice as likely to have purchased a mutual fund and thereby increased the effectiveness of their promotions.

Statistics Are Essential for Effective Use of a Data Warehouse

Powerful, flexible, and usable statistical tools are must-haves in a data warehousing environment. There is no purpose to saving and storing data beyond using it to make more informed business decisions. Statistics lets

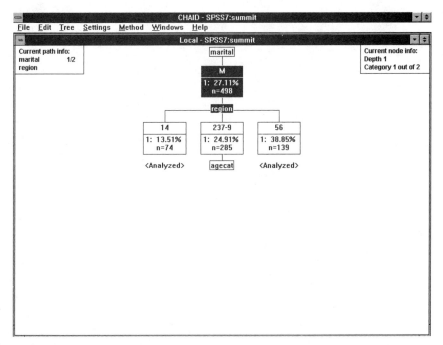

Figure 15.6 Variable interactions: The combination of marital status and region variables is the best predictor of Summit Fund ownership.

you begin to explore the data and discover interesting hypotheses to test further. It lets you test whether the data is truly reflecting what you think it measures or not. Most importantly, good statistical tools make it easy to add new data to the analysis with facilities for aggregating data from multiple sources, adding new data (either new variables or additional cases in the same fields), and determining which piece of data provides the most useful information. Statistical analysis fits comfortably with the approach of getting started with your warehouse rather than spending years specifying the ever-changing data requirements before you begin bringing data elements together.

Chapter 16

Neural Networks and Business Data Systems

STEVE RUSSELL
Senior Principal Consultant, dbINTELLECT
Technologies

Business opportunities often depend upon finding useful groupings of clients, detecting advertising that works best for certain customer segments, determining what manufacturing and product storage strategies are optimal, and predicting the rise and fall of pertinent financial markets. Techniques from intuition to statistics are applied to such tasks, until the number of distinct driving factors becomes unmanageable. Biological systems, however, deal well with multiple inputs, contradictory information, and missing values in promptly assessing threats and opportunities. So, methods that can emulate the brain's abilities in pattern recognition and control might be expected to provide great value in selected business applications.

A *neural network* is a digital programming simulation of a biological nervous subsystem. The simulation represents data by virtue of its structure and activation patterns. The facts present in a neural system typically are stored in a somewhat distributed manner, with no single element of the network representing any given fact by itself. Like the human sensory systems and brain, a neural network adjusts to inputs from the environment. This adjustment is a form of learning. The neural network (*neural net*, or just *net*) adjusts by means of a reward or feedback system that can change the operations of the net as it is exposed to successive learning trials over time.

Biological Foundations

Because neural networks are modeled after neurons, a brief review of neural anatomy and physiology can help in understanding the terminology and goals of the users of this technology.

Biological neurons are specialized cells, with a central cell body and extended wirelike projections called *axons* and *dendrites*. Nervous signals in a neuron normally flow from the end of a dendrite along the dendrite to the cell body, then along the cell body to the axon, and finally along the axon to its endpoint, called a *synapse*. The outside layer of the neuron is a thin membrane that actually conducts the electrical and chemical pulses, by means of a locally selective and sudden flow of electrically charged substances, such as sodium and potassium ions. As sets of spiking pulses travel across the membrane over time, permanent changes can occur in response. Such changes in membrane responsiveness are a type of neural cell learning. (See Figures 16.1 and 16.2.)

A neuron can be activated by a neighboring neuron or one whose axon ends just next to it. This signal transmission occurs when an electrochemical pulse, or *activation spike*, travels to the end of the sending neuron's axon. The synaptic end of that axon converts the signal into the release of transmitter chemicals. These chemicals flow across a very small synaptic gap to an adjacent neuron's dendrite end. The dendrite's synaptic end can react to these incoming chemicals by starting a new electrochemical wave in this receiving neuron. So signals can flow from sensory cells to processing neurons, then between processing neurons for analysis, and finally to motor neurons to cause movement.

As with the neural membrane, the synapse can adjust with use—another type of neural learning. If the neuron responsiveness adjusts to favor or diminish reactions to the output from another neuron, the neuron is effectively giving more or less weight to the stimulation from that predecessor neuron. Also, the neuron can become more or less predisposed over time to react and fire in general, depending on a set of such learning experiences and the health and chemical environment of the neuron and its recent activity.

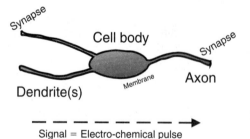

Figure 16.1 Neuron.

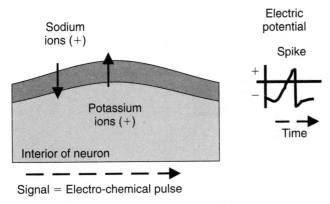

Figure 16.2 Membrane.

The message flow of most interest here occurs among chains and families of neurons. The flow most generally modeled is from neuron to neuron via axon-to-dendrite synapses. In some cases, though, the axon of the sending neuron might branch to conduct to the middle of the receiving neuron's dendrite, its cell body, or even its axon. Connections that are not axon-to-dendrite can weaken or strengthen the flow of other signals. The sending neuron thus can either increase or decrease the likelihood of the receiving neuron for firing. The receiving neuron can even connect its axon output back to itself or to the sending neuron, in a recurrent connection, and so strengthen, lessen, or perpetuate its own input. As an organism ages, individual neurons can grow new dendrites or axonal branches, connecting in new ways and to new neurons in the neighborhood or perhaps even far away in the body. Conversely, unused or inhibited branches can become ineffective, allowing for the forgetting of expired data or bad habits. (See Figures 16.3 and 16.4.)

The nerve cells of biological organisms often are arranged into families of specialized structure and activity. In visual systems, for example, columns of neurons feed signals forward, with perhaps some sideways or lateral connections, to reinforce the recognition of image features, such as lines or faces. Brain structures such as the hippocampus have circularity connected sets of nerve cells that can reinforce or diminish dynamic patterns of input to help recognize familiar versus novel data situations. Sensory and motor neurons often are simply involved in relaying long-distance signals between the brain and the body. Some higher brain processes are thought to involve highly interacting communities of similar neurons that rapidly interchange data and settle their activations into local subgroups of neural cells with correlated activity patterns for categorizing input data and for analyzing facts.

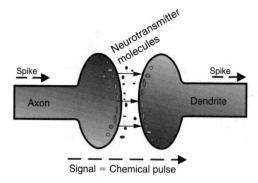

Figure 16.3 Synapse.

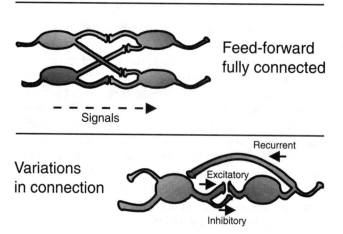

Figure 16.4 Connections.

For each of the network geometries, adjustments in neural structure and function must be possible over the lifetime of the organism to meet emerging situations and unexpected environments. The nervous system is able to learn by changing some of its ongoing operating characteristics, as well as by the storage of data for recall at appropriate times. Some changes in neurons are structural, such as in the membrane and synapse and in new neural connections. Some changes in system reactions simply are due to the variability in real-world inputs encountered and in the various dynamic states of all neural systems when these inputs arrive.

History of Neural Modeling

The role of the nervous system in signal transmission and the processing of data and ideas have long been known to science. Yet it was only in the 1940s that McCulloch and Pitts laid out a fledgling theory of biological neural networks using excitation, inhibition, and off/on threshold activation. During this same time period, Hebb discussed synaptic modification through usage.

The 1950s and 1960s saw the beginnings of computer simulation and the recognition of the role of statistics in modeling biological neural processing. The mathematics of matrix algebra and energy also were applied in this time period, and correlations and associative memories were explored. Rosenblatt promoted the so-called multilayer perceptron in 1958. Unfortunately, in 1969, Minsky and Papert were able to show that the perceptron with a linear transfer function is quite limited in power, stopping much of the neural network research for the decade of the 1970s.

In 1982, Hopfield showed mathematically that an energy model can be used to characterize recurrent neural networks that store information by dynamic pattern stability, thereby encouraging physicists and mathematicians to reconsider neural network research. Around this time, work on self-organizing maps and simulated annealing further expanded the role of mathematics in clarifying and certifying the science of neural networks.

In 1986, Rumelhart, Hinton, and Williams popularized the back-propagation multilayer perceptron, an idea that had been published and forgotten over a decade before. Work continues in many theoretical areas to this day, and efforts are continuing to recognize neural and connectionist computation as more than a simulation of the brain but as a new data processing tool in its own right.

Artificial Neural Network Basics

An Artificial Neural Network (ANN) begins with individual neurons simulated by a computer subprogram. Neurons are dynamic entities, which react to input signals by producing firing activity behaviors. These activation patterns can change over time, as each neuron learns new behavior through experiencing more stimuli and criticism. Neurons can convey firing signals to other neurons, which react in turn. The signals are carried along from neuron to neuron, sometimes feeding signals back to neurons earlier in the activation chain. Software communications between neurons effectively arrange the neurons into groups visualized as rows, grids, and layers.

Single-neuron simulation

A software model of neural activity typically consists of a series of discrete processing steps to update each of the network's neuron elements. In each complete set of update steps, which is called a *trial* or *epoch*, all of these processing elements are evaluated for their inputs and resultant output activations. Such neural models use the same working assumptions for determining the activation and learning for all of the neurons in the simulation. The axon-dendrite connections are modeled as communication paths or data sent between the processing elements. The various types of neural learning (such as chemical, membrane, synaptic, and connections) are partially encoded by altering the processors and the ways in which they receive and respond to inputs.

The neuron's current state and, in some cases, its recent history are used along with the current stimulation from all connected neurons or external inputs to calculate the neuron's next state. The excitatory and inhibitory inputs to a given neuron typically are treated in a common way, as a simple weighted sum, which usually is referred to as a *linear addition*. A less common variation uses the product of the inputs instead of the sum so that, if one of the inputs is zero, then the net input also is zero. This is referred to as a *gating function*. The neurons usually are all processed in a series of full sweeps or trials, but there also are models that use a random process to select a subset of the neurons for synchronized or asynchronous updating at various times. (See Figure 16.5.)

Activation functions

The calculation of a neuron's output firing level, or *activation*, usually is based on the sum of the weighted excitations and inhibitions at the time, combined in some models with the bias and recent firing history of the neuron. Activation is either on-off like a spike (a classical McCulloch-Pitts binary threshold neuron) or is dependent in a smoothly increasing manner upon its inputs. A spiking type of activation is modeled from an inactive (zero) or inhibitory (minus one) state to full activation (plus one) when the input exceeds a given threshold value. (See Figure 16.6.)

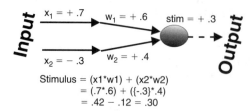

Input $x_1 = + .7$ $w_1 = + .6$ stim $= + .3$ Output

$x_2 = - .3$ $w_2 = + .4$

Stimulus $= (x1*w1) + (x2*w2)$
$= (.7*.6) + (\{-.3\}*.4)$
$= .42 - .12 = .30$

Figure 16.5 Single-neuron stimulation.

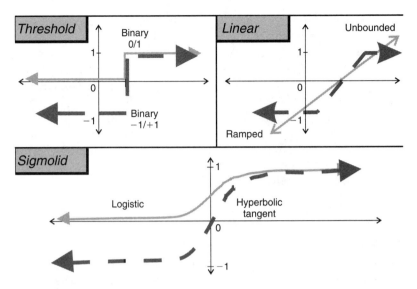

Figure 16.6 Activation functions.

A smoother activation function is essentially a model of the average of the neuron's firing over a brief time interval. As stimulation in the interval increases, the firing rate also increases. Smooth firing functions can increase directly with increasing input. Purely linear increases are used, but there is no upper or lower bound on their activation. Ramped linear activations are used to give a bounded if somewhat nonsmooth firing model. Nonlinear functions reflect the increased responsiveness of neurons to stimulation at certain moderate levels, giving an S-shaped or sigmoid activation function. Functions such as the logistic or hyperbolic tangent are convenient for smooth and bounded activation, varying from inactivity or inhibition to full excitatory activation as input from other neurons increases from strong inhibition to strong excitation. The choice of activation function contributes strongly to the power and speed of the net as well as the provability and understandability of its operations.

The specific calculation for whether a neuron will fire uses the inputs to that neuron, its weights for the individual inputs, and its current bias value. The weight factors are the neuron's evaluation as to the importance of each of its input sources. The neuron might weigh a given input as a strong influence, while computing exactly the opposite signed numeric value for the same input level from another source. The weight factors usually are from negative one to positive one—from opposite acceptance to full acceptance of the input. A weight factor of zero is equivalent to no connection between the two neurons. The total stimulation at any step for this neuron is the sum of the weighted inputs to the neuron at that point in time (i = Inputs):

$$\text{Stimulation} = \Sigma \left[(\text{Activation}_i) \times (\text{Weight}_i) \right]$$

The bias of the neuron to fire also can be added in. The bias is related to each neuron's current sensitivity and perhaps its recent firing history. This predisposition is added to the net stimulation to give the overall disposition to fire. The net disposition is used as input to an activation or transfer function, which determines the firing strength for the neuron in this processing cycle. The resulting output activation level is transmitted equally to each neuron that is stimulated by the firing neuron. The activation can be determined by a threshold function, which fires only if a certain net stimulus and bias combination is met. The activation function also can be an S-shaped curve that specifies a smooth increase in activation output when driven by increasing input stimulation:

Activation = f(Stimulation + Bias) = Threshold Off/On, or Sigmoid

Learning rules

The simplest and most direct way of affecting the next iteration of a neuron's processing is to change the way in which it weighs each of the inputs connected to it. This generally corresponds to the changes that biological systems accomplish in the synapses between neurons. Successive processing also can cause changes in the inclination for a given neuron to fire, which is referred to as its *bias*.

Network learning procedures involve adjustments to reinforce helpful neural weights and biases, to reduce the negative impact of improper settings, or to minimize the overall error or energy level of the network. If there is an external process that guides the updates, the adjustment is called *supervised learning*. Supervision simply can be an evaluation of performance as acceptable or not, or there can be more extensive training toward desired numerical output values. As opposed to using external criticism, a net can be constructed to learn in a self-organizing manner. Such unsupervised learning is accomplished by letting the firing pattern itself cause ongoing adjustments in the activated network components and their correlated or competing neural neighbors.

In some cases, learning requires a flexibility that exceeds any purely local stepwise improvements. A component of random (stochastic or probabilistic) activation adjustment can provide exploratory power in such cases. Alternatively, a human evaluator can intervene in various ways, taking whatever random or formula-driven adjustment actions deemed most appropriate to meet the objectives of the network.

Neuron connections

As with biological neural systems, the connectivity between neurons depends upon the task to be accomplished. Some tasks require quick learning and flexible readjustment. Other tasks require slower learning but eventual inflexibility so that a task can be mastered once and for all. The component neurons can be connected in feedforward or feedback layers or rings or in complex multidimensional cubic arrangements with data-signals flowing in one or more directions concurrently. (See Figures 16.7 and 16.8.)

Neuron elements typically are modeled as being chained together like biological nerve cells. For a simple sequence of two or more elements, a signal is transmitted along from cell to cell from the initial external input to the last processor's external output, with feedback in some models.

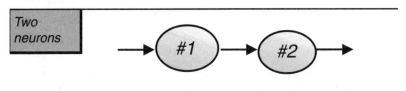

1st cell's output = 2nd cell's (weighted) input

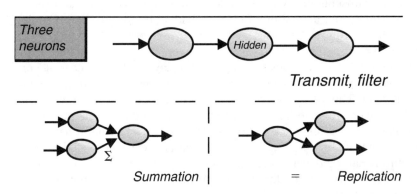

Figure 16.7 Neuron chains: Feed-forward (not recurrent).

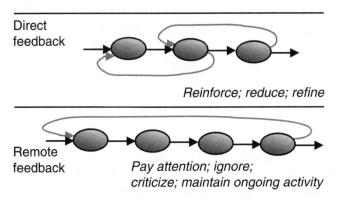

Figure 16.8 Neuron chains: Feedback (recurrent).

The computer simulation program that models such a connected sequence of neurons starts by processing those neurons receiving external stimuli. Their inputs and biases are used to determine their firing strength outputs, which are recorded for use in the subsequent processing step of the neural network simulation program. In the next step, these output levels are used as inputs to any neurons connected to these activations. Neurons in the center of the chain do not have external input or output, so they are called *hidden neurons*. In the processing sequence of successive neural elements, a nervous signal is filtered and otherwise modified due to the characteristics and current state of any processor involved.

Neural architectures

The most common neural network configurations visualize the neurons as being organized into one or more rows, or *layers*. In this case, the input layer accepts data values corresponding to external activation. Each neuron in the subsequent layer receives as input a copy of the data representing the output activation of each individual neuron in the preceding layer. This is referred to as a *fully forward-connected network*. The number of neuron elements in successive layers usually is the same or less than the number of neurons in the preceding layers. The processing continues layer by layer, through any hidden or internal layers to the final or output layer. The list of one or more output data values is the result from the final layer processed. For recurrently connected nets, the processing eventually causes feedback cycles between some or all neurons. In this case, there is no final output value. As processing cycles proceed, subsets of neurons can be observed to respond to separate portions of the input signal, apparently responding to unique features in that input data set. (See Figure 16.9.)

A given series of input value cases can be applied one at a time to a feedforward network. For each input case (such as a single loan application), the input signal attributes sweep from neuron to neuron and layer to layer until reaching the output neurons, where the last layer's firing level is the output of the net for that input. If the neurons are adjusted after such a processing sweep from input to output activations, the net hopefully can exhibit improved behavior (such as predicting the likelihood of defaulting on the loan) on a subsequent learning trial. At some point, the learning can be stopped, and the net can be put into production use (say in filtering loan applications for signs of trouble).

Now, if there is any feedback of activation to preceding neurons, the signal can be reinforced to augment or diminish it and to refine the time series of firings. Recurrent feedback from neurons farther downstream in the chain can be useful for criticism-based learning or for focusing the attention of the earlier neurons.

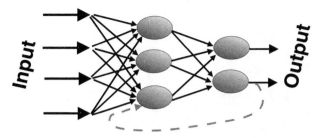

—Process one layer at a time
—Usually fully forward connected
—May have recurrent feedback loops

Figure 16.9 Neuron layers.

Recurrent neural nets can keep active indefinitely due to the circular stimulation of at least some neurons. Such nets typically have output points where the net can be examined when desired to see if it is settling down into a more or less fixed pattern of activity. The neurons also can be directly adjusted by external routines, in response to convergence behavior, to speed up or tune the net. After a network has been trained or primed with many input cases, the waves of activity from new input data sets can lead to varying patterns of convergence or cycles of similar collective neural firing that correspond to the detection of useful features in the input data.

Biological vision processing systems often are modeled by organizing the artificial neural elements into two-dimensional grid layers. Such models can be used for particular tasks in computer vision processing or in similar feature-sensitive tasks like optical character recognition. If only one planar layer is used, the neurons might be fully interconnected or particular groups of neurons might have limited lateral connectivities for mutual excitation or inhibition.

The one-layer neural grid arrangement can be presented with an initial activation pattern, to eventually settle its neurons into an activity pattern that might represent the recognition of key features in a visual scene. In this situation, the network's flat format allows neurons to work like humans in a committee, breaking into interest groups and focusing on preferred issues. If individual neurons or groups in the layer are connected in a circular fashion, behavior can be seen that simulates a ring of two-dimensional layered segments processing the activation subset repeatedly. (See Figure 16.10.)

As with the layered rows of neurons discussed previously, grids of neurons also can be organized into layers. Layers can feed signals forward, sideways within the layer, and even back and forth between two layers. It is assumed that there is an advantage in the two-dimensional representation, such as a correlation to the arrangement of pixels in a photographic image.

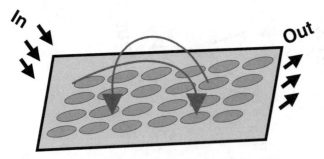

—Each processor connects to some or all others
—Initial activation settles into a pattern
—Certain areas detect certain input features

Figure 16.10 Single grid.

Otherwise, for example, a feedforward two-dimensional grid could be equivalently represented as a simpler arrangement of layers with one-dimensional rows of neurons. In situations where three directions or independent factors are of natural value, the grid model can be extended to a cubic arrangement of neurons in each layer. This example can be extended to modeling a set of neuron processors in a lattice specified by four or even more independent coordinate dimensions.

Common Neural Net Structures

Neural models can be considered in a building-block fashion. Single neurons are the basic processing units, with their code modules for activation or firing. Next, the learning-theory and time-sequencing algorithms are used for adjusting the neuron behavior over trials. Finally, the interconnection specifications give the architectural and dynamic structure for the participating components.

A common form of supervised learning in a layered feedforward network is the *Delta Rule*. The difference, or delta, between the desired and actual output is calculated for each output neuron. This error difference term then is used to change the weight for connections back from the output neuron to its predecessor neurons. The magnitude of this weight change is the product of the error, the strength of the stimulation from the connected predecessor, and a learning-rate parameter. If all of the weights are changed in this manner, then the answer in a subsequent trial with the same input will give less error. The net then is said to be learning the desired output for this input pattern.

The Delta Rule is:

$$\Delta W_{ki} = [\delta_k] \, x_i \, \eta$$

This is the weight update formula, where:

$$[\delta_k] = [(t_k - o_k)] = \text{error in the } k^{\text{th}} \text{ neuron's activation}$$

t_k is the target or desired activation of neuron k in the output layer
o_k is the actual activation of output neuron k
x_i is the ith neuron's activation from the prior neural layer
η is a learning rate parameter

The Delta Rule's error-reduction adjustment can be illustrated with a single neuron having two inputs. To keep matters simple in this example, the neuron is assumed to add its inputs in a weighted linear manner. The activation function is assumed to be the (linear) identity function, with the output activation level exactly equal to the total stimulation. (See Figure 16.11.)

The Delta Rule also is called Widrow-Hoff learning. A version of the Delta Rule sometimes is referred to as the *Least Mean-Square* or *LMS* rule, where an error cost function is used that involves calculating the errors $(t_k - o_k)$ and minimizing the average of their squares.

A generalization of the Delta-LMS procedure is the *Gradient Descent* method. Algorithms using such a Generalized Delta Rule and the gradient, or steepest, descent minimize the mean-squared error to move in the direction of most rapid error reduction. (See Figure 16.12.)

The Gradient Descent states that, for the kth output neuron's connection to its hidden neuron predecessors, the weight for this connection is updated according to the formula:

$$\Delta W_{kh} = [\delta_k] \times x_h \times \eta \quad \text{where } [\delta_k] = [(t_k - o_k) \times f'_k(\text{stim}_k)],$$

where all of the factors are as in the Delta Rule above, except for $f'_k(\text{stim}_k)$, which is the (partial) derivative of the activation function with respect to the summed and weighted stimulations to the kth output unit, evaluated for the output unit's current net stimulation from hidden neurons x_h. (See Figure 16.13.)

A hidden neuron can be considered in error by the sum of the deltas it helps to produce in the output neurons, adjusting for the weight on the connection to each of those neurons. The hth hidden neuron to i^{th} input neuron weights thereby are adjusted by a back-propagation of the error corrections from the higher levels in the network. So, for the hth hidden neuron, the (recursive) error correction formula for input-to-hidden weights is:

$$\Delta W_{hi} = [\delta_h] \times x_i \times \eta \text{: where:}$$

$$[\delta_h] = [\Sigma \; (\{(t_k - o_k) \; f'_k(\text{stim}_k)\} \times w_{kh}) \times f'_h(\text{stim}_h)]$$

$$[\delta_h] = [\Sigma \; (\{\delta_k\} \times w_{kh}) \times f'_h(\text{stim}_h)]$$

This says that a hidden neuron is in error to a degree measured in a sort of backward chain by the kth output neurons that it activates. Their error

Some learning environments are not well modeled by the previous supervised learning schemes. One example is a large party where people might tend to cluster together. Their talking to one another becomes more or less strengthened over time to eventually develop themes. No external reinforcement or assessment is involved as the party attendees form loosely organized "birds of a feather" clusters. Each person at the party listens most attentively to certain people and speaks most forcefully to selected people. The pairwise strengthening of such conversations is the underlying force that draws subgroups together. Because too much external chatter can be distracting, there also is a tendency to tune out any conversations that are not in the selected theme. Eventually, clusters of partygoers gravitate into pockets of similar communication activity. From perhaps dozens of individuals with a starting level of unorganized discussions, an ultimate state might be reached with only a handful of dominant subjects. The starting stimulation, the nature of the individuals, and their attentional links to others all combine to the evolution of activity that leads to a more stable state with a subset of a few common interests.

There are similar observations of organized behavior for unsupervised neural assemblies in biological nervous systems. If presynaptic stimulation is followed by postsynaptic activation, then there should be a strengthening of the neural synapse involved in that connection. This often is referred to as *synaptic learning*. Extending this somewhat, if there is an input neuron firing that ends up helping to cause a connected neuron's firing, then there should be an increase in the weighting factor for such a contributing connection.

Artificial neural network models use an extension of this type of learning. The sign and amount of activation from a predecessor neuron are associated with the sign and level of a receiving neuron's activation. The connection weights are strengthened for those neurons that are excitatory when a receiving neuron consequently fires. If a neuron fires, the weights for any

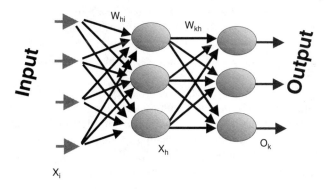

Figure 16.12 Gradient descent.

Error (cost) function surface

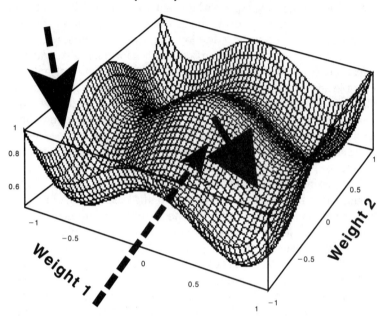

**Negative gradient
Direction = downhill
(actual path will change
direction with descent)**

Figure 16.13 Steepest descent.

inhibiting inputs can be minimized. If a neuron does not fire, its stimulating neurons also can be reduced in weighting. Over iterations, neurons with more correlated positive activity will have their connecting weights amplified, while other weights will be reduced. This automatic reinforcing of utilized and effective pathways is a form of unsupervised learning referred to as *Hebbian learning*. (See Figure 16.14.)

In Hebb Learning, the weight associated with a given neuron-to-neuron signaling path is strengthened if an excitatory input is correlated with a resulting positive activation for the neuron receiving the stimulation. If the input activation differs in motivational sign from the resulting activation output, the particular connection is reduced in value. So, the weight update rule for the given path is modified according to the *Hebb Law*:

$$\Delta w_{ij} = \alpha \times a_i \times a_j$$

where α is a learning-rate parameter, a_i is the (positive or negative signed) activation from the ith sending neuron, and a_j is the resulting (positive signed) activation for the jth receiving neuron. Usually the weights are constrained to be nonnegative, and conditions are added to stop exponential growth of the weights. (See Figure 16.15.)

Hebb Learning tends to reinforce similarities in sets of data inputs or iterations. Stronger reactions and associated weight updates are obtained where data commonalities can be reduced to a few common theme patterns so that several inputs can activate a given link similarly and so lead to its strengthening. This sort of data reduction into main themes or categories is useful in isolating principal components of interest in large data sets, such as defaulted bank loans.

The layered and gridlike configurations discussed earlier, along with their activations and connectivities, embody the primary features in neural systems. Table 16.1 briefly categorizes some of the major systems that have been developed over the years. Several of these and other systems have special designed-in and historical uses. Back-propagation is by far the most common in general applications today.

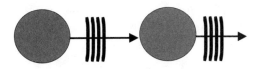

If #1 fires, and then #2 fires, then strengthen the weight between them

Otherwise, reduce the weight

Figure 16.14 Hebb learning.

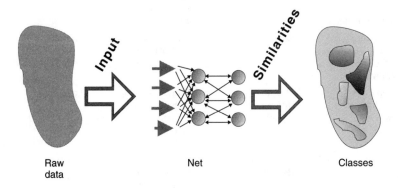

Raw data

Net

Classes

Figure 16.15 Input clustering.

TABLE 16.1

Name	Activation	Learning	Architecture
Perceptron (1957, Rosenblatt) Feedforward	Logistic	Supervised, Delta Rule	Layered
Adaline (1960, Widrow-Hoff) Feedforward	Binary threshold	Supervised, Least Mean-Square (LMS)	Layered
Reinforcement (1961, Minsky) feedforward and feedback	Binary, probabilistic	Environmental evaluation, Delta Rule	Layered
Brain State In A Box, BSB (1977, Anderson and others) Fully interconnected and self-activating Adaptive resonance	Values in [-1,+1], dependent on current activation	Unsupervised, then supervised	Single-layer
Theory, ART (1980, Grossberg) Feedforward and feedback	Binary threshold	Unsupervised, self-organizing, competitive	Layered
Hopfield Network (1982, Hopfield) Fully interconnected	Binary threshold, probabilistic	Hebb Rule, asynchronous updating, energy reducing	Grid
Kohonen Self organizing			
Feature Map, SOFM (1982, Kohonen) Fully interconnected	Nonlinear bounded, such as ramped linear	Unsupervised mapping using neighborhood function, dependent on nearby elements, energy reducing	Grid
Boltzmann Machine (1985, Ackley, Hinton, Sejnowski) Fully interconnected	Binary threshold, probabilistic	Unsupervised, minimize energy, random updating	Layered
Back-Propagation (1986, Rumelhart, Hinton, Williams) Feedforward	Logistic	Back-propagation of error correction	Multiple layer
Counterpropagation (1987, Hecht-Nielsen) Feedforward and feedback Bidirectional	Determined by differential equation	Unsupervised Kohonen, then supervised, by layers	Layered
Associative Memory, BAM (1988, Kosko) Fully connected	Ramped linear, dependent on prior neuron state	Unsupervised, stability-reaching, minimize energy	Two layer

Current Directions

Neural network research is extending the range of neural architectures and learning strategies, while further proving the utility and reliability of existing systems. In addition, combinations of neural systems with other hot areas of analysis are emerging. For example, nonlinear dynamics and chaos theory have been applied to neural systems. Hybrid systems have been formed, with genetic algorithms helping to structure and tune neural nets and with neural systems providing guidance in the construction of fuzzy logic rules for expert system applications.

Business Problems Solved

Neural networks have been shown to be effective for visual pattern recognition and motion prediction. These areas were not possible to analyze with standard programming languages and techniques. Transferring this capability to business, neural nets have found new patterns in customer behavior and have predicted financial market behavior.

Business Situations Addressed

Patterns range from simple facts like the effect of employment status on granting a loan to much more subtle combinations of factors such as histories of overextending credit versus ability to recover financially. The opportunity is twofold here:

- New factors and combinations of factors can be discovered to help understand one's business.

- A new source of advice exists that can flag possible problems and speed some kinds of processing, even without explicitly needing to spell out any verbalizable reasons.

The first point bears on the common business needs to understand the customer, the product, and the marketplace. There often are hidden dependencies, unanticipated correlations, and undeveloped opportunities. Although much of the business sense and acumen will likely escape any programming, some of the pattern and feature-related characteristics can be uncovered with a suitable neural network approach. The key is payback. If effectiveness and quality can be improved and market share can be increased, then the time spent looking into a new technology will be worthwhile. It is certain that the worldwide competitors are investing large amounts of time and money in exploring such innovations.

With respect to pattern discovery, concerted efforts are underway to mine very large databases in business and technology. It is felt that patterns will be found with better, simpler techniques working on sufficient volumes of data. Now that data collaboration, standardization, data sharing, data warehousing, and indexed long-term archiving are becoming more real, the wealth of data "capital" is primed for this prospecting. Patterns that have been discovered already enable marketers to attend to only the best prospects and for manufacturers to more effectively track down and prevent product faults. The cost savings and opportunity prospects are on a potentially vast scale, if more can be detected on why people buy products and how to provide better goods and services to customers.

Neural nets have captured the imaginations of many young scientists and entrepreneurs. It is nearly certain that new products and ideas will emerge as forces in the business world as more of their work becomes profitable. The appeal of working on such exciting and powerful technologies can be a drawing card for an infusion of drive and morale into a business unit, drive that can translate into innovation and new markets in unanticipated ways.

The following is an example of how to employ neural network technology:

1. Get a *lot of input* situational data.
   a. Take a broad-brush overlook. Is anything *new* or really different? Should attention be paid to the situation? Is there opportunity or danger?
   b. Carefully compare the current situation with historical records and business knowledge.

2. Put the data through a *category* sifter—eliminate redundancies and reinforce commonalities.
   a. Arrive at a few key clusters of similarity—attempt to name or understand these drivers.
   b. Reducing the number of key features or variables helps to focus attention.
   c. Clustering depends on the internal redundancy and correlations in the input data.
   d. Use step 1 to see if these are novel categories or just the same old stuff.

3. Use the categories and their activity levels to make *predictions* and determine *actions*.
   a. Use the most significant input features to associate with desired outputs.
   b. Train nets with these key drivers and their association with success factors.
   c. Use the nets to further identify and score potential customer groups and actions.

Note how this is like the development of astronomy, psychology, and economics. The driving and parametric factors were not revealed at once but had to be uncovered as novelties or combinations of old ideas. When new features were categorized, they had to be assessed over time as to their place among other ideas (note that the ideas are like variables or objects and had to be capable of expression and combination in ordinary English and mathematics). The cause-and-effect dependencies, temporal sequences and predictability, co-occurrences of other items, and so on had to be laid out. Then the formulae and shortcuts for dealing with these ideas and objects became standardized, often replacing older notions.

Neural Network Software Products

Neural network product offerings run a wide range of capabilities, reliability, and price. There are companies that have been selling this technology for decades, and there always are emerging competitors. A newcomer to the field should take the time to review all of the currently available products and their fit for a desired application. Product advertisements can be found in magazines and journals on artificial intelligence, as well as in more mainstream publications that periodically highlight advanced technologies.

Special-purpose journals on topics such as neural nets in finance will have current product reviews and recommendations, as well as the addresses of common-interest groups. If a manager does not have the time to become conversant in the technology, the use of consultants or inhouse experts is recommended for any long-term investment in neural approaches.

Personnel with a background in neural network theory should be more common over time, with increased academic coverage of the field and with growth in the number of workers with some exposure to neural applications.

Application Examples

Neural networks have been successfully employed for corporate bond rating. They have been used to analyze Standard & Poor's bond prediction risks and have been compared against linear regression. Networks have been used for forecasting global markets and prioritizing financial indicators. Swedish economic strength has been predicted, with sensitivity analyses to find the best indicators. In this case, the network outperformed traditional forecasting methods, even with fairly bad data.

Pap smears were analyzed by a neural net product for better cancer detection. The net outperformed human technicians in spotting bad cells in smear slides. However, the technicians caught some cancers that the net did not, underscoring the need for judicious use of neural nets along with other traditional approaches. Note here that earlier cancer detection means better and cheaper treatment and more saved lives.

A neural net controller was developed for a steel-rolling mill, where the net outperformed traditional control programs in a systems test. This can mean a better and cheaper product. Also, at the same company, there was a separate development of a neural network for modeling the yield strength, giving better process understanding, control, and product quality.

A recent conference on artificial-intelligence applications on Wall Street included sessions on:

- Forecasting Currency Exchange Rates: Neural Networks and the Random Walk
- Training Neural Networks to Predict Profit
- Financial Classification: Performance of Neural Networks in Leptokurtotic Distributions
- Predicting Quarterly Excess Returns: Two Multilayer Perceptron Training Strategies
- Automatic Understanding of Financial Statements Using Neural Networks and Semantic Grammars
- Using Neural Networks to Predict the Degree of Underpricing of an Initial Public Offering
- Bank Failure and Classification: A Neural-Network Approach
- Forecasting Currency Futures Using Recurrent Neural Networks

EDS' subsidiary dbINTELLECT includes the marketing-analysis neural net tool ModelMax in its set of features. ModelMax can help to determine who to mail to and otherwise advertise to. It can help to segment and stage campaigns and to better understand marketing success drivers.

Data Warehouse Connections

A neural network operates on sets of data that are organized as learning trials. A neural net is somewhat insensitive to a small amount of bad data or outlier cases, but more subtle features can be detected when bad data "noise" is minimized. Less common or less powerful attributes can be difficult to detect in small samples, and strong features can mask any small influences unless a lot of cases can be examined.

A data warehouse supplies a larger volume of read-only data available in longer and dedicated runs that build pattern knowledge. The data often is filtered for uniform formats and representations. Data errors generally are caught more quickly because the data warehouse's main job is to enable the sharing of good data. The data warehouse contains multisource data that can be readily joined for analysis. When uniform data is merged from separate areas, the patterns that are found can help in unforeseen ways to reveal departmental dependencies, bottlenecks, duplications, and synergies. Such joined data is ripe for the detection of novel and important features arising from the comparison of attribute values when matched with other data sets.

Neural net technology can help to mobilize the information capital in the data warehouse's pooled and standardized data. The categorization and predictive capabilities of neural systems when applied to very large databases (from a few gigabytes to several terabytes) should enable enhanced corporate business practices and should help to discover more opportunities for new profits.

References

Blum, Alan. *Neural Networks in C++: An Object-Oriented Framework for Building Connectionist Systems*. New York: John Wiley & Sons, Inc. 1992.

Haykin, Simon. *Neural Networks: A Comprehensive Foundation*. New York: Macmillan College Publishing Company. 1994.

Taylor, J.C., ed. *Neural Network Applications*. London: Springer-Verlag. 1992.

Wasserman, Philip D. *Advanced Methods in Neural Computing*. New York: Van Nostrand Reinhold. 1993.

Neural Networks. Official Journal of the International Neural Network Society. New York: Pergamon Press.

The Magazine of Artificial Intelligence in Finance. New York: A Miller Freeman Publication.

17

Neural Networks: Net-Modeling Market

KATHY PIPPERT
Documentation and Training Manager
Advanced Software Applications

Neural networks, which are based on a nonlinear computing technology, excel at complex pattern recognition and prediction. Rather than simply grouping customers or prospects into broad segments or subgroups, neural networks quickly learn to distinguish specific patterns of behavior and relate these patterns to *known outcomes* for the behavior being modeled. Once a neural network is trained to recognize the patterns associated with a behavior, it can assign scores, which indicate the likelihood of exhibiting this behavior, to records where *outcomes are not known*. Because these scores are assigned on a case-by-case basis, a neural network can easily identify those people who do not "make the cut" in the linear calculations of traditional segmentation techniques. The end result is that neural network models are at least as good as—and when relationships are complex or nonlinear, are far better—than those generated by other modeling strategies.

Direct marketers in all business disciplines can increase the effectiveness of direct mail and telemarketing campaigns as well as strengthen database marketing strategies by taking advantage of neural networks. A neural network can generate predictive models that enable you to:

- Differentiate between prospective buyers and nonbuyers, drastically reducing the amount of money previously wasted pursuing nonbuyers

- Distinguish between single-time buyers and multiple-time buyers so that you can market to them accordingly (or use what you learn to find ways of converting single-time buyers to multiple-time buyers)

- Identify people who are likely to lapse from a program so that you can use what you learn to offer them special incentives to stay

- Rank current buyers based on estimated future purchases so that you can market to them accordingly

- Identify potential new markets and quickly respond to changes in the current market by being able to spot new trends

- Launch new products and services more effectively

- Identify cross-sell and up-sell opportunities

- Reactivate buyers who have been inactive by reanalyzing their needs and marketing to them accordingly

Direct marketers in banking, publishing, telecommunications, and retail are in especially envious positions from a modeling perspective because their databases contain volumes of transactional and historical data, which is the data that neural networks thrive on.

What Are Neural Networks?

While the basis for neural computing has been around for over 50 years, computing power has only recently become powerful enough for neural networks to emerge from the laboratory to play an important role in business. Unlike other information processing technologies, *neural networks actually learn* by generating knowledge in the form of weighted relationships. This learning process is based on mathematical algorithms that "adapt" or change network connection weights in response to example inputs and known outcomes. A simplified representation of a neural network appears in Figure 17.1. This neural network has three layers of nodes arranged in a tree structure. These three layers are the input layer, hidden layer, and output layer.

The nodes in the *input layer* are passive, meaning that they do not perform any computations. Because they serve only to accept data from an input record, the number of input nodes is always equal to the number of variables used in a model. In addition, there is always one other input node known as the *bias element*. Always equal to one, the bias element provides a thresholding function that is similar to that provided by the cell body of a nerve cell. (A *neural network* is a mathematical construct that arose from attempts to model human nervous activity, particularly learning.)

Each input node is associated with a network connection weight. These weights, which change with respect to a variety of input patterns, connect

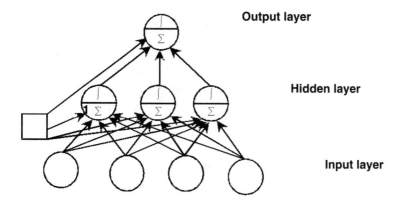

Figure 17.1 Simple representation of a neural network.

each of the input nodes to each of the nodes in the next higher layer, which usually is referred to as the *hidden layer*. (This intermediate layer also is often called the *feature-detection layer* because this actually is its function.) The number of hidden nodes is always at least two and increases as the number of input nodes increases.

Each hidden node gets its value by performing an internal activation, I, which is the sum of the pair-wise products of each input and its respective connection weight:

$$(1 \times W_0) + (X_1 \times W_1) + (X_2 \times W_2) + (X_3 \times W_3) + (X_n \times W_n)$$

then passing this activation through a nonlinear transfer function. A representation of a hidden node and its network connections with the input layer is shown in Figure 17.2.

Each hidden node has a different value, even though it receives the same inputs, because each hidden node has a different set of connection weights.

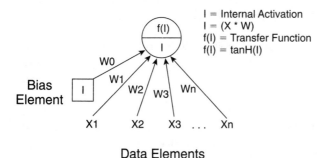

Data Elements

Figure 17.2 Hidden node and network connections with the input layer.

In other words, because the connection weights of the hidden nodes vary, the first input might have a big impact on the value of the first hidden node but not on the value of the second hidden node. This is how the neural network learns the features within the data, with the weights of each hidden node adjusting to learn about a particular behavior pattern.

The third layer is the *output layer*. There is only one output node. It gets its value by summing the values of the hidden nodes, after multiplying these values by another set of connection weights, and then passing this activation through yet another nonlinear transfer function. The value of the output node, which is always between 0 and 1, is the neural network score assigned to the given input record.

A neural network begins the learning process with a guess for each network connection weight. The preprocessed data in a carefully selected training sample is fed through the neural network and network outputs are computed. Because the outcome for each record is known, the neural network is able to subtract the network output for a record from its actual known outcome to produce a network error. The measured error for the network is the root mean square (RMS) of the network errors produced over a set of randomly selected input records. After measuring the RMS of a record set, the neural network adjusts the network connection weights. It then randomly selects another record set and measures the RMS error again. By watching whether the RMS error increases or decreases, the neural network knows how to adjust the connection weights for the next record set. The training goal is to minimize the measured network error over the entire set of data in a training sample.

Why Use This Particular Technology for Modeling?

When the connection weights are correct, a neural network can calculate responses for records that it has never seen before. This is very important. When you use the model to score a set of records *for which the outcomes are not known*, the neural network will see records with combinations of input values that did not exist in the training data. Nevertheless, the neural network can compare the input values to patterns found during training and still give each record a score. In many ways, this is analogous to how you prepare for a math exam. You drill on problems so that, when it comes time to take the test, you can apply what you have learned from your drills to solve new and different problems.

To demonstrate how effective neural networks are when applied to direct mail applications, the next few pages describe how two-pass logistic regression, an expert system, and a neural network would each select recipients for a direct mail offer.

Using two-pass logistic regression

Let's assume that you are currently using two-pass logistic regression—one of the most popular statistical methods—to identify people who are likely to respond to a direct mail offer. Your first step would be to find the best way of classifying your audience into two segments (for example, by income and age). The second step would be to limit the amount of errors by identifying a second plane that intersects the first.

A graphic representation of this problem appears in Figure 17.3. The gray areas show sections of the population that were incorrectly classified by this statistical method. These areas exist because the statistical method is linear and the pattern is nonlinear. While the results from the two-pass logistic regression method are good, you can see that other ways of selecting recipients might be better.

Using an expert system

Expert or knowledge-based systems are based on rules that define the characteristics of the subject. A graphic representation of how an expert system would perform on the same direct-mail example appears in Figure 17.4. The rules governing the selection process for this particular example are quite complex but can be summarized as follows:

- If Age > A2 and I1 < Income and Income < I3, then mail.
- If A1 < Age and Age < A2 and I1 < Income and Income < I2, then mail.

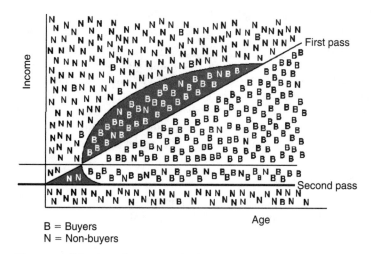

B = Buyers
N = Non-buyers

Figure 17.3 Selection using two-pass logistic regression.

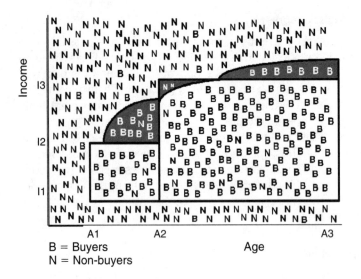

B = Buyers
N = Non-buyers

Figure 17.4 Selection using an expert system.

Once again, the gray areas show sections of the population that were incorrectly classified. While the number of cases is fewer than when two-pass logistic regression was used, the rectangular boundaries resulting from the if-then rules of an expert system still result in segments that are overlooked.

Using a neural network

The challenge is being able to pick and choose the individual people who are most likely to respond, regardless of what segment or subgroup they might be associated with. Figure 17.5 shows the nonlinear, curve-fitting solution that a neural network provides for this same direct mail example.

Even though a few buyers were overlooked and a few nonbuyers were selected, the neural network's solution is much better than those provided by the other two methods. Typically, overall improvement over statistical methods and expert systems in a direct marketing application is *between 8% and 15%*, which is substantial in terms of potential revenues.

Summarizing the differences

Two-pass logistic regression uses linear boundaries on heuristically determined, nonoverlapping subsets of data. This statistical method is best used when:

- Information flow is sequential
- Large volumes of data exist

- Many set processes are necessary
- Information is rather stable

Expert systems use if-then rules to create rectangular boundaries. An expert system is best used when:

- The domain is well understood
- Rules and facts are dominant
- Explicit rules can be formed

Neural networks use adaptive learning algorithms to produce nonlinear boundaries. A neural network is best used when:

- The domain is dynamic
- Judgment is required
- No explicit rules can be formed
- Time is critical
- The application is highly interactive and has multiple constraints

You can see how this last set of characteristics closely matches the basic nature of direct-marketing applications. Because there are no hard boundaries that limit where neural networks can look to find your next buyer, you pick up prospective buyers who otherwise would have been left out, and

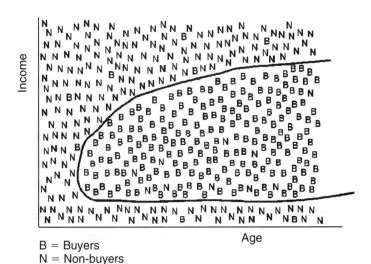

B = Buyers
N = Non-buyers

Figure 17.5 Selection using a neural network.

you eliminate those people who are the most unlikely to purchase, even if they happen to be in a promising segment.

If you are hesitant about investing in neural networks, the results that ModelMAX users are receiving demonstrate why this neural network-based application now is the standard in predictive model-building. (ModelMAX is an automated predictive modeling application from Advanced Software Applications, Pittsburgh, PA. It currently is the only software package to use this advanced computing technology in the direct-marketing industry in a manner that does not require extensive training in neural computing and its application.) ModelMAX has helped leading marketers to:

- Identify 97% of an offer's likely responders in only 25% of the population
- Identify 90% of the likely account closures (or people who are likely to lapse from a program) in only 35% of the population
- Identify 79% of the people who are likely to purchase another product (or service) in only 50% of the population
- Identify the 30% of the population who are likely to be responsible for more than 68% of the product revenue in the next six months
- Identify the 25% of the population who are likely to be responsible for more than 70% of the donations from the next fund-raising drive

While the quality of any model ultimately is dependent upon the quality of data upon which it is built, the previous results are typical for ModelMAX's users. What is even more amazing than the results themselves is the speed at which these models are generated. Because ModelMAX is designed specifically for direct marketers, its users are shielded from the steep learning curves that are associated with neural network tools and statistical packages. Results such as these actually are possible within hours of installing this PC Windows application.

With ModelMAX, you no longer have to spend weeks manually preprocessing the necessary data and then adjusting the model to make it perform well. You do *not* have to be a talented statistician to apply the model. With ModelMAX, you only need to supply it with the input data and respond to a series of prompts that use standard direct-marketing terminology. The application does the rest, including the automatic generation of models and management-level reports.

What Kind of Models Can I Build?

Neural networks offer you the opportunity to perform several important kinds of modeling very quickly. The first is modeling discrete behaviors, which indicate whether or not members of a population are likely to exhibit some action. For example, you can build discrete models to distinguish between:

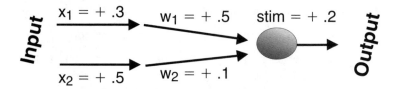

How does better weighting (listening) to inputs give better decision-making performance for an output-level node?

Assuming a simple linear combiner for output activation, the stimulus is $(.3)*(.5) + (.5)*(.1) = .20$.
A very simple activation function is the (linear) identity relationship with output simply equal to stimulus:

$$\text{STIMULUS} = f(x) = f(.2) = x = .2 = \text{INPUT}$$

Suppose that the target or desired output was $t = .1$

Then the delta or difference is:

HOW FAR OFF?
$$\delta \ (\text{target}-\text{output})$$
$$= (.1-.2) = -.1$$

Now, suppose that the learning rate parameter, n is simply set to one, and that the Delta rule is used:

HOW TO FIX?
$$\Delta w1 = {}^*\delta \times 1^* \qquad n$$
$$= \{-.1\} * .3 * 1 = \{-.03\}$$
$$\Delta w2 = {}^*\delta \times 2^* \qquad n$$
$$= \{-.1\}*.5*1 = \{-.05\}$$

Then:
$$w1 = w1 + w\Delta$$
$$\text{new} \quad \text{old}$$
$$= .5 + (-.03)$$
$$= .47$$

$$w2 = w2 + w\Delta$$
$$\text{new} \quad \text{old}$$
$$= .1 + (-.05)$$
$$= .05$$

So the new activation level, which is equal to the stimulus level in this case, is:

$$\text{Stim} = x1 \ w1 + x2 \ w2$$
$$= (.3)*(.47) + (.5)*(.05)$$
$$= .141 + .025 = .166$$

Which is then closer to the desired output value of .1

Figure 16.11 Error reduction.

corrections then are propagated back to this level for correction, thus the term *back propagation*. It can be shown that this iterative correction scheme does indeed give error reduction along a steepest-descent or gradient descent direction for the overall error or cost function. Adjustments thus are corrections of weights, in weight space. The weight vector follows a precisely defined and usually nonlinear trajectory along the error surface, terminating on the optimal solution.

- Responders versus nonresponders
- Buyers versus nonbuyers
- Single-time buyers versus multiple-time buyers
- High-volume buyers versus low-volume buyers
- Cross-sell or up-sell opportunities versus nonopportunities
- Retained customers versus lapsed customers

To predict a response, which is one of the most common applications of a discrete model, you must either use historical data or, when no such data exists (for a new product or service for instance), send out a test mailing to people randomly selected from your marketing database and track their responses. You then feed the relevant data that you have on this population to the neural network for building of a model that predicts responders.

To build a discrete model that predicts repeat customers, you feed the neural network what you know about both your present single-time and multiple-time customers, including information such as the first items or services purchased, how much was spent, and the selected payment method. You do *not* include information that is available only on multiple-time buyers because the file to be scored will consist of only first-time buyers.

If you did include an independent variable that provided values for only multiple-time buyers, the neural network would quickly learn that, when a value appears in this field, the record belongs to a multiple-time buyer. Using the data that you supply, the neural network generates a model that predicts whether a first-time customer is prone to purchase again. You then might use these predictions to promote to only those people who are likely to purchase again or try to find ways to convert single-time buyers to multiple-time buyers.

Based on the knowledge of what your customers are like and what their first purchases are, you also can use neural networks to build performance models, which predict some performance level over a specified time period. For example, you could use a neural network to create performance models to predict behaviors including but not limited to:

- How much a customer is likely to spend (when the period of time is exceptionally long, such as 5 to 10 years, this also is called a *lifetime value model*)
- How many items a customer is likely to purchase
- How often a customer is likely to purchase
- How often you should send out a promotion
- How often or when you should attempt to collect payments

Examples of the variables that generally are good candidates for predictive models appear in Figure 17.6. You can see that neural networks readily accept a variety of data, including transaction and promotion history, demographics, and lifestyle information.

How Is the Data Preprocessed?

When you use traditional segmentation methods, you must manually construct and refine mathematical models. When you use neural network tools, you must manually set parameters for preprocessing the input data, selecting the variables that are to be used in the model, and training of the neural network. When you use ModelMAX, the model-building process is entirely automated. To preprocess the input data, ModelMAX uses UDT (Universal Data Transformation), a powerful variable analysis process pioneered by A.S.A. Totally transparent to the user, UDT uses several proprietary algorithms to automate data transformations and optimize variable selection.

UDT is dramatically faster than any other method in accurately determining which variables are best suited for a given prediction. Because the *less is more* philosophy long held by statisticians is reflected in UDT's non-parametric capabilities, ModelMAX is a great tool for anyone who wants to quickly and reliably reduce large sets of variables to an optimum subset. As

Good Predictors for Response and Performance Models

Complete transaction history
- date customer first came on file
- date of first purchase
- date of last purchase
- method of payment
- bad debts
- returns
- frequency of purchases
- recency of purchases
- average dollar value of purchases
- types of merchandise/services purchased (major areas)
- Total dollars spent in each major area

Complete promotion history
- original media
- original source number
- package(s) mailed by key codes
- dates package(s) mailed
- number of times mailed to

Individual demographic data
- geographic designations
- age
- gender
- income
- occupation
- education
- product (subject) interest

External overlay information
- demographics
- lifestyles
- behaviors
- values/attitudes
- geographic information
- psychographics

Figure 17.6 Good predictors for predictive models.

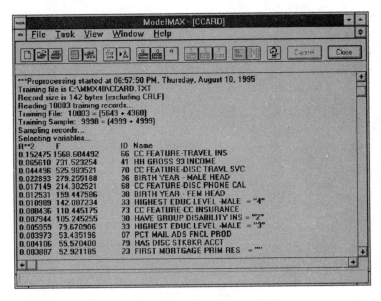

Figure 17.7 R-squared and F statistic values written to the log.

part of the variable selection process, ModelMAX calculates R-squared and F statistic values for the network input variables and uses step-wise regression to determine whether the percent of variation accounted for by a variable is likely to be explained by pure randomness. ModelMAX also detects any colinearity that exists, removing redundant variables from a model. During the variable selection process, ModelMAX writes out both R-squared (R^2) and F statistic (F) values to the project's log (Figure 17.7).

The end result is that ModelMAX is able to recommend the optimal variable set for any given prediction, indicating its selections in both the project's log and its Network Inputs report. The portion of the Network Inputs report where ModelMAX stopped selecting network input variables for a credit card response model appears in Figure 17.8. Of 100 possible network input variables, 67 were selected for use in the model. Most models are built on somewhere between 10 and 40 variables because the available input data is not nearly as strong as that which is used here.

After the optimum variable set for a model has been identified, you have quick insight to key market factors. Studying the selected variables can help you to identify market trends and adapt to changes. You also can quickly perform "what if" scenarios by removing selected variables from a model to determine how much the model's performance is impacted. This is especially important when considering how much external overlay information might help you in your prospecting efforts. Perhaps the results of "what if" modeling indicate that you can reduce the number of overlay vari-

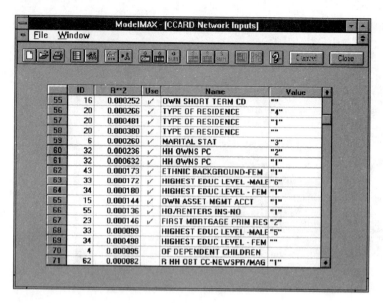

	ID	R**2	Use	Name	Value	
55	16	0.000252	✓	OWN SHORT TERM CD	""	
56	20	0.000266	✓	TYPE OF RESIDENCE	"4"	
57	20	0.000481	✓	TYPE OF RESIDENCE	"1"	
58	20	0.000380	✓	TYPE OF RESIDENCE	""	
59	6	0.000260	✓	MARITAL STAT	"3"	
60	32	0.000236	✓	HH OWNS PC	"2"	
61	32	0.000632	✓	HH OWNS PC	"1"	
62	43	0.000173	✓	ETHNIC BACKGROUND-FEM	"1"	
63	33	0.000172	✓	HIGHEST EDUC LEVEL -MALE	"6"	
64	34	0.000180	✓	HIGHEST EDUC LEVEL - FEM	"1"	
65	15	0.000144	✓	OWN ASSET MGMT ACCT	"1"	
66	55	0.000136	✓	HO/RENTERS INS-NO	"1"	
67	23	0.000146	✓	FIRST MORTGAGE PRIM RES	"2"	
68	33	0.000099		HIGHEST EDUC LEVEL -MALE	"5"	
69	34	0.000498		HIGHEST EDUC LEVEL - FEM	""	
70	4	0.000095		OF DEPENDENT CHILDREN		
71	62	0.000082		R HH OBT CC-NEWSPR/MAG	"1"	

Figure 17.8 Network inputs report showing the variable selection cutoff.

ables from 20 to 6 without adversely affecting the model, thereby saving
you from having to purchase 14 more variables for the tens of thousands or
even millions of names in the file that you want to score with the model.
(ModelMAX provides for scoring files on the PC or exporting the model for
scoring on another platform such as UNIX or a mainframe.)

Once the input data is preprocessed, you can view a report that indicates
the number of unique values for each variable as well as displays the number
of records with "good" and "bad" values and the number of bins to which
these values are mapped for use by the neural network. Preprocessing results for the first several variables in a model to predict acceptance of a
credit card featuring frequent flyer miles appear in Figure 17.9.

From this report, you can generate variable distributions or profiles in either bar chart or table format. A bar chart for a categorical type variable
named MARITAL STAT appears in Figure 17.10. From this bar chart, you
can determine approximately how many times each unique value for MAR-
ITAL STAT occurs in this project's training file. (Please note that a variable
that has numbers assigned as its values is not necessarily a numeric scale
type variable. If the values do not have numeric significance, then the variable should be defined to the neural network as a categorical type.)

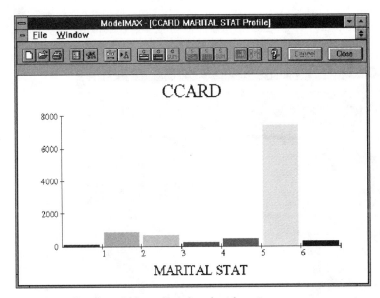

Figure 17.9 Sample variables report.

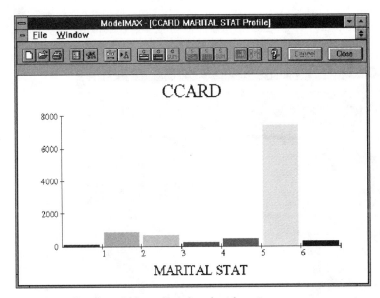

Figure 17.10 Sample variable profile in bar chart format.

A variable profile for MARITAL STAT in table format appears in Figure 17.11. From this table, you can determine exactly how many occurrences of each unique value occur in the training file. These profiles are important because the frequency distribution for each variable should mirror that of the entire population from which the model's input file was randomly selected. The frequency distribution for each variable used in the model also must closely resemble that of the population in the file that the model will be used to score. For example, if MARITAL STAT is used in a model, you might not want to use a model built on a population of married people to score a population of single people.

How Do I Evaluate a Model?

Once a neural network is trained, you can view a *Gains Table*, which distributes the records over table rows by equal counts. A Gains Table is so named because it reflects the "gains" that can be expected over mailing randomly. This type of report also is commonly referred to as a *"decile" report* because early, hand-drawn tables typically had 10 rows. Even though the number of rows in a Gains Table varies, the name decile report still persists. A Gains Table for the credit card response model appears in Figure 17.12.

The strength of a model can be gauged by the spread between the neural network cutoff scores for the top and bottom segments as well as the spread between the segments. The larger the spread, the larger the

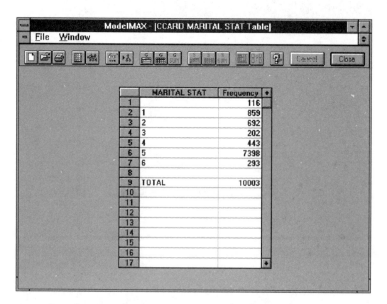

Figure 17.11 Sample variable profile in bar chart format.

			ModelMAX - [CCARD Gains Table]						▼ ▲
File	Window								↕

Seg #	Records	CC FEATURE	Profit / CC FEATURE FREQ Cost Per Record	Cum. Profit	% of Records	Response Rate (%)	Cum. % Records	Cum. % CC	Cutoff Score
			0.0000						
1	502	493	0.00	0.00	5.02	98.21	5.02	11.31	0.9841
2	512	485	0.00	0.00	5.12	94.73	10.14	22.43	0.9771
3	499	479	0.00	0.00	4.99	95.99	15.13	33.42	0.9501
4	499	499	0.00	0.00	4.99	100.00	20.11	44.86	0.9155
5	492	491	0.00	0.00	4.92	99.80	25.03	56.12	0.8991
6	504	502	0.00	0.00	5.04	99.60	30.07	67.64	0.8892
7	496	494	0.00	0.00	4.96	99.60	35.03	78.97	0.8662
8	495	480	0.00	0.00	4.95	96.97	39.98	89.98	0.7918
9	495	327	0.00	0.00	4.95	66.06	44.93	97.48	0.4757
10	501	55	0.00	0.00	5.01	10.98	49.94	98.74	0.2158
11	497	7	0.00	0.00	4.97	1.41	54.90	98.90	0.1289
12	507	2	0.00	0.00	5.07	0.39	59.97	98.94	0.1160
13	501	0	0.00	0.00	5.01	0.00	64.98	98.94	0.0984
14	497	1	0.00	0.00	4.97	0.20	69.95	98.97	0.0843
15	499	6	0.00	0.00	4.99	1.20	74.94	99.11	0.0481
16	500	15	0.00	0.00	5.00	3.00	79.94	99.45	0.0259
17	494	2	0.00	0.00	4.94	0.40	84.87	99.50	0.0126
18	500	3	0.00	0.00	5.00	0.60	89.87	99.56	0.0049
19	500	15	0.00	0.00	5.00	3.00	94.87	99.91	0.0012
20	513	4	0.00	0.00	5.13	0.78	100.00	100.00	0.00000
Tot	10003	4360							

Figure 17.12 Sample Gains table.

differences between those who are most and least likely to exhibit the selected behavior. The key columns in the previous Gains Table are the CUM. % RECORDS and the next column, which is the cumulative percent of the dependent variable (CUM. % CC). By row 9, this model has accounted for 97.48% of the responders in only 44.93% of the population. This key information also is graphed in a Lift chart (Figure 17.13) so that you can quickly compare the results from this model to those from a random mailing. (ModelMAX automatically calculates values for the CUM. PROFIT column if you enter profit and cost parameters as part of the scoring process.)

To determine whether a model will do well when used to score records that it has never seen before, you must use it to score at least one validation file, which is another input file where the outcomes are known. (Scoring does not result in any further learning or adjustment to the network connection weights. The mathematical algorithms generated during network training are used to assign neural network scores to these input records.) When the percentages for the validation file are similar to those from the file used to build the model, then you know that the model will do well when used to score a similar population where the outcomes are not known.

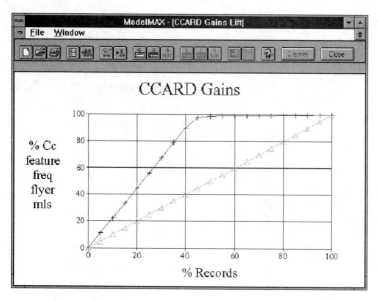

Figure 17.13 Sample lift chart.

Is There Any Way to Tell What Segments Look Like?

The end result of the modeling process is the assignment of a neural network score. However, ModelMAX also makes use of an unsupervised neural network, which is known as a *self-organizing map*, to cluster the data in a project's training sample. From the back-end Segment reports that ModelMAX generates, you can gain an idea as to what the people placed on the rows of a Gains Table look like. The two types of Segment reports are Variable Analyses and Segment Comparisons. A *Variable Analysis* represents the impact of either one variable or two variables over the rows of the Gains Table (Figure 17.14).

A *Segment Comparison* represents the average characteristics for either one row or two rows of the Gains Table (Figure 17.15). Whenever two rows are graphed, you can look at whether the bars move in the same or opposite direction to determine how different the patterns for these two rows actually are.

Because ModelMAX is designed to be predictive rather than descriptive, it must make use of the preprocessed data in a project's training sample to generate these back-end reports. If you are interested in performing precise profile analysis quickly and easily, you might consider dbPROFILE. Designed by A.S.A to be either a standalone product or a complement to ModelMAX, dbPROFILE is a sophisticated data-analysis and decision-support tool. It features an unsupervised neural network that uses the multiple dimensions in *raw data* to group together the records of people who behave similarly.

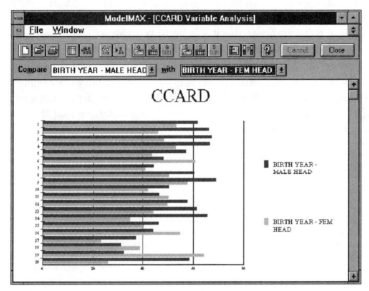

Figure 17.14 Comparison of BIRTH YEAR-MALE HEAD and BIRTH YEAR-FEM HEAD.

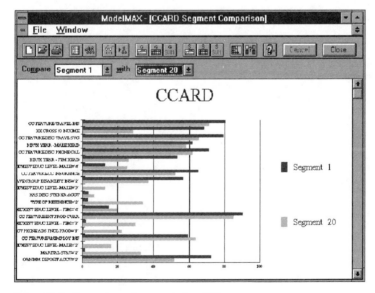

Figure 17.15 Comparison of segments 1 and 20.

Putting Neural Networks to Work

Successful direct marketing is more than a numbers game. It requires a keen understanding of people and their motivations. The answers to the questions "Exactly who will respond?", "To what degree will they respond?", and "Why will they respond?" are in your database. Yet, ironically, the more extensive the data that you collect, the harder it can be to transform it into useful information about individual prospects and customers because, at some point, no matter how sophisticated your information system, you run up against the limits of traditional data-analysis techniques. Neural networks enable you to take that data and turn it into useful information. With a product such as ModelMAX, you can realize the full power of your database and the full promise of database marketing.

18

Putting the Data Warehouse on the Enterprise *Intra*net

RICHARD TANLER
Chairman, Information Advantage, Inc.

We now are witnessing the third major event in an information technology revolution that began two decades ago. The latest event, like the previous two, will signal a fundamental change in how each of us acquire and use information.

In 1975, a revolution in the computer industry was started by a rather innocuous cover story in *Popular Electronics* magazine. The Altair 8800, based on the Intel 8080 microprocessor, was introduced. The personal computer was born, promising computer power at affordable prices for all—at least for those with sufficient technical skills.

The second major event redefined the rules for personal computer software. In 1983, Apple demonstrated the Lisa personal computer. Lisa was the first commercial attempt at providing a graphical user interface (GUI) and mouse. Apple followed with the Macintosh, and Microsoft created a standard for ease-of-use. The personal computer evolved into a tool truly for everyone.

Now, it is safe to conclude that the Internet is yet another paradigm shift in information technology. The Internet is defining how personal computer users acquire and use information from a worldwide network of databases. The *personal* computer has transitioned into the *networked* computer.

The microprocessor changed the rules for the hardware industry and, in doing so, accelerated innovation and the creation of a new lineup of industry leaders. The software industry now is dominated by Microsoft, a company that recognized the importance of developing software for a new class of computers and users. The companies that will emerge as the leaders in the next era will find ways to advance the power of the networked computer.

The Internet is where I, as a casual user, can retrieve just about any trivial bit of information: "What was the temperature in Liverpool?" Importantly, I can "surf the Net" easily and without great expense. I am a self-taught user, a testament to how easy Internet access has become. The Internet is more than a source of information. The Internet provides communication and collaboration capabilities that transform the personal computer into a networked computer.

Contrast the Internet user, with the majority of users within business organizations. How easy is it for a nontechnical decision maker to access information stored in the enterprise data warehouse? Is there much real collaboration occurring among decision makers? Can the Internet serve as a model for business systems development?

The Enterprise *Intra*net

The "*Intra*net" is a concept borrowing from the *Internet*. The *Intra*net is not a product; rather it is a vision of how information could be provided to users inside an enterprise. An *Intra*net should provide a simple means of accessing information on customers, sales, financial performance, marketing plans, etc. An *Intra*net also should provide communication and collaboration capabilities well beyond simple e-mail. The *Intra*net must provide data security layers and provide meaningful guidelines for how information is appropriately used in decision-making.

Some of the most valuable assets of the enterprise are the operational data used in managing the business. The data is being organized in data warehouses to make data more accessible to users. The data warehouse is the foundation of the *Intra*net. The challenge in providing users access to data stored in the data warehouse is that an analysis layer is required. This layer converts masses of raw data into meaningful information, presented as reports, graphic visualizations, or mathematical functions. This is the key difference between the Internet, which focuses on the retrieval of text and image data types, and the *Intra*net that also must support the processing of numeric data via some form of data reduction method to present useful information.

The amount of information available on the Internet is mind-boggling. So too, the business enterprise is capable of amassing enormous amounts of data in a data warehouse. The *Intra*net concept is a way to begin to think about how the data warehouse will be integrated into an enterprise information architecture.

Communications and Shared Decision-Making Responsibility

Decision making improves with timely, accurate, and complete information. Information types that are useful in decision making include numeric data (weekly sales trends), text (marketing objectives), image (advertisement), management experience, and new ideas. The decision-making process requires the integration of *all* of the information types, which means that decision making improves as a result of a "collaborative effort."

Currently data warehousing is concerned with the archiving of hard numeric data extracted from operational systems. This is an important first step. The *Intra*net will place added emphasis on the integration of text and image data. The *Intra*net also will influence how the ideas and experience of a workgroup are exchanged during the decision making process. (See Figure 18.1.)

Today, most users can communicate via a corporate e-mail system. An e-mail system allows text files to be exchanged but *does not* facilitate true collaboration. E-mail systems sometimes actually *avoid* collaborative communication. LotusNotes is one step closer to a collaborative method of exchanging valuable information, but the focus still is text file sharing. True collaboration requires the sharing of "live" information in such a way that the recipient can immediately continue an analysis or branch off in an entirely new direction without assistance. For an effective use of the *Intra*net,

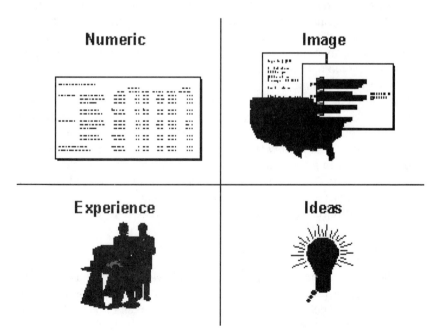

Figure 18.1 Types of information on the *Intra*net.

if I receive a report from another *Intra*net user, I should immediately be able to drill down, drill up, or skip hierarchy levels on any dimension, perform analyses, pivot, rotate, and analyze the results, then pass "live" work in progress to others in the organization.

There is a subtle but critically important capability that is required to support the *Intra*net. The management of the data warehouse, access and reporting middleware, and the communications infrastructure must be presented to the user as a tightly integrated package. The *Intra*net will require its own form of logic server to manage the integration of tools and communications layers.

Security on the *Intra*net

The liberal sharing of information and collaboration among users on the *Intra*net immediately raises data security issues. The data warehouse should be viewed as one of the enterprise's most valuable assets. Data must be secured; however, if it is too tightly controlled, the value of the warehouse will never be fully realized.

The security issue is indeed complex. To illustrate, a Sales Vice President has authorization to view financial data at a U.S., Region, and Sales Territory level. At the territory level, the financial data would include all salary data for sales representatives. If the Sales Vice President creates a report and decides to share it, the regional managers should have access to only territory information for their region and be blocked from accessing territory information for other regions. In other words, if I am not authorized to receive and access the report, I should not be able to view the report or drill into areas where I do not have authorization.

Again, there is a subtle capability that is being described. Reports that are created from data stored in the warehouse should *not* simply be shared as text files. All reports should be "live," giving the recipient the ability to immediately analyze and modify the report as well as the "live" logic and assumptions supporting the analyses. For effective collaboration that yields productivity, the report along with the template, "live" logic, and assumptions *must* be shared throughout the workgroup and enterprise. If the recipient is not authorized, the report logic should fail to execute.

Intelligent Agents on the *Intra*net

One of the common complaints about e-mail and even phone mail is that the mail box fills up faster than a user has time to isolate and address the really important issues. Agents are intended to work on behalf of users to isolate important information sought by a user. An agent can be triggered by some predefined event or at a specified time interval. The agent sends an alert to notify specific users on a "need-to-know" basis.

Triggers, agents, and alerts *must* have the ability to run continually as background processes on an *Intra*net logic server even when a user's PC is powered off or physically disconnected from the server, providing a means of automating the routine analysis process. When the PC is reconnected to the network, the agents must be smart enough to then notify users of conditions that occurred during the disconnect. Because data warehouses tend to grow exponentially, it is critical that agents proactively monitor and manage activities, alerting decision makers *only* when specific conditions exist. It is unrealistic to believe decision makers would be productive by aimlessly data surfing through potentially hundreds of gigabytes of data looking for answers. The decision maker should be free to concentrate on the immediate critical issues while the system ensures that developing conditions will not go undetected.

An example of the use of triggers, agents, and alerts is a forecasting accuracy-monitoring application. When each week's actual sales are updated to the data warehouse (trigger), the system automatically calculates the mean absolute percent error between forecasted and actual results over the latest six weeks for every product (agent). The mean absolute percent error is a simple way of representing forecast error over time. An alert is sent to each marketing manager responsible for the product forecast if a threshold for the mean absolute percent error calculation is exceeded. The marketing manager then can take appropriate actions to avert out-of-stocks or excessive inventory buildup.

Longer-term agent technologies will support closed-loop decision support and electronic authorization. This takes communication and collaboration to a very high level. Closed-loop decision support is a process whereby agents trigger other agents to actually formulate a recommended action for user authorization. In the sales forecasting, the system might trigger a second agent to recompute a statistical forecast based on inclusion of most recent data or increase the safety stock level provided to manufacturing. (See Figure 18.2.)

Architecture of the *Intra*net

The foundation for the *Intra*net is a data warehouse. The data warehouse must be flexible enough to be managed on one or multiple data servers. An *Intra*net logic server is required to manage data access, analysis, and reporting logic. The logic server also provides for centralized security control and communications as well as background and batch processing required to implement robust trigger, agent, and alert functionality. (See Figure 18.3.)

The *Intra*net logic server also will house metadata—data about data—that is essential to link the analysis logic to the data warehouses. Metadata is a road map for describing the data warehouse and transparently managing analysis rules in business terms for applications and users. Metadata

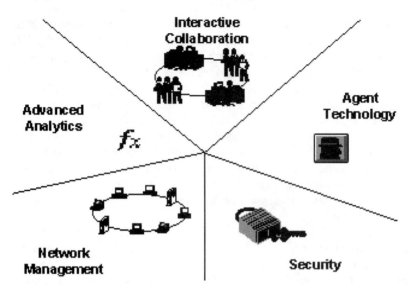

Figure 18.2 Requirements for an *Intra*net Application Logic Server.

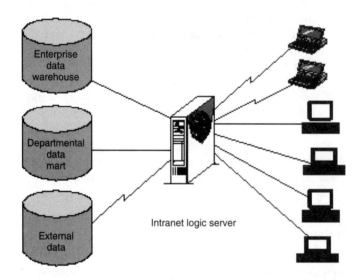

Figure 18.3 The Enterprise *Intra*net Architecture.

standards will evolve from the need to create a common set of navigation capabilities and the synchronization rules to align multiple data types within an application.

In some cases, the data warehouse and the logic server might be the same physical hardware platform; however, it might be beneficial to scale separate hardware platforms to their specific task. In large *Intra*net installations, the data warehouse often spans multiple hardware platforms in combination with many departmental logic servers. It is essential that business analysis applications *simultaneously* access multiple databases on multiple servers and perform the necessary analysis on the fly.

The most important aspect of the *Intra*net architecture is that it must be capable of supporting a small number of users to a very large number of users. *Intra*net is a viable concept only if everyone within the enterprise has access, even if for some users data access is limited. The *Intra*net is as much about communications and collaboration as it is about data access.

Implementing an *Intra*net

As noted previously, *Intra*net is a concept, not a product. Certainly, the creation of a data warehouse is a key step in developing a foundation for the *Intra*net. The data warehouse should contain data about operating performance, competitors, customers, and financial information. Each of these types of data will be used by workgroups to address different business issues, but all must share information and collaborate on decisions. Marketing can't change a major program to respond to a competitor's action without spending approvals from management and finance.

The second step in the implementation of an *Intra*net is senior management support. The *Intra*net can be a catalyst for change and improvements, but this will require senior management enthusiastic support.

The *Intra*net concept must be deployed rapidly and broadly throughout the enterprise. To date, many organizations have concentrated on developing their data warehouse with less emphasis on how it will be used. Initial user access has been limited to a small number of data knowledgeable users. For an *Intra*net to be successful, a large number of users must be provided immediate access. Rather than building a very large data warehouse and adding users slowly, the *Intra*net model enables all users to access some portion of the data warehouse. The data warehouse then can be expanded in phases.

The missing link in implementing an *Intra*net vision has been the logic server. Since its formation in 1990, Information Advantage has never strayed from a view that the business logic had to be partitioned from the presentation layer (PC-resident GUI and information display) and the data warehouse. This partitioning must be both logical (a published application programming interface) *and* allow physical partitioning, with the logic residing on its own network server. For several years, Information Advantage has evolved a very sophisticated set of server-resident capabilities that meet the requirements of an *Intra*net logic server.

The model for a logic server is AXSYS from Information Advantage. AXSYS is a software development technology for creating advanced custom business analysis applications. AXSYS has been used in production environments since 1991. Recently, Information Advantage announced DecisionSuite 3.0, an integrated set of business-analysis tools architected to perform relational multidimensional analysis *directly* against data warehouses and data marts in an open, three-tiered environment. DecisionSuite delivers the power of the logic server to the user's desktop.

With years of proven results using a three-tiered architecture for business analysis, DecisionSuite and AXSYS are mature products in an emerging market. Information Advantage has been leading the three-tiered market with automated analysis, detect and alert agents, workflow and desktop integration, business information objects, and collaborative decision making using "live" reports without having IT predefine drill paths or write stored procedures. Decision makers point-and-click to identify trends and exceptions, draw comparisons, share "live" enterprise data, and get answers fast. DecisionSuite provides various levels of functionality to address the needs of different types of users throughout the enterprise. Included in the Suite are: InfoAlert, NewsLine, Analysis, and Workbench.

Information Advantage is leading the marketplace as the latest industry paradigm shift takes shape. Users now know that they can easily get information, collaborate using "live" reports, and use information to make informed decisions. Look at the Internet to see the future for data warehousing and the effective distribution of information.

Chapter 19

Visualization in Data Mining

JIM AUCOIN
*Product Manager, Advanced Visual
Systems Inc.*

Why Data Mining?

A corporation's historical data provides a useful means of analyzing business performance measures and identifying the factors that influence them. Buried within the vast amount of data that represents a corporation's transactions is a history of global patterns, such as a relationship between a customer and the products that he or she purchases regularly. These relationships represent valuable knowledge about the database, objects in the database, and, if the database is a faithful mirror, the real world registered by the database. The data's all there at the organization's fingertips.

The introspective analysis of an organization's data has proven to be so valuable that it has been given its own name: data mining. *Data mining* is defined as the process of applying artificial-intelligence techniques, including advanced modeling and rule induction, to large data sets to determine patterns in the data. From a business perspective, data mining can be defined as the process of scanning through very large data sets to glean information.[1]

Data mining recently has seen a surge in popularity, largely because the benefits it offers are so tangible: accurate identification of buying trends, optimization of promotional programs, and precise definition of market seg-

---

[1]Reeves, Laura. "Data Mining." *Data Management Review*. Vol. 5, No. 7, July/August 1995, p. 92.

ments. Data mining can be used to uncover sales patterns to support new product development. It also can be used to identify the common elements in failure situations and detect weaknesses in complex power distribution systems.

Data mining has not been limited to one type of industry or function but is invaluable to virtually all organizations. Organizations have used data-mining analyses to improve revenue, decrease costs, and enhance their competitive position. Data mining has been applied in industries such as retail, health care, insurance, and finance. By far, however, the most common applications for data mining are in marketing and financial areas.

What Are the Tools Used in Data Mining?

Data mining is concerned with analyzing the transactional data of an organization to spot trends and patterns. This data often is buried deep within very large databases, which in some cases contain data from several years. It therefore is not uncommon to find databases exceeding 100 GB, or even a terabyte. Organizations frequently transfer their operational data to a data warehouse to support data mining.

On the front-end (client) side, a set of tools typically is provided that allows the user to analyze the contents of the data warehouse via graphical, tabular, geographic, and syntactic reports. The primary role of the front-end data-mining tool is to provide the user with an intuitive, graphical tool for creating new analyses and navigating the data warehouse. The goal of data mining is to help focus the user's analysis so that relevant information is obtained faster and so that his or her time is used more effectively.

Data-warehouse vendors probably would claim that any query tool that supports their products is a data-mining tool. The fastest-growing data-mining tool actually might be the spreadsheet. Most now have been enhanced to allow users to "pivot" data (i.e., to perform fairly sophisticated cross-tabulations simply by grabbing and dragging an attribute or field). Multidimensional spreadsheets and databases also are becoming popular for data analysis. Data-mining technologies also include analysis techniques that can help enhance the value of the data exploration ("drill down," "drill up," and summarization along various dimensions) supported by multidimensional tools.

Information extracted from the data-mining process typically is presented to the user in the form of numbers in rows and columns within a spreadsheet. Most front-end data-mining tools also provide business graphics such as line graphs, histograms, and pie charts. These simple graphical methods allow the analyst to capture and present some of the information in the databases. However, their usefulness is limited by the number of dimensions being examined. For example, for two dimensions, a vector representation is suitable (line graph). For three dimensions, a matrix display sometimes is adequate, with the rows and columns representing the elements of two different dimensions and the cells of the matrix representing the summarized fact data for each grouping.

Past three dimensions, it becomes increasingly difficult for the user to visualize multidimensional data. Data display is easier if the dimensions are "flattened out," similar to the traditional report containing "control breaks." However, displays of that sort might obscure patterns that otherwise would be apparent. Basic bar and pie charts will suffice only for data along two or three dimensions. Given the complexity of the data stored in data warehouses, these methods limit the dimension of the data presented and tell little about the relationships among the variables in the database.[2] Is there any easy and intuitive way to glean information from these massive databases?

Visualization

We appreciate bar and pie charts because they convert pages of hard-to-understand numerical and textual data into something that is easily comprehensible. We all know the adage, "A picture is worth a thousand words." The benefits of graphical presentation of numerical and textual data are self-evident. Graphics provide us with one of the most effective means of communication, because our highly developed 2D and 3D pattern-recognition capabilities allow us to perceive and process pictorial data rapidly and efficiently.

Bar and pie charts are very simple examples of the use of graphics to quickly convey information about the data that they represent. At the other end of the graphics spectrum are sophisticated 2D and 3D interactive graphics tools that have been critical analytical components for years in many scientific disciplines. These disciplines include engineering analysis, computational fluid dynamics, computational chemistry, molecular modeling, medical imaging, oil and gas exploration, environmental studies, and remote sensing. What these industries have in common is the need to analyze extremely large data sets, produced and collected by a diverse range of methods, to understand particular phenomena.

Visualization is a term used to refer to the more-or-less real-time depiction of scientific data. It is enabled with the use of interactive computer graphics. Interactive computer graphics probably is the single most important means of producing pictures since the invention of photography and television. However, it has the added advantage that, with the computer, you can make pictures of not only concrete, "real-world" objects, but also of

---

[2]Weldon, Jay-Louise. "Managing Multidimensional Data: Harnessing the Power." *Database Programming & Design*. Vol. 8, No. 8, August 1995, p. 26. © Miller Freeman, Inc.

abstract, synthetic objects, such as mathematical surfaces in 4D, and of data that have no inherent geometry, such as survey results.[3]

The goals of data mining in the business world bear many similarities to the needs of several of the scientific fields referenced previously. Like the scientists and engineers in those scientific fields, the business analyst needs to analyze enormous quantities of data. One of the means by which the scientist attacks the problem is visualization. By using visualization, they are able to summarize the data and highlight trends and phenomena through various kinds of graphical representation. Let's take the field of oil and gas exploration as an example.

Plain and simple, the goal of oil and gas exploration is to find and extract oil as quickly and as cheaply as possible. The science of geophysics is largely concerned with analyzing and defining subsurface geology to improve the probability of success in drilling for oil and gas. The key problem in oil and gas exploration is to locate geologic structures that trap hydrocarbons. Hydrocarbons, being lighter than water, tend to be trapped in the top of porous layers (i.e., sand) that are overlaid by tight fine-grain geographic layers (i.e., shales). Figure 19.1 illustrates four of the typical types of hydrocarbon traps that are sought with this technology.

There are several techniques used to predict where oil is likely to be found. For the sake of simplification, let's look at an example of reflection seismology. The underlying principle of reflection seismology is to measure the seismic energy from an artificial seismic source as it travels through different layers of geologic strata (i.e., rock types). The "artificial seismic force" to start the movement of seismic waves typically is an explosion of dynamite. Essentially, holes are drilled in the earth, and the dynamite is put down the hole and exploded. Through the measurement of the resultant seismic reflections, the geologist is able to obtain data that can be used to predict the rock formations in the area surveyed.

The data sets generated by these acquisition techniques are enormous, frequently on the order of many gigabytes. A number of different processes are run on the data to convert it into a form that can be used to create a representation of a seismic section. The data then is available to be interpreted.

To visualize the data, it typically is read in as a 3D block of data, called a *volume*. Because the data sets are so large, the data is not read into the computer all at once but is converted in "chunks." Each point of data in the selected area represents a physical location (i.e., an x,y,z location) in the three-dimensional "space" represented by that particular area. The value (or values, depending on the data-acquisition methods used) at each data point can represent many attributes. In this reflection seismology example, it will

---

[3]Foley, James and Andries van Dam. *Computer Graphics: Principles and Practice*. Addison-Wesley Publishing Company, 1990, p. 3.

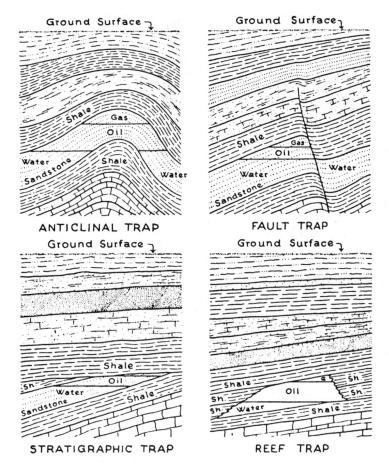

Figure 19.1 Typical examples of hydrocarbon traps.

represent some value associated with the seismic reading at that point (seismic amplitude, phase, frequency, velocity, etc.). A collection of surrounding values in a given area will in turn identify (to a certain degree of probability) the type of rock formation at this location.

Several visualization techniques can be used to analyze this data. One of these is to view the volume of data as a surface plot on a workstation or PC screen. To enhance the analysis of the data, the data can be represented in several different ways. One method is to assign a value to each data point (or, more typically, to a certain range of data points) that will correspond to a color to display for that range of values. All the points that fall within the selected range of values will have the same color. In a 3D representation of the object, the colors will smooth out to form layers. (See Figure 19.2.)

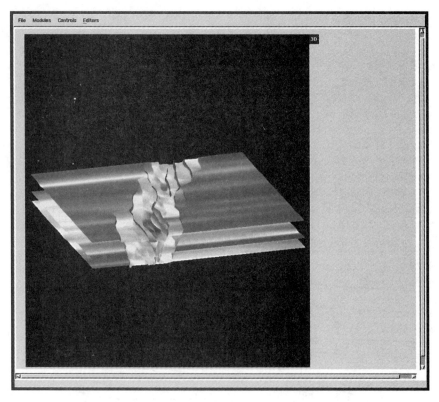

Figure 19.2 A 3D representation of the object. Royal Holloway College, University of London

Visually, then, the geophysicist can see, on the screen, where the rock formation goes from shale to sand, to limestone, and so forth. Some visualization software packages allow the user to interactively rotate the object to analyze the surface from all angles. Other advanced visualization techniques allow the user to "slice" and "dice" the data—that is, to move a horizontal or vertical plane through the surface. In this manner, the geophysicist can analyze each layer of the volume in detail.

A host of other visualization techniques are available that assist the user with his or her analysis of the data. These include functions such as picking (which allows the user to click on an area of the visualization and get back the data values at that point), different render modes such as wireframe and bounding boxes, pan and zoom functions, a number of graphing methods, etc.

Relationship to Data Mining

Data mining also is confronted with the task of converting enormous magnitudes of data into meaningful insight. As in the scientific field, an effective means with which to analyze this data is to use visualization to summarize the data and highlight trends and patterns.

Let's look at direct marketing, for example. The goal in direct marketing is not to locate oil but to identify among potentially millions of clients or prospects the people who are likely to respond to an offer, then to target a specific mailing or telesales campaign to them. The response rate for a mass mailing is incredibly low (typically around 2%) and incredibly costly. By better targeting the candidates, not only could the response rate increase, but the cost for each positive response could go down.

The data that is available to the business analyst will not come from seismic readings, but rather through the course of its normal business operations. A company's business records contain detailed information on each customer and the products that he or she has purchased, as well as how much and when. A telecommunications company, for example, has detailed reports of its customers' transactions (phone calls), including "how much" (number of calls and call duration), "when" (time of day), "where" (geographic area called), and so forth.

In many cases, this data will have been summarized according to some criteria and stored in a data warehouse. The "science" of data mining involves exploring this data in an attempt to uncover patterns or detect anomalies. "Striking it rich" often means finding an unexpected result that requires users to think creatively. Tools for the data "miner," therefore, should allow for heuristic, iterative analysis where the user is looking for something but doesn't know quite what (but will recognize it once he/she sees it).

Typically, however, the techniques available in data mining are restricted to spreadsheets and reports or simple bar charts or pie graphs. Why not extend the capability of traditional business graphics to support the visualization of multidimensional data? Why not use the graphical methods available with visualization to transform multidimensional databases into images that would allow patterns inherent in the data to reveal themselves?

Let's suppose that you are a long-distance telecommunications company with 10 million customers. Which ones do you target with your direct-marketing campaign?

This is an instance where visualization could be used effectively. Your method to narrow your mailing list might to be perform an analysis where you go through all your records and select everyone who has registered a certain number of long-distance phone calls within the past six months. One method of visualizing the results of this search could be to use a scatterplot display in a three-dimensional grid. (A *scatterplot* is a visualization technique that displays each data point as a colored sphere, or bubble. Scatterplots sometimes are referred to as *bubble viz*.) The size, shape, and color of the bubble can each be used to represent a variable in the data (Figure 19.3).

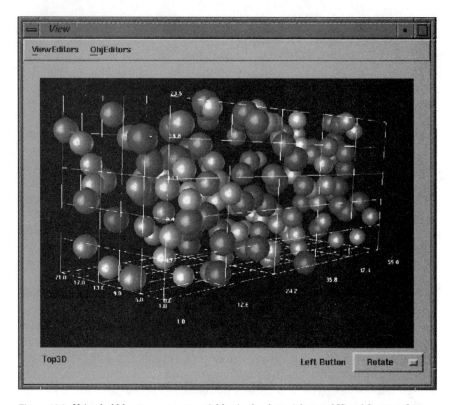

Figure 19.3 Using bubbles to represent variables in the data. Advanced Visual Systems Inc.

The three axes in this visualization ideally should be able to represent any dimension within your data and should be able to be randomly selected and modified by the user. For example, he or she might select "day of month," "time of day," and "phone call duration" as his three axes. The scatterplot display will quickly identify the "hot" points within the data set.

In the example depicted in Figure 19.3, the search criterion has been defined as long-distance calls between 1 and 60 minutes from a particular area code on a daily and hourly basis over a three-week period. The three axes (X, Y, Z) depict: day of month for three weeks of data (a number from 1 to 21), time of day in half-hour increments (0.0 to 24.0), and call duration (number of minutes from 1 to 60). The presence of bubbles represents long-distance phone calls at a particular data point. The color of the bubble indicates the total number of minutes logged for that particular timeframe. (This book is unfortunately able to include only black-and-white images.)

At this point, the user can choose to more fully explore those data points using visual methods or perhaps click on the data and see a traditional numerical display in a spreadsheet. The volume of data points also can be rotated to observe clusters in different areas.

Here, then, by preparing and presenting the data graphically, the user can uncover properties of the data and quickly and easily detect any patterns or deviations from expected results. He or she can get a picture of what the data is trying to tell him/her, then perhaps confirm the observations with other statistical analysis. As with traditional data-mining tools, visualization allows the user to focus in on what is important, but it's critical to have the detail data behind the summary data. Detail data should be available to help provide the rationale for discovered trends. Visualization, therefore, will not replace numeric analysis but can be used effectively to show the user which numbers to look at.

Let's look at some more examples of visualization in data mining.

Figure 19.4 depicts visualization used in the context of stock portfolio analysis and introduces shape to represent additional variables. Each object within the rectangle on the right-hand side represents the price of a particular stock within a user-defined period (the past two weeks, for example). The size of the object represents the value of the stock (the bigger the object, the larger the value). A shape that gets wider from bottom to top is a stock whose price has been increasing within the timeframe being exam-

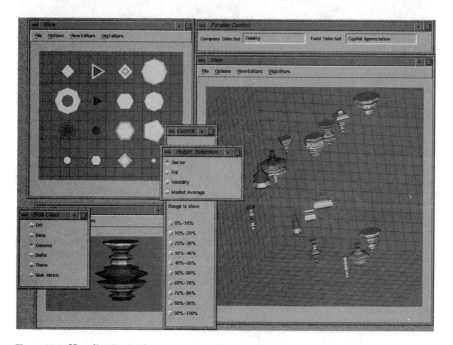

Figure 19.4 Visualization in the context .f stock portfolio analysis. Fusion Systems Limited

ined; conversely, one whose shape gets thinner from bottom to top is decreasing in value. The distance of the object from the "floor" indicates the stock's movement within the timeframe of reference. Color also is used to depict the overall risk exposure of the stock (triggered by a threshold that the user sets), with red being the highest risk and green the lowest. (This is unfortunately not easily visible in these black-and-white images.)

Figure 19.5 is an example of the use of three-dimensional bar charts to represent the closing price of a number of high-technology company stocks over a seven-month period. The height of each bar represents its closing price on a given day. Color also is used in this example to represent the closing price. This image can be rotated to more clearly focus in on a particular stock or group of stocks.

Clicking on any particular stock will bring up a line graph, as shown in Figure 19.6.

Figure 19.7 is an example of visualization used within a telecommunications company's real-time network monitoring and control system. This particular visualization plots values in 3D of the network traffic load on any given day of the month and at a given time of day. Both height and color are used to depict the value at any data point. Peaks and valleys in the load thus

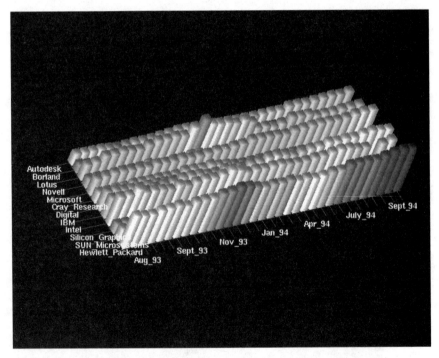

Figure 19.5 The use of 3D bar charts to represent data. Advanced Visual Systems Inc.

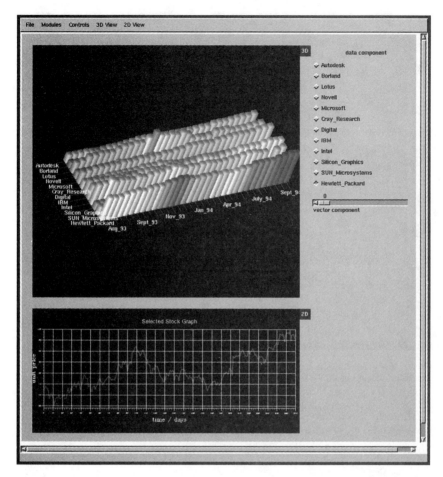

Figure 19.6 The line graph for a particular stock. Advanced Visual Systems Inc.

can be easily identified in this visualization. The average daily network load also is depicted by the colored bars on the back "wall" of the visualization.

Figure 19.8 shows a multidimensional visualization that allows the user to quickly analyze the performance of a particular currency over a given time-frame against those of various other countries. Both the height and color of each cube represents a currency's relative strength or weakness versus that of another country.

Finally, the example in Figure 19.9 uses visualization to depict the changing population of the United States per decade, from 1790 through 1990. The visualization application shown here consists of a three-dimensional map of the United States that the user can interactively interrogate for population statistics. The height and color of each state depicts its population

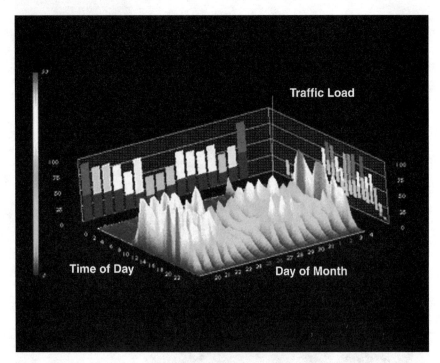

Figure 19.7 Visualization in a real-time network monitoring and control system. British Telecommunications plc.

in the selected decade (the taller the state, the greater the population; the color ranges from blue for lowest to red for highest). The numeric value of the population also can be displayed for each state.

Data-Visualization Architectures

Visualization has evolved over a period of time, and users have many options to choose from when selecting visualization software. There are two general categories: turnkey visualization applications and application builders.

Turnkey visualization applications

Turnkey visualization applications offer a fixed functionality to solve a limited range of specific problems. The user supplies the data and the computational instructions, and possibly some geometric mapping, to the main program. The application supplies the main program and usually has an attractive user interface.

Many products in this category are extremely application-specific. Examples in oil-and-gas exploration, molecular modeling, and architectural modeling, for instance, are common but of limited use in other fields. They also are often available only on selected hardware and operating system platforms in those industries. More general examples include: Application Visualization System and Gsharp (AVS, Inc.); PV-Wave (Visual Numerics); Data Visualizer (Wavefront Technologies); Plot, Transform, and Dicer (Spyglass); Data Explorer (IBM); Explorer (Numerical Algorithms Group); and Khoros (Khoros).

The user does not have to program these packages and can obtain results very quickly. Their disadvantage is that they have limited extendibility and, therefore, often might provide only a part of the solution a user requires. They all have reached a high level of maturity, and many users applying visualization in their work will likely be using one of these packages.

Application builders

Application builders offer a series of modules linked by interfaces that are connected interactively at runtime. They combine features of graphics li-

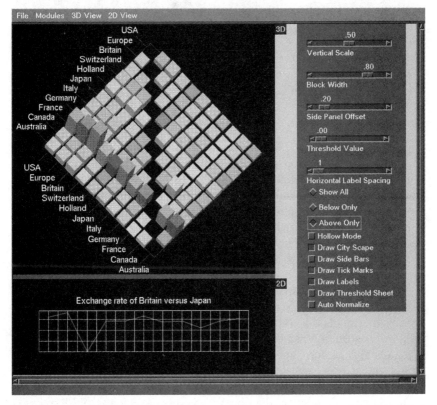

Figure 19.8 Visualization of the performance of a particular currency. Advanced Visual Systems Inc.

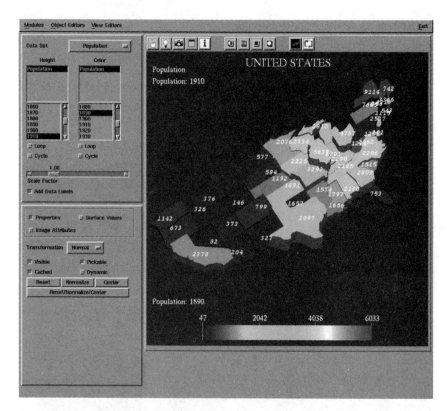

Figure 19.9   Visualization of the U.S. population. Advanced Visual Systems Inc.

braries and presentation packages with turnkey solutions for individual parts of the program, while providing the flexibility to customize the user's final solution. The supplied modules can be replaced or augmented by user-written modules, as required, for greater extensibility.

In these systems, virtually everything that the user needs is provided by the program. The user only has to direct the execution path of the program and provide the data and, optionally, his or her own computational modules if required.

Applications are constructed via a mouse-driven interface with the user manipulating icons on screens and linking them with data paths. With graphical symbols that represent programming elements, applications are built by constructing visible connections between modules, which represent programs that perform specific operations on the data (pseudocoloring, filtering, and so on). New applications can be prototyped quickly by connecting modules in different ways.

An example of such a product is AVS/Express (AVS Inc.). AVS/Express is a multiplatform application-development environment that runs on all of the major UNIX platforms as well as Windows. It uses object-oriented visuals of programming and lets the user rapidly prototype and construct technical applications. AVS/Express incorporates both traditional visualization tools—such as 2D plots, graphs, and image processing—as well as advanced tools—such as 3D interactive rendering and volume visualization.

The developer using AVS/Express is provided an extensive set of modules that he or she can graphically connect together to build visualization objects. These objects are combined to construct a higher-level application. The developer also can easily incorporate his or her own programs written in C, C++, or FORTRAN by encapsulating them in modules that can be saved and added to the standard set of AVS/Express' module libraries.

Some of the standard libraries provided with AVS/Express are described in the following paragraphs.

The *Graphics Display Kit* includes the full spectrum of rendering technology required to display and manipulate text, 2D images, and 2D and 3D geometric images. Key elements include display elements (such as views, cameras, and lights), rendering primitives (such as images, lines, polygons, and text), user interface editors (such as properties, transformations, and drawing modes), interactors (such as object selection and transformations), and picking operators (such as data probing).

The *Data Visualization Kit* contains the objects, data structures, and libraries specifically designed to visualize and analyze real-world, 2D, and 3D data (such as that found in the examples given in this chapter). Key features include data analysis (such as divergence, gradient, magnitude, and probe), data processing (such as crop, extract scalar, scale, and threshold), scalar display (such as contour, isosurface, and slice), and vector display techniques (such as advector, glyph, and streamlines).

The *Image Processing Kit* is an extensive library of functions for analyzing and manipulating images. Supported functions include analysis (such as image probe, measure, register, and histogram), arithmetic (such as floating point operators, logical operators, and shift operators), draw/edit (such as region-of-interest, grid, and look-up), geometric ops (such as reflect, rotate, warp, zoom, and translate), filters (such as convolve, edge, kernel, and median), and fast Fourier transforms (such as real, magnitude and phase, multiply FFT, and inverse FFT).

The *User Interface Kit* lets the user specify the construction and layout of an application's user interface (including pull-down menus with buttons, sliders, dials, etc.) in both native Motif and Windows. The User Interface Kit is integrated with the visual programming environment.

The *Database Kit* provides interfaces to several SQL-based relational database management systems (RDBMSs), such as Oracle, Sybase, and Informix. It also contains an Open Database Connectivity (ODBC) interface that provides connectivity to any ODBC-compliant database. Key functionality provided with the Database Kit includes: database logon validation, selective extraction and presentation of data from the database, modification of table data, commit and rollback operations for individual transactions, and a host of other miscellaneous SQL operations, including table and view management operations.

Figure 19.10 shows the AVS/Express visualization environment that was used to create the visualization in Figure 19.3 (long-distance call analysis). The graphical user interface menus on the left-hand side of Figure 19.10 are part of the AVS/Express Database Kit and provide a high-level method for the developer to interact with the underlying modules. They allow the user to type in SQL instructions, display lists of tables and columns in the database, and view the result of his query in an output window.

On the right-hand side of Figure 19.10 is the set of underlying Database Kit modules themselves, linked together to perform the functions of connecting to the database, selectively retrieving data, and importing the data into a visualization viewer.

Figure 19.11 shows the visualization itself in a viewer window of the AVS/Express application. In addition to the 3D geometric representation of the data, a 2D graph also has been selected to display the data.

The other visualization examples provided in this chapter were all created using AVS/Express.

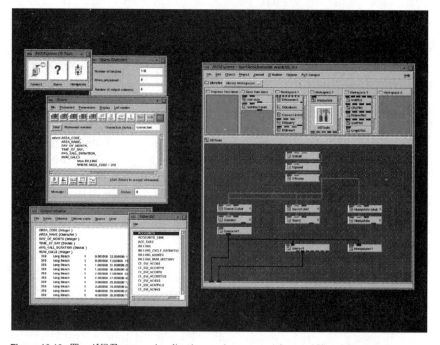

Figure 19.10 The AVS/Express visualization environment. Advanced Visual Systems Inc.

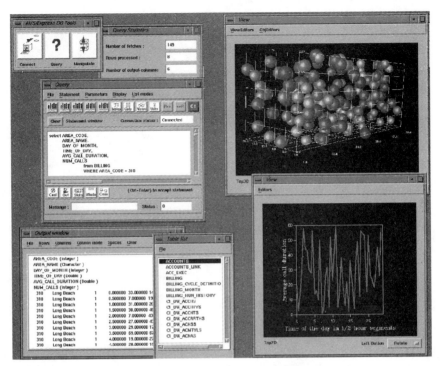

Figure 19.11 A visualization in a viewer window of the AVS/Express application. Advanced Visual Systems Inc.

Summary

Data mining is critical to the enterprise that wants to exploit operational and other available data to improve the quality of decision making and gain critical competitive advantage. Companies that do not employ data mining might find themselves increasingly vulnerable in highly competitive marketplaces. Moreover, while an organization can achieve a degree of expense reduction by investing in operational systems, companies using data mining can identify opportunities to increase revenue by orders of magnitude.

The enabling power of data mining is substantially enhanced when combined with another technology: data visualization. Data visualization has helped scientists and engineers make sense of natural phenomena for years. Adding data visualization to data mining makes it possible for the user to gain a deeper, intuitive understanding of his or her data. The result is more efficient and productive use of data that ultimately leads to higher profits.

20

Prediction from
Large Data Warehouses

DR. KAMRAN PARSAYE
CEO, Information Discovery, Inc.

Ask anyone involved in a competitive business if he or she would like to have a crystal ball, and you are likely to get a quick "yes." As data warehouses become widespread, the use of predictive modeling is becoming a key application area. Automated data-mining systems use large warehouses of historical data to find patterns, see trends, and make predictions by themselves to provide a significant business edge.

Prediction often is done in the context of decision support and "data mining," with "discovery" as a closely related component. I define *data mining* as a "decision-support process in which we search for patterns of information in data." This search can be done just by the user (e.g., just by performing queries), in which case it is quite hard, or it can be assisted by a smart program that automatically searches the database for the user and finds significant patterns. Once the information is found, it needs to be presented in a suitable form, with graphs, reports, etc. (See Figure 20.1.)

A computer system that finds patterns in data is called a *discovery system*. A computer system that aims to make predictions based on the patterns is called a *predictive modeling system*. These are two quite distinct forms of activities. The first approach can help a user change his or her perception with respect to the data and make different decisions as a result, while the second simply can make a prediction. Prediction on a data set can be performed with or without discovery, but transparent modeling is preceded by discovery.

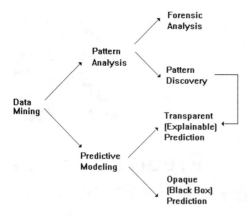

Figure 20.1 The data-mining hierarchy.

A predictive modeling system selects among a set of alternatives (e.g., the highest response group) or assigns a value (e.g., a response rating or a profitability value) to a population. It might or might not help a decision maker understand anything about the prediction process. While a predictive model selects among a set of values, a discovery system provides explicit information that explains the nature of a database; it tells the untold story of the data. Prediction based on explicit pattern discovery is transparent and explainable, while opaque prediction just provides answers with no explanation.

While discovery and prediction form the basis of data mining, it is worth noting that three related areas of decision support include:

- Automatic pattern discovery, whereby a program looks for patterns by itself with no queries posed by a user. This is an approach based on system initiative.

- Multidimensional analysis (or OLAP), whereby the program helps a user visualize patterns from various viewpoints. This is a mixed-initiative approach.

- Query and reporting, for providing answers to questions the users already know to ask. This is a user-initiative approach.

Note that neither OLAP nor query and reporting do either discovery or prediction by themselves. They require "user-supplied hypotheses" and help the user get specific answers from the data, not provide predictions. For a detailed discussion of these issues see "The Four Spaces of Decision Support," *DBMS Magazine*, November 1995.

Categories of Models

At the top level, there are two ways to build a predictive model: let a human design the model and implement it as an algorithm or let a computer system learn by looking at examples. Hence a predictive modeling system can be:

- An *algorithmic system* developed by writing a specific program (e.g., a scoring model) in some programming language.
- A *learning system* trained by providing it with examples.

In an algorithmic system, a human somehow comes up with a model and an algorithm (e.g., by performing statistical analysis, etc.). The algorithm then is coded into a program for execution. Later, new data is submitted for prediction. A learning system, on the other hand, looks at historical data and is trained, or trains itself, to predict the future. At times, an underlying set of assumptions needs to be supplied to the system, but there is no direct effort by humans for inventing and coding an algorithm, as in Figure 20.2.

Learning systems themselves can be categorized as:

- Opaque—Blackbox systems
- Transparent—Explainable systems

An opaque system learns and predicts, but its specific behavior on each case is unknown to the user and it does not explain its behavior. A transparent system, on the other hand, can provide a detailed account of why it performs a specific operation, and its internal methods of operation are visible to the user. For example, most neural nets are opaque, while rule discovery is transparent.

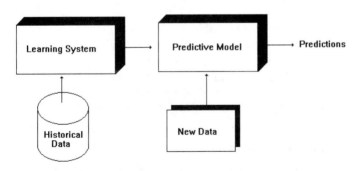

Figure 20.2 Learning and predicting models.

Thus a transparent learning system has two distinct modes of use:

- As a learning system used for "prediction."
- As an exploratory data-analysis tool used to provide "insight."

A traceable predictive system can trace back through its actions to say which indicators led it to make a recommendation. For example, some neural networks can trace back to say that, for a specific prediction, they made a recommendation based on the indicators.

However, this form of traceability should not be viewed as transparency, because it tells you about the behavior of the *predictive model*, not about the *data set*. In other words:

- *Traceable systems* provide information about their own actions.
- *Transparent systems* provide information about the data that they analyzed, as well as their own actions.

A transparent system is always traceable, but a traceable system is not necessarily transparent.

Transparency is a highly desirable feature in a predictive model because:

- People often hesitate to fully rely on opaque/black-box models.
- The user can understand the behavior of the transparent model and hence can apply it more effectively in conjunction with other business decisions.
- Transparent models with explanations are easier to control and manage when the nature of the world changes, and the model needs modification.

A predictive model is called *restrained* if it sometimes refuses to provide a prediction, because the data presented to it looks unusual. A predictive model is called *unrestrained* if it always provides a prediction anyway, regardless of what it is shown. It generally is advisable to use restrained models, not only because they are more reliable in the face of noisy, inaccurate, or unreliable data, but because they can detect a changing world and signal the fact that perhaps the future is no longer like the past.

There are several approaches to building predictive models such as statistical models, rule-based systems, and neural networks. I will discuss these later. First, I will consider the data on which the model is built.

Looking at the Whole Warehouse

Large data warehouses provide an unprecedented opportunity for looking at historical patterns by making more data than ever before accessible for analysis.

Sometimes it might seem daunting to look a really large warehouse straight in the eye and try to make predictions from all of the data. It is tempting to try and obtain a smaller "sample" of the data to build a predictive model. This shyness to look at the whole warehouse often is very expensive. In most cases, the temptation to sample must be resisted.

At times, when you have a 100,000,000-record retail database, someone might suggest that a 100,000-record sample might be good enough. This is not so. Sampling will almost always result in a loss of information, in particular with respect to data fields with a large number of nonnumeric values.

It is easy to see why this is the case. Consider a warehouse of 10,000 products and 500 stores. There are 5 million combinations of how a product sells in each store. However, how one product sells in a store is of little interest compared to how products "sell together" in each store—a problem known as *Market Basket Analysis* (e.g., how often do potato chips and beer sell together). There are 50 billion possible combinations here, and a 100,000-record sample can barely manage to scratch the surface. Hence the sample will be a really "rough" representation of the data and will ignore key pieces of information.

In using a small sample, you might as well ignore the product column. Therefore, you no longer have a large warehouse because, in effect, you have reduced it by removing fields from it. Hence sampling a large warehouse for analysis almost defeats the purpose of having all the data there in the first place.

Apart from sampling, aggregation can be used to reduce data sizes. However, aggregation can cause problems, too. As shown in Figure 20.3, the aggregation of the same data set with two sampling or aggregation methods actually can produce the same result, and the aggregation of the same data set with two methods can produce two different results.

As another intuitive example of how "information loss" and "information distortion" can take place through aggregation, consider a retail warehouse where Monday to Friday sales are exceptionally low for some stores, while weekend sales are exceptionally high for others. The aggregation of daily sales data to weekly amounts will totally hide the fact that weekdays are "money losers," while weekends are "money makers." In other words, key pieces of information often are lost through aggregation, and there is no way to recover them by further analysis.

Statistical Approaches

People have wanted to make predictions for centuries but have only recently obtained the appropriate tools for doing so. Short of reading star charts, the earliest approaches to prediction were based on statistics. In 1647, Chevalier de Mere began to look for a method of "predicting dice" to

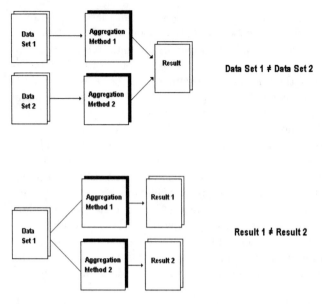

Figure 20.3 Aggregation and results.

improve his chances in gambling. He asked the well-known mathematician Blaise Pascal for help and with a short correspondence between Pascal and Pierre de Fermat the theory of probability was born—mostly based on arithmetic operations. This in turn led to the study of statistics, which then was based on the use of polynomial equations. For a review of how statistics has evolved into automatic discovery, see chapter 4 of *Intelligent Database Tools and Applications*.

Statistical approaches are discussed in such detail elsewhere that there is no need to expand on them here. However, a brief look at one popular statistical method, namely regression, will help clarify some issues through comparison with other approaches.

In the simplest form, the idea behind regression is to find the parameters for a line that minimizes the distances from an existing set of points. This is called the *regression line*, as shown in Figure 20.4a. The equation for the line is expressed as a *polynomial expression*, such as $ax + by = c$. Note that polynomials have their roots in the mathematics of the 17th century, where tracing trajectories of cannon balls was one of the key sources of funding in Europe. This is not the mathematics to use for analyzing large data warehouses.

Figure 20.4b shows how two rules characterize a different set of points. Rather than using polynomials, rules use *logical statements*. As Figure 20.4b shows, these statements are more boxlike and often can be understood by users. To approximate the points in Figure 20.4a with rules, you need to use a set of smaller boxes, as seen in Figure 20.4c. This figure also makes it easy to see why inexact rules are "universal approximators" (i.e., they can approximate the surface of any function).

Traditional statistics certainly is valid and rigorous. The main problem is that it comes from the 1930s. Its tools are too rough and do not scale up to large nonnumeric data sets. We have better tools now, as discussed later in this chapter in the section "What can IDIS do that statistics cannot?"

One way to note how statistics is limited is to observe that it will give the same answers based on samples. Look at it this way: as the warehouse size goes up, the information content of the data increases, yet the ability of a sample-based system remains almost the same (i.e., as a whole, its effectiveness in obtaining information from the data diminishes as the data size increases).

Rule-Based Prediction

In rule-based prediction, you first generate a set of rules from a database, then use them for prediction. A rule-based predictive modeler thus uses the rules generated from a warehouse to predict values for new data items.

Transparent, discovery-based models usually work much better on larger (and real) data sets, not just on samples of data. There are two phases to rule-based prediction:

- *Rule discovery*—You analyze a historical database and generate a set of rules by automatic discovery. (See Figure 20.5.)

- *Prediction*—You apply the rules to a *new data set* and match the rules to make predictions. (See Figure 20.6.)

So the basic idea shown in Figure 20.5 is simple:

- You use a historical database to generate rules.

- You match the rules to new data to predict values that you have not seen before.

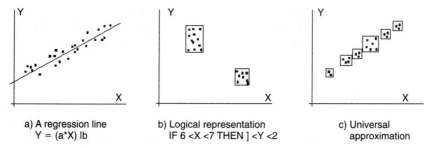

a) A regression line
Y = (a*X) lb

b) Logical representation
IF 6 <X <7 THEN] <Y <2

c) Universal
approximation

Figure 20.4 Clustering of results.

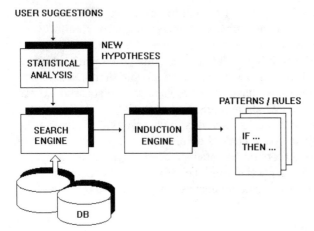

Figure 20.5 Rule discovery.

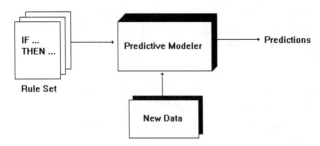

Figure 20.6 Prediction.

However, a sophisticated rule-based predictive system, such as the predictive modeler for IDIS (Information Discovery System), has an intermediate step. Because you sometimes might generate too many rules, and many of these rules might overlap anyway, the *rule-refinement phase* improves the rule-set, as shown in Figure 20.7.

Rule-based models usually are transparent, traceable, and restrained. Rule-based predictive models also are more accurate because rule-discovery systems can look at the whole warehouse and do not ignore information through sampling.

Decision Trees

Decision trees sometimes are used for making predictions from databases, but they should not be confused with rule sets. Decision trees are a simpler and less powerful form of rules. A rule set actually is many decision trees grouped together (i.e., it really represents a forest, not a tree). A decision tree can be turned into a set of rules, but not vice versa, because rule sets are more powerful.

A decision tree is a hierarchical organization of "attribute-value" pairs, as shown in Figure 20.8. Note that, in a tree, the order of attributes is fixed. For example, if the attribute Age is used as the first level, then in all rules obtained from the tree, this attribute appears. You can never have a rule without the attribute Age.

Predictive models based on decision trees often go wrong when the values for some of the fields are unknown or when value combinations in new data are slightly different. Moreover, they usually deal only with clarification and no other method of prediction.

Furthermore, the ranges used by decision trees typically are fixed and inflexible. For example, once you have broken Age into the threefold range (Age < 30, 30 < Age < 60, and Age > 60) then you can no longer use the range (25 < Age < 37) within the tree. This will cause many patterns to be missed.

In all my experiments with predictive models, I have found trees to be far less successful than rules—the previous indications being only some of the issues that cause problems.

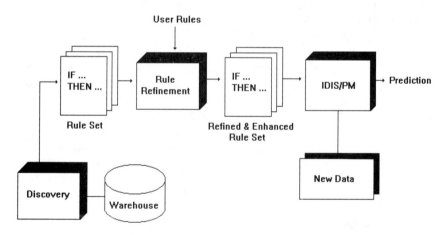

Figure 20.7 Rule-based predictive modeling.

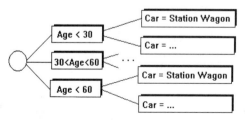

Figure 20.8 Attribute value pairs.

Neural Net Models

A neural network consists of a number of interconnected elements (called *neurons*) that learn by modifying the connection strengths between the elements. As with other learning systems, there are two phases to the use of a neural net:

- You train the net by feeding it examples until it stabilizes.
- The net makes predictions when presented with new data.

A neural net normally contains many neurons. The basic functions of each neuron are to:

- Evaluate input values
- Calculate a total for the combined input values
- Compare the total with a threshold value
- Determine what its own output will be

While the operation of each neuron is fairly simple, complex behavior can be created by connecting a number of neurons together. The input neurons are connected to a middle layer (or several intermediate layers) that then is connected to an outer layer, as in Figure 20.9.

Each neuron usually has a set of weights that determines how it evaluates the combined strength of the input signals. Inputs coming into a neuron can be either positive (excitatory) or negative (inhibitory). Learning takes place by changing the weights used by the neuron in accordance with classification errors that were made by the net as a whole. The inputs usually are scaled and normalized to produce a smooth behavior.

The training phase for the net sets the weights that determine the behavior of the intermediate layer. A popular approach is called *backpropa-*

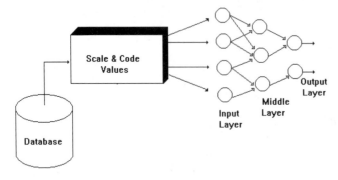

Figure 20.9 Neuron arrangement.

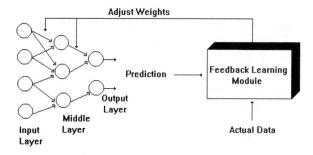

Figure 20.10 Feedback.

gation in which the weights are adjusted based on how closely the network has made guesses. Incorrect guesses reduce the thresholds for the appropriate connections, as shown in Figure 20.10.

Neural nets can be trained to reasonably approximate the behavior of functions on small- and medium-sized data sets because they are universal approximators. However, in practice, they work only on subsets and samples of data and at times run into problems when dealing with larger data sets (e.g., failure to converge or being stuck in local minima), as is well documented in the literature.

It is well known that backpropagation networks are essentially equivalent to regression. There are several other network training paradigms that go beyond backpropagation but that still have problems in dealing with large data sets. One key problem for applying neural nets to large data warehouses is the data preparation problem (i.e., the data in the warehouse has to be mapped into real numbers before the net can use it). This is a difficult task for commercial warehouses with many nonnumeric values.

The Data-Preparation Problem

Because input to a neural net has to be numeric (and scaled), interfacing to a large data warehouse can become a problem. For each data field used in a neural net, you need to perform scaling and coding.

The numeric (and date) fields are *scaled* (i.e., they are mapped into a scale that makes them uniform). For example, if ages range between 1 and 100 and the number of children between 1 and 5, then you scale these into the same interval (e.g., − 1 to +1). This is not a very difficult task.

However, nonnumeric values cannot easily be mapped to numbers in a direct manner because this will introduce "unexpected relationships" into the data, leading to errors later. For example, if you have 100 cities and assign 100 numbers to them, cities with values 98 and 99 will seem more related together than those with numbers 21 and 77 (i.e., the net will think these cities are somehow related). This might not be so.

To be used in a neural net, values for nonscalar fields—such as City, State, or Product—need to be coded and mapped into "new fields," taking the values 0 or 1, as shown in Figure 20.11. This means that the field State, which can have seven values (CA, NY, AZ, GA, MI, TX, and VA) is no longer used. Instead, you have seven new fields—called CA, NY, AZ, GA, MI, TX, VA—that each take the value 0 or 1, depending on the value in the record. For each record, only one of these fields has the value 1, and the others have the value 0. In practice, there often are 50 states, requiring 50 new inputs.

Now the problem should be obvious: "What if the field City has 1000 values?" Do you need to introduce 1000 new input elements for the net? In the strict sense, yes, you have to. However, in practice, this is not easy because the internal matrix representations for the net will become astronomically large and totally unmanageable. Hence bypass approaches often are used.

Some systems try to overcome this problem by grouping the 1000 cities into 10 groups of 100 cities each. Yet, this often introduces bias into the system because, in practice, it is hard to know what the optimal groups are. For large warehouses, this requires too much human intervention. The whole purpose of data mining is to find these clusters, not ask the human to construct them.

Eventually, the best way to use neural nets on data warehouses will be to combine them with rules, allowing them to make predictions within a hybrid architecture.

Forecasting and Time Series

The term *forecasting* often has been used in the context of the prediction of the behavior of a single variable (e.g., total sales for a product) based on

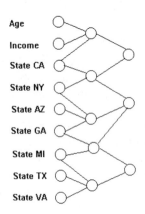

Figure 20.11 "States" example.

the past behavior of the same variable (e.g., past sales of the same product). Many traditional approaches have used time-series modeling for this purpose. Forecasting with time series often assumes that the past behavior of the predicted variable has sufficient information in itself to tell us about its future performance. In many practical cases this assumption needs to be fully revisited, if not discarded.

The techniques for time-series-based prediction are well covered in many publications, and I will simply mention that the basic idea often revolves around Auto-Regression and Moving Average (otherwise known as ARMA), with the integration of these into a model yielding ARIMA. The auto-regressive technique goes back to 1927, while models based on Box and Jenkin's work have remained popular since the 1970s.

One of the main problems in building a traditional forecasting model, such as a Box-Jenkins system, is *model identification*, which is highly dependent on the level of sophistication of the model designer. Significant effort is needed to get the model right. Yet, examples where linear forecasting models easily break down are easy to find. Only in the 1980s did the work of Tong and Lim eventually step beyond linear models, but these models often require even more effort to construct.

Needless to say, these types of forecasting models are opaque and it is unlikely for a manager to grasp any of the details of the model or the underlying assumptions that go into building it. Also, these models typically will ignore many of the data items stored in the warehouse. A simple moment of reflection and some common sense suggest that, by refusing to look at all of the relationships in the warehouse, the model must be missing something really big. It also is possible to perform forecasting with the other models discussed earlier, simply by a suitable mapping of variable values. Other models can be combined with some elements of traditional forecasting theory.

Predictive-Model Refinement

A key feature of transparent learning systems is *predictive-model refinement*. In this approach, discovery is used to improve the success rate of a predictive model by producing a critique of the behavior of the model, as shown in Figure 20.12.

The basic idea is simple: any predictive model has a success rate (e.g., it works 90% of the time). Yet this success rate is hardly ever uniform (e.g., the model might work 99% of the time on some segments and 80% of the time on others). By keeping track of where the model succeeds and fails, you can improve its performance.

Please note that the predictive model used here can be *any* model, either built with discovery itself, or an old statistical model, etc. Hence discovery can improve itself or any other model. This feature is very useful because,

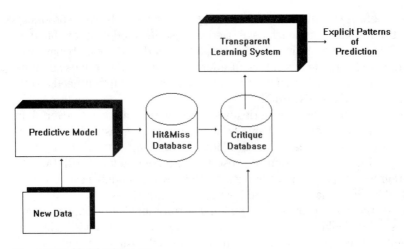

Figure 20.12 Model refinement.

over time, a predictive model needs to change in response to a changing world.

By knowing exactly how the model's success rate is being affected by changes in the environment, the parameters used for prediction are adjusted and other strategic steps can be taken to avoid problems. A *dynamic* and *transparent* model with *automatic predictive-model refinement* is essential for success in a changing world.

What Can IDIS Do that Statistics Cannot?

IDIS (Information Discovery System) is an automatic discovery system that analyzes large databases and discovers patterns, rules, and often unexpected relationships. It uses statistics and machine learning to generate easy-to-read rules that characterize data, providing insight and understanding. It has made automatic discoveries in fields ranging from forest protection to the oil industry, medicine, and financial analysis.

IDIS includes both a *statistical module* and an *artificial-intelligence module*. It continues to form and test various hypotheses about possible relationships in the database and uses machine-learning algorithms to generate rules. Although IDIS uses statistics, it is not intended to be a statistics program, but a discovery machine.

Because IDIS is a novel idea, people often have asked us: "But couldn't you do that with statistics?" Interestingly enough, we have seen three categories of IDIS users:

- Those who do not know statistics at all
- Those who know statistics very well
- Those who know some statistics, but not very much

The previous question usually is asked only by people in the third group, while those in the second group recognize that IDIS differs from statistics programs because it aims to do different things from statistics.

In this section, I will discuss how IDIS differs from statistics and why it is a novel and important approach to data analysis. This section is structured as follows: "An overview of IDIS" outlines how IDIS works and what it does while the rest of the section discusses three example databases analyzed by IDIS:

- A database of disk-drive failures, where IDIS identified the cause of the manufacturing problem. In this case, it would be very hard to get the results that IDIS obtained with a statistics package.

- A classic statistics data set, Fisher's Iris data from 1936, listed in many statistic textbooks manuals (e.g., pages 324 to 329 of the SAS user manual or as part of the Systat demo disk). To be *fully convinced* of how IDIS is different from statistics, all you have to do is look at these pages of the SAS manual, or the Systat demo, alongside the IDIS output in the section "The Fisher Iris Study" later in this chapter.

- A medical database of lead-poisoning data, where IDIS identified errors in the application of statistics. Here, the data previously had been fully analyzed with statistics, but IDIS discovered underlying factors that distorted the statistical analysis.

Thus, each example will make a different point. The disk-drive example illustrates how IDIS aims to perform a different task than a statistics program, the Fisher study shows how IDIS can more easily produce results superior to statistics, and the lead-poisoning example shows how IDIS can detect errors in the way statistical programs are applied and suggests that IDIS should be used in conjunction with most statistical analyses, even if one aims to do pure statistics.

"IDIS characteristics and some application areas" then discusses some characteristics of IDIS and provides case studies of the application of IDIS to different fields. The last section concludes and summarizes this discussion.

An overview of IDIS

The roots of IDIS go back to our attempts at providing a different paradigm for using databases, to make them *active*, rather than *passive*. Traditionally, a database is a passive and static repository of information that will provide answers when a human initiates a session and asks a set of pertinent questions. IDIS changes this point of view by turning the database into an *active* repository of information, automatically posing queries to the database and uncovering useful and unexpected information.

Thus, from an evolutionary point of view, IDIS can be viewed as the first step towards intelligent databases [Parsaye et al, 1989]. There are three basic steps in dealing with a database:

1. You *collect* data (e.g., you maintain records on clients, products, sales, etc.).

2. You *query* data (e.g., you ask "which products had increasing sales last month?").

3. You try to *understand* data (e.g., "what makes a product successful?").

When using a query language, you need to know what to ask about. If you ask a relevant question, you will get an interesting answer. However, there often is so much data that you might not know what the relevant questions are. IDIS discovers the relevant questions by performing an intelligent analysis of the data. Often this points out totally unexpected relationships that can be pursued further with queries.

IDIS can be viewed as a layer on top of the database query system. A query language, such as SQL, can deal with step 2, but it cannot automatically answer questions posed in step 3 because you do not know what to ask for. All you might have are hypotheses that can be tested with repeated queries. You need to form the hypothesis, but SQL will not form it for you. The answers to questions posed in step 3 often are unexpected.

To deal with step 3, a "human analyst" who is well versed in statistics and query languages has to take the following steps:

1. Form a hypothesis.

2. Make some queries and run a statistics program.

3. View the results and perhaps modify the hypothesis.

4. Continue this cycle *until a pattern emerges*.

These are *exactly* the steps taken by IDIS *automatically*. The human analyst would have to perform these tasks him- or herself, again and again. However, as you know, there will never be enough statisticians to analyze all of the world's databases.

In essence, IDIS has a closed-loop architecture with respect to hypothesis formation and analysis. It continues to query the database and performs statistics and induction until knowledge is discovered. Statistics programs, on the other hand, have an open-loop architecture for their operation—that is, a human analyst has to close the thinking loop.

While IDIS is discovering unexpected knowledge, it formulates hypotheses. However, the hypotheses are not generated at random, and various heuristics are carefully built into the program to avoid performance pitfalls. Thus hypothesis formation in IDIS is intelligent. IDIS is a combination of:

- A built-in query processing module and database interface
- A built-in statistical module for data analysis
- A discovery and induction module for rule generation

See Figure 20.13. The analyses of IDIS can be shaped by the user towards a specific task, or IDIS can be set to roam freely through the database. Moreover, the user can determine the minimum level of confidence in the generated rules, the way missing values should be treated, and other specifications.

IDIS and statistics

Since Blaise Pascal first expounded on probability theory in 1645, statistical techniques have been the basic tools for describing and analyzing large amounts of data. In the right hands, statistical methods can be very useful in providing insight into the overall structure of data.

There is no doubt that statistics should play an important role in any program that tries to learn from data. However, while statistical techniques are useful, conventional statistics should not be viewed as the only available tool for data analysis.

Due to their roots in numerical processing, statistical techniques almost always provide their conclusions in terms of mathematical equations expressed in the language of *polynomials*. Statistical findings are expressed with curves, equations, and matrices—in contrast to the language of *logic*, which

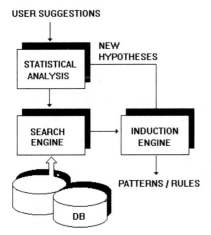

Figure 20.13 IDIS components.

expresses information in terms of logical relationships. This is a reflection of the influence of Newton and Leibnitz on today's mathematical culture, which has overshadowed the work of logicians such as Frege and Russell.

To capture knowledge, you need to discover logical relationships that are expressed in terms of rules rather than polynomial equations. *Rules are much more readable than mathematical equations.*

Many people who have databases do not really know statistics well enough to interpret statistical findings, but anyone can easily read through a set of rules. A discovery program with a built-in "expert" statistician can interpret statistical findings, then summarize them as rules.

The basic strategy of most statistical techniques is to look at differences in data sets and use equations to characterize these differences. Statistics packages do not look into a database to find the specific *values* that lead to the formation of logical rules.

IDIS can automatically produce rules such as the following one, which refers to actual values in a database:

```
% Rule 11
CF = 80
   Field-1 = Value-1
IF
   Field-2 = Value-2
AND
   Value-3 < Field-3 < Value-4 ;
% Margin of Error: 6 %
% Applicable percentage of sample: 30 %
% Applicable number of records: 837 ;
```

This rule automatically establishes a concrete relationship between *field values*. When a database is very large, analyzing each of the values with a separate statistics command is practically impossible, and the value of automated rule generation becomes obvious.

Until now, statistical techniques have been used by statisticians rather than "nonstatisticians" because:

- Their use requires an understanding of statistics.
- They need iterative processing—that is, an analyst has to run some statistics, think about the results, and then run some more statistics.
- Their results generally rely on the language of polynomials and require interpretation by a statistician.

There will *never* be enough human statisticians to analyze all of the data in all of the databases. The only solution is to provide large numbers of users with intelligent user-interface technology combined with statistics and artificial intelligence.

IDIS forms hypotheses and models itself. A statistical analyst would have to first form a model, then test various hypotheses. Again, due to its closed-loop architecture, IDIS is superior here and can suggest interesting models to a statistician.

To do some of what IDIS does using a statistics package, an analyst would have to write a program. However, IDIS is self-installing and requires no programming. It attaches itself to the database and generates knowledge.

IDIS does more than statistics; it generates knowledge. IDIS can provide valuable information that might never be discovered by a traditional statistical package.

In general, IDIS is characterized and distinguished from statistics by:

- The language of logic, not the language of polynomials
- Not abandoning, but enhancing statistics
- Facility in handling large amounts of multiple-type data
- Robustness in dealing with inexact and missing data
- The ability to define "concepts" for discovery
- Generation of both exact and inexact results
- Efficient implementation on either personal computers or client server
- Easy use by "nonexperts" in statistics

IDIS uses *deduction* as well as *induction*. This is an important point, because data often is not available in terms of the concepts that the user wants to analyze. For example, while the database might include fields about "Date of Purchase" and "Date of Return," what the user really wants to explore has to be expressed in terms of "New" and "Old." This is done by expressing concepts.

These fields then act as "virtual attributes," allowing the use of *compound* (or aggregate) attributes within induction. For example, the concept "underweight" might be defined in terms of a person's height, age, etc. Then this concept itself might be used recursively in further concept definitions. Not only are recursively defined attributes permitted, but rules themselves can be recursive. Furthermore, deductive induction allows you to use fuzzy logic and inexact reasoning.

When you have a large database that needs to be analyzed, IDIS's *efficiency* becomes evident. Describing a phenomenon in a format that is easily read by nonstatisticians can be a painstaking and time-consuming task with traditional statistical packages. On the other hand, IDIS asks you to specify any concept that you would like to explore (or it will select the goals for you). It then explores all available information in your database and automatically generates logical, easy-to-read rules that describe your data in a nutshell.

In general, IDIS can be viewed as the evolution of statistics. However, from a mathematical point of view, IDIS is not purely an enhanced statistics package. The induction method used in IDIS relies on a solid mathematical foundation.

Following statistical discovery, IDIS constructs topological neighborhoods for database records, then draws generalizations on these neighborhoods to discover rules.

First example: Causes for manufacturing errors

This example deals with data obtained from the disk-drive division of a well-known computer manufacturer. The disk drives had sporadic defect problems whose cause could not be identified. A sample from the database (3354 records) is shown in Table 20.1.

To use statistics on this data set, you first would have to convert alphanumeric data to numbers. Then you would have to specify a hypothesis and select a suitable method of analysis.

Obviously, this database is too large for visual analysis, although descriptive information (provided by IDIS) would be a good start. Regression is not going to provide meaningful results with this type of data. So you might consider clustering, discriminant analysis, etc. In sum, analyzing this database with a statistics package will be very complicated and time-consuming.

On the other hand, in less than five minutes, IDIS revealed that one particular operator was causing most of the problems in one particular manufacturing step. One of the rules that IDIS produced very quickly to identify the source of the problem looked like this:

```
% Rule 10
CF = 82
  "FAILURE MODE" = "932"
IF
  "OPER" = "213272"
AND
  "STEP" = "FSI"
;
% Margin of Error: 4.7 %
% Applicable percentage of sample: 11.3 %
% Applicable number of records: 379
```

This means that, when operator 213272 performs the manufacturing step FSI, he will make error 932 82% of the time. As it turned out, some operators were not properly trained. It would have taken a lot longer to find the source of the problem any another way.

The real problem that statistics faces here is that the useful information in this database pertains to values, not trends. IDIS can discover this; statistics cannot. Statistics alone thus would fail to use this database to its full potential.

TABLE 20.1 Database Sample

Serial no.	Step	Product code	Lot no.	Operator number	Failure mode
NI81400800	FSI	Xmb19	24	176613	419
NI81130796	MA1	XMI14	24	32787	932
NI81809313	FSI	XMI14	24	213272	931
....	...	.....	..	......	...
....	...	.....	..	......	...
....	...	.....	..	......	...
NI81000875	CB2	X418172	37	213272	932
NI81201054	CAM	X418172	44	32787	931
NI81000878	FSI	A418172	37	51512	932
NI81201022	FSI	X418172	43	213272	932
NI81400817	MA1	XMI14	24	38978	931

TABLE 20.2 "Species" Example

Sepal L	Sepal W	Petal L	Petal W	Species
5.1	3.5	1.4	0.2	SETOSA
5.6	2.9	3.6	1.3	VERSICOLOR
5.9	3.0	5.1	1.8	VIRGINICA
4.9	3.0	1.4	0.2	SETOSA
...	...	...	...	....
...	...	...	...	....
6.7	3.1	4.4	1.4	VERSICOLOR
6.2	3.4	5.4	2.3	VIRGINICA
4.7	3.0	5.2	2.0	VIRGINICA
5.6	3.0	4.5	1.5	VERSICOLOR

Second example: The Fisher Iris study

The Fisher Iris study, a classic in statistics, was published in 1936 by the renowned statistician Sir Ronal Aylmer Fisher. It frequently is employed as a standard test case and is listed in many statistics text books and user manuals. For example, it appears in both the SAS manual and in the Systat demonstration literature. Table 20.2 shows the schema for the database.

Petal-L means Petal Length, and Petal-W means Petal Width, etc. The database contains only 150 records—50 for each species of iris. Using this information, the objective is to identify the species of an iris based upon its physical characteristics—that is, petal and sepal length and width measurements.

A quick look at pages 324 to 329 of the SAS Statistics manual, or the Systat demo literature, is all that is necessary to see how IDIS is different from statistics and to see its striking advantages over traditional statistics. These pages show polynomial equations whose parameters are adjusted to accommodate the test data. They use terms such as covariance matrix, Chi-square, and canonical correlation that are intimidating to the average user. The results of the analysis really are usable only by statisticians and, in the end, do not tell you how to characterize irises in an intuitive way. IDIS, on the other hand, can produce pragmatic knowledge from this data.

Here are some of the base rules that IDIS discovered from this database:

```
% Rule 1
CF = 98
  "SPECIES" = "VIRGINICA"
IF
  "4.8" <= "PETAL LENGTH" <= "6.7"
AND
  "1.8" <= "PETAL WIDTH" <= "2.5" ;
% Margin of Error: 5.4 %
% Applicable percentage of sample: 30.0 %
% Applicable number of records: 45

% Rule 7
CF = 98
  "SPECIES" = "VERSICOLOR"
IF
  "1.7" <= "PETAL LENGTH" <= "4.9"
AND
  "0.6" <= "PETAL WIDTH" <= "1.7" ;
% Margin of Error: 5.1 %
% Applicable percentage of sample: 32.0 %
% Applicable number of records: 48

% Rule 15
CF = 100
  "SPECIES" = "SETOSA"
IF
  "1" <= "PETAL LENGTH" <= "1.9" ;
;
% Margin of Error: 1.0 %
% Applicable percentage of sample: 33.3 %
% Applicable number of records: 50

% Rule 16
CF = 100
  "SPECIES" = "SETOSA"
IF
  "1" <= "PETAL LENGTH" <= "3.5"
AND
  "0.1" <= "PETAL WIDTH" <= "0.4" ;
% Margin of Error: 1.0 %
% Applicable percentage of sample: 32.0 %
% Applicable number of records: 48
```

Once IDIS is instructed to include concepts such as Long, Short, etc. even better rules are produced:

```
% Rule 7
CF = 100
  "SPECIES" = "SETOSA"
IF
  "PETAL LENGTH" = "SHORT" ;
;
% Margin of Error: 1.0 %
% Applicable percentage of sample: 33.3 %
% Applicable number of records: 50

% Rule 8
CF = 100
  "SPECIES" = "SETOSA"
IF
  "PETAL WIDTH" = "THIN" ;
;
% Margin of Error: 1.0 %
% Applicable percentage of sample: 33.3 %
% Applicable number of records: 50
```

With this knowledge, a user should be able to distinguish an iris setosa from other irises. The following is an example of what a statistical package might produce after analyzing this database. Do *not* be alarmed if these results seem confusing to you; they are only comprehensible by statisticians:

```
SUM OF PRODUCT MATRIX M,
M = B'A' (A(X'X)-1 A')-1 AB (Hypothesis)

S-LENGTH S-WIDTH P-LENGTH P-WIDTH

S-LENGTH 61.332
S-WIDTH -15.583 14.193
P-LENGTH 163.141 -52.047 417.330
P-WIDTH 73.197 -23.239 175.126 84.230

MULTIVARIATE RESULTS:

HOTELLING-LAWLEY = 35.727
F-STAT = 584.923 DF = 8 286 PROB = .000

WILKS' LAMBDA = .033
F-STAT = 196.491 DF = 8 288 PROB = .000

PILLAI TRACE = 1.219
F-STAT = 56.636 DF = 8 300 PROB = .000

THETA = .708 S = 3 M = .6 N = 70.1 PROB = .000

( SUM 1 - 1 ) 2P2 + 3P - 1
RHO = 1.0 - ( N(J) - 1 N - G ) 6(P + 1)(G - 1)
```

Based on the comparison of these results with those produced by IDIS, it is clear that "equations do *not* help you understand how to distinguish the species of irises, rules do."

IDIS rules quickly tell you that all irises with short or thin petals are iris setosa (i.e., IDIS gives you practical knowledge). This example also illustrates that "knowledge is better grasped in terms of logical rules than polynomial equations."

IDIS produces clean, easy-to-read rules that can be understood by everyone, including people who do not know statistics. IDIS produces intuitively understandable knowledge, while statistics typically produces abstruse mathematical results.

Third example: Lead-poisoning data

This case study deals with lead-poisoning data from the USC cancer registry. This case examined toxic damage to the kidneys of subjects who were exposed to lead in their work environment. The schema for the part of the database is shown in Table 20.3.

The field names refer to various physiological measurements (e.g., PBB means Blood Lead Level, ZPP means Zinc Protoporphyrin Level, NAG means N-Acetyl-Glucosaminidase, and UCREAT means Urine Creatinin Level). As you can see, the database includes missing and unknown values.

The data had been carefully analyzed with SAS prior to analysis with IDIS. When IDIS was applied to the data, it quickly generated the following rule:

```
% Rule 7
CF = 75
  "NAG" = "HIGH"
IF
  "Sex" = "f"
AND
  "10-25-30" <= "Birthdate" <= "8-10-41"
AND
  "MEDIUM" <= "PBB1" <= "HIGH"
% Margin of Error: 15.5 %
% Applicable percentage of sample: 18.6 %
% Applicable number of records: 18
```

TABLE 20.3 Clinical Example

Birthdate	Sex	PBB1	ZPP1	PBB2	ZPP2	PBB3	ZPP3	NAG	UCREAT
06-08-30	f	26	38	8	35	16	23	2.300	5.69
12-10-33	f	12	58	10	58	4	51	0.890	6.10
04-16-55	m	29	16	16	20	18	19	1.560	1.22
01-18-35	m	31	49	22	38	21	34		
05-28-60	m	22	15	12	23	10	19	0.260	2.12
01-28-67	m	22	24	15	15				
08-10-46	f	26	50	22	24	14	28	0.240	2.30
10-26-64	f		7	36	6	32		1.500	2.66
.....	..	...	...	...	...	...	...	......	.....
.....	..	...	...	...	...	...	...	......	.....
05-11-59	f	10	80	4	62	13	58	1.080	2.05
03-09-67	m			6	65			1.360	2.49

This rule was very surprising, because heretofore there was no medical basis for a relationship between gender and the level of lead in the blood.

However, the enzyme N-Acetyl-Glucosaminidase was used to measure the level of lead in the blood, and it was later recalled that this enzyme is affected by iron levels. Females have varying concentrations of iron in their blood, affecting the enzyme and skewing the results of the statistics. Thus IDIS discovered that the statistical results were biased, unless males and females were distinguished.

The statistical program SAS alone was unable to reveal the gender bias. Lead-poisoning studies with N-Acetyl-Glucosaminidase now are evaluated differently as a result of IDIS's discovery. Of course, hindsight is 20/20, and perhaps a physician "could have" guessed these findings. Nevertheless, all humans are fallible, and everyone can benefit from the insight of IDIS.

We can only wonder how many other statistical studies in other hospitals all over the world have overlooked important factors—such as sex, iron level, sugar level, or other important factors—by focusing on statistical details.

IDIS characteristics and some application areas

What's unique about IDIS? What does it do that no other program can? It combines artificial intelligence, databases, and statistics to discover information. It produces rules in an intelligent way by detecting patterns, forming hypotheses, and adjusting its own search criteria. It produces easy-to-read rules rather than mathematical statements. Most important of all, it produces *unexpected* information.

To use a query language, you need to know what queries to ask—that is, you need to have a hypothesis, then test it. However, with a query language, you will not find anything unexpected. IDIS, on the other hand, forms queries automatically and executes them; you don't even need to know a query language to use IDIS.

IDIS uses statistics, then extends beyond statistics. In other words, IDIS can produce statements that statistics cannot. For example, in the faulty disk drives example, ICL produced a rule identifying the operator responsible for errors. Statistics, on the other hand, can only give you a curve, a matrix, an equation, or a test statistic.

Mr. James Brown, a consultant to the oil industry in Houston, Texas, was an early user of IDIS. He has used IDIS to analyze various proprietary oil company databases, including geological data related to the quality of oil products and economic data on the oil industry. Mr. Brown has an extensive background in statistics and has analyzed oil industry data for over 20 years. He routinely uses IDIS in addition to statistical packages.

With IDIS, Mr. Brown was able to predict how many barrels of oil a field would produce on an annual basis. "We have not seen another program capable of doing what IDIS can do," said Mr. Brown. "In every case, something useful has come out of the analysis with IDIS. In some cases, IDIS has produced startling results. Even in the area of your own expertise, you will find that IDIS continually gives you reasons to say, 'I didn't know that!'"

Mr. C. Nathan of the U.S. Forest Service in Redding, California, used IDIS to predict the fire-damage potential of forest stands and to explore preventive measures for controlling fire losses. "We began our analysis with SAS, then ran IDIS to see if it would show us anything similar to or beyond our SAS analysis," said Mr. Skinner. "The results of IDIS's analysis gave us other areas to explore that we hadn't thought of before."

David Barnhart of the Army and Air Force Exchange Service used IDIS to determine sales patterns based on the demographics (age, sex, marriage, income, children, etc.) of customers. The main retailer for military installations around the world, the AAFES controls approximately 17,000 businesses and has 2 to 3 million customers. "IDIS has helped us locate ways to make more money from our customer base," said Mr. Barnhart. Before using IDIS, the AAFES paid one person $30,000 annually to do all of the demographic analyses manually with statistics. Now, with IDIS, the same analyses can be done in a matter of days.

Mr. Ronald Cook of Eltron Research, Inc. has used IDIS for complex scientific analyses relating to catalysts and crystallization processes. One such application was the discovery of how different properties influence a catalytic reaction. "We looked at the physical, structural, and thermodynamic properties of catalytic reactions," said Mr. Cook. "Our analysis with IDIS suggested ideas for new catalysts and ways to make known catalysts work better."

Mr. Cook also has used IDIS to analyze the structure of crystals. Before using IDIS, Cook used statistical and factor analysis, in addition to pattern recognition techniques. "There are no science-oriented programs available that do what IDIS can," said Mr. Cook. "What is especially important to the research that I'm doing is that IDIS also reads databases with words and fuzzy meanings, along with numerical statements."

Mr. Jeff Brunner, of Gilman Securities, uses IDIS to analyze data relating to financial markets and makes decisions based on these analyses. "What is relevant to the market today is not necessarily relevant tomorrow," said Mr. Brunner. "You cannot apply the market system to a statistically based program diagnostically, because the focus changes throughout the day. We use IDIS to figure out how the market reacts to the volatility in various industrial sectors."

The risk/benefit ratio for automatic discovery is very attractive. IDIS has to discover only a few unexpected relationships to pay for itself. Because the discoveries can always be rechecked with queries, there is little chance of loss due to errors, but there is great potential for gain. This is in contrast to expert systems that mimic human experts. If an expert system errs, the consequences can be serious. IDIS can turn the passive data in a database into active information and knowledge that can be used to gain productivity.

Conclusions

Today, at every level of society, we need better information and more knowledge, yet the world's databases are overflowing with data! How can we accelerate the discovery of information and the generation of knowledge? Simply working harder is not the answer. There would never be enough statisticians and scientists to meet the demand. The answer is to automate the discovery of information—to *generate* knowledge *automatically*. Unlike the statistical packages that output curves and equations, IDIS automatically generates rules that characterize a database.

Today it is almost impossible to find a large organization that does not utilize a database system. Those who do not use information-management tools to stay productive cannot compete and will inevitably become extinct. In the next decade, it will be hard to find a large organization that does not strive to remain competitive by discovering information and generating knowledge. Within the next few years, almost every aspect of science, technology, and business will benefit from automatic discovery.

References

Blum, R. "Discovery, Confirmation, and Incorporation of Causal Relationships from a Large Time-Oriented Clinical Database: The RX Project." *Computers in Biomedical Research*, 1982.

Box, G. and F. Jenkins. *Time Series Analysis*. Oakland CA: Holden-Day, 1976.

Gale, W. ed. *Artificial Intelligence and Statistics*. Reading: Addison-Wesley, 1986.

Gaines, B. and M. Shaw. "Induction of Inference Rules for Expert Systems." *Journal of Fuzzy Sets and Systems*, 1986.

Holland, J. et al. *Induction*. Cambridge: MIT Press, 1986.

Hunt, E. et al. *Experiments in Induction*. New York: Academic Press, 1966.

Mahnke, J. "IDIS Tools Discovers Database Patterns." *MIS Week*, December 1988.

Michalski, R. et al. *Machine Learning*. Vol. I. Palo Alto: Tioga Books, 1983.

Michalski, R. et al. *Machine Learning*. Vol. II. Los Altos: Morgan Kaufmann Publishers, 1986.

Michie, D. "Automating the Synthesis of Expert Knowledge." ASLIB Proceedings. London, 1984.

Parsaye, K. "Machine Learning: The Next Step." *Computer world*, October 1987

Parsaye, K., M. Chignell, S. Khoshafian, and H. Wong. *Intelligent Databases*. New York: John Wiley and Sons, 1989.

Parsaye, K. and M. Chignell. *Intelligent Database Tools and Applications*. New York: John Wiley and Sons, 1993.

Parsaye, K. "The Sandwich Paradigm." *Database Programming and Design*, April 1995.

Parsaye, K. "The Four Spaces of Decision Support." *DBMS*, November 1995.

Quinlan, R. "Discovering Rules from Large Collections of Examples." *Expert Systems in the Micro Electronic Age*. D. Michie ed. Edinburgh: Edinburgh University Press, 1979.

Tong, H. and K. Lim. "Threshold Autoregression." *Journal of the Royal Statistical Society*. B-42, 1980.

Tukey, J. "Statistician's Expert Systems" in [Gale 86]

Theoretical Perspective on Data Warehousing

When you begin to analyze the visions that different people have for the warehouse, you will more than likely begin to see a lot of fruitful types of opportunities. The next thing that comes to mind probably will be why and how:

- Why does a data warehouse represent the solution to challenges presented by such a wide variety of the types of applications that are in demand by business today?

- How do you begin to calculate what the total impact of taking a data-warehousing approach will have on the overall business and data processing environment?

To address these questions, you need to take a step back and look at these computer systems from a different perspective.

The Efficiency of the Data-Management Process Itself

In chapter 2, I introduced a bit of the history on the relationship between business and the computer. I established that computer systems were applied to the business on a case-by-case basis, and in each case, the application that was adopted inevitably brought a good return on investment. (See Figure A.1.) I also talked about how, as businesses and computers became more sophisticated, new efficiencies were gained by copying or sharing the data between applications. (See Figure A.2.)

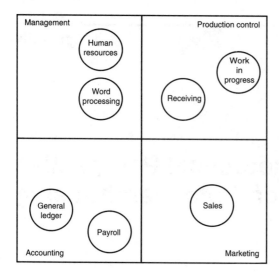

Figure A.1 Functional clusters.

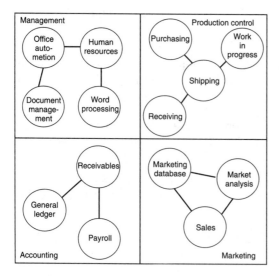

Figure A.2 Data sharing.

At a certain point in the evolution of computer systems, there was a revolution in the management of data. From the days of simple sequence files (tape and card) to the days of random disk access, we saw a gradual improvement in the ability to share data. However, between 1960 and 1970, the database was introduced to business. A database is simply a large, sophisticated computer program that manages data in a more efficient way than you could without it.

With the creation of the database, we suddenly created quantum leaps in the ability to integrate systems, in ways never before imagined. Unfortunately, this new integration capability was accompanied by a corresponding set of problems. Whenever you tie two systems together to achieve improved integration efficiency, you also create a dependency between those two systems (a deficiency). So while the developers of these large, integrated systems continued to squeeze greater efficiency out of their systems with this type of integration activity, they were simultaneously building increased interdependency into those same systems.

The Cost of Interdependency

The costs that system interdependency place on a computer system are in no way as straightforward as the benefits received. When you tie two systems together, you immediately get the benefits that the integration provides, and if everything would stay as it is, there would be no downside. However, as I already have established, business needs change, technologies change, and so computer systems also must change. It is when it comes time to change one of these systems that you begin paying the integration price.

When you tie two computer systems together by forcing them to share the data that they utilize, you create a situation where it is not possible to make changes to one of those systems without concern for the implications those changes will have on the other systems. This interdependency might be trivial. It might even be nonexistent (you can make the changes that you want and it will have no impact whatsoever). In some cases, the change will have a big impact. When you decide that it's time to change a system, you can no longer simply make the changes to that system alone. You also must determine the impacts these changes will have on systems that have been linked with it. (See Figure A.3.)

In its simplest form, this data-sharing dependency presents no big problem. When you connect two systems (represented by the two nodes in the diagram), you create one linkage between them and two interfaces (one interface for system A and one for system B). (See Figure A.4.)

The problem becomes more complicated as you add more applications to the system and increase the number of linkages. While you usually do not end up linking every system to every other system, that is what this kind of approach dictates as a theoretical possibility. From this perspective, you can see (at least in theory) that, as you add applications to your system, you exponentially increase the number of interfaces and linkages that need to be maintained. (See Figure A.5.)

Mathematically, what this boils down to is that, for every n applications within your environment, you have a total of n (the number of systems) times $n-1$ the total number of interfaces that each system must be ready to

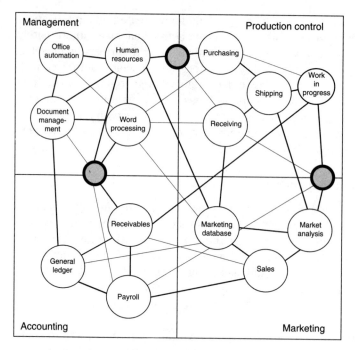

Figure A.3 The data glut.

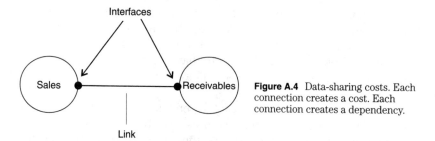

Figure A.4 Data-sharing costs. Each connection creates a cost. Each connection creates a dependency.

maintain. For example, if I have four systems, each of those systems will need three interfaces, for a total of twelve interfaces. (See Figure A.6.)

As your systems become larger, more multifaceted, and more interdependent, the time that you must spend maintaining these interdependencies becomes a growing part of the overall computer systems budget. In a classical application of Brooks' Law, you can conclude that you eventually will end up with so many interdependencies that you will not be able to afford to make changes to any systems. This is due to the cost of making the corresponding changes to the connected systems. This is precisely the situation that most large systems managers are facing today.

The Data Warehouse as a Solution

From the overall perspective, you can begin to see how a data warehouse could be used to reduce much of this complexity. You do this by attacking the basic model upon which system integration has been based on until now.

At first glance, you are stuck with a no-win situation. On the one hand, you have an imperative that demands that every operational system work to maintain its own operational integrity. That means each operational system should change as quickly as possible, if those changes can yield good productivity. On the other hand, you have an imperative to share data so that you can better control the overall processes and expenses at higher levels.

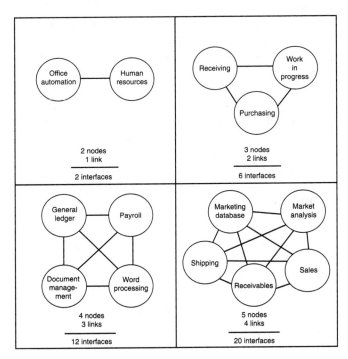

Figure A.5 The accumulation of interfaces.

For *n* systems you could end up needing $n \times (n-1)$ interfaces.

100 applications = 9,900 interfaces

1,000 applications = 999,000 interfaces

Figure A.6 System interdependency math.

As a result, you are stuck with an approach that demands that, every time you do something, you lose something. Make a system more independent and efficient, and you lose on the integration front. Make a system more integrated with other systems, and you lose efficiency.

Breaking the Deadlock

The data warehouse can offer you some relief from this data deadlock. By developing new systems that pull their information off of the warehouse and by developing feedback mechanisms into those applications, you can create an environment where the number of system interdependencies is greatly reduced on both sides.

Figure A.7 illustrates my model for the data warehouse. Notice that, by establishing the formal rules for the development of backflush and feedback mechanisms, I have greatly simplified the interconnectivity possibilities. (See Figure A.8.)

On a theoretical level, what I have done is used the warehouse as a common ground for the exchange of data between systems. Systems no longer need to move between each other to stay synchronized. The connections between old and new systems have been reduced to a total of $n \times 2$ possibilities as opposed to the $n \times (n-1)$ that were required earlier.

This theoretical exploration should help you understand how and why the warehouse seems to solve so many problems. The reason is that it greatly simplifies the overall architecture of the system at a fundamental level.

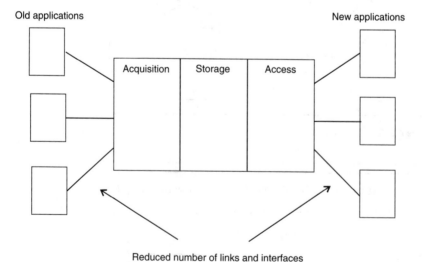

Reduced number of links and interfaces

Figure A.7 Reduced number of links.

For n systems you will need $n \times 2$ interfaces.

100 systems = 200 interfaces

1,000 systems = 2000 interfaces

Figure A.8 Data-warehouse math.

Index

A

access component, 83-87, 95
  feedback from, 99-101
  managing, 169-174
  types of users, 162-165
  validating, 275
acquisitions component, 79-83, 95
  platform allocation for, 192
  tracking, 175
  validating, 277
Advanced Software Applications, xviii
Advanced Visual Systems Inc., xviii
Analysis, 350, 424
analysis (*see* data analysis)
applications, 102-105
  access-only, 121
  business focus, 112-116
  contiguity of, 110-111
  data-only, 121-122
  definition, 110
  developing, 127-129
  developing more than one at same
    time, 118-119
  developmental sequencing, 116-118
  financial systems control, 11-12
  integrated marketing, 11
  layering, 121
  quality control, 10-11
  skills required for developing, 314-316
  solution-development phase, 132-133
  validating, 281
  validating development of, 279-280

architecture, 68
  artificial neural network, 384-386
  client/server, 343-346, 349-351
  data-storage, 143-148
  Enterprise Intranet, 421-423
  network, 92-93
  storage, 148
  visualization, 436-440
artificial neural network (ANN), 379-386
  activation functions, 380-382
  architecture, 384-386
  learning rules, 382
  neuron connections, 382-384
  single-neuron simulation, 380
autonomous layering, 121
autonomous value-based segmentation
    approach (AVBS), 61-62
AVS/Express, 439-440
AXSYS, 424

B

back-flush mechanisms, 99, 143
back propagation, 388, 452-453
Barnum, P.T., 32
Barnum's law, 32-33
benchmarking, 153-154, 231-232
Box-Jenkins system, 455
Brooks' law, 26-29
Brooks, Frederick P. Jr., 26
browsing, 347
business, economic cycles of, 39

ABOUT THE AUTHOR

Rob Mattison is one of the world's leading authorities in databases, data warehousing, and data mining. For over a decade, he has been helping organizations discover new and better ways to manage and capitalize on their massive data stores. Through his work with over 100 different organizations and as a columnist and speaker, he is well-known for promoting common-sense, practical, cost-effective systems development solutions. Many of his time-tested, proven capabilities and approaches have been shared in this book.

Rob currently works as a senior consultant with dbINTELLECT Technologies based in Golden, Colorado, helping clients develop data-mining solutions. He is the author of *Understanding Database Management Systems: An Insider's Guide to Architectures, Products, and Design* and coauthor with Michael J. Sipolt of *The Object-Oriented Enterprise: Making Corporate Information Systems Work*, both of which were written for The McGraw-Hill Companies.

Rob and his wife Brigitte have their home in Des Plaines, Illinois, and can be contacted via CompuServe at 70451,207. Your comments, opinions, and questions are encouraged.